Jonathan Edwards and the Church

Jonathan Edwards and the Church

RHYS S. BEZZANT

OXFORD
UNIVERSITY PRESS

OXFORD
UNIVERSITY PRESS

Oxford University Press is a department of the University of Oxford.
It furthers the University's objective of excellence in research, scholarship,
and education by publishing worldwide.

Oxford   New York
Auckland   Cape Town   Dar es Salaam   Hong Kong   Karachi
Kuala Lumpur   Madrid   Melbourne   Mexico City   Nairobi
New Delhi   Shanghai   Taipei   Toronto

With offices in
Argentina   Austria   Brazil   Chile   Czech Republic   France   Greece
Guatemala   Hungary   Italy   Japan   Poland   Portugal   Singapore
South Korea   Switzerland   Thailand   Turkey   Ukraine   Vietnam

Published in the United States of America by
Oxford University Press
198 Madison Avenue, New York, NY 10016

Library of Congress Cataloging-in-Publication Data
Bezzant, Rhys S.
Jonathan Edwards and the church / Rhys S. Bezzant.
pages cm
Includes bibliographical references.
ISBN 978-0-19-989030-9 (cloth : alk. paper)   1. Edwards, Jonathan, 1703-1758.
2. Church—History of doctrines—18th century.   I. Title.
BX7260.E3B49 2013
230'.58—dc23
2013020564

9 8 7 6 5 4 3 2 1
Printed in the United States of America
on acid-free paper

*This book is dedicated to President Josiah (Jed) Bartlet,
who has made Jonathan Edwards
a household name.*

Contents

Preface

WHAT WE BELIEVE about the church matters, for our ecclesiological perspective changes how we approach God. If the church is primarily a gift from God to believers and not merely an instrument for mission toward unbelievers, new opportunities for encounter with God can be enjoyed. The church is certainly a body of believers who are joined together for service, but in more exalted theological categories, the church is also Christ's bride, for we are united with the divine life forever. Indeed, in the language of Jonathan Edwards, the whole world was created so that "the eternal Son of God might obtain a spouse" (*WJE* 25: 187).[1] The church is not an afterthought in the otherwise individualistic plans of God, but is the focused domain where God's promises, presence, and purpose are to be discovered. Jonathan Edwards's ministry, writings, and example have proven powerfully effective in shaping my own approach to ecclesiology, and they continue to provide resources that enable me to contribute to present heated debates over the nature and life of the church. I hope this book persuades the reader of the theological significance of the church in God's world.

The following are the types of concerns I regularly encounter in conversations about the church. Some people question the very need of any organized church given the post-modern revulsion toward institutions or the more general disgust with clerical abuses. In other circles, church planting is de rigueur and raises fundamental issues of how structures of authority and accountability might be expressed, how sacraments are to be celebrated (if at all), and how much distance should be created between new and old forms. Since World War II, evangelical parachurch agencies have made extraordinary achievements in leadership training, campus evangelism, and worldwide publishing, creating excitement and allegiance that once was channeled toward local

---

1. Throughout this book, I will locate Edwards's writings using the abbreviated title of the Yale series (*WJE*) followed by the volume and page number.

parishes or congregations. Some even ask if there is a need to attend church at all if my needs are being met in a university fellowship or if a university fellowship becomes a church when sacraments are administered there. In some circles, reductionism reigns, arguing that where the Word of God is preached, there is church, or church can only exist where a certain liturgy is practiced. I have greatly valued all the questions of my friends and students concerning ecclesiology, which have animated this book. If any of these concerns are yours, I hope what follows will begin to address them.

It may be a surprise to the reader, as it was to me the student, that no one before now has written a book on Edwards's ecclesiology. It has been widely assumed that Edwards did not believe in the church or had no developed views on how it is to be understood theologically. After all, he was a revivalist, preaching for conversions, and therefore interested in individual's souls but nothing more. His infamous sermon "Sinners in the Hands of an Angry God," known better by its title than its content, surely provides validation to Edwards's attenuated vision for the church. Perhaps there have been others who just assumed that whatever view Edwards held regarding the church, it was the same as his Puritan forebears, and thereby inadequate to become a model for the life of the church in the modern world. In either case, no one went searching, apart from Tom Schafer in the 1950s, and Doug Sweeney and Amy Plantinga Pauw in the 2000s. It may have simply been the case that Edwards in no single document made ecclesiology his leading topic of investigation, so that until the publication of all twenty-six volumes in the *Works of Jonathan Edwards* by Yale University Press, and now a further forty-seven volumes in the online edition, there was never the opportunity to draw together the extraordinary variety of ecclesiological material that peppered all of his writings, whether treatises or sermons or miscellanies or letters. I hope what follows begins to make good the deficit.

On a more personal level, it is my dream to see the development of the study of evangelical history in universities, seminaries, and colleges outside of the United States, not only in Australia where I teach. The study of patristics, medieval history, and the European Reformations is well established, but to narrate the story of evangelicalism—of which Edwards is a fountainhead who has made an enormous impact not only in North America—seems to me to be a pressing need. In those enlightened places like Australia where Christian faith has been written out of the record, the evangelical contribution to society, science, education, unionism, politics, and theological debates in the church needs to be redressed. The broader study of evangelical texts and Edwardsean traditions has more recently been encouraged by the staff of the Jonathan Edwards Center at Yale, who have overseen not only the publication of Edwards's works, but also the establishment of satellite Jonathan Edwards Centers around the world in Leuven, Amsterdam, Heidelberg, Budapest, Wrocław, Krakow, São Paulo, Bloemfontein, Chicago, Tokyo, and Melbourne, with others on the way. The conversation emerging from these centers amply rewards my aspirations.

This book traces the life and career of Edwards chronologically and asks at each juncture what his writings and ruminations contribute to his emerging ecclesiology. Against the backdrop of Reformation debates and early New England commitments, we investigate how Edwards held fast to fundamental Protestant convictions while creating space for fresh expressions of church life. My basic contention is that, by preserving its strengths and adapting its expression, Edwards refreshes an ossified New England ecclesiology. He acknowledges the church's dynamic relationship with the created order, history, and the nations, and advocates renewal in ecclesial life through revivals, itinerancy, Concerts of Prayer, missionary initiatives outside of the local congregation, and doctrinal clarification. Edwards accommodates the Christendom model of ecclesiology to the new philosophical, political, and social realities of the mid-eighteenth century British Atlantic world. He is prepared to relinquish an understanding of the church in which the clergy primarily served the wider community and the national interests of New England, but also distances himself from separatist ecclesiology, which draws strong lines of demarcation between the kingdom of this world and the Kingdom of Christ. Edwards's ecclesiology can be aptly summarized as prophetic insofar as the church makes identification with its social context, while still providing an alternative millennial vision for human flourishing. He embeds a revivalist ecclesiology within a traditional ecclesiology of nurture and institutional order.

Some scholars have approached Edwards as a theological metaphysician whose opinions on ecclesiology are abstracted from the life of the congregation, while others have seen him as a product of social forces and constrained by the vicissitudes of the revivals. In this light, his dismissal is seen as the result of reactionary attempts to reinstitute the prevailing conditions of an earlier vision of the church. Neither approach is ultimately satisfying. Using the overarching categories of ecclesiological thoughts, passions, visions, and life, we deal in each section with a piece of writing by Edwards that anchors the theological investigation, allowing as well for historical pressures to shape our reading. Long before it became fashionable to use a tree as the symbol of Romanticism, Edwards fittingly used the tree as an image of the church. Rooted deeply in one place and yet responsive to its environment, Edwards's understanding of the church requires from him and from us theological principle and contextual plasticity. His philosophical and ministerial nuance is a gift to the church today.

What joy it is, then, to thank those who have encouraged my reading and writing for their ultimate contribution toward the life of the church. Foremost among supporters are Peter Adam and Ridley College Melbourne, who granted extended periods of leave for me to work without the normal responsibilities of college life. My sabbaticals in 2007–2008 and 2011 not only were productive periods of research but also gave me the immense privilege of meeting Edwards scholars from around the world and of immersing myself in the life of the Jonathan Edwards Center at Yale, where the hospitality of Ken Minkema, Adriaan Neele, and Harry Stout has been extraordinarily generous. Life in New Haven would not have been the same without the fellowship and prayers of brothers and sisters at Trinity Baptist Church, where this Australian Anglican was warmly welcomed, and the community of Helen Hadley Hall, especially John, Diana, and Andrew, who put it all in perspective. Kyle Strobel, who sat with me for almost a semester at the big desk in the Edwards Center at Yale, read an earlier chapter of my dissertation and has never failed to stimulate my thinking about Edwardsean theology and spirituality. Bo and Brooke Crockett and their family deserve a special mention for allowing me to complete the manuscript while staying in their home, and Gerry and Jean McDermott offered hospitality and important tips for making sure that the book is read. The staff at OUP, especially Cynthia Read, has been wonderfully gracious and professional in guiding this novice through the process of book publication. Nick Coombs ought to be congratulated for trying to get into the bibliography by offering to me one of his own college essays on church polity! My parents have offered unstinting support for my labors in the Lord, and themselves saw what a delight it is to work in New Haven when they bravely visited the United States in 2011. Boniface—not the saint but a Staffordshire terrier—is to be thanked as well: some of my best ideas came when he forced me to leave my desk and take him for a walk. Gifts often come in the form of interruptions.

Jonathan Edwards and the Church

I

Puritan Search for Ecclesiological Order

1.1 The Disordered Edwards: His Misunderstood Ecclesiology

> Ah paradise! Edwards,
> I would be afraid
> to meet you there as a shade.
> We move in different circles.[1]

WHETHER IN POETRY, prose, or the public imagination, Jonathan Edwards (1703–1758) has often been misrepresented. As a philosopher, theologian, revivalist, and pastor, he easily eludes facile categorization. Perhaps, having lived on the distant side of the American Revolution in colonial America, wearing a wig and a gown, his understanding of society and politics appears quaint and distant, easily distorted. Perhaps, by virtue of his Reformed convictions, he was painted in a pejorative light after the American Civil War, when his brand of theological reflection seemed destined for ignominy in contrast with more convenient Arminian notions. Perhaps, in today's world where Christian faith has been marginalized and hopes for revival are dim, his preaching of heaven and hell as realities to confront seems intolerant or embittered.[2] Certainly, his often anthologized but less often appreciated sermon, "Sinners in the Hands of an Angry God," draws together themes of his ministry with virulent voices of disapproval.[3]

---

1. Robert Lowell, "Jonathan Edwards in Western Massachusetts," in *Life Studies and For the Union Dead* (New York: Farrar, Straus and Giroux, 2007), 41.

2. Mark Twain, with a measure of predictable hyperbole, described Edwards as a "drunken lunatic." See Philip F. Gura, "Edwards and American Literature," in *The Cambridge Companion to Jonathan Edwards*, ed. S. J. Stein (Cambridge: Cambridge University Press, 2007), 266.

3. See Wilson H. Kimnach, Caleb J. D. Maskell, and Kenneth P. Minkema, *Jonathan Edwards's Sinners in the Hands of an Angry God: A Casebook* (New Haven: Yale University Press, 2010) for examples of the history of reception of the sermon.

The twentieth century has witnessed, however, attempts to rehabilitate the reputation of Edwards, understanding him on his own eighteenth-century terms as well as within the bigger picture of American history, and beyond. The neoorthodox saw in Edwards's doctrine of original sin an antidote to naïve approaches to evil.[4] Perry Miller encouraged him to lie on the Procrustean bed of modernity, albeit a little uncomfortably.[5] Yale University Press has produced a letterpress edition of his works, totaling twenty-six volumes, giving academic respectability and copious material to begin construction of a more nuanced Edwards. Fresh questions concerning family and gender, Empire and communication, slavery and freedom, experience and rhetoric have led scholars and students alike to search out Edwards's mind and ministry for clues concerning the present state of religion, politics, and evangelical faith, and ways forward when the path is otherwise dim.[6] Max Lesser's bibliographic work attests the proliferation of studies on Edwards.[7]

It is therefore surprising to note that when it comes to Edwards's explicit and systematic understanding of the church, very little commentary has been attempted.[8] There have been, of course, studies on Edwards's position in the Communion controversy of 1750 and his attitude toward itinerancy.[9] Much has been written on his place in discussions of the Puritan covenant ideal and millennial assumptions concerning the church and the world.[10] These, however, easily atomize the debates and distort the representation of his convictions

---

4. Stephen D. Crocco, "Edwards's Intellectual Legacy," in *The Cambridge Companion to Jonathan Edwards*, ed. S. J. Stein (Cambridge: University Press, 2007), especially 310–13.

5. Perry Miller, *Jonathan Edwards* (Lincoln: University of Nebraska Press, 2005).

6. See Stephen J. Stein, ed., *The Cambridge Companion to Jonathan Edwards* (Cambridge: Cambridge University Press, 2007) for such topics as these addressed.

7. Max X. Lesser, *Reading Jonathan Edwards: An Annotated Bibliography in Three Parts, 1729–2005* (Grand Rapids: Eerdmans, 2008).

8. Notable exceptions, though written fifty years apart, include: Thomas A. Schafer, "Jonathan Edwards' Conception of the Church," *Church History* 24(1) (1955): 51–66, and Douglas A. Sweeney, "The Church," in *The Princeton Companion to Jonathan Edwards*, ed. S. H. Lee (Princeton/Oxford: Princeton University Press, 2005), 167–89. See also bibliography for Amy Plantinga Pauw's recent contributions to ecclesiological debate on Edwards.

9. For example, see: Alan D. Strange, "Jonathan Edwards on Visible Sainthood: The Communion Controversy in Northampton," *Mid-America Journal of Theology* 14(1) (2003): 97–138; William J. Danaher, "By Sensible Signs Represented: Jonathan Edwards' Sermons on the Lord's Supper," *Pro Ecclesia* 7(3) (1998): 261–87; Timothy D. Hall, *Contested Boundaries: Itinerancy and the Reshaping of the Colonial American Religious World* (Durham: Duke University Press, 1994).

10. For example, see Carl W. Bogue, "Jonathan Edwards on the Covenant of Grace," in *Soli Deo Gloria: Essays in Reformed Theology: Festschrift for John H. Gerstner*, ed. R. C. Sproul (Nutley: Presbyterian and Reformed Publishing Company, 1976); Gerald R. McDermott, "Jonathan Edwards and the National Covenant: Was He Right?" in *The Legacy of Jonathan Edwards: American Religion and the Evangelical Tradition*, eds. D. G. Hart, S. M. Lucas, and

through connection with only a select range of doctrinal foci. Not infrequently one meets the opinion that Edwards actually did not have a settled ecclesiology or that his concern for the revivals must necessarily have eclipsed any residual concern for the church, its structures, life, and ministry. Bainton summarizes just such an assumption when he states that due to "his preoccupation with individual conversion Edwards appeared at times to have lost sight of the divine community."[11] Likewise, Hart suggests that "in so striving for a gauge to heart religion, the church for Edwards becomes superfluous."[12] It is just such assumptions that this thesis seeks to refute.

When faced with the tumultuous circumstances of the rebirth of vital piety on a large scale in eighteenth-century America, one might, in the end, be forgiven for focusing on the foreground of individual experience. Bainton or Hart may have succumbed to just such a myopic distortion in the case of Jonathan Edwards. However, while it is palpably evident that Edwards did act as midwife to scores of individual rebirths, this by no means necessitates the view that he had marginal concern for the nurture of corporate Christian maturity. In fact, it is my contention that Edwards's ecclesiology must be viewed as an essential coordinating principle in his response to the vicissitudes of revival. I shall track the development of his ecclesiological commitments, establishing their substantial connection with other major theological themes and arguing for the ways in which Edwards's depiction of the Lord's Supper is consonant with these broader concerns.

Edwards's doctrine of the church and its place in God's economy were not merely an amorphous shadow cast by the bright fires of spiritual ardor or a knee-jerk reaction to the pressures of revival, but rather was itself a compass by which he was enabled to navigate the currents and reefs of the revivals' waters. It is not impossible for an evangelist to be an ecclesiologist at the same time. It is not unreasonable to look for some deeper ordering of Edwards's thoughts in matters of the church. He was, after all, the legatee of just such a Puritan search for order in the century before him. Even those suspicious of his teaching acknowledge the rigors of his intellect and his capacity to unify ideas:

> White wig and black coat,
> all cut from one cloth,

S. J. Nichols (Grand Rapids: Baker, 2003); Brandon G. Withrow, "A Future of Hope: Jonathan Edwards and Millennial Expectations," *Trinity Journal* 22(1) (2001): 75–98.

11. Roland H. Bainton, *Yale and the Ministry: A History of Education for the Christian Ministry at Yale from the Founding in 1701* (New York: Harper & Brothers, 1957), 31.

12. Darryl G. Hart, "The Church in Evangelical Theologies, Past and Future," in *The Community of the Word: Toward an Evangelical Ecclesiology*, eds. M. Husbands and D. J. Treier (Downers Grove, IL: IVP, 2005), 31.

and designed
like your mind!¹³

It is my contention that the flow of evangelical piety from the eighteenth century onward can contain a high view of the church within its banks.

1.2   The Gospel, Reformations, and Puritans: The Unstable Church

Jonathan Edwards stood within the flow of debates concerning the church,
which had threatened to burst their banks since the Reformations of the sixteenth century. Indeed, these debates were themselves an attempt at resolv-
ing concerns expressed over the nature of church in the late medieval period,
which had arrived at some degree of ecclesiological pluriformity within the
Augustinian conception of the church's essential unity. Debates about the relationship between church and state—refracted through dangerous appeals to
church councils to initiate reform, set against the travesty of rival papacies
with the rise of millennial aspirations turning into apocalyptic critique of the
Pope as Antichrist—were altogether a combustible mix when Luther lit the
spark of sacramental controversy.¹⁴

Luther focused ecclesiological debates on his understanding of the Gospel,
which would become for him an instrument of leverage to remove the great
weight of medieval excess and corruption. In his Ninety-Five Theses, he could
state that "[t]he true treasure of the church is the most holy gospel of the glory
and grace of God."¹⁵ As well as an anti-indulgence polemic, Luther intended
here to focus the center of the church's life on an account of God's character
expressed in terms of God's movement toward human beings for their salva-
tion.¹⁶ The objective reality of the enfleshed Son of God and a passion for the
uncluttered purity of the Gospel gave Luther's ecclesiology a Christological

---

13. Lowell, "Jonathan Edwards in Western Massachusetts," 42.

14. Jaroslav Pelikan, *Reformation of Church and Dogma (1300–1700)*, vol. 4 of *The Christian Tradition: A History of the Development of Doctrine* (Chicago/London: University of Chicago Press, 1984), 38, 68, 81, 104, 127.

15. John Dillenberger, "The Ninety-Five Theses," in *Martin Luther: Selections from his Writings*, ed. J. J. Dillenberger (Garden City, NY: Anchor Books, 1961), 496.

16. Pelikan, *Reformation of Church and Dogma*, 128.

core.[17] His own existential trials in desperately seeking a gracious God, coupled with practices of penance that were pastorally unable to secure assurance of sins forgiven, led him to configure the Gospel in terms of Christ as Savior, a sharp soteriological offer and demand. Luther gave momentum to the later devotional intensity of Puritanism.[18] Indeed, Luther's espousal of the apostolic message of the Gospel as the *norma normans* of the church became a way of reconciling the unity, holiness, and catholicity of the church, which had been debated in the medieval period.[19]

While the second-generation reformers, like Melanchthon and Calvin, built on Luther's foundations, they nevertheless conceived their doctrine of the church within a slightly different set of architectonics. Assuming this Christological core, they nevertheless gave more attention to organizing the whole biblical narrative around that Christological focus, which coordinated nature and grace, or law and Gospel, and lent new seriousness to attempts to reform the structures and ministries of the church.[20] These second generation reformers were concerned about the "purity of the church" and Christ's authority to reform it according to his Word[21] "with a consistency and a rigor that went considerably beyond Luther."[22] The rule of Christ through his Word gave deliberate shape to the church and set the church within an eschatological framework insofar as it represented the coming Kingdom.[23]

17. Paul D. L. Avis, *The Church in the Theology of the Reformers* (Atlanta: John Knox Press, 1981), 3, 13.

18. John Coffey and Paul C. H. Lim, "Introduction," in *The Cambridge Companion to Puritanism*, eds. J. Coffey and P. C. H. Lim (Cambridge: Cambridge University Press, 2008), 2.

19. Pelikan, *Reformation of Church and Dogma*, 110.

20. Robert Doyle, "The Search for Theological Models: The Christian in His Society in the Sixteenth, Seventeenth and Nineteenth Centuries," in *Christians in Society*, ed. B. G. Webb, vol. 3 of *Explorations* (Homebush West, New South Wales: Lancer Books, 1988), 36, 41. Likewise, Edwards sought to reintegrate the orders of grace and nature, in reaction to the Enlightenment disenchantment of the world: Avihu Zakai, "Jonathan Edwards, the Enlightenment, and the Formation of Protestant Tradition in America," in *The Creation of the British Atlantic World*, eds. E. Mancke and C. Shammas (Baltimore and London: Johns Hopkins University Press, 2005), 193.

21. Avis, *The Church in the Theology of the Reformers*, 13, 33.

22. Pelikan, *Reformation of Church and Dogma*, 186.

23. See, for example, John Calvin, *Institutes of the Christian Religion*, trans. F. L. Battles, Library of Christian Classics (Philadelphia: Westminster Press, 1960), IV/ii/4. In this book, I adopt the convention of quoting the section number from the *Institutes*, and not the page number.

Such leaders also developed a more transformative expectation of the church's relationship with secular authority, regarding which Luther had never been forced to take anything other than a conservative position.[24] Calvin understood the Gospel as God's purposes for the world centered in Christ, which generates not just individual conversions, but the very foundation of the church itself.[25] Calvin's developed doctrine of predestination reinforced this framework, for human beings have been elected in Christ, who is the head of the body, which is the church. Doctrines concerning predestination focus on individual privilege and responsibility, which has necessary expression within the body. The church is understood in relation to God's past decree and to the purposes for which it was formed, according to the Apostle Paul in Ephesians 1:22–23. It is said of Calvin that "[h]is entire object was to bring human life in its totality under common obedience to God in Christ,"[26] of which the church is an essential means.

A new concern for the circumference of the church, its membership, and extent was demonstrated in the application of godly discipline, though Calvin did not formally make such discipline a mark of the church.[27] His Anabaptist contemporaries, however, reconfigured ecclesiological discussion by promoting as essential to church life baptism (as a believing adult) as the front door to church life, and the ban (disciplinary exclusion from the godly fellowship) as the back door.[28] It was their contention that deferring to princes or town councils, as the magisterial reformers did, could not bring substantial reform to the church, nor was such deference modeled in the New Testament. They rejected coercion as a compromised model of participation in the life of the church and worked to establish a voluntary system of membership in which unforced accountability would most likely secure congregational purity. This ethical vision was itself implicitly an eschatological vision as well, and one that served as a "device for passing judgment on contemporary society."[29] Their separatist inclinations, therefore, were unlikely to be graciously received. Such

---

24. Coffey and Lim, "Introduction," 3.

25. G. S. M. Walker, "Calvin and the Church," *Scottish Journal of Theology* 16(4) (1963): 371–89, especially 376–77.

26. Walker, "Calvin and the Church," 371.

27. Avis, *The Church in the Theology of the Reformers*, 35.

28. It should be pointed out that Martin Bucer also maintained the necessity of the ban, though not coupled with the rejection of paedobaptism. See Avis, *The Church in the Theology of the Reformers*, 45.

29. See F. H. Littell, *The Origins of Sectarian Protestantism: A Study of the Anabaptist View of the Church* (New York: Macmillan, 1964), 51.

an ecclesiologically radicalizing narrative could either inspire or destabilize further attempts at Protestant church reform, according to the prevailing social and political conditions in which they were held.

The ideological interplay between these various ecclesiological agendas was clearly in evidence within the Puritan movement, initially nestled within the Church in England but spilling over into independent structures and reflecting distinctive existential commitments and an emphasis on the Holy Spirit from the late sixteenth century.[30] Such factionalism was expressed in the Admonition to the Parliament in 1572 by John Field and Thomas Wilcox requesting further purifying reform of the church, as well as during conflict between King and Commons over episcopacy and Arminianism during the reigns of James I (1603–1625) and Charles I (1625–1649). This antagonism played out militarily in the Civil Wars of 1642–1649, which affected all of the British Isles and ideologically shaped the British colonies in North America. Internecine ecclesiological instability was brought to its constitutional end with the downfall of the Independent, Oliver Cromwell, and his Interregnum, the Restoration of the monarchy in 1660 under Charles II, the consequent Ejection of Puritan clergy in 1662, and the imposition of a revised Book of Common Prayer in the same year. The Puritan Bible Commonwealths in New England, though sequestered by distance and ideology, were nevertheless conversation partners in these disputes, and the history of New England, at least until the time of the American Revolution, would reflect the competing aims of comprehension and establishment, or separation and purity, which were contested in the first few generations of sixteenth-century European reformers and beyond.[31] Interaction with each of these polarities shaped developments in ecclesiology in early New England settlement.[32]

Jonathan Edwards inherits these debates in the early eighteenth century. While unreflective attention might divorce the revivals from antecedent ecclesiological instability, it has recently been cogently argued that the Great Awakening of the 1730s and 1740s cannot be understood without ecclesiology

---

30. Coffey and Lim, "Introduction," 3–7. See also Jerald C. Brauer, "The Nature of English Puritanism: Three Interpretations," *Church History* 23(2) (1954): 99–108, especially 101–02.

31. Calvin, too, attempted in Geneva to unify these ideals. See Walker, "Calvin and the Church," 382.

32. Ecclesiological debate was not restricted to Anglo-Saxon contexts. The Dutch Further Reformation and the concern to anchor the theological enterprise in simplified forms, appealing to the deductivist epistemology of Petrus Ramus, was very influential; Petrus van Mastricht, William Ames, and Francis Turretin might be included in this school. In their ecclesiology, however, they "stand for no great fundamental variations of thought." See John T. McNeill, "The Church in Post-Reformation Reformed Theology," *The Journal of Religion* 24(2) (1944): 96–107, especially 98.

in the foreground. James F. Cooper, using the often-neglected records of individual Massachusetts Congregationalist churches, argues that the revivals of the eighteenth century are attributable in large part to the tensions existing within the ecclesiological order of New England from its earliest days, rather than to sociological developments of the eighteenth century alone:

> Rather than the democratizing turning point that historians have described, Massachusetts's Great Awakening is better understood as an event whose onset reflected ongoing tensions within the colony's religious life and whose consequences accelerated changes in both Congregationalism and the larger culture that had long been under way.[33]

He goes even further to suggest that, just as ecclesiology was at the heart of the Great Migration of the 1630s and 1640s,[34] so the second and third generation of New England men and women maintained a conversation with their forebears insofar as they modified or defended the ecclesiological principles espoused through the language of covenant.[35] The genius of appeal to the covenant is clarified when we understand that this flexible terminology provides both individual assurance in the face of an inscrutable God and reasons to believe that the Lord is not only committed to an individual believer but also has intrahistorical intentions for churches and nations as well.[36]

The merits of this intergenerational discourse as a framework for interpretation are themselves a significant scholarly debate. Delbanco argues, for example, that because the first Puritans were somewhat bewildered in the New World, they could not resolve ecclesiological tensions easily, leaving it to their children to provide an adjusted sense of ecclesiological purpose.[37] Conversely, some have

---

33. James F. Cooper, *Tenacious of Their Liberties: The Congregationalists in Colonial Massachusetts*, Religion in America Series (Oxford: Oxford University Press, 1999), 198.

34. Cooper, *Tenacious of Their Liberties*, 11.

35. Avihu Zakai furthermore maintains that this conversation had begun a significant time before the migrations. He holds the position that their origins are to be discovered not merely in a sense of "crisis" in the seventeenth century but also as the result of longer-term social and political trends in Britain. See Avihu Zakai, "The Gospel of Reformation: The Origins of the Great Puritan Migration," *Journal of Ecclesiastical History* 37(4) (1986): 584–602, and especially 585. The "Exodus" model of migration, precipitated by the desire to escape oppressive powers, is suggested by Zakai as the leading paradigm for understanding Puritan migration. See Avihu Zakai, *Exile and Kingdom: History and Apocalypse in the Puritan Migration to America*, Cambridge Studies in Early Modern British History (Cambridge: Cambridge University Press, 1992), 9.

36. Pelikan, *Reformation of Church and Dogma*, 240–41, 371.

37. Andrew Delbanco, *The Puritan Ordeal* (Cambridge: Harvard University Press, 1989), 116.

argued that the late seventeenth century saw a declension in piety among the children and grandchildren of the plantation's founders.[38] The very terms under which such putative declension was debated extended the ecclesiological debates of the earliest period. Conversations concerning the Half-Way Covenant (1662), the Reforming Synod (1679), and the Saybrook Platform (1708), to list but a few, may have been exacerbated in part by nonecclesiological pressures, but resulted in decisions that had profound ecclesiological impact. Stephen Foster helpfully defines Puritanism and leads the case for this multigenerational model of meaning:

> Two notions fundamental to this study are…the sense of Puritanism as a "movement"—a congruence (more than an alliance) of progressive Protestants…thrown up by the fortuitous circumstance that England's official Reformation took root unevenly. The second follows directly from the first: a commitment to establishment was native to English Puritanism….This understanding of the English Puritan movement endows the New Englanders, even in 1630, with a vital, evolving culture, one based on long practice and developed institutions….Accordingly, further change in America in the later seventeenth century merely continues a long story.[39]

While the "long argument" was certainly integral to the development of the churches in New England in the seventeenth century, this concern must not necessarily take as its starting point the allegedly perfect and settled ecclesiology of either the Pilgrim Fathers or the Puritan founders of Massachusetts Bay. American history might have a date, or dates, as its discrete starting point, but the ideological concerns that generated the migrations predate and postdate stepping onto any rock. Puritanism in the Old World as much as in the New continued the

---

38. This thesis of declension is primarily attributable to Perry Miller, *The New England Mind: From Colony to Province* (Cambridge: Belknap Press of Harvard University Press, 1953), where even his section headings build on this language. More recently, this thesis has been contested in Harry S. Stout, *The New England Soul: Preaching and Religious Culture in Colonial New England* (New York: Oxford University Press, 1986), who has argued that rather than limiting the preaching of early New England to those sermons given on public occasions like election days, fast-days, and military remembrances, often known as jeremiads, a more balanced reading takes into account pastoral sermons preached on Sundays, where the declension of the colonies is not in the foreground.

39. Stephen Foster, *The Long Argument: English Puritanism and the Shaping of New England Culture, 1570–1700* (Chapel Hill: University of North Carolina Press, 1991), xiii.

"duality between the insular and the comprehensive that had always been at the heart of the movement."[40]

Patricia Bonomi has also repudiated the declension theory as the guiding narrative of the first century of British American life. It cannot be denied that the ideals set by the earliest migrants were so high that they were unlikely to be easily reached, but she makes clear that church attendance was still a valued part of social life and that clerical training and status occupied an increasingly significant social role. It suited, however, later denominational history writing to advance the thesis that the earlier forms were inevitably ill-suited to New World conditions for which later arrivals, such as the Baptists and the Methodists, were better prepared.[41] There were indeed "tensions generated by territorial and demographic growth," and the seventeenth century may accurately be viewed as "a time of strain and conflict," but the conclusion that these reflected a falling away from an ordered pristine beginning is inadequate, since it is "unlikely that by about 1650 the colonists possessed sufficiently stable church establishments from which to decline."[42] Religious confusion was more the order of the day.

Debates concerning the church, which the Reformations generated and which Edwards inherited, are more substantially debates concerning the nature of the Gospel, its authority, and its scope. Concerning authority, if the church has primacy over the Gospel, as Roman Catholicism espoused, reform was made difficult and access to salvation was only to be found within the structures and sacramental ministry of that church. If, on the other hand, the Word of the Gospel is understood as the progenitor of the church, persistent appeal to that Word enables ongoing reform, and access to salvation is to be found through means of grace, themselves dependent on that Word. It thus became a maxim in Protestant thought that the Gospel had the preeminent authority to create, shape, and reform the life of the church.

However, the scope of the Gospel's content was not yet settled among Protestants, with Lutheran emphasis on individual forgiveness and salvation,

---

40. Foster, *The Long Argument*, 27. Plantinga Pauw has most recently made this same point, suggesting that the Puritans, drawing on Calvin and shaping Edwards, struggle to maintain the "persistent tension between the ideals of inclusiveness and holiness," and often resort to the use of the imagery of mother and bride respectively to resolve the tension. Amy Plantinga Pauw, "Practical Ecclesiology in John Calvin and Jonathan Edwards," in *John Calvin's American Legacy*, ed. Thomas J. Davis (Oxford: Oxford University Press, 2010), 92, 97.

41. Patricia U. Bonomi, *Under the Cope of Heaven: Religion, Society, and Politics in Colonial America*, updated ed. (Oxford: University Press, 2003), xix.

42. Bonomi, *Under the Cope of Heaven*, 8, 15.

for example, and Reformed emphasis on divine purposes for communal life.[43] The Puritan Gospel straddled this debate. It made much of sin and atonement, but situated this within a more comprehensive vision of Scriptural priorities: "Gospel preaching centers always upon the theme of man's relationship to God, but around that center it must range throughout the whole sphere of revealed truth."[44] Puritanism wove together variegated sources of doctrinal emphasis, within an English context colored by internationalist experience and concerns, producing a labile ecclesiological mix. It will be critically germane to our thesis not merely to describe the development and determinations of Edwards's doctrine of the church but also to locate Edwards's understanding of the church in its historical flow, as well as to locate the Gospel that Edwards preached in its relationship with the church. Not only did Edwards face the challenge of providing for the already-conflicted Puritan church in New England renewed clarity, stability, and unity, but he had to do this in the midst of revivalist fervor and new fissures within the received polity. His ecclesiological recalibration was a timely work.

1.3 Parties, Polity, and Purpose: The Church in New England

Edwards was an eighteenth-century New England interlocutor with, and ultimately a New World leading voice in, Puritan ecclesiological debate. Although the broadest historical connections between the late medieval, Reformation, and Puritan periods in their relationship to ecclesiology have been traced in the preceding section, it is my intention here to provide a brief survey of particular theological issues supporting those reflections in New England. While ecclesiology is commonly approached through the application of word studies, a better foundation upon which to build a doctrine of the church is more exacting and therefore challenging because it involves the process of coordinating other doctrines. If, for example, we are the body of Christ, debates concerning

---

43. Calvin says that the Gospel is "the clear manifestation of the mystery of Christ" or "the proclamation of the grace manifested in Christ" and sets these within the perspective of the progressive revelation of the Kingdom. He grants that there is a "broad sense" in which forgiveness under the law might be understood as the Gospel, but wants to draw our attention to a "higher sense" that focuses on Christ and God's ultimate purposes. See Calvin, *Institutes*, II/ix/2. See also Walker, "Calvin and the Church," 379.

44. James I. Packer, "The Puritan View of Preaching the Gospel," in *How Shall They Hear? A Symposium of Papers Read at the Puritan and Reformed Studies Conference, December 1959* (London: Evangelical Magazine, 1960), 17.

Christology will have a profound impact on our expectations of church, as will debates concerning eschatology, because the purposes for which God made this world will at some level be reflected in the ways in which the church promotes God's good plans. As the concrete expression of Christ's body and mission, the doctrine of church has both fixed and flexible elements and is at the intersection of the mind of God, the life of God, and the benefits of God bestowed on the people of God. Ecclesiology is necessarily a cumulative and synthetic doctrine.

This section purports neither to be an exhaustive treatment of colonial America nor a survey of all Puritan theological enterprise, but an introduction to ecclesiological concerns as they affected Edwards. He had to navigate between competing Puritan parties, diverse approaches to ministerial authority, and questions concerning the ultimate social role of the gathered Christian community. The church's philosophical grounding within the Puritan period, understood here through the Aristotelian vocabulary of causation, forms the structure of this section.

The Church and God's Relationship to the Creation

God's relationship to the material order and, by implication, whether the church is expendable or necessary to divine rule and involvement in the world lies at the heart of much theological disputation.[45] One of the most fundamental theological questions concerns the relationship between God's power and will, relative to his love and design, which has an ecclesiological entailment. A traditional theological debate between those who would speak of God primarily in terms of transcendent power and freedom and the contingency of the creation (known as voluntarists), and those who would espouse God's self-imposed restraint, highlighting not his freedom but his design and the pursuant necessity for him to act consistently within the world (known as realists) was reprised in early New England's debates concerning salvation and the church. In seventeenth century terms, if God is more like a constitutional monarch, ruling through the conventions of law, than a capricious dictator, ruling by divine fiat, then the church, too, has a more permanent and dignified role in fulfilling God's purposes for the world.[46] This might be described as

---

45. See Dennis L. Okholm, "The Fundamental Dispensation of Evangelical Ecclesiology," in *The Community of the Word: Toward an Evangelical Ecclesiology*, eds. M. Husbands and D. J. Treier (Downers Grove, IL: IVP, 2005), 44–45, for a contemporary discussion of this point between evangelicals and dispensationalists.

46. Roy Porter, *Enlightenment: Britain and the Creation of the Modern World* (London: Penguin, 2000), 100.

a debate concerning the formal cause of ecclesiology, as it is the most fundamental principle by which any understanding of the church is made intelligi-
ble. Puritans in New England belonged to informal parties taking up differing
position on this issue.

Although it might be easy to assume monolithic ecclesiological agreement between the Pilgrim Fathers of 1620 and the audacious leaders of the
Puritan Great Migration of the 1630s,[47] this position is increasingly seen as a
construct of Whiggish nationalist ideology,[48] rather than the result of detailed
and discriminating historical research. Janice Knight, for example, in conscious though nuanced distinction from the book by Perry Miller of almost
the same name,[49] argues that not only did the Plymouth Fathers maintain a
separatist ecclesiology in distinction from the nonseparating Puritans of the
Massachusetts Bay Colony, but even these nonseparating Puritans in Boston
disagreed among themselves concerning God's attributes and relationship
to the world.[50] God might approach the world through command or through
promise.[51] The cosmological constitution of this world has a bearing on the
formal cause of the church.

One school of thought, shaped by William Perkins (1558–1602) and William
Ames (1576–1633), stressed the transcendence of God, his unknowability and
even unpredictability, the nature of sin as the positive presence of evil that
needs to be progressively eradicated, and God's condescension in the form
of covenants to give beggarly human beings some confidence in his mercy
towards them. While covenants had previously been attempts to encourage
accountability and godly living, in the mind of Ames, they became "nothing
less than the essential core of the church."[52] Just as God had in past covenants
with Israel limited his power for the sake of his chosen, so now God would
invite those in whom his grace was preveniently stirring to commit themselves to a life of discipleship by striving for moral improvement and owning

---

47. See Francis J. Bremer, *The Puritan Experiment: New England Society from Bradford to
Edwards*, rev. ed. (Lebanon, NH: University Press of New England, 1995), chapter 3.

48. See Delbanco, *The Puritan Ordeal*, 215–218, where he suggests, for example, that the
work of Perry Miller, Sacvan Bercovitch, Daniel Webster, and Sidney Lanier has distorted
Puritan motivations.

49. Perry Miller, *Orthodoxy in Massachusetts 1630–1650* (Boston: Beacon Press, 1959).

50. See Janice Knight, *Orthodoxies in Massachusetts: Rereading American Puritanism*
(Cambridge: Harvard University Press, 1994).

51. Oliver O'Donovan, *Resurrection and Moral Order: An Outline for Evangelical Ethics*
(Leicester: Apollos, 1994), 40–42, 151.

52. Zakai, *Exile and Kingdom*, 227.

God's covenant offer for themselves.[53] Drawing on medical paradigms of the day, the purgation of sin required exertion on the behalf of those committed to overcoming its effects.[54] Paradoxically, this position, which stresses God's majesty and consequent unapproachability, encourages the human activity of preparation for the reception of salvation,[55] which would be at work within the structures of the human soul gradually and reasonably, like "a tiny seed planted...that is up to the soul to water and cultivate."[56]

An alternative position, espoused by Richard Sibbes (1577–1635) and John Cotton (1585–1652), acknowledged the sovereignty of God and desperation of sinners, but emphasized "divine benevolence over his power," the Augustinian conception of sin as a privation of the good, and the necessity of God filling the individual with grace, this experience perhaps being described in apocalyptic terms.[57] There is nothing the individual can do but wait passively on God, praying for such an endowment of grace. While the former position gravitated toward forensic fine distinctions and explanations, this latter view drew heavily upon organic metaphors of the relationship between God and the individual in salvation. Sibbes's antipreparationism exemplifies this model.[58] Rather than an appreciation of the continuities between the structures of this world and the appropriation of salvation, this school would emphasize the radical discontinuities experienced in the nature of conversion.[59] Miller, representing an earlier generation of scholarship, would smooth out the differences

---

53. In Brauer's estimation, the genius of the covenant was its ability to hold together "the emotional and the rational, the subjective and the objective," though this framework "constantly threatened to separate and finally did." See Brauer, "The Nature of English Puritanism," especially 104.

54. Delbanco, *The Puritan Ordeal*, 81–82.

55. Human preparation, or cultivation of the moral life, was a strategy to combat the seductions of Antinomianism and thereby social degeneration as well as to encourage prosperity and stability within the covenanted nation. See Thomas A. Schafer, "Solomon Stoddard and the Theology of the Revival," in *A Miscellany of American Christianity: Essays in Honor of H. Shelton Smith* ed. S. C. Henry (Durham: Duke University Press, 1963), 338–39.

56. Perry Miller, *Errand into the Wilderness* (Cambridge: Harvard University Press, 1956), 57–58.

57. Knight, *Orthodoxies in Massachusetts*, 3.

58. Knight takes the view that Sibbes, contrary to much traditional scholarship, was not essentially a preparationist, in as far as he refused to believe that the capacity to prepare for salvation betokened election. See Knight, *Orthodoxies in Massachusetts*, 111–12, 131.

59. See Norman S. Fiering, "Will and Intellect in the New England Mind," *William and Mary Quarterly* 29(4) (1972): 515–58, for a discussion of these schools of thought in relation to the faculty psychology of the seventeenth century.

between these schools,[60] while Francis Bremer more recently acknowledges their subtle distinctions: "unity but not uniformity."[61]

As much as these positions appear to lie quite close to each other, they nevertheless occasioned a significant breach of the peace in the very earliest settlement of New England. The Antinomian Crisis (1636–1638), as it became known, pitted the defenders of preparationist piety against Anne and William Hutchinson, who, along with the Reverend John Wheelwright (Anne Hutchinson's brother-in-law), Henry Vane, and William Coddington, argued that the notion of cultivating grace within one's own experience was tantamount to performing works as a condition of salvation.[62] This is certainly the danger when one stresses the performance of the provisions of the covenant as a means of owning salvation. For their part, the prosecutors of those dubbed "Antinomian" presented the extreme position of these "Hutchinsonians" as equivalent to denying the need for obedience to the law in the life of faith. Anne Hutchinson and her party were subsequently banished by the Massachusetts General Court for their "heresy," after which they founded new colonies in Exeter, Portsmouth, and Newport. While the preparationist party had been in the minority in England, in the colonies, its leadership was determined not to waste an opportunity for ascendancy.[63] Their later expectation of a narrative of grace in the process of applying for membership of the covenant community reinforced linear and predictable patterns concerning salvation.

In this model, the discipline it was expected such individuals would exercise in their combat against sin and in their pursuit of holiness and fulfillment of the dream of congregational purity had its ecclesiological reflex in the increase of ministerial authority, through oversight of the "incremental process of spiritual reformation that always fell short of consummation."[64] Furthermore, obsessive focus on the experience of stages of grace in the individual (the *ordo salutis*) could obscure a vision for God's international purposes.[65] Such a millenarian mindset had earlier developed with Luther's critique of the papacy as the Antichrist, as well as among Puritans. English

---

60. See, for example, Miller, *Errand*, 59–60.

61. Bremer, *Puritan Experiment*, 22.

62. This crisis may have had the further sociological explanation that there was disorganization and a shortage of clergy in the earliest settlement, encouraging women to be more actively involved in leadership. See Bonomi, *Under the Cope of Heaven*, 18–19.

63. Knight, *Orthodoxies in Massachusetts*, 69.

64. Knight, *Orthodoxies in Massachusetts*, 3, 52–53, 80.

65. Bremer, *Puritan Experiment*, 42.

Calvinists, because of persecution, had been exiled to the continent during Mary Tudor's reign (1553–1558), and continental Reformed scholars like Martin Bucer (1548–1551) and Peter Martyr (1548–1553) had found refuge in Cambridge and Oxford respectively during the reign of Edward VI, cross-pollinating such views.[66] Knight points out that those of the party of Sibbes and Cotton (dubbed by her the "Spiritual Brethren") perpetuated such internationalist and providentialist concerns, though this attraction to the millenarian purposes of God was not equally shared with the "Intellectual Fathers" (the school of Perkins and Ames), who were more concerned with doctrinal and personal purity in the local congregation where sin could be more easily "contained and controlled."[67] Sibbes and Preston and Cotton and Davenport, known as the Cambridge Circle,

> focused intensely on the Christian's duty to work for the world church and formulated specific practical programs for change. Insisting that the "common good is to be preferred before private good," they consistently expanded the sphere of Christian concern, from the personal to the congregational, the national to the international church. And in the current crisis of international, indeed cosmic proportions, action rather than lamentation or retreat was the only adequate response.... Far more than their preparationist counterparts, the Brethren read the signs of the times, prayed for the millennial dawn, and worked on its behalf. Rather than conceiving of the Kingdom as the product of cataclysm or the shattering of the natural world, they believed in the unfolding of the Kingdom on earth and in time.[68]

Delbanco makes the further connection that the preparationist model of piety, in which divine contracts with individuals (often with covenantal legalism as the result) reflect the insidious pressures of emergent capitalism, was keenly felt but not always welcomed by the Puritan middle-classes:

> The doctrine of preparation...was as much a response to the threat of disorder as were the poor rates and the laws of settlement. It was an

---

66. Jeffrey K. Jue, "Puritan Millenarianism in Old and New England," in *The Cambridge Companion to Puritanism* eds. J. Coffey and P. C. H. Lim (Cambridge: Cambridge University Press, 2008), 260–63.

67. Knight, *Orthodoxies in Massachusetts*, 166, 179.

68. Knight, *Orthodoxies in Massachusetts*, 50, 154.

endorsement of regularity in the itinerary of the soul as well as in the household and the street.[69]

In his analysis, the migration to the New World was therefore for some a flight from encroaching insecurity and from temptations to worldly pride as much as it was a "confident journey towards the millennium" to found a church with a transnational agenda.[70]

These fundamental debates concerning sin, salvation, and service were continuing issues in Edwards's own day. Though the Great Awakening was an intrusive movement or "surprising work" for the recrudescence of vital piety, it played out among debates concerning God's relationship with the world and the degree to which God might use the regular and the natural to achieve his ends. It fell to Edwards to explain how this outpouring of the Holy Spirit received as a fresh experience of grace was both an interruption within individual experience as well as subordinated to the shape and order of clerical ministrations and eschatological expectations. The church was an integral part of God's design for human flourishing, even when God chose to put his mark on human experience in this world in irregular ways.[71]

The Church and Its Means of Grace

Edwards is heir to a more specialized debate concerning the means used by God to promote the Gospel of grace in human experience and the polity that would best defend it. The nature of Christian leadership and ecclesiastical organization, the role of the sermon and sacraments, and the responsibilities and pious affections of lay church members all provide ways into understanding divine intentions through secondary causation in the world. The language of the body of Christ is helpfully used as a metaphor to coordinate the various means of divine operation, by giving the opportunity to speak of head, members, organs, growth, and nurture. It also has the possible entailment of legal or mystical union with Christ as the universal foundation of the church, for any connection with the head raises questions concerning absorption within or distinction from divinity. This debate may be summarized by speaking of the efficient cause of the church, for here we discuss the ways in which God's rule is mediated in the life of the church.

---

69. Delbanco, *The Puritan Ordeal*, 51.

70. Delbanco, *The Puritan Ordeal*, 80.

71. Delbanco, *The Puritan Ordeal*, 236, 249.

Although the prosecution and defense of Anne Hutchinson in the Antinomian Crisis centered on her claims to direct spiritual illumination,[72] this episode opened up further ecclesiological fault lines in New England, which concerned the authority of the church, the place of clerical leadership in the colonies, and the responsibilities of members of the congregations to provide correction to their teachers if need arose.[73] Anne Hutchinson is a particularly celebrated example not only because of the passion of her prophesyings, but also because she was a woman, married, articulate, and teaching men.[74] Such challenges had not been anticipated in the Bible Commonwealth. It had seemed self-evident to both Plymouth and Massachusetts Bay believers wherein God's authority was instituted: they came to the New World clear about the corruptions of church authority from which they were fleeing, and armed with the Scriptures to guide them confidently toward a new application of the minutiae of church faith and order.[75]

The 1640s saw particular developments within England and the colonies that necessitated further elaboration of issues of polity. The Civil Wars in Britain between the Roundheads, or Parliamentary forces, and Charles I over the prerogatives of the King in Parliament and his rapprochement with Roman Catholic powers, notably Spain, exposed the migrants to the accusation that they were shirking their duties by remaining in New England and not returning to Europe to fight for the grand cause (the removal of episcopacy and the limitation of monarchy). Some did indeed return to England, which left those remaining even more vulnerable to the charge that they "had abandoned the purpose for which they had come."[76] The purity of the congregational polity and their commitment to its preservation and extension was called into question.

Furthermore, the new systematization of beliefs and structures through the deliberations of the Westminster Assembly of Divines, called in 1643, caused friction among the *émigrés* who were divided among themselves on

---

72. Bremer, *Puritan Experiment*, 69.

73. Delbanco, *The Puritan Ordeal*, 171.

74. It is, however, Cooper's thesis that lay-clerical relations were in the background of the Antinomian Crisis and that this crisis did nothing immediately to change the balance of these responsibilities within the churches of the Bay Colony. See Cooper, chap. 3 in *Tenacious of Their Liberties*.

75. Cooper, *Tenacious of Their Liberties*, 18–19.

76. Delbanco, *The Puritan Ordeal*, 202. See also the demographic and ideological analysis of remigration in Susan Hardman Moore, *Pilgrims: New World Settlers and the Call of Home* (New Haven: Yale University Press, 2007).

the issue of Presbyterianism and feared its imposition in Congregational New England. The Cambridge Platform (1648) was the response to these challenges, outlining the commitment of the New Englanders to the doctrine of the Westminster Confession of Faith, though they diverged from its clauses on polity. The New England Way was to be congregational,[77] appealing to the malleable language of covenant to provide the mechanism whereby the responsibilities of God, minister, and people were coordinated[78] with checks and balances provided by five different offices of leadership.[79] Most significantly, the innovation of a "relation of conversion," or a personal testimony of faith, for those wishing to become members of the fellowship was formalized.[80] This attempt to close the gap between the visible and the invisible church was one mechanism for quality control and the beginnings of association between a "highly developed morphology of conversion with an ecclesiastical institution."[81] It is Bushman's contention that essential to the Puritan experiment in the new world was its transformation from "an instrument of rebellion [in England] to one of control."[82] Indeed, the Cambridge Platform (Chapter X, § 3) does explicitly acknowledge the limitations of authority from below.[83]

Restrictions on membership may well have served the interests of the clergy and the colonies in the 1640s and 1650s, but it proved less amenable to the developing demographics of New England in the 1660s.[84] Dispersed settlement, shortage of clergy, the allure of a pervasive proto-capitalist economy, the failure of the Puritan Commonwealth under Cromwell, the Restoration

---

77. See the relevant sections of the Cambridge Platform in Alden T. Vaughan, ed., *The Puritan Tradition in America, 1620–1730*, rev. ed. (Hanover, NH: University Press of New England, 1972), 107, 111.

78. E. Brooks Holifield, *Theology in America: Christian Thought from the Age of the Puritans to the Civil War* (New Haven: Yale University Press, 2003), 41–42.

79. Bremer, *Puritan Experiment*, 108.

80. Bremer, *Puritan Experiment*, 106.

81. Edmund S. Morgan, *Visible Saints: The History of a Puritan Ideal* (Ithaca: Cornell University Press, 1963), 77. More recently, describing the requirement of a "relation of conversion" as innovative has been challenged. See Patricia Caldwell, *The Puritan Conversion Narrative: The Beginnings of American Expression*, Cambridge Studies in American Literature and Culture (Cambridge: Cambridge University Press, 1983), where she outlines the cases for and against incremental or radical shifts in the nature of membership hurdles in the New World (especially at 83–86).

82. Richard L. Bushman, *From Puritan to Yankee: Character and the Social Order in Connecticut, 1690–1765* (Cambridge: Harvard University Press, 1967), 147.

83. Vaughan, ed., *The Puritan Tradition*, 105.

84. See the detailed description of Connecticut's own demographic development in Bushman, chap. 10 in *From Puritan to Yankee*.

of the monarchy in 1660, and the palpable presence of those like Quakers not subscribing to orthodox Christian ways all led to a reflexive anxiety in New England. The "sub-apostolic" generation, not having endured the crucible of Stuart and Laudian oppression nor the terrors of migration and settlement, did not maintain their parents' spiritual fervor. The high standard for entry into the church may have kept many away from accessing full membership, though these same children, now become parents, were still sufficiently respectful of the church to request the sacrament of baptism for their own offspring.[85] New England's Half-Way Covenant, formalized in 1662 on the recommendations of a ministerial advisory convention of 1657, was the resulting compromise, allowing the grandchildren of regenerate members to be presented for baptism while not yet permitting the parents of the baptisands, who had no testimony of grace to recount, to partake of the Lord's Supper or to vote in church matters.

This recalibration of ecclesiological norms was achieved within one generation of settlement. While H. Richard Niebuhr could describe this as a "transition from a movement toward the future into an order conserving the past,"[86] such a dramatic development must not simply be seen as conservative or reactionary, for the new arrangement engendered a renewed social vision. The Half-Way Covenant registered a new missiological phase in the development of ecclesiology in New England, allowing greater authority to the clergy. To give those who were not full members of the church access to sermons and sacrament demonstrated a commitment to reach out through a program for Christian education and pastoral evangelism in which the church was viewed as a training ground for the gradual equipment of the saints.[87] This trajectory reached its zenith in the ministry of Solomon Stoddard in Northampton, who even opened up participation in the Lord's Supper to those who could not give a relation of faith, as he saw the sacraments as "converting ordinances."[88] While the New England Way traditionally highlighted the dignity of the laity

---

85. See the summary of conditions impacting those of "tender conscience" in Joseph A. Conforti, *Saints and Strangers: New England in British North America*, Regional Perspectives on Early America (Baltimore: John Hopkins University Press, 2006), 100–03.

86. As quoted in James T. Meigs, "The Half-Way Covenant: A Study in Religious Transition," *Foundations* 13(2) (1970): 142–58.

87. Meigs, "Half-Way Covenant," 151–52.

88. Perry Miller, "Solomon Stoddard, 1643–1729," *Harvard Theological Review* 34(4) (1941): 277–320. Stoddard effectively makes observance of the sacrament part of preparation for conversion, and not a means of sanctification: W. Reginald Ward, *The Protestant Evangelical Awakening* (Cambridge: Cambridge University Press, 1992), 284. See also Bonomi, *Under the Cope of Heaven*, 62.

in church polity, by the end of the seventeenth century, the power of some clergy was increasing, perhaps fostered by frontier conditions but more likely as a reflection of the desire to mimic cosmopolitan fashions and trends, which itself positioned them as players on an international field.[89] Morgan highlights clerical aspirations:

> Historically the magnification of the minister's office has often gone hand-in-hand with a comprehensive policy of church membership, while a limited membership, emphasizing purity, has been associated with a restriction of clerical authority. . . . [A]s ministers become independent of the laity, they tend to magnify the importance of their own role in the process of redemption and to feel a keener obligation to the unconverted. The clergy of New England follow this pattern.[90]

Conversely, the Half-Way Covenant generated in some minds a degree of social instability, insofar as the ostensibly settled relationship between clergy and laity needed redefinition.[91] Order within the churches was meant to secure the channels of grace to God's people, but confusion resulting from changes to the status of the ministry had its concomitant impact on confusion over the status of the laity. Doubt about the means of grace affected assurance of the experience of grace. A polity dominated by the purity of the membership runs the risk of losing the objectivity of grace, represented by a settled clerical caste, but serves to highlight greater dignity for the laity. Cooper points out how the Half-Way Covenant had the potential, despite the development of the status of the clergy, to ennoble concomitantly the laity and its self-confident assertion: "This loss of unanimity permanently eroded clerical authority in church affairs, forcing a more active role in government upon ordinary churchgoers."[92] Division among the clergy

---

89. Cosmopolitanism was the social and intellectual movement, spawned by the Enlightenment, that held that thinkers and writers outside of the metropolis were nevertheless active participants in the Enlightenment project and not merely passive observers from a distance, thereby functioning as a model opposed to provincialism. See Ned C. Landsman, *From Colonials to Provincials: American Thought and Culture, 1680–1760* (Ithaca: Cornell University Press, 1997), 62–63.

90. Morgan, *Visible Saints*, 143.

91. Miller, "Solomon Stoddard," 308–11. The Half-Way Covenant had less impact on the churches in the Connecticut River Valley than in eastern Massachusetts, where provisions for membership had been historically stricter (especially since the decision of the colony of New Haven to amalgamate with the more relaxed arrangements of the Hartford churches).

92. Cooper, *Tenacious of Their Liberties*, 89.

undermined their social prestige.[93] The head and its members need each other for healthy life.

It was therefore no great wonder that a church fearing disorder in an Empire already shaken by political innovations could fall prey to the rhetoric of those influenced by Enlightenment categories, who advocated the benefits of centralized authority to be found within the Anglican polity. The New England Way had been challenged from within during the Antinomian Crisis, and also from without given redefinitions of covenant and clergy, which left serious questions concerning its long-term viability. A new *modus vivendi* was reached during the turmoil of the Great Awakening, when revivals prompted a reevaluation of lay and clerical responsibility, experience of the covenant, and the propriety of sacramental means. Edwards had to provide not merely theological clarity but stability in the forms of ministry available, while resisting corrupting influences from abroad.

The Church and the Future of the World

Edwards inherits a conversation concerning the purpose of the church within the world, its identity, independence, and goal, and to what degree it may be assimilated to the cultural conditions in which it is set. The contingencies of the church's *Sitz im Leben* suggest pneumatological and eschatological themes for these are doctrines, which explore the ways in which God makes his grace particular to individuals' lives as well as to corporate experience, and also perfects his purposes for the creation.[94] If Christ as Lord universalizes the purposes of God beyond their Jewish origins, then the Holy Spirit localizes the designs of God in time and space and brings them to completion. We deal here with the final cause of ecclesiology, the teleology of the church, and its role in the divine economy. This whole schema of course presupposes the church's existence *sine qua non* as a local assembly of God's people and preempts later discussion of the church's trinitarian shape.

Significant models of corporate life, which had guided New England since its foundation, reflected questions of the place of Christians within the broader culture. Whether it was the language of "an errand into the wilderness" or the "city on the hill," it was not just the relationship between God and an individual believer, nor the relationship between the clergy and the laity, that defined the parameters of the earliest Puritans' ecclesiology. It was also the

---

93. Bremer, *Puritan Experiment*, 165.

94. Roger Haight, *Christian Community in History: Comparative Ecclesiology* (New York: Continuum, 2005), 7, 54.

relationship between the church and the watching and often warring world, which powerfully formed their assertions concerning the church. As Roger Haight suggests, an ecclesiology from below, recognizing the contingencies and provisionality of the situation in which the church finds itself, usefully reminds us that the church is necessarily creaturely and does not yet entirely conform to the perfect will of God for his people.[95]

Picking up on the language of "errand into the wilderness," Perry Miller made the case that the first Puritans wanted to establish an exemplary ecclesiological model by taking their message and ministry into a new world. He saw them leaving England behind in order to purify the church's structures in the New World. Basing his view on the sermon preached by John Winthrop in 1630 aboard the *Arbella*, entitled "A Modell of Christian Charity," the duty of those first Puritan quasi-secessionists was to create a godly order that might both transform the wilderness and give fresh impetus for reform of the church at home.[96]

This view has been contested more recently by, among others, Andrew Delbanco who, in his provocative work *The Puritan Ordeal*, wants to argue that the Puritans were fleeing something at home as much as they were looking forward to something new on the other side of the ocean.[97] Furthermore, the language of the "light on the hill" in its context not only allowed for the new settlement to provide hope to others still in darkness but also reminded those traveling that, such was their visibility, their cause could bring great dishonor to God if it failed.[98]

In either case, whether the reading is simple or more nuanced, of fundamental concern to the earliest settlers was their relationship to the world around them. They deliberately appropriated the model of Israel in the wilderness as the type of which they were the antitype, crossing the waters,

---

95. Haight, *Christian Community in History*, 25–36.

96. Miller, *Errand*, 12.

97. In Delbanco, *The Puritan Ordeal*, we are reminded that their migration was a "flight from chaos" (80, 93), though a clear delineation of an enemy could be transformed in time into a more positive agenda (59). This position is taken up also by Bozeman, who argues that Winthrop's sermon is not as focused on futurity as the incidental image of the "city on a hill" might suggest, but rather is an anti-triumphalist preachment, warning of the dangers of their new lives and encouraging "primitivist-archetypal" enjoyment of pure ordinances with the background of "avoidance, flight and asylum." See Theodore Dwight Bozeman, *To Live Ancient Lives: The Primitivist Dimension in Puritanism* (Chapel Hill: University of North Carolina Press, 1988), 113, 111.

98. John Winthrop, "A Modell of Christian Charity," in *The Puritan Tradition in America, 1620–1730* ed. A. T. Vaughan (Hanover and London: University Press of New England, 1972), 146.

facing foes in the land, owning the covenant, and beginning a nation.[99] The earlier settlement at Plymouth, consisting of those who had separated from the Church of England first at Scrooby in Nottinghamshire and then who sojourned at Leyden in the Netherlands, had no such rhetoric as part of their holy cause.[100]

While the nonseparating Puritans may have had personal or economic as well as theological motives for migration, there could be no doubt that the contingencies they faced upon disembarkation made their most robust hopes seem more fragile. The welcome they received from indigenous North Americans was initially mixed: both aid and aggression. Conversely, their own dreams of evangelizing the Amerindians, suggested in the seal of the Massachusetts Bay Colony in which the English are bidden "to come over and help," was both pious yearning and naïve missiology, contaminated by their own importation of diseases, against which the Indians had no immunity.[101] Congregationalism, which assumed the ideal of a Christian commonwealth it had inherited from the late Middle Ages, had yet no structures for sending missionaries, because it assumed a sedentary ministry of one parson to one parish.[102] A turning point came in the King Philip's War (1675–1678), when a coalition of Indian tribes, led by Philip or Metacom, asserted their military capacity to win back territory lost to the invading Englishmen. The Puritan terms of engagement with Amerindians changed dramatically hereafter, as the indigenous were increasingly seen as a "race apart,"[103] and Puritan efforts to reach them by and large faltered, though the ministry of John Eliot and his Praying Towns and later David Brainerd proved exceptions to the rule.[104] It is therefore indeed remarkable that Eliot translated the Scriptures into the Algonquian tongue before 1663.

Agricultural arrangements also had an impact on the ways of the church. Though the New Haven colony, for example, had initially sought to make every landholder's entitlement contiguous with the central Green and its church, thus providing unfettered access for farmers to connect with church

---

99. Delbanco, chap. 3 in *The Puritan Ordeal*.

100. Bremer, *Puritan Experiment*, 31–32.

101. Conforti, *Saints and Strangers*, 24–28.

102. Bremer, *Puritan Experiment*, 202.

103. Bremer, *Puritan Experiment*, 205.

104. See John B. Carpenter, "New England Puritans: The Grandparents of Modern Protestant Missions," *Missiology: An International Review* 30(4) (2002): 519–32, for the place of the Puritans in the development of the modern missions movement.

and central authority, or conversely for the town council to keep watch over outlying farms, this provision proved too cumbersome within a generation.[105] The shape of the farm proved inefficient for farming and for subdivision; children wanted their own holdings that parents could only with difficulty under this model provide, and prospects for autonomy and prosperity in other newly settled areas proved too attractive for the churches to retain all of their members within the parish bounds. Social mobility militated against the sedentary models of Old England and the Puritan polity, as did the very topography and demographics of the colonies.[106]

Adaptation to the new land had political ramifications as well. The first Puritans had arrived under the charter of the Massachusetts Bay Company, which unified them through their participation in a commercial joint stock company: governance was structured through investors. This gave them adequate funds for survival, though not adequate accountability for life in such a difficult environment. It was to John Winthrop's great credit that he reorganized the company charter to provide for a broader franchise, such that it was not just members of the company who could elect assistants, but also all freeholders, who were nevertheless also required to be church members.[107] The assumptions of standardized polity had also to be revisited, as it became evident that in the seventeenth century, Massachusetts, Connecticut, and Rhode Island were established in different ways and defined their franchise differently.[108]

One of the greatest external threats to the New England Way in the seventeenth century was the revocation by James II of the Massachusetts Bay Charter in 1684, upon which Joseph Dudley was appointed acting governor of Massachusetts, New Hampshire, and Maine, and then Sir Edmund Andros was appointed governor of the newly formed Dominion of New England in 1686, eliminating the popular basis for government in the colonies, previously so highly prized. The voice of the people was ignored, with the exception of those who had returned to England due to their dissatisfaction with colonial order: their outspoken views at the English court had since 1660 created bad sentiment toward the American colonies.[109] After 1685, James increased

---

105. Bushman, *From Puritan to Yankee*, 54.

106. Miller, *Errand*, 9.

107. Conforti, *Saints and Strangers*, 55.

108. Conforti, *Saints and Strangers*, 52.

109. See Delbanco, *The Puritan Ordeal*, 184–214 for a substantial report on the often-neglected issues of remigration.

intolerance toward all Protestant dissent, both at home and abroad. There were increasing attempts at imperial integration, even ecclesiastical Anglicization, of the colonies and a kind of political centralization anathema to the founding Puritan vision. Though the Glorious Revolution (1689) and the accession of William and Mary as co-regents put a halt to this previous totalizing pressure, their politics of toleration still affected the Puritans of New England, but in a different way. The New Englanders were no longer subject to persecution, but they also could not make a claim for hegemony, either political or ecclesiological, in New England life. Their purity of polity seemed part of an older, fading world.[110] Such cultural pressures on the Puritan experiment severely tested the boundaries of distinctiveness at the heart of their reasons for migration.

While agricultural and political pressures are readily observable, or at least identifiable, it was the less obvious epistemological and metaphysical pressures that, in the end, perniciously affected the identity of the Congregationalist churches in the New World. It was the growth of deist thought in England— generated, for instance, by Sir Isaac Newton's discoveries of "Nature viewed as matter in motion, governed by laws capable of mathematical expression,"[111] and the philosophy of Locke—who argued that all knowledge of the world was to be derived inductively from the senses, which in time created ruptures in the Congregational Way. Unlike the animosity expressed toward the church by philosophers in France, these thinkers were confessedly Christian. As Porter explains, "Enlightenment in Britain took place within, rather than against, Protestantism."[112] The Enlightened proclivity in England to work within and through the structures of the world and the church made for a more "reasonable" faith. Indeed, the independence of Congregational churches was increasingly interpreted as "disorderly" in a world dominated by Anglican and Latitudinarian conceptions of "order."[113] In the long term, the Enlightenment project undermined still further the already unstable order of Puritan ecclesiology by forcing apart options for renewal. At the same time, however, the

---

110. The changes to Puritan conceptualizing of faith and polity are exemplified in the demise of marital imagery in Puritan preaching, which had stressed covenanted, corporate, and organic frameworks. Voluntary and contractual relationships between autonomous individuals undermined the power of images of union, though this transformation occurred later in the colonies than in Britain itself. See Michael P. Winship, "Behold the Bridegroom Cometh! Marital Imagery in Massachusetts Preaching, 1630-1730," *Early American Literature* 27(3) (1992): 170–84, especially 178–80.

111. Porter, *Enlightenment*, 138.

112. Porter, *Enlightenment*, 99.

113. Landsman, *From Colonials to Provincials*, 107.

Enlightenment did give new tools for describing, propagating and experiencing the Christian Gospel, which came to expression in the revivals.[114]

The Congregational churches of New England began their "mission" in the New World at a time in Western history when many of the ecclesiological assumptions taken for granted for so long were coming unraveled. Despite painful disagreements with the established Church of England, the churches of New England were born with the expectation that they, too, would monopolize the polity of the new territory. They were ill prepared not just for the contingencies they would meet but also for the political and cultural changes soon to overtake both them and the land from which they had fled, though such were not easy to anticipate. Their very *raison d'être* would be distorted, causing them to ask fundamental questions of God's purpose for them and for the church beyond New England, and how they might better serve God's intentions within history. The purpose of the church as a prophetic contrast with the world, or as a more meager aspiration to house and protect those rejected by the world, was at issue.

In all of these ways, the century preceding Jonathan Edwards's birth saw an extraordinary ecclesiological recalibration, the results of which he managed and adapted in his own ministries in New Haven, New York, Northampton, Stockbridge, and Princeton. The "light on the hill" appeared to have been eclipsed by the "candlelamp of the human spirit" (Proverbs 20:27), or perhaps was in danger of being smothered altogether. The mission of the church was to be redefined in Edwards's teaching given the breakdown of assumptions concerning Christendom. The purposes of history in relation to the church were likewise to be clarified by him as he renewed his vision for Christian community by first engaging with the debates from within his own family concerning faith, conversion, and covenant ownership. The disputed place of Edwards himself in these debates becomes the burden of the following section.

---

114. See David W. Bebbington, "Evangelical Christianity and the Enlightenment," in *The Gospel in the Modern World: A Tribute to John Stott*, eds. M. Eden, David F. Wells (Leicester: IVP, 1991), Gerald R. McDermott, *Jonathan Edwards Confronts the Gods: Christian Theology, Enlightenment Religion, and Non-Christian Faiths* (Oxford: University Press, 2000), and Josh Moody, *Jonathan Edwards and the Enlightenment: Knowing the Presence of God* (Lanham: University Press of America, 2005).

2

Ordered Ecclesiological Thoughts (1703–1734)

2.1 Church of Early Experience: Negotiating Family and Faith

EDWARDS HAD TO decide in his earliest years how to appropriate the gift of his New England ecclesiological heritage and how to nail his own theological colors to the mast without damaging or disowning thanklessly the patrimony preserved for him. First of all, he had to come to terms with the impact of his own immediate family, especially Timothy his father and Esther his mother, on his formation and nurture.[1] Then, he had to confront the long shadow of his maternal grandfather, Solomon Stoddard, whose own ecclesiological innovations and revered reputation, among other authority figures in a world of hierarchical deference, were no less intimidating.[2] He resolved to pursue independence of mind:

> Monday, Sept. 23. [1723]...Resolved, if ever I live to years, that I will be impartial to hear the reasons of all pretended discoveries, and receive them if rational, how long so ever I have been used to another way of thinking.[3]

In effect, Jonathan had to renegotiate spiritual allegiances with members of his own family in order to begin his ecclesiological journey of discovery. The

---

1. Jonathan Edwards, "Resolutions," in *Letters and Personal Writings*, The Works of Jonathan Edwards 16, ed. G. S. Claghorn (New Haven: Yale University Press, 1998), 756. This resolution was drafted early in 1723.

2. See Ralph J. Coffman, *Solomon Stoddard* (Boston: Twayne Publishers, 1978) for a substantial biography.

3. Edwards, "Diary," in *Letters and Personal Writings*, The Works of Jonathan Edwards 16: 781. Note that throughout this book, the actual piece of writing by Edwards is only named when a volume contains multiple pieces.

angst of an earnest young man coming to terms with his own familial and social context in his "Resolutions" and "Diary" sets up his ecclesiological deliberations.

Upbringing and the Challenge of Ecclesiology

There was sufficient of the new and the old within his immediate family to make this process of discernment an onerous task. Edwards was born into the manse, with his father, Timothy Edwards (1669–1758), a clergyman of rigorous and intelligent stamp. Serving in East Windsor for sixty-four years and having overseen a number of periods of revival in his congregation, Timothy Edwards had lived and worked in a near-wilderness setting, with responsibilities for farming, local politics, erecting palisades against Indian incursions, and educating his eleven children, of whom Jonathan was the fifth and the only boy. Being prepared for pastoral leadership from his earliest days was, not surprisingly, Jonathan's lot. Timothy was from an established Puritan family of Welsh extraction, was trained for the ministry at Harvard under the prevailing philosophical deductivism of Petrus Ramus,[4] graduating in 1691, and held fast to the traditions as handed down to him both in his family and in his education. Agreeing that God's grace was uncontrollable, he simplified the steps of preparation which a seeker might be expected to travel to find grace to just three: conviction, humiliation, then regeneration.[5] He had, however, exacting views of the requirements for admission to the Lord's Supper and maintained the traditional New England defense of local church autonomy.[6] His bias was toward preserving purity of church membership, even while loosening, to some degree, the pattern for preparation for grace.[7]

Solomon Stoddard, on the other hand, who occupied the pulpit of the Congregational church in Northampton, Massachusetts, from 1672 to 1729[8]

---

4. William Sparkes Morris, *The Young Jonathan Edwards: A Reconstruction*, The Jonathan Edwards Classic Studies Series (Eugene, OR: Wipf and Stock, 2005), 70.

5. George M. Marsden, *Jonathan Edwards: A Life* (New Haven: Yale University Press, 2003), 26–28.

6. Kenneth P. Minkema, "Jonathan Edwards: A Theological Life," in *The Princeton Companion to Jonathan Edwards*, ed. S. H. Lee (Princeton: Princeton University Press, 2005), 1–2.

7. Zakai notes that even with three steps distinguished, this morphology of conversion was distinct from the original Lutheran model, which could be reduced to two, namely a repentant response to law and a believing response to grace. See Avihu Zakai, "The Conversion of Jonathan Edwards," *Journal of Presbyterian History* 76(2) (1998): 127–38, especially 133.

8. Jonathan's father Timothy had married Esther, the first child of Stoddard to Esther Mather Stoddard, in 1694. She was the widow of the first minister of Northampton, Eleazer Mather.

and who had proved himself to be a giant in matters ecclesiastical along the Connecticut River Valley, was an irascible defender of the preparationist model of salvation, although on his own terms.[9] Stoddard held that stages in conversion were indeed necessary in order to rid those seeking faith of any notion that their own efforts were meritorious. Jones reminds us that "[p]reparation was a safeguard against presumption in a most presumptuous age. It was not a guarantee of salvation but a purely negative doctrine that taught men not to trust their own works."[10] He upheld the remarkable position that the Lord's Supper should function not merely as an affirmation and seal of conversion already won but also as an opportunity to receive grace at the beginning of the Christian walk. During the period of preparation for salvation, the sacraments ought to be open to any who shunned a scandalous life and were credally sound.[11] Stoddard privileged the pursuit of conversion over the provisions for purity of church membership.[12] His oversight of five "harvests" in Northampton, spiritual seasons of intensified and revived commitment to the claims of Christ, encouraged by "hellfire preaching," appeared to validate his approach.[13]

Such a diluted view of church membership was further supported by Stoddard's view of leadership, which stressed the advantages of top-down authority and which marginalized the Congregationalist commitment to the participation of the laity in the affairs of the church.[14] The incipient Presbyterianism of Connecticut's Saybrook Platform (1708) was more congenial to Stoddard as a framework for the rights and responsibilities of the leadership of the fellowship. Essentially, a national covenant, designed to secure God's providential blessing, was of greater importance to Stoddard than

---

9. Stoddard "never doubted the truth of the preparationist, step-by-step description of conversion; he did doubt that any reliable procedure for distinguishing true faith from its imitations could be constructed on the basis of that description." See David Laurence, "Jonathan Edwards, Solomon Stoddard, and the Preparationist Model of Conversion," *Harvard Theological Review* 72(3–4) (1979): 267–83, especially 267.

10. James W. Jones, *The Shattered Synthesis: New England Puritanism before the Great Awakening* (New Haven: Yale University Press, 1973), 119.

11. Ward, *The Protestant Evangelical Awakening*, 284.

12. Minkema, "A Theological Life," 2.

13. Edwards, like his grandfather, saw the value of awakening sinners through the preaching of hellfire. See Schafer, "Solomon Stoddard," 330, 341.

14. Cotton Mather with other contemporaries in Boston were particularly aggrieved by this innovation and the threat that it represented to the New England Way, expressing his concern through veiled allusions in his work *Magnalia Christi Americana* (1702). See Miller, "Solomon Stoddard," 294–302.

protecting the purity of the local congregation, guaranteed through representative leadership.[15] Indeed, Stoddard was of the view that the people of the frontier were not able to govern responsibly in church affairs due to a critical lack of education and time.[16] His geographical context shaped his "instrumental ecclesiology" greatly.[17] He countenanced the expectation that God would act in this world using means to form a people for himself albeit gradually,[18] and that the best means to promote the Gospel was to form something like a national church, drawing on Old Testament models.[19] While sharply worded, Miller makes a not unhelpful contrast between western and eastern Massachusetts:

> Frontier individualism, common-sense and contempt for tradition resulted in benevolent despotism, while loyalty to the past and sophistical speculation in Boston resulted in a defense of personal freedom and the liberty of the covenant.[20]

Giving further weight to his already high view of the authority of the clerical caste as God's messengers, Stoddard viewed the divine covenant, focused in God's ministerial representative, as necessary to mitigate the potentially capricious power of God.[21] In his discourse of 1687 entitled *The Safety of Appearing at the Day of Judgment in the Righteousness of Christ*, the themes of preparatory humiliation, grace, and covenant were outlined,[22] and membership of the covenant community was, in the words of De Jong, "completely externalized."[23] A covenantal ministry of Word and sacraments, mediated by the clergy, was adequate without tightly circumscribed criteria for congregational membership to provide both objective and subjective assurance of divine benevolence

---

15. Schafer, "Solomon Stoddard," 332, 339.

16. Miller, "Solomon Stoddard," 310–12.

17. Meigs, "Half-Way Covenant," 150.

18. Meigs, "Half-Way Covenant," 151–52.

19. Ward, *The Protestant Evangelical Awakening*, 285. Marsden points out that Stoddard increasingly affirms Old Testament conceptualities, while others like Timothy Edwards made efforts to create purity in the congregation, drawing on significant New Testament themes. See Marsden, *A Life*, 31.

20. Miller, "Solomon Stoddard," 311.

21. Miller, "Solomon Stoddard," 287–88.

22. E. Brooks Holifield, *Theology in America: Christian Thought from the Age of the Puritans to the Civil War* (New Haven: Yale University Press, 2003), 66–68.

23. Peter Y. De Jong, *The Covenant Idea in New England Theology: 1620–1847* (Grand Rapids: Eerdmans, 1945), 130.

for individual Christians.[24] Signs of regenerating grace in an individual's life were neither required nor sufficient for assurance when confronting either the limited epistemological capacity of human beings or the absolute and naked power of God.[25] If clerical authority in New England had traditionally been based on received prestige, then in Solomon Stoddard we see a new stage, in which aristocratic control and professional expertise or success are added to the established measures.[26] His epithet of "Pope of the Connecticut River Valley" reflected his social position. Stoddard promoted both national and individual covenants, while demoting the significance of covenant with the local church.[27] It was puzzling to Stoddard, therefore, that despite his openness to more indiscriminate participation in communion, there were still many in Northampton who declined to participate in the Lord's Supper.[28]

The stakes were high for Jonathan.[29] He would have had to make a decision between the different ecclesiological approaches espoused by his father and grandfather, even if he had not been invited in 1726 to work alongside his grandfather in the congregation at Northampton, and to be prepared as Elisha to take over the mantle from Elijah.[30] It is from his "Personal Narrative,"[31]

---

24. Morris, *Young Jonathan Edwards*, 228.

25. Holifield, *Theology in America*, 34–42. The case is made here for the connection in traditional Reformed thought between the doctrine of divine accommodation or condescension and the appeal to the doctrine of the covenant, which allows for apparently divergent doctrines to be reconciled through use of the flexible term of covenant, in this case the absolute power of God and the moral responsibility of human beings.

26. J. William T. Youngs, *God's Messengers: Religious Leadership in Colonial New England, 1700–1750* (Baltimore: Johns Hopkins University Press, 1976), 138.

27. Schafer, "Solomon Stoddard," 358.

28. David D. Hall, "The New England Background," in *The Cambridge Companion to Jonathan Edwards*, ed. S. J. Stein (Cambridge: Cambridge University Press, 2007), 71. The declension theory of religious commitment in Puritan New England does not adequately deal with the possibility that a decrease in the numbers of communicant members is the result of increased religious scrupulosity.

29. While the immediate circle of Edwards's family was pursuing a ministry of practical divinity, Jonathan's earliest extant writings were not chiefly concerned with theology narrowly defined but with topics current in transatlantic natural philosophy, for example, the discourse "Of Insects" in 1719, then "Of the Rainbow," "Of Light Rays," "Of Atoms," and "Of Being" during 1721, reflecting a precocious mind and keen powers of scientific observation. See Jonathan Edwards, *Scientific and Philosophical Writings*, The Works of Jonathan Edwards 6, ed. Wallace E. Anderson (New Haven: Yale University Press, 1980) for suggestions of other interests and distractions.

30. At Stoddard's funeral, William Williams made this very comparison. See Schafer, "Solomon Stoddard," 332.

31. Edwards, "Personal Narrative," *WJE* 16: 790–804.

an extended autobiographical reflection describing events and attitudes from the early 1720s, in particular his conversion, that shifting allegiances within his wider family can be plotted and his later desire to demonstrate independence of mind from an early age can be traced.[32] In Puritan New England, any revision of received understanding of conversion had ecclesiological ramifications, for "conversion was the means whereby the purity of the church and the stability of the state were to be maintained," though in the course of the Great Awakening, "conversion became the religious source to express an intense dissatisfaction with the religious and the social status quo."[33] Either way, Edwards's reflections on his conversion would have serious consequences for his understanding of the church.

Conversion and a Decision for Ecclesiology

Purportedly written by Edwards at the behest of his future son-in-law, Aaron Burr, to provide some kind of relation of his own conversion, the "Personal Narrative" was brought to print in 1765 by Samuel Hopkins, a later disciple of Edwards.[34] It is a narrative in which Edwards describes his devout childhood, irresolute adolescence, and formative college years from the perspective of his own experiences of saving grace; indeed, it first had the title (provided by others) "An Account of His Conversion, Experiences and Religious Exercises, Given by Himself," then "The Conversion of President Edwards," both of which suggest more distinctly than the title "Personal Narrative" its character as a document intended for public consumption.[35] The account of two personal "seasons of awakening" and the ultimate discovery of a "new sense of things," appealing judiciously to the Scriptures but replete with references to and words cognate with "holiness," is the core of the narration.[36] Significantly, Edwards sets his personal awakening against the backdrop of Reformed

---

32. It should be noted that this narrative was written substantially later, in December 1740, even though it treats early incidents in his life.

33. Jerald C. Brauer, "Conversion: From Puritanism to Revivalism," *The Journal of Religion* 58(3) (1978): 227–43, especially 238.

34. W. Clark Gilpin, "'Inward, Sweet Delight in God': Solitude in the Career of Jonathan Edwards," *Journal of Religion* 82(4) (2002): 523–38.

35. Kenneth P. Minkema, "Personal Writings," in *The Cambridge Companion to Jonathan Edwards*, ed. S. J. Stein (Cambridge: Cambridge University Press, 2007), 49–51.

36. The progress from self-absorption to an acknowledgement of Christ's achievements and climactically an appreciation of the "divine being," before personal appropriation of salvation, marks the suspenseful trajectory of the piece. Zakai, "Conversion," 129–31.

theological debates as to the sovereignty of God and self-consciously within the realm of the material order:

> And as I was walking there [in my father's pasture], and looked up on the sky and clouds; there came into my mind, a sweet sense of the glorious majesty and grace of God, that I know not how to express. I seemed to see them both in a sweet conjunction: majesty and meekness joined together: it was a sweet and gentle, and holy majesty; and also a majestic meekness; an awful sweetness; a high, and great, and holy gentleness.[37]

What is most striking at first reading is the almost complete absence of any ecclesiological content at all. New insights are not received by listening to the preached Word, nor is there any reference to attending divine service or participating in the sacraments. At one place, he acknowledges that he stops on a Sunday—"At Saybrook we went ashore to lodge on Saturday, and there kept Sabbath; where I had a sweet and refreshing season, walking alone in the fields"[38]—but makes no reference to church attendance and deliberately remarks on being alone. Indeed, many of his most astounding experiences of God are connected to his own solitary perambulations in nature.[39] Although he acknowledges that even as a boy he would chart a course towards "secret places...in the woods, where I used to retire by myself," it was as an adult that he "walked abroad alone, in a solitary place in my father's pasture, for contemplation" and "used to spend abundance of my time, in walking alone in the woods, and solitary places, for meditation, soliloquy and prayer, and converse with God."[40] It almost appears at points in the narrative that nature functions quasi-sacramentally, being the material means by which God's grace is conveyed to him, obviating any Protestant suspicion that such means are

---

37. Edwards, "Personal Narrative," *WJE* 16: 793.

38. Edwards, "Personal Narrative," *WJE* 16: 798.

39. However, unlike early New English conversion narratives, Edwards does not give precise details when he describes geographic places. See Caldwell, *Puritan Conversion Narrative*, 26. DeProspo concurs: "What Edwards considers to have been his true conversion is related in the personal narrative without a single mention of time, place, or person. Companions and locales are associated with the false conversions that precede it." See R. C. DeProspo, "The 'New Simple Idea' of Edwards' Personal Narrative," *Early American Literature* 14(2) (1979): 193–204.

40. Edwards, "Personal Narrative," *WJE* 16: 791, 793, 794.

generated by human activity.[41] However much these incidents are couched in language reflecting debates from the 1730s, it remains true that these experiences of aloneness were critical to the sequence of growing acceptance of divine purposes. Gilpin suggests an eschatological motif:

> Solitude gave the foretaste of heaven, not because Edwards was alone but because there he expressed his affections toward the other or the one, unimpeded.[42]

Of great ecclesiological interest to us, nonetheless, is the way this account positions Edwards in the debate about preparation for salvation, insofar as he sidesteps any advocacy for a morphology of conversion.[43] He does not identify a single moment at which he might apply the soteriological transfer language of moving from death to life, or from darkness to light. Indeed, he confides in his diary from the period in a more straightforward fashion that the absence of a clear experience of saving grace "in those particular steps" was for him destabilizing.[44]

He had experienced intense religious emotions as a boy and had had "seasons of awakening" as an adolescent when God dangled him "over the pit of hell,"[45] but even his growth toward an experience of the "new sense" defied categorization. He remarks that "it never seemed to be proper to express my concern that I had, by the name of terror," nor "never could give an account, how, or by what means, I was thus [eventually] convinced."[46] Remarkably, it never dawned on him that "there was anything spiritual, or of a saving nature

---

41. George S. Claghorn, "Introduction," in *Letters and Personal Writings*, The Works of Jonathan Edwards 16, ed. G. S. Claghorn (New Haven: Yale University Press, 1998), 749. Edwards does not experience a light, like Paul, nor does he feel tormented like Augustine or Luther, but he enjoys spiritual harmony and proportion, and reconciles with the absolute power of God: Zakai, "Conversion," 135.

42. Gilpin, "Solitude in the Career of Jonathan Edwards," 537.

43. In this, he echoes traditional Calvinist views, in which penitence is radically displaced from first position in the *ordo salutis* and yields to faith as the primary response to grace. See Morris, *Young Jonathan Edwards*, 48.

44. Jonathan Edwards, "Diary," *WJE* 16: 779.

45. Edwards, "Personal Narrative," *WJE* 16: 791.

46. It is significant that Edwards uses here the language of "terror," known as a conversionary strategy in the preaching of Stoddard and common to significant conversion accounts from history, which exhibit "dramatic occurrences of supernatural power or nature's violence." Zakai, "Conversion," 133.

in this."[47] Indeed, Edwards is quick to point out that if there were no clear steps toward conversion at the beginning of his story, nor is there toward its end.[48]

Most tantalizing of all is the oblique reference to a conversation with his father after arriving at his "new sense." Having expatiated on a new "inward sweetness," and on being metaphorically "alone in the mountains, or some solitary wilderness, far from all mankind, sweetly conversing with Christ, and wrapped and swallowed up in God...that I know not how to express," he is able prosaically to express the account that he gave to his father "of some things that had passed in my mind." Concrete validation of his experience was sought, even though Timothy maintained the expectation of a more rigorous sequence. This is immediately followed up by a description of further sweet transports "that I know not how to express."[49] It is unclear, nonetheless, just how satisfying the conversation was, as he describes his resulting state ambiguously as "pretty much affected by the discourse we had together."[50] I take it that it was a difficult exchange, not least because of the contrast between the warmth of Christian fellowship, which he so enjoyed with the Smith family, his spiritual kin, while ministering in a Presbyterian congregation in New York, and from which he so reluctantly departed, perhaps at his father's prompting, and the experience of his return to his biological family in Windsor.[51]

Kimnach most helpfully draws our attention to contemporaneous entries in Edwards's "Diary" and "Resolutions," which further support the contention that Jonathan had been struggling with a significant disagreement with his

---

47. Edwards, "Personal Narrative," *WJE* 16: 793.

48. Edwards, "Personal Narrative," *WJE* 16: 803.

49. Edwards, "Personal Narrative," *WJE* 16: 793.

50. Though the language describing his meeting with his father is restrained in contrast to the descriptions around it, and though that conversation is summarized as a *discourse* with quasi-technical precision, Morris merely asserts that Jonathan met with his father to have "confirmed the inner testimony of the Holy Spirit." See Morris, *Young Jonathan Edwards*, 553. My reading suggests that the encounter was less cordial than Morris believes. DeProspo highlights the independence of Jonathan's divine dependence from his filial one: DeProspo, "The 'New Simple Idea,'" 200. Grabo comments briefly that the reference to the Smiths and to Timothy Edwards functions as a narrative strategy of intensification: Norman S. Grabo, "Jonathan Edwards' *Personal Narrative*: Dynamic Stasis," *Literatur in Wissenschaft und Unterricht* 2(3) (1969): 141–48. Zakai takes a more positive reading: Zakai, "Conversion," 131–32.

51. Edwards, "Personal Narrative," *WJE* 16: 798. The church in New York in which Edwards served as supply preacher was a small house fellowship resulting from a church split (rather than a formally instituted congregation), enabling a particularly intense experience of Christian fellowship. See Jonathan Edwards, *Sermons and Discourses, 1720–1723*, The Works of Jonathan Edwards 10, ed. W. H. Kimnach (New Haven: Yale University Press, 1992), 262.

father for some time over his own suitability for Christian ministry given his unorthodox progress. In Kimnach's estimation:

> On the issue of the proper morphology of conversion he [Timothy] seems to have been a liberal traditionalist, adhering to a simplified step theory while admitting the possibility of unpredictable personal variations from the norm. Perhaps his distinguishing trait, however, was an intense desire for personal oversight and control...he probably tended to dominance, if not manipulation...there is little to support the notion of Timothy Edwards' being either very tolerant of the unconventional or particularly responsive to idiosyncratic approaches to spirituality, especially in the case of his own dear son whom he was carefully molding to fill the expectations of family and the profession of the Puritan ministry.[52]

Jonathan hesitates to adopt the kind of relation of grace, which had been expected by his father in East Windsor, a relation that assumed an experience that could be described with certitude and confidence. Even if grace was not controllable, in this model it was definable. Demonstrating his aversion, when he writes the "Personal Narrative," his recital of early spiritual developments is expressed in the philosophical vernacular of the eighteenth century, appealing to "sense" and with a caution concerning the adequacy of words. Though expression of a relation of grace before acceptance into full membership was essentially crossing a narrative threshold, he self-consciously contrasts his relation of grace to that upheld by his father through narrative summation, written not to win new entry to the church but to confirm new morphology. This artifice made the distinction from his father's ecclesiology all the more powerful.[53]

Furthermore, a less personal and more theological antipathy toward precision in conversionist morphology is expressed by Edwards in other writings

---

52. Wilson H. Kimnach, "Preface to the New York Period," in *Sermons and Discourses, 1720–1723*, The Works of Jonathan Edwards 10, ed. W. H. Kimnach (New Haven: Yale University Press, 1992), 271–72, 275.

53. Such a pastoral narrative, as distinct from larger grand narratives or narratives to demonstrate the relation of grace, allows for personal disorientation, provisional conclusions, and slow achievements, making a significant statement concerning his ultimate position. See Amy P. Pauw, "Edwards as American Theologian: Grand Narratives and Personal Narratives," in *Jonathan Edwards at 300: Essays on the Tercentenary of his Birth*, eds. H. S. Stout, K. P. Minkema, and C. J. D. Maskell (Lanham, MD: University Press of America, 2005), 18.

from the 1720s. In "Misc." 317,[54] headed "The Work of Humiliation," Edwards affirms some level of self-conscious decision on behalf of the seeker to move toward owning Christ, for "it is necessary for the soul to suppose that he can't be his own savior and that he deserves ruin, when he actually receives Christ and his salvation as a free gift. 'Tis impossible to receive him as a free gift without supposing so at the same time." However, Edwards is not persuaded that individuals are "always brought to a conviction of the insufficiency of their own strength and righteousness by their own experience of its ineffectualness, as in the multitudes that were in a few hours converted by the preaching of the apostles."[55] Indeed, God may choose to bring a sense of conviction to an individual using their "rational consideration" as much as by appealing to "lively strong imaginations of misery and danger," for in such cases "God don't make so much use of the imagination as he does in others; they ben't so disposed to it, neither is there that need of it."[56] He sits loose to monomaniacal methods of ecclesiological incorporation.

Preparation, Purity, and Ecclesiological Principle

It appears that Edwards is making a most delicate ecclesiological case in his early writings and in the "Personal Narrative." He is distancing himself from his grandfather's preparationist model of conversion, dependent on the preaching of terror to invoke contrition, which relied on traditional means of grace, such as sermons, sacraments, and clerical ministrations, to enable the possibility of ownership of a social as much as spiritual covenant.[57] On the other hand, he appears only on the surface to be endorsing the alternative frame of reference of his father, distancing himself from Timothy's expectations of a more traditional experience and relation of grace.[58] As Jonathan later wrote in his preface to *Freedom of the Will*, he was

---

54. I follow in this book the citation system for miscellanies that is adopted by Sang Hyun Lee. See Sang Hyun Lee, ed., *The Princeton Companion to Jonathan Edwards* (Princeton: Princeton University Press, 2005), xxi.

55. "Misc." 317, Jonathan Edwards, *The "Miscellanies" (Entry Nos. a–z, aa–zz, 1–500)*, The Works of Jonathan Edwards 13, ed. Thomas A. Schafer (New Haven: Yale University Press, 1994), 398.

56. "Misc." 325, *WJE* 13: 405. A similar point is made in the sermon, "True Repentance Required," where Edwards writes: "I do not say that a true penitent's thoughts always run exactly in this order, but I say that they are of this nature, and do arise from this principle." See Jonathan Edwards, "True Repentance Required," *WJE* 10: 514.

57. It is nevertheless true that in preaching to his New York congregation, Edwards was prepared to advocate the traditional means of grace, though warning against their observance with no inward reality. See Jonathan Edwards, "The Value of Salvation," *WJE* 10: 335, and "The Importance of a Future State," *WJE* 10: 367, 375.

58. Minkema, "A Theological Life," 2–3.

beholden to no one in formulating his own views, not even those closest to him.[59] Effectively, he had navigated himself toward an ecclesiological position akin to the minority Puritan party of seventeenth-century New England, in which neither preparation nor narrative were sufficient indicators of true religion.

Edwards's view of God permits of surprising intrusions of grace into individuals' lives, potentially marginalizing the church, which it appears had played little formal role in discretely mediating grace to him, while lacking confidence in the divine work in his experience. Although he never dismissed out of hand God's capacity and desire to use means to appointed ends, such predictable channels were not constitutive of the shape of grace. Grace could be unpredictable in its effusion, but it confirmed for Edwards his exalted and yet dependent place within the natural order, which served as a venue to glorify God's immanence.[60] In traditional language, grace served to perfect nature and not destroy it. Edwards ignored neither the theological nor the ecclesiological debates that preceded him, pretending that he could, in primitivist fashion, reconstruct the nature of the church from scratch, based on either biblical or pragmatic considerations. Rather, he takes both a principled and moderating stance in an attempt to resolve the most recent debates endangering both delicate New England ecclesiological stability and responsibilities to filial piety. Church neither channels nor controls the mediation of grace, but, as we shall see, conscripts such an experience into larger redemptive purposes for the world.[61]

2.2 *Church in Two Worlds: Reconciling Providence and Apocalypse*

Jonathan Edwards's conversion in the summer of 1721 almost immediately began to recalibrate his thought. He acknowledged that he had developed an appreciation for the sovereignty of God, which formerly was lacking. He added to his interest in scientific reflection concern for philosophical questions concerning the mind, being, and the nature of knowledge. While at Yale as an undergraduate student (1716–1720) and then as a graduate student (1720–1722), he began to defend Reformed teaching, not least the doctrines of justification and postmortem judgment, which occupied him in his master's defense in 1723, and began to pursue opportunities for a ministry of the Word in New York (1722–1723), Bolton (1723–1724), and at Yale as a tutor (1724–1726).

59. See Jonathan Edwards, *Freedom of the Will*, The Works of Jonathan Edwards 1, ed. Paul Ramsey (New Haven: Yale University Press, 1957), 131.

60. Zakai, "Conversion," 136.

61. Zakai, "Conversion," 135.

His apprenticeship under Solomon Stoddard (1727–1729), before taking on sole responsibilities in the Northampton church upon Stoddard's death in 1729, was to be his chief venue for sermonic instruction. What is most striking in his earliest sermons before 1729, however, is the almost complete absence of preaching on the topic of ecclesiology itself, or reference to eschatology beyond questions of individual retribution or bliss, perhaps due to the fact that he has not yet been faced with sustained leadership challenges in an institutional setting. The corporate nature of salvation could easily be overlooked in the sermons of Edwards from the 1720s.

However, the material containing some of the most helpful early explanations of the role of the church in the world appears in Edwards's apocalyptic writings, notably, "The Notes on the Apocalypse,"[62] begun in October 1723. It is of great significance then that the "Apocalypse"[63] has been published by Yale University Press after being virtually unknown, and in substance unquarried, for most of the nineteenth and twentieth centuries.[64] The only Scriptural book to have its own dedicated notebook in Edwards's corpus, the Revelation to St John, plays a significant part in Edwards's attempts to combat the "desacralization" of history, which had been promoted through Enlightenment historiography, itself espousing a vision of *historia humana*.[65] He also wanted to reposition New England in Puritan apocalyptic speculation by reinterpreting the elements of the Apocalypse and distancing himself from seventeenth-century assumptions concerning the particularism of the New World project. Of note is the fact that, as a private repository of thoughts,

---

62. The section in the Yale edition entitled "Notes on the Apocalypse" contains several smaller units: a brief exposition of the book of Revelation chapter-by-chapter; a sequence of ninety-three notes on particular exegetical issues from the book of Revelation known as the "Apocalypse Series"; a ninety-fourth entry consisting entirely of quotations from Moses Lowman's *Paraphrase and Notes* outlining world history and its connection to Revelation; a brief essay critiquing Lowman called "Remarks"; a scrapbook or "apocalyptic ledger" composed after 1747 listing events that may be confirmed through the book of Revelation called prosaically "An Account of Events Probably Fulfilling the Sixth Vial on the River Euphrates, the News of Which Was Received since October 16, 1747"; a list of events describing evangelical successes called "Events of an Hopeful Aspect on the State of Religion"; and finally, a "Tractate on Revelation 16:12." The final section of this Yale edition volume contains *An Humble Attempt*, to be dealt with elsewhere in this work. See Jonathan Edwards, *Apocalyptic Writings*, The Works of Jonathan Edwards 5, ed. Stephen J. Stein (New Haven: Yale University Press, 1977), 95–305.

63. Note that I shall use the title "Apocalypse" in quotation marks to identify this notebook of Edwards; otherwise, without quotation marks, the Apocalypse refers to the Book of Revelation, the last book of the canonical Scriptures.

64. Stephen J. Stein, "Editor's Introduction," in *Apocalyptic Writings*, The Works of Jonathan Edwards 5, ed. S. J. Stein (New Haven: Yale University Press, 1977), 79–82.

65. Avihu Zakai, *Jonathan Edwards's Philosophy of History: The Reenchantment of the World in the Age of Enlightenment* (Princeton: Princeton University Press, 2003), 141.

Edwards confided in the "Apocalypse" notebook in ways he was not prepared to do through sermons. This notebook, alongside the sequence of theological commonplaces known as the "Miscellanies," of which those composed before the death of Solomon Stoddard in 1729 are numbered a–z, aa–zz, 1–386,[66] functions as initial ruminations on themes that were to be made public and used more systematically later in his writing or preaching, containing, for our purposes, several that expound apocalyptic themes.

The "Apocalypse" contains significant ecclesiological content because, like his predecessors in New England, Edwards affirms that stream of historical interpretation that views the book of Revelation as a confirmation of the centrality of the sixteenth-century Reformation to church history, and that consequently attests the significance of the ongoing struggle between the Protestant interest[67] and Roman Catholic nations' grasp at international hegemony. His guiding hermeneutic is the identity of papal authority with the counterfeit ministry of the Antichrist,[68] and his approach to Revelation is to assume that the first half of the book presents a broad perspective on world history, and the second half is concerned more narrowly with the fate of the church within it.[69] Edwards takes an historicist reading of the text,[70] which sees its prophecies corresponding to events within history and significantly equates the prophecy of the two witnesses (Revelation 11:3) with the Waldenses and the Albigenses,[71] and the resurrection and ascension of the two witnesses after persecution (Revelation 11:11–12) with the Reformation of the sixteenth century:

> They are now got forever out of the reach of their enemies. Antichrist will never be able again to quell Christianity, and conquer the Reformation, do what he will.[72]

---

66. Edwards, *WJE* 13: 95–305.

67. See Thomas S. Kidd, *The Protestant Interest: New England after Puritanism* (New Haven: Yale University Press, 2004), which describes the process in New England of creating a pan-Protestant interest after the emasculation of Puritan categories of identity formation.

68. Stein, "Editor's Introduction," 12.

69. This is the model developed by Joseph Mede (1586–1639), who argued that the "little scroll" of Revelation 10:2 provides the content for the latter half of the book of Revelation. See James West Davidson, *The Logic of Millennial Thought: Eighteenth-Century New England* (New Haven: Yale University Press, 1977), 46. See also Edwards, *WJE* 5: 106–07.

70. Such an approach to the book of Revelation contrasts with a preterist or a futurist reading, which places its substance in the past or the future respectively. See Clarence C. Goen, "Jonathan Edwards: A New Departure in Eschatology," *Church History* 28(1) (1959): 25–40.

71. Edwards, *WJE* 5: 137.

72. Edwards, *WJE* 5: 105.

Under Edwards's schema, the vials or bowls of God's wrath (Revelation 15–17) are poured out on the Roman Catholic Church, beginning most recently with the triumphs "in Wicliff's, Hus's, and Jerome of Prague's days" followed by the second vial "at and after Luther's days."[73] The third vial corresponded to the drying up of the rivers of Roman Catholic teaching and teachers, in essence calamities upon the Kingdom of France as a "source" of popery, which Edwards may have understood to be contemporaneous with his writing.[74] Though Edwards had cause to adjust the schedule of the vials in the course of later writing, intimating that his own day witnessed the fulfillment of the prophecy of the sixth vial,[75] either way the impact of his case was most significant. The power of antichristian opposition to the Gospel was being undermined with every vial poured, the most treacherous days of the church lay in the past, the life of the church must shortly prosper, and any future tribulations for the pilgrim people of God in this world must surely be interpreted as the darkness immediately before the dawn or the increasing travails of a woman about to give birth.[76] In Edwards's estimation, it is the Protestant Reformation and the impending Millennium that are the parameters constraining any understanding of the life of the church in his own day.

Edwards writes several topical entries about the church, both in the "Apocalypse" and in the "Miscellanies." He describes the importance of the clerical ministry to teaching and the administration of the sacraments,[77] the propriety of quasi-synodical courts of appeal in matters of dispute,[78] the necessity of aspiring to be a visible Christian to qualify for admission to the Lord's Supper,[79] and the love of Christ, which is expressed toward his spouse, the church.[80] We learn further that the strength and joy of the

---

73. Edwards, *WJE* 13: 196.

74. Edwards, *WJE* 13: 196.

75. See Edwards, "Account of Events Probably Fulfilling the Sixth Vial," in *WJE* 5: 253–84, compiled after 1747. Moses Lowman held that all but the last two vials had been poured out. See Edwards, *WJE* 5: 202.

76. See also Edwards, "Misc." 356, *WJE* 13: 429, where the picture is drawn of the sun returning seasonally from its southernmost latitude, though the weather in the north grow yet colder.

77. See Edwards, "Misc." *mm*, *WJE* 13: 187.

78. See Edwards, "Misc." *qq*, *WJE* 13: 188–189.

79. See Edwards, "Misc." 338, *WJE* 13: 413.

80. See Edwards, "Misc." 189, *WJE* 13: 332.

church is foreshadowed in the ministry of Deborah as prophetess,[81] that the book of Revelation is "dedicated to the church of Christ in all ages,"[82] that the church was born not on the day of Pentecost, but existed from the time of Adam,[83] and that the Antichrist is Christ's rival "for the same spouse, even the church."[84] Even a cursory reading attests the presence of ecclesiological topics in Edwards's early mind.

A closer reading of such notebook entries during the 1720s yields further ecclesiological reflection.[85] It is not just that the word "church" or descriptions of structures for ministry constitute theologizing of the church. Though Edwards distances himself from a rigorous preparationism for locating the experience of conversion in a sequence, he nevertheless shows appreciation of the natural processes of history in which the church is embedded and that correlate the order of nature with the order of grace. His very presuppositions concerning the reading of the book of Revelation support this. Stein makes clear that Edwards's interpretation of Revelation "was based on the belief that God works through the historical process to achieve his will, not in spite of or apart from that process."[86]

Indeed, not only does God accommodate himself to the givens of time and space, but within that realm, the church itself is also, from divine perspective, the particular "object of providential care."[87] In "Misc." *ww*, entitled "Four Beasts," Edwards argues that the vision of Revelation 4 provides an important framework for the remainder of the book, such that after we learn about God, "the great Beginning and Ending of all," we learn of "the church of God, represented by the four and twenty elders, the subject of all dispensations."[88] The second paragraph of this entry uses the word "providence" five times, fourteen in all in the entry, making it the theme of this vision and thereby the theme of

---

81. Edwards, *WJE* 5: 127.

82. Edwards, *WJE* 5: 98.

83. Edwards, *WJE* 5: 136.

84. Edwards, *WJE* 5: 139.

85. No doubt Edwards had also been exposed in this early period to the defense of the Anglican polity espoused by Benjamin Hoadley, Bishop of Winchester, which had appeared in the Yale library. See Iain H. Murray, *Jonathan Edwards: A New Biography* (Edinburgh: The Banner of Truth Trust, 1987), 66.

86. Stein, "Editor's Introduction," *WJE* 5: 15.

87. Stein, "Editor's Introduction," *WJE* 5: 51.

88. See Edwards, "Misc." *ww*, *WJE* 13: 192.

the book of Revelation itself. Stein's thesis is that "Edwards's interpretation of the vision of the living creatures in Revelation 4 provides such an organizing focus by disclosing theological and literary order in the Apocalypse relating to the theme of providence,"[89] for through the "concept of providence, history and prophecy formed a continuum."[90] Although Edwards is often tarred with an apocalyptic brush, suggesting a distance from this-worldly concerns, his early commitment to the doctrine of providence makes room for a positive ecclesiology as essential to his theological constructions, highlighting "the fortunes of the church militant through the ages and in the present, as well as in his concern with the glories of the church triumphant."[91]

Consequently, Edwards is able to present the internationalist credentials of the church. It had been a common feature of the Puritan worldview to defend a particularist notion of the nation. For example, in John Foxe's *Acts and Monuments*, the nation of England could embody the fruit of Protestant victories in the sixteenth century, or New England could be described by Brightman as a nation in covenant with God when it appeared that Laudian persecution of Puritans or the Stuart Restoration made England's Protestant status untenable.[92] The "sacralization" of New England at the expense of Old England drew on the "Exodus-style" model of the people of God fleeing the persecution of Egypt and, despite trials, arriving in the Promised Land.[93] Such a mindset would undercut any possibility or desire to demonstrate the universal fellowship of believers, or the common Gospel inheritance of the church, as it was more likely to draw crisp lines of apocalyptic demarcation between those who belonged to the beast and those who belonged to the Lamb. Edwards's providentialist groundwork, on the other hand, along with changing fortunes of Protestants in English constitutional and imperial arrangements, made for new appreciation of the universal church of Christ. Localism had been transcended:

---

89. Stephen J. Stein, "Providence and the Apocalypse in the Early Writings of Jonathan Edwards," *Early American Literature* 13/3 (1978): 250–267, especially 252–253.

90. Stein, "Providence and the Apocalypse," 261.

91. Stein, "Providence and the Apocalypse," 263.

92. Indeed, Brightman makes a correspondence between England and the compromised church of Laodicea in Revelation 3. See Zakai, *Exile and Kingdom*, 52.

93. Zakai, *Exile and Kingdom*, 9. Zakai contrasts the "Exodus" model of migration with the "Genesis" model, the latter stressing the pilgrimage of Abraham in response to promise, and the former focusing on the expulsion of the Hebrews in response to threat.

[I]n contrast to New England Puritan historians who construed the Puritan migration to America during the seventeenth century as a great eschatological and apocalyptic event, establishing an essential gulf between the Old and New Worlds, Edwards abandoned the vision of the glorious New World in providential history. The redemptive process concerned all Protestants, regardless of their location.[94]

Edwards made this point in the sermon, "True Nobleness of Mind," preached early in 1728, while expounding the civic responsibilities of the virtuous citizen:

A natural man may be concerned for the good of the country he belongs to, but a Christian is concerned for the universal church and the world of mankind, has an universal benevolence.[95]

Contrary to much popular opinion, Edwards, in his earliest writings, did not argue that the millennial reign of Christ was to begin in North America. His international perspective provided him with just cause to expect the coming kingdom to be centered on the Middle East.[96] Kidd sets such a view within the broader framework of the 1720s in which "one can sense weariness among some New England observers who had long waited for the destruction of Rome and the conversion of the Jews.... New England's religious and cultural leadership seemed more than ready to turn their attention to an internationalist, ecumenical, and evangelical vision of conversions at the end of the world."[97]

Even when Edwards uses a large canvas upon which to paint the glories of the church, his millennial expectations in the period before 1729 are relatively modest. The entries entitled "Millennium" for this period in the "Miscellanies" (Nos. 26, 262, and 356) contain nothing describing a historical crisis, divine judgment, or apocalyptic intervention. Rather, "Misc." 26 relates the spread of the knowledge of God throughout the world such that barbarous nations become "as bright and polite as England," "excellent books and wonderful performances" might come from "Terra Australis Incognita," and disparate nations of the world "join the forces of their minds in exploring the glories of the Creator, their hearts in loving and adoring him, their hands in serving

---

94. Zakai, *Jonathan Edwards's Philosophy of History*, 162.

95. Jonathan Edwards, "True Nobleness of Mind," in *Sermons and Discourses, 1723–1729*, The Works of Jonathan Edwards 14, ed. K. P. Minkema (New Haven: Yale University Press, 1997), 238.

96. Edwards, *WJE* 5: 133–34.

97. Kidd, *The Protestant Interest*, 157.

him, and their voices in making the world to ring with his praise."[98] "Misc." 262 suggests a gradually increasing likeness of this world to heaven, insofar as "those things that more directly concern the mind and religion, will be more the saints' ordinary business than now." Secular activity will occupy less of the average person's time because of "a more expedite and easy and safe communication between distant regions," for example through the invention of the mariner's compass![99] A sense of conflict is, however, suggested in "Misc." 356, where an illustration from geography sets out the possibility that, just as we still sense increasing cold even after the sun has begun its course northward after the winter, so also "vice and wickedness may increase...after knowledge and light begin to increase."[100] Most instructively, in the "Exposition on the Apocalypse," under the heading of Chapter 20, no explanation of the thousand-year rule is given until an amendment is made in 1746 or 1747.[101]

More detail is provided in the exegetically oriented "Apocalypse Series." Entry No. 16, headed "Chapters 13 and 20," provides some calculations that suggest that Satan's kingdom will be finally overthrown around the year 2000, and the means used to fell the enemy will not be military but rather "blowing the trumpet of the gospel and preaching the Word of God."[102] This entry is, however, more concerned with establishing the correspondence between the type of the Sabbath rest after six days of creation and the antitype of the millenarian Sabbath after six thousand years of the world's labors.[103] It is surely significant that it is the world that will rest in the "peaceable reign of the saints,"[104] rather than the church that will rest after her trials and tribulations. The work of the church, and especially her ministers, is outlined in Entry No. 21, entitled "Chapter 20," where the apocalyptic focus is meager:

> So are ministers, the stewards of God's house, to labor, that they may present the church a chaste virgin to Christ.... And God makes use of

---

98. Edwards, "Misc." 26, *WJE* 13: 212.

99. Edwards, "Misc." 262, *WJE* 13: 369.

100. Edwards, "Misc." 356, *WJE* 13: 429.

101. Edwards, *WJE* 5: 123, note 8.

102. Edwards, *WJE* 5: 130. See also Entry No. 50, in which a similar argument is mounted, describing the metaphoric call of the trumpet in the preaching of the Gospel at the beginning of the seven thousand years.

103. Edwards, *WJE* 5: 129–30.

104. Edwards, *WJE* 5: 129.

his ministers to adorn and beautify souls, that they may be fit to be the spouse of Christ; that is their work.[105]

The conclusion of history will come when Christ, having ruled over the world for the sake of his church and having defeated all the enemies of his kingdom of grace, will relinquish his mediatorial rule to God the Father and enjoy union with his bride.[106] The church in this entry is so much a part of the warp and woof of the order of nature that she is entirely passive in the movement toward her consummation in glory, entirely dependent on the supernatural intervention of Christ to achieve her appointed ends.

Edwards, during the 1720s, was provoked to defend God's place within the order of nature, both in terms of its physical and temporal properties, because Enlightenment philosophy had attempted to describe and systematize the operations of nature without recourse to the operations of the deity. Edwards's reflections on the book of Revelation, both public and private, are a fertile ground to demonstrate his understanding of God's work in the world, of which the church is at its heart. His forays into apocalyptic exposition are indeed a major source for our understanding of Edwards's early ecclesiology, though Zakai reminds us that his "attempts to formulate his philosophy of history went on slowly and gradually" in this period.[107] These themes will be revisited regularly in the course of this book as we unpack their nuanced and evolving role.

2.3 Church under Threat: Confronting Enlightenment Epistemology

Although any disagreement with his family would be painful, Jonathan Edwards's most significant contretemps during his formative years (and indeed beyond) was with those teachers, both religious and otherwise, whose commitment to Enlightenment philosophy, whether rationalist or empiricist, left no room for the supernatural or for morality shaped by Christian convictions. The pressure to conform to the light of most recent scholarship and to the centralizing spirit of New England's new status as province of the Empire

---

105. Edwards, *WJE* 5: 131–32.

106. Edwards, "Misc." 86, *WJE* 13: 250–51.

107. Zakai, *Jonathan Edwards's Philosophy of History*, 191.

was seductive.[108] In this section, we will have particular reason to look at sermons and discourses, where Edwards's analyses of threats to the theological life of the church are most accessible and his capacity to respond to them most organized. The threat of Enlightened thought would jeopardize New England's convictions concerning salvation, but significantly would also have an ecclesiological reflex, which Edwards presciently saw and guarded against.

Since Perry Miller's contribution to the rehabilitation of Edwards in the middle of the twentieth century, a common approach to Edwards has been to view him through the prism of the philosophy of John Locke (1632–1704), an Englishman who had most responsibility for laying the groundwork of the Enlightenment project in the seventeenth century through his treatises *Essay Concerning Human Understanding* (1690) and *The Reasonableness of Christianity* (1695).[109] Locke, in turn, can be described as applying to anthropology and the study of humankind the insights of Sir Isaac Newton (1643–1727) in the realm of natural science, in whose writings varied motions of the universe were systematized to produce fixed laws and regular patterns. The analog in the realm of human relationships would be "general principles that could explain all of the wide variations in human behavior in diverse societies."[110]

Locke's philosophical modesty shied away from the extreme claims of certainty found in those schemes of thought that stressed *a priori* deductivism. On the other hand, he also shunned unbridled skepticism: he permitted divine revelation so long as it could be supported through the exercise of reason. Locke overturned the suspicion of sense perception germane to Platonic streams of Western philosophy and developed a fresh approach to epistemology, in which a human being is pictured as a blank slate or *tabula rasa*, passive in receiving sensory data and yet capable of some high degree of probability in the knowledge gleaned. Simple ideas are interpreted by us through sensations from without and are not innate to us, though we do have some capacity to organize or connect them through reasoning, creating complex ideas.[111]

---

108. Alongside *philosophical* adversaries, described by Edwards as Arminians, deists, freethinkers, or Socinians, we must also reckon with the *geopolitical* adversaries of England in North America, namely, the French and the Spanish.

109. See Moody, *Edwards and Enlightenment*, 11n16, for a bibliographical summary of the debate.

110. Landsman, *From Colonials to Provincials*, 60–62.

111. Porter, *Enlightenment*, 64. See also John Locke, *An Essay Concerning Human Understanding*, The Clarendon Edition of the Works of John Locke (Oxford: Clarendon Press, 1975), 104, 668, 698.

The Collegiate School, founded in 1701 and later known as Yale College,[112] whether at Saybrook, Killingworth, Wethersfield, Hartford, or New Haven, had developed an eclectic syllabus that early included Locke. Availability of such new ideas was due in part to the gift from Jeremiah Dummer (1681–1739) to the nascent institution of a library including latitudinarian books, collected in London in 1712–1713, and also to the deliberate intention of Yale to develop skills in logic and oral exercises drawing on a variety of metaphysical and philosophical schemes.[113] Locke was studied, alongside Virgil, Burgersdijck, Ramus, Mastricht, Heereboord, and Ames.[114] That Edwards read Locke may be assumed. Famously, Hopkins could describe Edwards's appreciation of *The Essay Concerning Human Understanding* by comparing him to a "most greedy miser in gathering up handfuls of silver and gold from some new discovered treasure."[115] Though Edwards may have enjoyed reading Locke, and it might even be argued from some of Edwards's own early writings that the psychology of Locke had been appropriated by him when he drew together the language of light and of sense,[116] we must nevertheless exercise a little caution in seeing Edwards as too reliant on Lockean empiricism. As Brown reminds us, Edwards's epistemology contained rationalist elements, and linguistic dependence might not suggest wholehearted agreement.[117]

For Edwards, then, recent philosophical developments were not in and of themselves an adversary. It is even true that he absorbed some of the method of Francisco Suárez (1548–1617), a Spanish Counter-Reformation Jesuit, in his approach to logic.[118] Edwards's "Catalogue of Books" (commenced in 1722 and

---

112. This name, and the title of rector for its president, were deliberately chosen to create ambiguity and to avoid the scrutiny and suspicion of London, which alone could grant licenses for establishing tertiary institutions.

113. Morris, *Young Jonathan Edwards*, 62, 101.

114. Morris, *Young Jonathan Edwards*, 65. It remains contested, however, whether any distinctive characteristics of Yale's syllabus are attributable to its founding in opposition to the kind of ministerial education that Harvard provided. Bainton sees Yale's founding in conservative terms, as does Harry Stout, while Morris is more circumspect. See Bainton, *Yale and the Ministry*, 1; Morris, *Young Jonathan Edwards*, 66; Stout, *The New England Soul*, 220.

115. Samuel Hopkins, ed. *The Life and Character of the late Reverend Mr. Jonathan Edwards, President of the College at New-Jersey, Together With a Number of His Sermons*, 2nd ed. (Glasgow: David Niven for James Duncan, 1785), 9.

116. See, for example, Jonathan Edwards, "Christ, the Light of the World," in *Sermons and Discourses, 1720–1723*, The Works of Jonathan Edwards 10, ed. W. H. Kimnach (New Haven: Yale University Press, 1992), 539.

117. Robert E. Brown, *Jonathan Edwards and the Bible* (Bloomington: Indiana University Press, 2002), 40.

118. Morris, *Young Jonathan Edwards*, 398.

in use the remainder of his life) contains works already completed, ordered, or desired, many of which were of contemporary philosophy, while his "Account Book" listed, alongside references to cattle and creditors, books he had lent out.[119] He remained abreast of recently published materials through reviews or excerpts in journals like *The Guardian, Republic of Letters, Bibliothèque Choisie,* or *Bibliothèque Universelle,*[120] where it is assumed he would have met the ideas of the Irish Anglican Bishop and philosopher George Berkeley (1685–1753) as well. Though Edwards's dependence on Locke has often been overstated, it is nevertheless true that Edwards did turn to Locke as well as to other thinkers to find forms in which he might commend true piety in an age more accustomed to tepid propositionalism.[121] Moody summarizes:

> It is better to picture the Enlightenment as Edwards' springboard, than as Edwards' data source. Edwards does make substantial withdrawals from the Enlightenment bank, particularly the proto-Enlightenment of Locke and Newton, but only to invest in his own, essentially Biblical, view of reality.[122]

It was not so much the Enlightenment project itself that Edwards regarded as an adversary as the use to which it was put by those radical thinkers who wanted to displace supernatural religion through their own deistic schemes. Such a naturalistic process tended to separate morality from its religious, more particularly Christian, validation and was strenuously resisted. If those dubbed "Arminian" or "Latitudinarian" were prone to collapse the transcendent into the immanent without remainder and to marginalize the ability of divine grace to intrude upon an individual's life, then Edwards would relentlessly rail against such leaders and their promotion of works-righteousness through his sermons, discourses, and miscellanies, which defended justification by grace, the righteousness of Christ, and the sovereign work of the Spirit.[123] The issue had become most pertinent for him, because the rector

---

119. Peter J. Thuesen, "Edwards' Intellectual Background," in *The Princeton Companion to Jonathan Edwards,* ed. S. H. Lee (Princeton: Princeton University Press, 2005), 24–25. See also Jonathan Edwards, *Catalogues of Books,* The Works of Jonathan Edwards 26, ed. P. J. Thuesen (New Haven: Yale University Press, 2008).

120. Morris, *Young Jonathan Edwards,* 457.

121. Morris, *Young Jonathan Edwards,* 576.

122. Moody, *Edwards and Enlightenment,* 7.

123. Minkema summarizes the Arminian challenge in New England thus: "Arminianism was named after the sixteenth-century Dutch theologian Jacob Arminius. Originally, it was narrowly understood as a repudiation of John Calvin's supralapsarianism, but by the early eighteenth century the term came to encompass a broad spectrum of theologians, including

of Yale, Timothy Cutler, and tutors Johnson and Browne, had, on October 16, 1722, declared their intention to join the Church of England, associated in many minds with incipient Arminianism,[124] for which their employment at Yale was not surprisingly abruptly terminated.[125] New England's Congregationalist leaders saw this incident "as a threat to international Protestantism from popery."[126] Edwards's preaching in New York during the fall of 1722 provides an early statement of his anti-Arminian position.[127]

Edwards's own M.A. oral defense in Latin, known as the *Quæstio*, presented a year later in September 1723, responded boldly to the theological challenge of Arminianism that had convulsed Yale in 1722 when he asserts that "a sinner is justified in the sight of God neither totally nor in part because of the goodness of such obedience, or of any works at all, but only on account of what Christ did and suffered, received by faith."[128] Of a piece with such theological *Zeitgeist*, Edwards finds himself during the 1720s often preaching to defend first the divinity of Christ against latter-day Socinians and then the atonement against Arminians for whom the radical rupture between grace and nature was unacceptable, and preaching to promote the sovereignty of the Spirit that so ably protects the priority of grace.[129]

---

the majority of the Anglican clergy, who emphasized good works over right doctrine and maintained the free will of humankind to accept or reject the grace of God." See Kenneth P. Minkema, "Preface to the Period," in *Sermons and Discourses, 1723–1729* The Works of Jonathan Edwards 14, ed. K. P. Minkema (New Haven: Yale University Press, 1997), 17. It ought to be added that antipathy toward Roman Catholic expressions of works-righteousness had been a consistent theme in Puritan preaching before the eighteenth century, which Edwards continued to address.

124. Anglicanism was particularly obnoxious to New England Puritans: "In ecclesiology the Puritans argued that congregational government was more biblical and less prone to corruption than prelacy. They also accused the Latitudinarian movement in Anglicanism of feeding the increased authority given to reason at Harvard. In Puritan vocabulary, Arminianism, Latitudinarianism, and Prelacy were synonymous with heresy, and Anglicanism possessed all three." See George G. Levesque, "Quaestio: Peccator non Iustificatur Coram Deo Nisi per Iustitiam Christi Fide Apprehensam," in *Sermons and Discourses, 1723–1729*, The Works of Jonathan Edwards 14, ed. K. P. Minkema (New Haven: Yale University Press, 1997), 50n5.

125. Kimnach, "Preface to the New York Period," *WJE* 10: 287.

126. Kidd, *The Protestant Interest*, 128.

127. Edwards, "Glorious Grace," *WJE* 10: 397.

128. Jonathan Edwards, "A Sinner Is Not Justified in the Sight of God Except Through the Righteousness of Christ Obtained by Faith," in *Sermons and Discourses, 1723–1729*, The Works of Jonathan Edwards 14, ed. K. P. Minkema (New Haven: Yale University Press, 1997), 61.

129. In jeremiad-like way, this sermon for a fast day gives important insights into spiritual trajectories in the land: Jonathan Edwards, "Sin and Wickedness Bring Calamity and Misery on a People," in *Sermons and Discourses, 1723–1729*, The Works of Jonathan Edwards

The theological tendency of the early eighteenth century toward deist innovations had begun to threaten the purity of the church. The infiltration of
Enlightenment ideas into New England reflected first of all on the impossibility of Puritan life remaining sealed from the outside world. Indeed, since 1707,
the very structure of English life itself had changed with the birth of the unified Kingdom of Great Britain in the merging of the parliaments of Scotland
and England. Politically, the British Isles and their dependencies had become
increasingly centralized, and this development found philosophical support
in the rationalizing and ordering that the Newtonian system made available
to science and sociology. The anarchy of the Civil Wars, the Commonwealth,
and the Protectorate encouraged many to long for a less chaotic and more settled Christian polity, which was achieved in the Restoration of 1660. Though
not driven to armed interventions in the New World, the labile nature of the
Congregationalist model, the desire by some for Presbyterian polity, and the
increasing attraction of English mores all led to a greater tolerance of Anglican
design and ordination, as the defection of the Yale teaching staff in the early
1720s attested.[130]

Edwards responded to the Arminians not just because their views were a
threat to the Protestant priority of divine grace in salvation but also because he
saw, more ominously, that these views represented a challenge to the authority
of the local congregation and hence its purity. Authority would be dangerously
relocated:

> The appeal of Latitudinarians in American was extremely broad.... In
> the provinces, where a dominant church hierarchy was lacking every-
> where, it had a wide resonance, appealing both to the dissenting
> majorities in most northern colonies and to the gentry-dominated,
> Low Church establishments in the south.... Another reason for the
> Latitudinarians' appeal...was to locate the ultimate authority in reli-
> gion not in the church but in the mind of the individual.... In attempt-
> ing to demonstrate the conformity of religion to the natural order, they
> assumed that hearers were to judge for themselves rather than take the
> pronouncements of the church for granted.[131]

14; ed. K. P. Minkema (New Haven: Yale University Press, 1997), 498–99. See also Edwards,
"Threefold Work," *WJE* 14: 396, and Edwards, "None are Saved," *WJE* 14: 350–51.

130. Youngs, *God's Messengers*, 30, 32, 78–79.

131. Landsman, *From Colonials to Provincials*, 66.

Though Edwards has little of explicit ecclesiological deliberation in the sermons and discourses of the 1720s, his soteriological arrows were nevertheless pointed at an ultimately ecclesiological target. Edwards found cause for alarm and adversaries to refute in the movement toward Arminianism in New England. The battle would be joined until the last years of his life.

2.4 Shape of the Church: Formulating Trinitarian Dynamism with Design

Edwards acceded to sole leadership of the church in Northampton on February 11, 1729, upon the death of Solomon Stoddard. A year after this new beginning, he had started to draft the "Discourse on the Trinity," drawing on formulations from earlier "Miscellanies," subsequently being revised for both private and public purposes until the mid-1740s.[132] The "Discourse" demonstrates Edwards's innovative defense of traditional trinitarian orthodoxy against the increasingly assertive claims of deist or rationalist opponents who wanted to leave behind fissiparous or disordering debates of earlier periods, and for whom the doctrine of the Trinity represented obscurantist and superstitious dogma. Among such adversaries were neo-Arians on the one hand (for example, the New England divine Jonathan Mayhew), who would undermine the deity of the Son and the Spirit or subordinate their ontological status to God the Father. On the other hand, Edwards writes against those of Arminian or perhaps Socinian persuasion (for example, the Archbishop of Canterbury John Tillotson), who, by virtue of their positive view of the human contribution to salvation, would demote the work of the Son and the Spirit. Both heterodox approaches rendered the Son and the Spirit marginal to the plan of salvation and elevated moralism based on the laws of nature to the quintessence of Christian faith.[133] As Lee summarizes, "Arminianism was fundamentally anti-trinitarian."[134]

From an ecclesiological perspective, Edwards's theological adversaries were a danger not just to the integrity of individual salvation but also to corporate expressions of faith, because their liberalizing agenda strengthened the authority and ultimately the autonomy of the individual and consequently weakened

---

132. Jonathan Edwards, "Discourse on the Trinity," in *Writings on the Trinity, Grace and Faith,* The Works of Jonathan Edwards 21, ed. S. H. Lee (New Haven: Yale University Press, 2003).

133. Porter, *Enlightenment,* 102–04.

134. Sang Hyun Lee, "Editor's Introduction," in *Writings on the Trinity, Grace, and Faith,* The Works of Jonathan Edwards 21, ed. S. H. Lee (New Haven: Yale University Press, 2003), 4.

or relativized the authority of the church in the world.[135] Edwards's trinitarian discourse provides a bulwark against such assaults (even while carefully using Enlightenment categories for his own ends). Such trinitarian reflection serves not just apologetic ends, but implicitly provides a constructive model for the church as a relational community to imitate, with the Trinity itself as the ultimate life in which the church is invited to participate. The dynamic life of the Trinity does not create imbalance or instability for the church, but rather the relations between Father, Son, and Spirit are ordered and so bequeath organic growth with design to our experience of fellowship within the church.[136]

A Model for the Life of the Church: God's Complexity with Consistency

Edwards's "Discourse" is of ecclesiological significance because it provides a window into his overall theological trajectory, broadly aligning him with the "Spiritual Brethren" rather than the "Intellectual Fathers" in the taxonomy of Janice Knight. In her schema, Knight describes the circle of Richard Sibbes (1577–1635), the teaching of which highlighted the unmediated work of God in an individual's life and consequently the derivative role of the church as ordering and sustaining such regeneration. With this she contrasts the school of William Ames (1576–1633), which stressed the power of God, the importance of incremental change in the life of the seeker through the discipline of preparation, and consequently the authority of the church in mediating grace.[137]

---

135. Some thinkers attributed blame to the clergy for all the ills of society and thereby undermined the church's moral and political authority. See Porter, *Enlightenment*, 102.

136. Recent commentators have pointed out the dangers in Edwards's trinitarian formulations. While Steve Studebaker makes the case that Edwards is essentially an Augustinian theologian who affirms the doctrine of inseparable external acts and appeals to the mutual love model of trinitarianism, this often remains camouflaged by the dominant language of *social relations*: Steve Studebaker, "Jonathan Edwards's Social *Augustinian* Trinitarianism: An Alternative to a Recent Trend," *Scottish Journal of Theology* 56(3) (2003): 268–85. Amy Plantinga Pauw, on the other hand, wants to point out the ways in which Edwards appropriates both Cappadocian/Victorine themes of social trinitarianism and Augustinian psychological tropes. She is, however, keen to leave unresolved in Edwards this attempt at a fusion between two classical models, which Edwards made to serve pastoral or polemical ends and which she claims creates an unstable mix. Amy P. Pauw, *"The Supreme Harmony of All": The Trinitarian Theology of Jonathan Edwards* (Grand Rapids: Eerdmans, 2002). Danaher is much more positive concerning the constructive synthesis achieved in Edwards's trinitarian thought, particularly as it relates to an ethical vision and so adjudicates between the former scholars: William J. Danaher, *The Trinitarian Ethics of Jonathan Edwards*, Columbia Series in Reformed Theology (Louisville: Westminster John Knox, 2004).

137. Knight, *Orthodoxies in Massachusetts*, 1–4. While Knight's contrast does provide fruitful spheres of association among earlier Puritans, there is also a case for demurring, as, for

She mounts the case that Edwards belongs to the former grouping. God's direct involvement in the world is nevertheless to be understood expressed through the agency of the Son and the Spirit, with the church as the secondary instrument.

Edwards's views can usefully be contrasted with those found in Ames's *Marrow of Theology*. After three chapters on theological prolegomena,[138] Ames begins his reflections on God proper in the fourth chapter entitled "God and His Essence," in which he stresses the transcendence of God and our incapacity to understand or to describe him.[139] Even with revelation, our comprehension is limited. The distance between God and us necessitates epistemic modesty such that we must be reserved in any propositions we make concerning him. There is no mention of the triune character of God in this section.[140]

The next section, Ames's brief presentation of the Trinity, appears under the rubric of "The Subsistence of God," and consists of three and one-half pages.[141] The language of subsistence is applied to both the singular essence of the Godhead and the traditional concept of the hypostatic distinction between persons of the Trinity: "The subsistence, or manner of being [subsistentia] of God is his one essence so far as it has personal properties," and "The same essence is common to the three subsistences."[142] Ames makes use of the traditional Augustinian psychological analogy of understanding and love to highlight God's unity while allowing relations within the Trinity, presenting the Father as "*Deus intelligens*," the Son as "*Deus intellectus*," and the Spirit as "*Deus dilectus*."[143] The next section, "The Efficiency of God," describes the power of

---

example, when we read not of Ames's presentation of God's rule but of God's love: "for in the old covenant God expressed his wise and just counsel in the form of sovereignty—but in the new there is only mercy." William Ames, *The Marrow of Theology*, trans. J. E. Eusden (Grand Rapids: Baker, 1997), 151. Amy Plantinga Pauw likewise cautions against the starkness of Knight's contrast, though she holds that Edwards's echoes of the Sibbesian party are a useful corrective to the depiction often made of his theology: Pauw, *Supreme Harmony*, 5–8.

138. These sections reflect the background of Ramist logic, which is characterized by "dichotomizing of concepts—subdividing them into pairs, and splitting those pairs into more pairs, and so on—as being the key to epistemological and educational mastery of all realities." See James I. Packer, "A Puritan Perspective: Trinitarian Godliness according to John Owen," in *God the Holy Trinity: Reflections on Christian Faith and Practice*, ed. T. George (Grand Rapids: Baker, 2006), 94.

139. It is one of the characteristics of premodern or classical philosophy that essence precedes existence, whereas modern philosophy inverts the assumption.

140. Ames, *Marrow*, 83.

141. There is no chapter entitled "The Trinity."

142. Ames, *Marrow*, 88.

143. Ames, *Marrow*, 89.

God at work in the world and in point number eight lists "[t]he proper order for conceiving these things is, first, to think of God's *posse*, his power; second, his *scire*, knowledge; third, his *velle*, will; and lastly his *efficere potenter*, efficient power."[144] Significantly, it is the power of God that both begins and ends this description, that is, the expression of God's power is both "the meaning of that efficiency which pertains to God's essence," and "in some ways follows after his knowledge and will."[145] Because Ames is concerned not to divide the Godhead by allowing for "compositeness or mutation of power...in God's perfectly simple and immutable nature,"[146] the Father, Son, and Spirit labor together "inseparably," though according to their own distinctive "manner of working."[147] In Ames's Chapter 7, called "The Decree and Counsel of God," a similar prioritizing is listed.[148] In each of these examples, the doctrine of the Trinity does not create the structure of the presentation, but rather is accommodated to philosophical theology exemplified in the exercise of God's power in the world. Nor does Christology play a significant role, as Ames is keen to defend the simplicity of the Godhead. God is dependable because God is essentially one.

John Norton (1606–1663), on the other hand, begins his introduction to *Orthodox Evangelist* (1654) with a description of love as the foundation of Christian ministry and of the whole teaching endeavor: "So as there is not to be found a more vigorous effusion of the Bowels of Jesus, in any of the hearts of the children of men, then [sic] is in the souls of the Ministry."[149] Like Ames, Norton names the first chapter "Of the Divine Essence," argues for the divine simplicity, and begins with the fundamental accommodation of God to human finitude. He defends the unity of the Godhead while acknowledging various pluralized names for God in the Bible. Significantly, unlike Ames, Chapter 2 of *Orthodox Evangelist* is entitled "Of the Trinity" and devotes some fifteen pages to this theological theme. Norton includes an explanation

---

144. Ames, *Marrow*, 92.

145. Ames, *Marrow*, 92.

146. Ames, *Marrow*, 91.

147. Ames, *Marrow*, 93.

148. Ames, *Marrow*, 94.

149. John Norton, *The Orthodox Evangelist, or A Treatise Wherein Many Great Evangelical Truths (Not a Few Whereof Are Much Opposed and Eclipsed in this Perillous Hour of the Passion of the Gospel,) Are Briefly Discussed, Cleared, and Confirmed: As a Further Help, for the Begetting, and Establishing of the Faith Which Is in Jesus. As also the State of the Blessed, Where; Of the Condition of Their Souls from the Instant of Their Dissolution: And of Their Persons after Their Resurrection* (London: John Macock, Henry Cripps, Lodowick Lloyd, 1654), 1.

of the mutual indwelling of each member of the Trinity,[150] which, by contrast, Ames has no need to expound because of his assertions of God's simplicity. Norton makes no reference to the legal covenant of redemption[151] (which Ames makes the precondition for the covenant of grace[152]) but instead in Chapter 2 expresses pastoral concern for "the consolation of believers."[153] Significantly, it is organic imagery applied to the effulgence of God and an almost mystical appreciation of the process of remanation, described rapturously, that helps to mark out Norton as distinct from the Amesian school with its propensity to forensic categories:

> God is a full fountain, or rather a fountain which is fulnesse it self; willing to communicate as the sun sends forth its light, a fountain its streams, and the prolifical virtue in plants, inclineth them to fruitful-nesse; and the seminal virtue in living creatures, disposeth them to generation.... Goodnesse so descends and cometh from God unto the creature, as that it stops not there, but ascends and returns again unto God.... Hence love is said to be both extatical [sic], that is, carrying the lover as it were out of himself unto the loved.... Unto that infinite and created sea, whence all created rivers of goodnesse come, thither they return again.[154]

Knight sees in Ames a "preference for images of domination" and "the master trope of sovereignty,"[155] while in Norton and his school she witnesses "neo-platonist visions of divine plenitude and effulgence" and "the master trope of benevolence."[156] Although Ames expresses reserve concerning God's involve-ment with the created order and human capacity to appropriate God's ben-efits, Norton is in no sense beholden to such caution. He affirms both the nature of mystery and the value of exploring it.[157] We must speak of the Trinity

---

150. Norton, *Orthodox Evangelist*, 31–32.

151. The covenant of redemption is that pretemporal consent of the Father with the Son to effect salvation for human beings, enacted through the temporal covenant of grace. Appeal is made to Psalm 2 or Ephesians 3:14–15 to support such a pact.

152. Ames, *Marrow*, 149.

153. Norton, *Orthodox Evangelist*, 34.

154. Norton, *Orthodox Evangelist*, 13.

155. Knight, *Orthodoxies in Massachusetts*, 75.

156. Knight, *Orthodoxies in Massachusetts*, 76, 82.

157. Norton, *Orthodox Evangelist*, 34.

even when such description of the life of the Trinity has the potential to disorder and overwhelm our experience. It is just such a risk that we observe in
Edwards as well. Here we find not a spirit of theological caution but rather of
trinitarian assertion, and this is based on our created likeness to God.[158] It is
not that Edwards wants to teach that all mystery is removed, but that, by analogy with nature and on closer inspection, we can be more confident of what
we will come to discover:

> I humbly apprehend that the things that have been observed increase
> the number of visible mysteries in the Godhead in no other manner,
> even as by them we perceive that God has told us much more about it
> than was before generally observed.... And if he views them [natural
> things] with a microscope, the number of the wonders that he sees will
> be much increased still. But yet the microscope gives him more of a
> *true knowledge* concerning them.[159]

Edwards's understanding of the Trinity aligns him with the school that maintains God's approach to this world through promise of consistent access.

The Grammar of the Life of the Church:
The Persons of the Trinity

Edwards's presentation of the Trinity in this discourse not only locates him
within a broader Puritan ecclesiological trajectory but also provides concrete
images and tropes that anchor his doctrine of the church for the life of the
people of God. The work of Father, Son, and Spirit provides the grammar with
which Edwards's doctrine of the church can be articulated.

A Bride For Christ

The security of the church is exemplified in the metaphor of the church
being a bride for Christ. Although the outpouring of God's life toward the
creation in love and grace could be potentially overwhelming,[160] this expansive
self-expression nonetheless has shape in the Son, whom Edwards describes
as "the face of God" or "the brightness, effulgence or shining forth of God's

---

158. Edwards, "Trinity," *WJE* 21: 113.

159. Edwards, "Trinity," *WJE* 21: 139–40 (emphasis mine).

160. The use of natural images (for example, God "communicates himself...as the ema-
nation of the sun's action, or the emitted beams of the sun") can create visceral reactions.
Edwards, "Trinity," *WJE* 21: 138.

glory."[161] Christ's luminescence is associated in Edwards's mind with his office as "the great prophet and teacher of mankind, the light of the world, and the revealer of God to creatures."[162] The potentially disordering elements of effulgence or the destabilizing distinction of the persons, such that the Godhead is a "society" or "family," are brought to focus Christologically in the revelation of the Son, despite the dynamism of the image.[163] He is the end for which God created the world and the constrained means by which God's extravagant love is expressed:

> Christ is divine wisdom, so that the world is made to gratify divine love as exercised by Christ, or to gratify the love that is in Christ's heart, or to provide a spouse for Christ—those creatures which wisdom chooses for the object of divine love as Christ's elect spouse, and especially those elect creatures that wisdom chiefly pitches upon and makes the end of the rest.[164]

The church, therefore, is the creation of God to gratify Christ's love, just as Christ's ministry is an agency of God's love for the church and the world. Conversely, God gives the church to Christ as his bride "so that the mutual joys between this bride and bridegroom are the end of the creation."[165] The church is necessary to the person of Christ. This ought not to be understood, however, as expressing divine dependence on the creation, as the formula here is not the trinitarian language of the Father and the Son, which, as a result of

---

161. Edwards, "Trinity," *WJE* 21: 118, 119.

162. Edwards, "Trinity," *WJE* 21: 120.

163. Amy Plantinga Pauw, "Practical Ecclesiology in John Calvin and Jonathan Edwards," in *John Calvin's American Legacy*, ed. Thomas J. Davis (Oxford: Oxford University Press, 2010), 95.

164. Edwards, "Trinity," *WJE* 21: 142. This point is made later in a sermon on Revelation 22: "Christ obtaining this spouse is the great end of all the great things that have been done from the beginning of the world[;] it was that the son of God might obtain his [c]hosen spouse that the world was Created…and that he came into the world…and when this end shall be fully obtained[,] the world will come to an [e]nd." Jonathan Edwards, "613. Unpublished Sermon on Revelation 22:16–17 (May 1741)," (accessed from the Jonathan Edwards Center at Yale University, 2011), L. 3v. Note that where normal pagination is lacking in unpublished works, references in this book refer to leaf number, either *recto* or *verso*.

165. Though there is only one reference in the "Discourse" to the provision of a spouse for Christ, and this being added later than the mid-1730s, Edwards has nevertheless made use of this imagery in an early essay. See Jonathan Edwards, "Misc." 271, in *The "Miscellanies" (Entry Nos. a–z, aa–zz, 1–500)*, The Works of Jonathan Edwards 13, ed. T. A. Schafer (New Haven: Yale University Press, 1994), 374.

Nicene debates, maintains a line between the Creator and the creation. Here, the functional terminology of "Christ," the one anointed for service, allows for economic distance from ontological concerns.[166]

The life of the church is framed by the church's role as the reward to Christ, who is the head of the body and the groom for the bride.[167] This union between Christ and the church will never be surrendered nor sundered, giving to Christ an eternal distinction among the members of the Trinity and to the church a stake in the life of the Godhead and a Christologically defined future.[168]

A Covenant between the Father and the Son

A detail pertinent to ecclesiology and connected to Edwards's trinitarian thought, which is adumbrated in the "Discourse" (though appearing more explicitly later in "Misc." 1062), concerns the pretemporal covenant of redemption between the Father and the Son:

> It is evident by the Scripture that there is an eternal covenant between some of the persons of the Trinity about that particular affair of man's redemption; and therefore that some things that appertain to the particular office of each person, and their particular order and manner of acting in this affair, does result from a particular, new agreement, and not merely from the order already fixed in a preceding establishment founded in the nature of things, together with the new determination of redeeming mankind.[169]

---

166. It must furthermore be acknowledged that in the book of Revelation, the language of *groom* or *Christ* is never used in relation to the bride. Consistently in Revelation, the imagery is derived from the domain of sacrifice in which the second person of the Trinity is presented as the Lamb. The language of *Christ* is however drawn from Paul's concerns in Ephesians 5.

167. Edwards, in a later sermon from 1737, makes the same point: "Christ is the bridegroom and his true invisible church is the bride." Jonathan Edwards, "448. Matthew 25:1 (Nov. 1737)," in *Sermons, Series II, 1737*, The Works of Jonathan Edwards Online 52 (Jonathan Edwards Center at Yale University, 2008), L. 3r. And again: "the church of Christ that I have described is the Bride[,] the Lamb[']s wife." Jonathan Edwards, "738. Unpublished Sermon on Colossians 1:24 (April 1744)" (accessed from the Jonathan Edwards Center at Yale University, 2011), L. 24v.

168. Jonathan Edwards, "Misc." 1062, in *The "Miscellanies" (Entry Nos. 833–1152)*, The Works of Jonathan Edwards 20, ed. A. P. Pauw (New Haven: Yale University Press, 2002), 440.

169. Edwards, "Misc." 1062, *WJE* 20: 432.

In recognition of the traditional weakness of Western thought and its propensity to stress the oneness of God at the expense of the distinctions with equality of the persons of the Trinity, Edwards expounds the pretemporal conversing of the Father and the Son, which demonstrates their equality as a result of their willingness to enter into a covenant of redemption with each other for the sake of those to be saved. The covenant of redemption helps Edwards to avoid the danger of subordinationism in the Trinity and so protect the deity of the Son and of the Spirit from the potential of Arianizing.[170] Indeed, Edwards goes on to describe not only the covenant of redemption but also a colloquium or "council of peace," possibly with overtones of the frontier, between the Father and the Son that takes place prior to the formal covenant in which they agree in principle "concerning the part that some, at least, of the persons are to act in that affair [of redemption]."[171] Such dynamism is nevertheless structured or designed, for the outcome of the agreement is regarded by members of the Trinity as "fit, suitable and beautiful."[172]

On the other hand, when Edwards highlights the equality of the triune persons by brazenly describing their hypostatic interactions as a "society of the Trinity," he must simultaneously assert the ordering and agreed leadership of God the Father, "who acts as the head."[173] Using such anthropomorphic

---

170. However, because the work of each member of the Trinity is not simply interchangeable, Edwards asserts that there is a "priority of subsistence" within the life of the Trinity, which "is more properly called priority than superiority." Subordination, in his estimation, exists when the language of volition is applied to one member of the Trinity in relation to another: "For one is not superior to another in excellency; neither is one in any respect dependent on another's *will* for being or well-being. For though one proceeds from another, and so may be said to be in some respect dependent on another, yet it is no dependence of one on *the will of another*. For it is no *voluntary* but a *necessary* proceeding, and therefore infers no proper subjection of one to the will of another." See Edwards, "Misc." 1062, *WJE* 20: 431.

171. Edwards, "Misc." 1062, *WJE* 20: 433.

172. Edwards, "Misc." 1062, *WJE* 20: 431. However, Edwards's later descriptions of relations within the Godhead appear to leave the Holy Spirit at some level disenfranchised, or at least depersonalized. The Spirit is referred to as Christ's "treasures," and the language of the Augustinian trinitarian model reemerges, in which the Spirit is presented as "the bond of union between the two covenanting persons," "the infinite love of God to himself and to the creature," the "moving cause of the whole transaction," and the "great good covenanted for." See Edwards, "Misc." 1062, *WJE* 20: 439, 443.

173. Edwards, "Misc." 1062, *WJE* 20: 433. It has been pointed out that such language is not original to Edwards but was used by Petrus van Mastricht, a Dutch Reformed theologian whom Edwards read and greatly admired. See Adriaan C. Neele, *The Art of Living to God: A Study of Method and Piety in the Theoretico-Practica Theologia of Petrus van Mastricht (1630–1706)*, Perspectives on Christianity 8:1 (Pretoria: Department of Church History, University of Pretoria, 2005), 223, 237. Mastricht takes his cue from the imagery of Psalm 2 and the vocabulary of Ephesians 3:14–15.

language as "society," he applies to the Godhead a structure that we would rather expect to encounter in a town or a church. Appropriating the terminology of covenant as a device to bring order to the relationships within the Trinity itself, he removes the fear that God's sovereign work in the world is capricious, arbitrary, or the result of internecine divine squabbling. Those who approach him are encouraged to expect consistency and compassion. As Christ orders the glory of God *ad extra*, so the covenant between Father and Son orders the glory of God *ad intra*. Christ's work in the world is the means by which the Son brings honor to the Father, insofar as the Son fulfills his part in the economy of God through his work as mediator of the new covenant.[174] Edwards concludes:

> The Redeemer shall present all that were to be redeemed to the Father in perfect glory, having his work completely finished upon them.[175]

The Spirit Of Union

Spiritual union is at the heart of Edwards's theological project.[176] The Spirit defines the unity that exists between Christ and the church, "for the Spirit is the bond of union and that by which Christ is in his saints and the Father in him."[177] While language of the covenant usefully orders eternity with time and God with humankind, it is in the end the Spirit and not covenant who mediates grace to believers, and so the covenant must not be interposed between Christ and the church. Most fundamentally, individuals participate in the Spirit who makes possible our common life:

> It is a confirmation that the Holy Ghost is God's love and delight, because the saints' communion with God consists in their partaking of the Holy Ghost. The communion of saints is twofold: 'tis their communion with God, and communion with each other. . . . In this also eminently consists our communion with the saints, that we drink into the

---

174. It is important to note that Edwards does not use the language of the economy of God exclusively to refer to the acts of God performed *ad extra* for the salvation of the elect. In his usage, *economy* speaks more generally of the ways in which God both determines and carries out his purposes.

175. Edwards, "Misc." 1062, *WJE* 20: 434.

176. Danaher, *Trinitarian Ethics*, 255.

177. Edwards, "Trinity," *WJE* 21: 144.

same Spirit: this is the common excellency and joy and happiness in which they are all united.[178]

Even when the Spirit is given to us without restraint, he comes to us chiefly as an overflow from Christ, for the "oil that is poured on the head of the church runs down to the members of his body and to the skirts of his garment."[179]

Despite this disclaimer, covenant is used by Edwards to relate vital piety and the benefits of salvation that accrue to the individual believer, albeit with Christological mediation. He defends this connection when, for example, he writes that "[t]he covenant was made with Christ, and in him with his mystical body," or "that [the covenant] that is made to men is a free offer; that which is commonly called the covenant of grace is only Christ's open and free offer of life, whereby he holds it out in his hand to sinners and offers it without any condition."[180] Notionally, a distinction between covenants may be entertained, but Edwards is at pains to maintain the substantial unity of the purposes of God, expressed through covenant but enjoyed through union with Christ.[181]

Similarly, the heuristic value of distinguishing covenants may support our understanding of order within the economy of God, but its usefulness is limited if the distinction between covenants is pressed too far. Edwards wants to eschew the implicit danger of making human faith a condition to receiving the covenant of grace, apart from the covenant God made with Christ to fulfill the covenant on our behalf, which is offered to us without condition:

> But, ye'll say, they explain themselves and say [that] though faith is the condition of salvation, yet they are not saved because of it as a work, but only a condition. But to this I say, I cannot think of any intelligible meaning of the word "work" in divinity, but something to be done as a condition.... Talking thus, whether it be truly or falsely, is doubtless the foundation of Arminianism and neonomianism, and tends very much to make men value themselves for their own righteousness. *But it seems*

---

178. Edwards, "Trinity," *WJE* 21: 129, 130.

179. Edwards, "Trinity," *WJE* 21: 136.

180. Jonathan Edwards, "Misc." 2, in *The "Miscellanies" (Entry Nos. a–z, aa–zz, 1–500)*, The Works of Jonathan Edwards 13, ed. T. A. Schafer (New Haven: Yale University Press, 1994), 198–99.

181. Edwards, "Misc." 2, *WJE* 13: 199.

to me, all this confusion arises from the wrong distinction men make between the covenant of grace and the covenant of redemption.[182]

A modification to the definition of personhood that is traditional in the Western church gives further integrity to Edwards's desire to reaffirm the nature of spiritual union as foundational to the church's life. As Danaher suggests, for Edwards, a person is not "an individual substance of a rational nature" but rather "a dynamic state of relationality in the self-consciousness, which is modeled after God's own triune personhood."[183] Such a psychological model provides Edwards with the framework to describe human moral life as a participation in the life of God through the Spirit, known as divinization or *theosis*, supported by the social model's description of the Godhead's interpersonal love.[184]

The church is in spiritual union with Christ as the body is to the head. Though members of that body receive Christ severally, the body of Christ as a metaphor for the church orders the diverse expressions of grace and gifts into a unitary whole. Covenant language in these texts is applied primarily to Christ as head over the church, and only secondarily to "Christ mystical."[185] The Spirit brings grace to individual lives and thereby derivatively forms a community. The church appears as a corporate instrument to give expression to the prior work of God in individuals' lives and, as we shall see, to order the work of grace for glory. Cherry summarizes such a progression:

Covenant theology was most valuable to Edwards for a description of the nature of the saints' relation to God in faith, and his church-covenant principles were ramifications of this primary use of the theology.[186]

---

182. Edwards, "Misc." 2, *WJE* 13: 197–98 (emphasis mine). Edwards would go on to qualify this language, arguing that it is indeed possible to describe faith as a condition of justification, if we simultaneously deny that faith is a cause of salvation. See Sang Hyun Lee, "Grace and Justification by Faith Alone," in *Princeton Companion to Jonathan Edwards*, 145.

183. Danaher, *Trinitarian Ethics*, 7.

184. Danaher, *Trinitarian Ethics*, 6–7.

185. Edwards, "Misc." 1062, *WJE* 20: 442.

186. Conrad Cherry, *The Theology of Jonathan Edwards: A Reappraisal* (Bloomington: Indiana University Press, 1990), 109. Cherry makes significant efforts here to demonstrate the importance of covenant imagery to Edwards, given Perry Miller's claims against just such a position.

The covenant between the individual and the church, though ultimately a fore-ground issue in later debates surrounding qualifications for full membership and Edwards's dismissal, are essentially secondary in Edwards's thinking. It is the Christian's participation in Christ through the Spirit for which the cov-enant language of redemption and of grace is chiefly a defensive epithet, and thereby a strategy protecting against crude theories of divine absorption.

The Trinity as Defense against the Implosion of the Church

Edwards has attempted to retool the fundamental doctrine of the Trinity to make it more robust in debates of the eighteenth century, which would oth-erwise discredit it as superstitious remnants of earlier philosophical plat-forms. In so doing, Edwards bears intellectual arms against those labeled "Arminians," an amorphous group that highlighted not only the positive role humans can perform in achieving salvation but also the liberal notion that individuals are the indivisible unit of society.[187] A complex web of theological (Arminianizing), philosophical (liberalizing), and political (individualizing) trends conflate to become an enemy in Edwards's apologias. The Arminian foe is in the end an ecclesiological foe who asserts that the ultimate locus of authority is the individual believer, in contrast to the body of Christ. As Jenson asserts:

> But what, univocally, was "Arminianism"? It was Protestantism without the Reformation. It was the assimilation of Protestant protest against spiritual bondage to Enlightenment protest against religious author-ity.... "Arminianism" was "Protestant principle" mustered not on behalf of threatened "catholic substance" but rather for the further mitigation of its offensive promises and demands.... Liberalism's refusal to regard communities as primary historical agencies, and its need to keep God out of the action, are closely linked phenomena.[188]

Edwards's doctrine of the Trinity provides positive ecclesiological definition to counteract such philosophical pressures. The very Spirit who unites Father to Son, who equals the cost of redemption and purchases life for believers is the

---

187. Henry F. May, *The Enlightenment in America* (New York: Oxford University Press, 1976), 14.

188. Robert W. Jenson, *America's Theologian: A Recommendation of Jonathan Edwards* (New York/Oxford: Oxford University Press, 1988), 54–55, 100.

one who brings individuals under the authority of the Father and who knits together those believers as a spouse for the Son. The outcome of emphasis on the sociality of the Godhead is not only to provide individuals with access to this triune life through the indwelling Spirit but also to present the church with the opportunity of defining itself in relation to this triunity and of modeling itself to some degree on the triune life. Though not explicitly argued in the "Discourse," such trinitarianism is outlined as necessarily exercising ecclesiological shape in the mind of Krister Sairsingh:

> Since the love which binds the Trinity together is the same love which binds the church to the Son and the saints to each other, we can rightly conclude that the structure of relationship which constitutes the glory of God or God's internal fullness is the same structure which constitutes the reality of the church.... The re-presentation of the societal and relational structure of God's trinitarian life in the community of the saints, is, in a manner of speaking, the visibility of God in the world.[189]

Trinitarianism keeps corporate and therefore ecclesiological expectations alive. The divine glory *ad intra* and *ad extra*, expressed in the Son and through the Spirit, is a model of order and not of confusion, appealing to philosophical rigor and not superstition, visible in God's work in the church. Edwards's conflation of the themes of the immanent and the economic Trinity, which becomes a "hallmark of Edwards's theology,"[190] serves our understanding of his ecclesiology well. His dynamic and ordered conception of Trinitarian relations has its echo in the dynamic yet ordered life of the church in the world.

---

189. Krister Sairsingh, "Jonathan Edwards and the Idea of Divine Glory: His Foundational Trinitarianism and its Ecclesial Import" (unpublished doctoral diss., Harvard University, 1986), 208–09.

190. Lee, "Editor's Introduction," *WJE* 21: 31.

3

Ordered Ecclesiological Passions (1735–1746)

3.1 The Revived Church in A Faithful Narrative

EDWARDS'S ASSUMPTION OF leadership in Northampton in 1729 coincided with unprecedented economic and social challenges in western Massachusetts, which involved changes to traditional family structure, the sufficiency of local production and desire for manufactured goods from elsewhere, and radical ruptures in received authority.[1] Traditional models of vital piety therefore appeared to many as a retardant against expeditious social transformation. More immediately, Edwards also had to provide confidence to those in the church that his leadership would perpetuate the emphases of his vaunted predecessor. Revivals, known locally as "harvests," had been a visible feature of Stoddard's long ministry, an expectation of which the grandson inherited along with the pulpit, font, and table. Edwards was to be responsible for the church in vastly different circumstances.

Revivals, expected yet surprising, reshaped the social order in unforeseen ways as they generated further instability in already labile times. Indeed, when Edwards writes publicly in the mid- to late 1730s about those revivals of 1734–1735, he parallels the experiment conducted on Schrödinger's cat: the observation itself changes the very phenomenon observed. Edwards's letter of May 30, 1735, to Benjamin Coleman in Boston relating events in Northampton and its subsequent publication with greater detail and length in London in 1737 under the title *A Faithful Narrative* shapes, as much as describes, the expressions of revival, whether intentionally or not.[2] This tract gives us some of Edwards's

---

1. Catherine A. Brekus, "Children of Wrath, Children of Grace: Jonathan Edwards and the Puritan Culture of Child Rearing," in *The Child in Christian Thought*, ed. M. J. Bunge (Grand Rapids: Eerdmans, 2001), 306.

2. See Jonathan Edwards, "Unpublished Letter of May 30, 1735," in *The Great Awakening*, The Works of Jonathan Edwards 4, ed. C. C. Goen (New Haven: Yale University Press, 1972).

first written thoughts on the nature of a revived church, which begins to draw together theological themes and ecclesiological concerns that had confronted him in the formative years of the 1720s. He must now decide whether his revised model of church life is sufficiently robust to bear the weight of revivalist corporate renewal.

A Faithful Narrative is essentially a defense of the events of the period of revival in Northampton from 1733 to 1735. It begins with the spiritual state of the town, proceeding then to an outline of the "surprising work of God" or the nature of the awakening within that compressed period in the Connecticut River Valley, followed by an appraisal of the variety of conversions in Northampton itself, concluding with two notable case studies and some final observations. Though presented as a narrative,[3] what is unexpected is that perhaps one-third of the account is given over to more intentional theological interaction with the nature of preparation for conversion in the appraisal section. Edwards seeks as his goal not merely to provide encouragement to those readers outside of Northampton to pray and work for revival. Essentially, he also seeks to make a theological case for his understanding of conversion, itself a locus of debate in New England. He takes this opportunity to submit to public scrutiny his arguments against the threats of Arminianism and Antinomianism, which stress respectively either the merits of preparationism or the value of the unmediated experience of God. This work is certainly occasional, but it is not thereby accidentally theological or responsive only to the events portrayed. Edwards's constructive ecclesiology is located in the importance attached to divine freedom, local authority, and international concern, which revival in the church magnifies. How contingent the church is, given new perspectives and pressures, is the question facing Edwards.

The historiography of the Great Awakening has been addressed recently by Thomas Kidd, who argues persuasively that rather than being an interpretative fiction, the events of the mid- to late eighteenth century in North America contain sufficient commonalities even without the branding of Whitefield and his unifying peregrinations. See Thomas S. Kidd, *The Great Awakening: The Roots of Evangelical Christianity in Colonial America* (New Haven: Yale University Press, 2007), especially xviii–xix. A summary of recent debate is found in Bruce Hindmarsh, "The Great Awakening Revisited," *Evangelical Studies Bulletin* 68 (2008): 1–5. These views are contrasted with Frank Lambert, *Inventing the "Great Awakening"* (Princeton: Princeton University Press, 1999), and Jon Butler, "Enthusiasm Described and Decried: The Great Awakening as Interpretative Fiction," *Journal of American history* 69/2 (1982): 305–25.

3. The title of the piece was not of Edwards's choice, but rather was assigned by his English editors, Isaac Watts and John Guyse, with whom Edwards had several editorial disagreements. See Clarence C. Goen, "Editor's Introduction," in *The Great Awakening*, The Works of Jonathan Edwards 4, ed. C. C. Goen (New Haven: Yale University Press, 1972), 37, 42.

Revival as an Antidote to Arminian Challenges

The Rand and Breck affairs were the focus of much energy and grief in Massachusetts in the early to mid-1730s. William Rand (1700–1779) and Robert Breck (1713–1784) were both Harvard graduates whose apparently heterodox opinions had won them notoriety in Hampshire county, the former for instigating in Sunderland "the great noise which was in this part of the country about Arminianism,"[4] and the latter for the "late lamentable Springfield contention."[5] Breck was to have accepted a ministerial settlement in Springfield, though his Arminian beliefs divided the congregation and caused unrest among local clergy before his eventual ordination on January 26, 1736. Though these cases may appear to be minor irritants rather than substantial causes, for Edwards, they were quickly connected to the incident in Yale in 1722 when leading Congregationalists defected to Anglicanism, and reflected a broader change of mood:

> [T]his is what "Arminianism" meant in mid-eighteenth-century New England: it had less to do with Jacobus Arminius (1560–1609), the Dutch theologian from whom it took its name, than with a mood of rising confidence in man's ability to gain some purchase of the divine favor by human endeavor.[6]

Breck's ordination, upheld on appeal to the Massachusetts General Assembly, not only represented local threats to the traditional theological order, but it also flagged for Edwards and those of his ministerial association the rights of the congregation being affirmed at the expense of the learned opinion of the clergy. The label "Arminian" implied a threat to the ecclesiastical order as well.[7]

The question remains in what ways the Connecticut River revival of 1733–1735 and the description of it in *A Faithful Narrative* maintain a stand against

---

4. Edwards, "Faithful Narrative," *WJE* 4: 148. Goen points out (Goen, "Editor's Introduction," *WJE* 4: 9, 17–18) the false conclusion of Goodwin that the "great noise" referred to the Breck rather than the Rand affair; in Goen's estimation, the Breck affair postdated the writing of the "Faithful Narrative." See Goen, "Editor's Introduction," 7–8, and Gerald J. Goodwin, "The Myth of 'Arminian-Calvinism' in Eighteenth-Century New England," *New England Quarterly* 41(2) (1968): 213–37, especially 221.

5. Edwards, "Faithful Narrative," *WJE* 4: 145.

6. Goen, "Editor's Introduction," *WJE* 4: 10.

7. William J. Scheick, "Family, Conversion, and the Self in Jonathan Edwards' *A Faithful Narrative of the Surprising Work of God*," *Tennessee Studies in Literature* 18 (1973): 79–89.

Arminian threats of the same period. To make this case, it must be shown that in Edwards's writing, these revivals are attested by explanation and examples of conversion, which allow for no human contribution to salvation and which do not disintegrate into disorderly enthusiasm and opposition to the means of grace. Indeed, in the "Preface to the First Edition," the editors make clear that "such blessed instances of the success of the Gospel" are attached to traditional doctrine "without stretching towards the Antinomians on the one side, or the Arminians on the other."[8] An outline of the preparationist debate in which Edwards finds himself can determine whether covenant terminology implicitly imports works righteousness into salvation. We are fundamentally asking questions of the ways in which God's grace works within the natural order, without breaching the created givenness of the church.

Edwards distances himself from the preparationist stream of Puritan piety by acknowledging the variety of ways in which human appropriation of grace occurs. "Legal awakening," or the individual's recognition of one's true status before God, can come quickly or slowly, but in either case ought not to be confused with the experience of salvation itself.[9] Although he does of course allow for a human experience of movement toward God, he is at pains to make clear that God is free to exercise his power to redeem without applying one method in particular. One ought to be modest in one's description of Christian beginnings in Edwards's estimation: "God has appeared far from limiting himself to any certain method in his proceedings with sinners under legal convictions."[10] Interestingly, such "legal convictions" are not consistently attached to exposure to the law but might well result from comparison with the assurance of others, the inability of strong pious affections to subdue anxieties, or through an apprehension of personal helplessness.[11]

Similarly, the moment of conversion itself might be experienced through a variety of categories: as a sudden "glorious brightness" or the gradual "dawning of the day," through the Spirit bringing "Scripture to the mind," being persuaded of the "truth of the Gospel in general" or "some particular great doctrine of the Gospel."[12] Edwards wants to protect those who are of tender conscience, who, by comparison with others or through preparationist teaching, deny themselves a genuine experience of grace:

---

8. Edwards, "Faithful Narrative," *WJE* 4: 132.

9. Edwards, "Faithful Narrative," *WJE* 4: 160–61.

10. Edwards, "Faithful Narrative," *WJE* 4: 166–67.

11. Edwards, "Faithful Narrative," *WJE* 4: 160, 164, 170.

12. Edwards, "Faithful Narrative," *WJE* 4: 177–79.

I believe it has occasioned some good people amongst us, that were before too ready to make their own experiences a rule to others, to be less censorious and more extended in their charity.[13]

Edwards recognizes the departure from the majority opinion that such a view represents, and this coming from a person relatively inexperienced in the ministry. He therefore validates his present ministry by association with the ministry and harvests of Stoddard.[14] He appears to sit loose to a commitment to a rigorous theological description of Christian beginnings, which had been characteristic of his Puritan predecessors. What gives assurance is not the ability to discern the first stirrings of grace in human experience (though this might be possible), but rather the outworking of grace in practical piety:

By the "sense of the heart" he meant the ability to promote and cherish grace, not the ability to discern its first invasion in the soul . . . he distinguished between the nature of true piety and the process whereby that piety is revealed.[15]

Edwards does not advocate the abolition of the language of preparation, and he does not deny God's freedom to use human psychology, experiences, or circumstances to achieve his own salvific ends. However, he is in this way presenting a picture of God in which God is free to take "the work into his own hands," and thereby acknowledges that "there was as much done in a day or two as at ordinary times."[16] God's grace might use natural processes more gradually to redeem individuals, but there is also a case to support God's more decisive intervention. Edwards's mediating position is significant, especially since he does not use the language of covenant in this work to express such a view. Essentially, he pushes back the notion of conversion to include those stages that formerly had been viewed as preparatory, and in so doing gives less room for any notion of human contribution to salvation.[17]

---

13. Edwards, "Faithful Narrative," *WJE* 4: 185.

14. Edwards, "Faithful Narrative," *WJE* 4: 176, 190.

15. Norman Pettit, *The Heart Prepared: Grace and Conversion in Puritan Spiritual Life*, 2nd ed. (Middletown: Wesleyan University Press, 1989), 210.

16. Edwards, "Faithful Narrative," *WJE* 4: 159.

17. Scheick, "Family, Conversion and Self," 85.

Revival as the Reordering of Social Relationships

The process of revival had a significant impact on the social world of the eighteenth-century English colonies of North America. In New England, the role of families, settled ministerial authority, the ministry of women, and the place of children and youth were all affected by this new work of God, as *A Faithful Narrative* relates. Edwards's account describes the reordering of social relationships in ways that both affirm and challenge his own status quo as God's clerical representative.

A new approach to youth ministry was the impetus for the 1733–1735 revival in Northampton. It had been a constant expectation of Puritan family life that parents had the responsibility to inculcate Christian faith in their children, both through private instruction and through public lessons in a school or church. Education to instruct the mind as much as to constrain the soul was a means of grace eagerly adopted by Puritan divines.[18] Common assumptions about the covenant of grace, under which the children of Puritans were in some sense privileged, provided the categories in which family, society, and church could be coordinated.[19] It was significant therefore when Edwards acknowledged a decline in this traditional order, which had been underway for some years. Edwards describes the degeneracy he faced after Stoddard's death:

> [I]t seemed to be a time of extraordinary dullness in religion: licentious-
> ness for some years greatly prevailed among the youth of the town; they
> were many of them very much addicted to night-walking, and frequent-
> ing the tavern, and lewd practices . . . they would often spend the greater
> part of the night in them, without regard to any order in the families
> they belonged to: and indeed family government did too much fail in
> the town.[20]

Though the family was understood as a commonwealth writ small, the pressures it faced in an increasingly dynamic economic setting influenced its capacity to maintain its previous functions.[21]

---

18. Edmund S. Morgan, *The Puritan Family: Religion and Domestic Relations in Seventeenth-Century New England*, new, revised, and enlarged ed. (New York: Harper & Row, 1966), 87–95.

19. Scheick, "Family, Conversion and Self," 80.

20. Edwards, "Faithful Narrative," *WJE* 4: 146.

21. Brekus, "Children of Wrath, Children of Grace," 307–08.

Edwards's response to this declension was remarkable for its day: he would target the demographic that needed a timely word. He began a new "service" that included preaching to address specific issues for the youth, organized neighborhood meetings of parents to discuss the matter, and encouraged those same heads of families to assert once again coordinated discipline. He had some reason for optimism, because the youth had responded well during previous harvests in Northampton. As it turned out, the youth decided through the preaching to modify their behavior, though serious local incidents had certainly prepared the ground. The death of "a young man in the bloom of his youth" from pleurisy and the death of a young woman after a lengthy illness with assurance of salvation being expressed at the last,[22] along with the conversion of a young woman "who had been one of the greatest company-keepers in the whole town,"[23] function in any age as spiritually sobering, not least to youth. This phenomenon was reported not only from Northampton but from surrounding towns as well.[24] The youth themselves began to meet in small groups for fellowship and discussion, which in turn the elder people imitated.[25]

The most striking examples given to validate the revival come at the end of the narrative. The conversion of a woman, Abigail Hutchinson, and of a girl, Phebe Bartlet, are fulsomely recounted. The former, a quiet person who worked in a shop, was not known for enthusiastic expressions of piety. Yet, despite the illness that soon took her life, she demonstrated extraordinary humility, assurance of salvation, commitment to the conversion of others, and love of the fellowship.[26] The process leading to her conversion was itself swift, taking place within a week, and while it does display some elements of method, for example the sensation of terror as a result of "a flash of lightning" followed by a "lively sense of the excellency of Christ, and his sufficiency to satisfy for the sins of the whole world,"[27] what is most evident is the variety of means appropriated by her to win and sustain a personal relation to Christ. She heard her brother speak of the importance of "seeking regenerating grace," she resolved to read through the entire Bible starting at the beginning,

22. Edwards, "Faithful Narrative," *WJE* 4: 147–48.

23. Edwards, "Faithful Narrative," *WJE* 4: 149.

24. Edwards, "Faithful Narrative," *WJE* 4: 152–59.

25. Edwards, "Faithful Narrative," *WJE* 4: 148.

26. Edwards, "Faithful Narrative," *WJE* 4: 191–99.

27. Edwards, "Faithful Narrative," *WJE* 4: 192–93.

and she engaged in "reading, prayer and other religious exercises."[28] Her
friends provided her with regular counsel, and she was concerned to "go to
the minister hoping to find some relief [from her spiritual anxiety] there."[29]
She spoke of having visions of Christ, though Edwards editorializes with the
parenthetical remark that she had seen Christ "in realizing views by faith."[30]
Words resounded spontaneously within her mind, while on other occasions,
she attended meetings and desired to be instructed further in the faith.[31] Her
heart was so aligned with God that she wanted to knock on each housedoor
to speak of the sweetness of Christ or simply to pull others near her that
they might be saved.[32] Her painful death reinforced in her a desire to be with
Christ, where grace would flow unimpeded. While reference is made here
to the ministry of Edwards, church services, and sermons, it is patently true
that the means God used to advance grace in Abigail's life were diverse and
dispersed. This youth reasserted her own filial piety toward her parents and at
one stage contemplated taking up residence in Edwards's manse for further
formation in the faith,[33] but on balance, the ordering of spiritual experience for
Abigail was provided chiefly through nonhierarchically defined means.

The case with Phebe Bartlet was different. As a four-year-old, she had limited opportunities to avail herself of means of grace outside of normal weekly
meetings, though the catechism, the visit of a neighboring minister, and texts
of Scripture played a role in her spiritual improvement. What is of most value
for our purposes is the ways in which Phebe inverted normal family roles and
set an agenda in piety for her parents and siblings. It was her eleven-year-old
brother, and apparently not her parents, who first introduced Phebe to the
"great things of religion."[34] Indeed, her mother tried to inhibit Phebe from

---

28. Edwards, "Faithful Narrative," *WJE* 4: 192.

29. Edwards, "Faithful Narrative," *WJE* 4: 193.

30. Edwards, "Faithful Narrative," *WJE* 4: 193–94. Edwards elsewhere explains how such
visions might be understood as "ideas strongly impressed, and as it were, lively pictures in
their minds," using categories of sensation, which highlight human passivity and divine
immanence: Edwards, "Faithful Narrative," *WJE* 4: 188.

31. Edwards, "Faithful Narrative," *WJE* 4: 194–95.

32. Edwards, "Faithful Narrative," *WJE* 4: 196.

33. It has been pointed out that it was not unusual for the children of Puritan families to be
sent away to live in other families, either for work or education, or simply to avoid excessive
doting from parents. See Morgan, *Puritan Family*, 77.

34. Edwards, "Faithful Narrative," *WJE* 4: 199. Morgan points out that the family is the
basic unit of church and society, deriving from the creation account. See Morgan, *Puritan
Family*, 135–36.

personal devotions "in her closet"[35] and refused to pray with another daughter, Amy, despite Phebe's importunate pleas.[36] Her mother in no way encouraged Phebe to believe in the possibility of assurance, but instead exhorted her merely to hope.[37] Phebe acknowledged that she loved God more than parents or siblings![38] The child was full of remorse when she discovered that taking some plums from a neighbor's yard without permission was stealing and was only pacified when a child was sent to the neighbor to make good the sin.[39] Her tender conscience was in evidence when she discovered that a poor local man had lost his cow: she begged her father (the only time he appears in the account) to give a cow to the man or to let the man's family come and live with them.[40] Finally, somewhat precociously, she longed to hear Edwards preach, and was thrilled when he returned to Northampton: "Mr. Edwards is come home! Mr. Edwards is come home!"[41]

While Edwards is obviously pleased with Phebe's exclamations of delight and the respect for his position that it entailed, what is most interesting in this account (and in the story of Abigail Hutchinson) is that traditional piety is established at the expense of received social and familial structures. Edwards's ministry, in kindling revival, actually serves to change the structures of Puritan culture, which it had been assumed were generative of fresh expressions of piety, but which in these accounts appear to have held them back. Tracy suggests that Edwards inadvertently undermined traditional social order through his targeted ministry:

> The problem in Northampton, as Edwards himself defined it in the *Narrative*, was the failure of family government. But while decrying the decline of parental authority, Edwards ironically eroded part of what

---

35. Edwards, "Faithful Narrative," *WJE* 4: 199.

36. Edwards, "Faithful Narrative," *WJE* 4: 204.

37. Edwards, "Faithful Narrative," *WJE* 4: 200.

38. Edwards, "Faithful Narrative," *WJE* 4: 201.

39. Edwards, "Faithful Narrative," *WJE* 4: 203.

40. Edwards, "Faithful Narrative," *WJE* 4: 204–05. A similar situation is described as occurring at the time of the sacramental season at Red River, where a young girl rebukes her father for his lack of charity, thereby illustrating the powerful redefinition of social roles through revival. See Leigh E. Schmidt, *Holy Fairs: Scotland and the Making of American Revivalism*, 2nd ed. (Grand Rapids: Eerdmans, 1989), 107.

41. Edwards, "Faithful Narrative," *WJE* 4: 205.

was left of it by appealing directly to the adolescents and intervening between child and parent in significant ways.[42]

It is of course true that Edwards began A *Faithful Narrative* with a critique of families that "did too much fail in the town"[43] and thereupon made attempts to coordinate their efforts at discipline, but we are not given the impression in this piece that Edwards wants to reinstate or advocate a model of social life that had proved inadequate to the needs of the day. His models of piety are not adults who resume former practices successfully, but young women who promote a new kind of religious devotion despite the dead weight of inert family norms, ordered ultimately by God.[44]

It may be justifiable for Tracy to eschew the interpretation that Edwards was brilliant while his congregation was stupid,[45] but her danger is to overplay the opposite contingency: that Edwards was naïve in his stewardship of the Northampton revival and ended up sponsoring the demise of Puritan structures of patriarchy from which his power base had benefited. He may well have been concerned about the excesses of the revival and situated the account of Hawley's suicide in nonchronological order in the narrative to highlight the revival's positive achievements, but this account in no sense disparages the newness of relations in Northampton, except to bemoan their untimely end. Edwards appears to value the diversity of means of grace that the revival engendered and that God had subsequently brought to order. It is not Edwards's ordination, nor his education, but his readiness for innovation that accredits his leadership in this piece.[46]

Revival as the Solution to Tribalist Concerns

The construction of regional identity in New England appealed to the terminology of covenant, which functioned as the grand unifying theory for social life. Its theoretical capacity to produce cohesive relations between individuals,

---

42. Patricia J. Tracy, *Jonathan Edwards, Pastor: Religion and Society in Eighteenth-Century Northampton*, The Jonathan Edwards Classic Studies Series (Eugene, OR: Wipf and Stock, 2006), 111, 122.

43. Edwards, "Faithful Narrative," *WJE* 4: 146.

44. Edwards, "Faithful Narrative," *WJE* 4: 209–10.

45. Tracy, *Jonathan Edwards, Pastor*, iii.

46. E. Brooks Holifield, *God's Ambassadors: A History of the Christian Clergy in America*, Pulpit & Pew (Grand Rapids: Eerdmans, 2007), 1–9.

families, churches, and the nation was prodigious. Indeed, though some commentators have suggested that the language of covenant applied to the nation was in decline in Edwards's time, others have reminded us that occasional sermons rather than the regular Sunday preachments may be the place to locate the ongoing power of the ideology of the national covenant.[47] The inherent sociological danger of New England viewing itself as the new Israel, in covenant with God, was tribalism, or protecting impervious boundaries between local life and movements elsewhere. Indeed, Morgan argues that Puritans succumbed to tribalism in several ways:

> Puritans of course thought of their God as the one God of the universe; but they made him so much their own, in the guise of making themselves his, that eventually and at times he took on the character of a tribal deity.... The Puritan system failed because the Puritans relied upon their children to provide the church with members and the state with citizens.[48]

Janice Knight identifies this trajectory in particular with that party of Puritans, including Hooker and Shepard, who privileged pastoral discipline, preparationist views of conversion and local church autonomy:

> [A] growing tribalism among the New England divines emerged in tandem with the rhetoric of preparationism. Their original devotion to pure church ordinances prompted these men to focus first on reform of their own hearts and then on the New England churches. Little energy or interest was left over for the millennial dreams that absorbed English radicals, to whom the preparationist emphasis on local purity may have seemed self-absorbed.... The truths of the faith now became the secrets

---

47. See Mark A. Noll, *America's God: From Jonathan Edwards to Abraham Lincoln* (Oxford: Oxford University Press, 2002), 45, 48. It should be pointed out, however, that Noll does not say that the covenant had no role for Edwards, only that its totalizing value was no longer necessary. Noll writes: "In his two published works, Edwards's key move was to repudiate a long history of New England thought by shifting emphasis on covenant away from the complex nexus of person, church and society to a simpler bond between the converted individual and the church.... To make the covenant more powerful for the church, Edwards was willing to relinquish its all-purpose functions for society." Noll here echoes earlier scholarship, which argued that Edwards surrendered the language of covenant in its social application. This position has been critiqued by Stout, among others. Harry S. Stout, "The Puritans and Edwards," in *The Princeton Companion to Jonathan Edwards*, ed. S. H. Lee (Princeton: Princeton University Press, 2005), 288.

48. Morgan, *Puritan Family*, 168, 185.

of the tribe…in general, they subscribed to a premillennialist reading of history, modeling their utopian ecclesiology on Old Testament precedent. While countering arguments for the importance of a general millennial fervor, this primitivist pattern supports claims of increasing tribalism based on congregational localism and preparationist individualism.[49]

The contours of the church presented in *A Faithful Narrative* are at odds with this prevailing ecclesiology. The very composition of this document attests an international concern and breadth. Edwards first conceives the idea of relating the events of the Connecticut River revival after Benjamin Colman, pastor of the Brattle Street Church in Boston and would-be editor, had solicited such news from him.[50] In time, this response was expanded and appended, though only as an excerpt, to a small volume of sermons by William Williams and published in Boston in November 1736. The first complete edition of Edwards's account was published in London in 1737, the second, also in London, in 1738, and finally, a version with errors expunged appeared in Boston in 1738. The account of the revivals held great interest from the earliest days not only in New England but in the metropolitan world of London too. An incidental feature of the first edition, which betokens the international reach of its content, can be found in the error on the title page. This *Faithful Narrative* was putatively set among the towns and villages of "New Hampshire in New-England." The 1738 edition overcorrected this geographical clumsiness by identifying more adequately that it took place in "the County of Hampshire, in the Province of the Massachusetts-Bay in New-England."[51] International concern is no assurance of typographical accuracy. Such collaborative efforts in publication registered the speed and nature of the republic of letters in the eighteenth-century transatlantic world.[52]

Indeed, it was becoming increasingly clear that not only would revival spill over into neighboring communities, but also the pressures Northampton faced were not to be isolated from concerns being faced elsewhere. The incident of Joseph Hawley's suicide appeared to create copycat aspirations among "multitudes in this and other towns."[53] The nature of events in Northampton

---

49. Knight, *Orthodoxies in Massachusetts*, 166–67.

50. Edwards, "Unpublished Letter of May 30, 1735," *WJE* 4: 99.

51. Edwards, "Faithful Narrative," *WJE* 4: 128–29.

52. Susan O'Brien, "A Transatlantic Community of Saints: The Great Awakening and the First Evangelical Network, 1735–1755," *American Historical Review* 91(4) (1986): 811–32.

53. Edwards, "Faithful Narrative," *WJE* 4: 206.

had become known in many places, prompting jealous and unfair reports of God's work elsewhere.[54] Edwards even used the interest of Watts and Guyse as a strategy to incite his own congregation to greater faithfulness, as he recounted to them such international exposure in a discourse on the image from Matthew's Gospel of the city on a hill.[55] This is itself significant, because it reflects Edwards's dream of the local revived congregation taking over the responsibility from the colony to become the model of the transformed community that others must imitate. Edwards's scope here is nothing less than revivals as precursors to the dawning of the New World, with churches as that world's most visible actualization. In another place, Edwards indulges his own dreams of a church not limited to the local congregation:

> There are many particular assemblies of Christians[,] multitudes of worshipping congregations of God['']s [p]eople and there are provincial and national churches and there is the church universal, which in the ordinary explanation of the [p]hrase [s]ignifies the whole Church militant upon Earth…[b]ut yet this don't [c]ontain the whole church of Christ and indeed is but a small part of the church in its [l]argest extent as consisting of the [s]aints both in Heaven and Earth.[56]

3.2 The Pilgrim Church in Charity and Its Fruits

At the same time that Edwards and his Northampton church were receiving international notoriety through the publication of *A Faithful Narrative* in 1737, Edwards himself was becoming increasingly agitated by the lack of long-term fruit displayed in the lives of those so affected locally. Instead of improvement in social and spiritual relations, Edwards witnessed deterioration, both formally and anecdotally. The second meetinghouse on the Northampton site had been abandoned upon the collapse of its gallery in March 1737, whereupon the design and construction of the new meetinghouse, dedicated in January 1738, drew out party spirit, dissensions, and callous disregard for others. Instead of the previous model of seating arranged with deference to age, the new

---

54. Edwards, "Faithful Narrative," *WJE* 4: 209.

55. Edwards, "Faithful Narrative," *WJE* 4: 210.

56. Jonathan Edwards, "546. Hebrews 12:22–24(c) (April 1740)," in *Sermons, Series II, January–June 1740*, The Works of Jonathan Edwards Online 55 (Jonathan Edwards Center at Yale University, 2013), 1.

floor plan gave priority to the wealth and family status of church members.[57] Husbands and wives could now sit together in family boxed pews, with those of higher status seated toward the middle. The youth, if not with their parents, would sit upstairs. The old-style architecture was adapted to new tastes: in line with contemporary English fashion, a steeple was added, making it look less like a meetinghouse and more like a church. Town meetings were now accommodated in a purpose-built town house. Preservation of Puritan ideals was not of chief concern, nor was charity for one's neighbor. The church's fellowship was in need of sustained ethical revival.

Edwards consequently undertook in the late 1730s three most significant sermon series to remedy the growing spiritual malaise in the town. These series, though paying formal homage to traditional Puritan homiletic conventions, were for Edwards himself unusual because they worked with smaller portions of the biblical text in sequence over a sustained period. The first of these was based on the parable of the ten virgins (Matthew 25:1–13), outlining the folly of indiscriminate and hasty recognition of the true church.[58] The last of these series in 1739, known as *A History of the Work of Redemption*, to be dealt with in the next section of this chapter, tried to resuscitate ailing spiritual health by locating the church of Northampton in the flow of redemptive history. The middle series, a sequence of sermons subsequently labeled *Charity and Its Fruits* and based on Paul's hymn to love in 1 Corinthians 13, consisted of fifteen preachments delivered in 1738. Like the other series, this one on the nature of sanctification in the Christian life had as its overall goal to provoke churchgoers to more serious Christian obedience through exposition of love's moral psychology and its corporate eschatology. Though the beginnings of the Christian walk were grounded in union with God, there was nevertheless a journey to be undertaken. His own summary of the series appears at the end of the last sermon: "As heaven is a world of love, so the way to heaven is the way of love."[59] Our corporate hope ought to have along the road to heaven an ecclesiastical reflex. We are a pilgrim people.

---

57. Marsden, *A Life*, 184–89.

58. See further Ava Chamberlain, "Brides of Christ and Signs of Grace: Edwards's Sermon Series on the Parable of the Wise and Foolish Virgins," in *Jonathan Edwards's Writings: Text, Context, Interpretation*, ed. S. J. Stein (Bloomington and Indianapolis: Indiana University Press, 1996), 3–18.

59. Jonathan Edwards, "Charity and its Fruits," in *Ethical Writings*, The Works of Jonathan Edwards 8, ed. P. Ramsay (New Haven: Yale University Press, 1989), 396.

The Way of Love: The Church Militant

A pilgrim people must grow in love, not presuming to have reached perfection. These sermons therefore contain exhortations, motivations, and warnings so that the past experiences of a revived church are consummated in godly order and not chaotic presumption. Love is binding, or, as expressed in a repreached sermon from Ephesians 5, "Love desires union."[60] Edwards exhorted his congregation to repent of their sin and to practice love. He questioned their inward intentions when he mused: "There are many here present who make a profession and show of religion, and it may be some who seem to do considerable things in religion…. But let us inquire whether we have sincerity of heart."[61] More pointedly, he named the sin of gossip, much in evidence in the town: "The iniquity which is committed by men in all our taverns by what they say of one another behind their backs is beyond account. Some injure others by making and spreading false reports of others, and so slandering them."[62] Economic sins are likewise addressed:

> And they are of a spirit and practice … who will take all opportunities to get all they possibly can of their neighbors in their dealings with them, asking more for what they sell to their neighbor or do for him than the thing is worth, squeezing and extorting to the utmost out of him.[63]

It has even been the case that such wrangling has been brought into relationships within the church: "There has been much anger in times past in this town on public occasions, and you or many of you here present are those in whose bosoms this anger has rested. Examine this anger."[64]

These sermons, however, do more than just exhort to love. Edwards's own perceptive distinctions within the realm of moral psychology lend to this series a constructive function, providing reasoned incentives to obey. In fact, the first sermon, "The Sum of all virtue," demonstrates its doctrine by outlining "what reason teaches of the nature of love."[65] Using language of eighteenth-century

---

60. Jonathan Edwards, "358. Ephesians 5:25–27 (1735/1752)," in *Sermons, Series II, 1735*, The Works of Jonathan Edwards Online 50 (Jonathan Edwards Center at Yale University, 2013), L. 15v.

61. Edwards, "Charity," *WJE* 8: 181.

62. Edwards, "Charity," *WJE* 8: 187.

63. Edwards, "Charity," *WJE* 8: 214.

64. Edwards, "Charity," *WJE* 8: 280.

65. Edwards, "Charity," *WJE* 8: 134.

moral theory, Edwards goes on in sermon four to make a further contrast between types of love: "as it respects the good enjoyed or to be enjoyed by the beloved, it is called love of benevolence; and as it respects good to be enjoyed in the beloved, it is called love of complacence."[66] The associated trinitarian foundations of love are summarized in the fifteenth sermon:

> The infinite essential love of God is, as it were, an infinite and eternal mutual holy energy between the Father and the Son, a pure, holy act whereby the Deity becomes nothing but an infinite and unchangeable act of love, which proceeds from both the Father and the Son.[67]

For Edwards, love is simply captured in the "disposition or affection by which one is dear to another,"[68] and this in turn for Christians is both a participation in the "Spirit influencing the heart"[69] and an imitation of "the eternal love and grace of God, and the dying love of Christ."[70] Our responsibility to practice love makes the church authentically Christian.

It must also be acknowledged that, according to Edwards, entirely disinterested love is not something that the Scriptures enjoin on believers.[71] In fact, he fully expects some elements of self-love in those who are growing in sanctification, as he writes in the seventh sermon entitled "Charity contrary to a selfish spirit":

> It is not a thing contrary to Christianity that a man should love himself; or what is the same thing, that he should love his own happiness. Christianity does not tend to destroy a man's love to his own happiness; it would therein tend to destroy the humanity. Christianity is not destructive of humanity.[72]

---

66. Edwards, "Charity," *WJE* 8: 212–13. Danaher points out the ways in which the traditional language of *agape, philia,* and *eros* relate to Edwards's contemporary labeling of the language of love. See Danaher, *Trinitarian Ethics,* 245.

67. Edwards, "Charity," *WJE* 8: 373.

68. Edwards, "Charity," *WJE* 8: 129.

69. Edwards, "Charity," *WJE* 8: 132.

70. Edwards, "Charity," *WJE* 8: 213.

71. He is in fact thereby critiquing the British school of moral sense philosophy, which espoused this position to create a foundation for ethics outside of revealed religion. See Zakai, *Jonathan Edwards's Philosophy of History,* 38.

72. Edwards, "Charity," *WJE* 8: 254.

The assumption in Edwards's reckoning is that as God diffuses his love and happiness to the creature, so we best promote our own happiness by seeking what God would give us. He does, however, qualify his argument by denying the possibility of "an inordinate self-love" in the believer. The experiential turning point in a believer's life at conversion is to be understood as a refocusing of our self-love rather than its extirpation.[73]

Such ethical deliberation has, of course, its roots in the diffusive love of God, but also serves contextually to distance Edwards from those of his peers who maintained that to love God disinterestedly is to make space for self-destruction in order to increase the glory of God.[74] Edwards avers that "[i]n some respects wicked men do not love themselves enough. They do not love themselves so much as the godly do. They do not love that which is their true happiness."[75] Edwards instead provides emotional boundaries for those of tender conscience, who, like his uncle Joseph Hawley, might be tempted to take their own life as a response to melancholy, and provides strategic boundaries for those who would disparage the revivals because of their propensity to extremism. Such abhorrent self-negation was exposed as lacking in sanctified grace in Edwards's mind through his moderate espousal of self-love. Stephen Post makes the case that:

> Edwards's suspicion of exaggerated demands for self-denial can be related to more than a respect for Puritan orthodoxy. Practical interests also persuaded him that proper self-regard must be included in the Christian ethic.[76]

Edwards also had to work against the tendency among the revived to judgmentalism. They could pursue self-abnegation as a kind of self-judgment, or in similar fashion judge others through a censorious spirit, to which he devotes an entire sermon, the ninth in the series. "Thinking evil of others," against which 1 Corinthians 13:5 warns, tends to fracture relationships and ultimately

---

73. Edwards, "Charity," *WJE* 8: 255.

74. Edwards's disciples and, in particular, Samuel Hopkins are responsible for distorting this view, suggesting that pursuing damnation for the greater glory of God would confirm one's status among the elect. See David C. Brand, *Profile of the Last Puritan: Jonathan Edwards, Self-Love, and the Dawn of the Beatific,* American Academy of Religion Academy Series (Atlanta: Scholars Press, 1991), 72, 125.

75. Edwards, "Charity," *WJE* 8: 257.

76. Stephen Post, "Disinterested Benevolence: An American Debate over the Nature of Christian Love," *Journal of Religious Ethics* 14 (1986): 356–68.

the church. Although there is a responsible form of judging, for example, that exercised by "judges in civil societies and churches, who are impartially to judge of the actions of others that properly fall under their cognizance, whether good or bad,"[77] Edwards is more concerned in this sermon with that type of irresponsible judging growing out of a "censorious spirit" that extends beyond the subject's competencies.[78]

God alone can judge the heart, according to Edwards in the late 1730s. His position here affirms the importance of the practice of charity in adjudicating church disputes, though ecclesiastical discipline is not inconsistent with this.[79] The church maintains boundaries, though they are necessarily provisional. In another place, Edwards acknowledges the mixed inclinations of any heart.[80] Ramsay notes that here, "Jonathan Edwards's discussion of the mixture of sincerity and hypocrisy remaining in the heart (the seat of both) shows that he did not expect 'purity of heart' in this life. The 'little sincerity' acceptable to God means that the Christian life was always *in via* toward holiness."[81]

Spiritual gifts are a major theme in several of Edwards's sermons in this series. With appeal to egregious displays of power by enthusiast leaders of the Connecticut River revivals, much damage had been done, in Edwards's estimation, to the cause of the Gospel.[82] Sermon two, entitled "Love more excellent than extraordinary gifts of the Spirit," presents the argument, foreshadowing later developments in *Religious Affections*, that although spiritual gifts are a great privilege and were used with extraordinary results in the time of the

---

77. Edwards, "Charity," *WJE* 8: 286.

78. Edwards, "Charity," *WJE* 8: 284.

79. Not long after preaching "Charity," Edwards excommunicated from the church a drunkard, Mrs. Bridgman, after repeated and appropriate warnings, which he outlined in a sermon where, unusually for Edwards, the individual is named. Jonathan Edwards, "482. Sermon on Deut. 29:18–21 (July 1738)," in *Sermons, Series II, 1738, and Undated, 1734–1738*, The Works of Jonathan Edwards Online 53 (Jonathan Edwards Center at Yale University, 2008). Excommunication had been an uncommon practice in Northampton, this being the first occasion since 1711. He argues in a sermon shortly after in July 1739 that though excommunicants are rightly cut off, significantly, this does not mean total disconnection from love: "They are cut off from being the objects of that charity of God's people that is due to Christian brethren. *They ben't cut off from all charity of God's people*, for they ought to love all men. There is a love of God's people due to the heathen and others that are not in the visible church of Christ." See Jonathan Edwards, "The Means and Ends of Excommunication," in *Sermons and Discourses, 1739–1742*, The Works of Jonathan Edwards 22; eds. H. S. Stout, N. O. Hatch, and K. P. Farley (New Haven: Yale University Press, 2003), 71.

80. Edwards, "Charity," *WJE* 8: 181.

81. Edwards, "Charity," *WJE* 8: 182n8.

82. See his references to extremes of experience later in this sermon. Edwards, "Charity," *WJE* 8: 168–69.

apostles, nevertheless "the ordinary influences of the Spirit of God working grace in the heart is a far greater privilege than any of them; a greater privilege than the spirit of prophecy, or the gift of tongues, or working miracles even to the moving of mountains."[83]

The way of love as described in 1 Corinthians 13 is bookended with descriptions in 1 Corinthians 12 and 14 of the value yet limitations of gifts, which are not necessarily the result of the Spirit abiding in the heart or mind:

> The Spirit of God communicates itself much more in bestowing saving grace than in bestowing those extraordinary gifts.... The Spirit of God may produce effects on many things to which it does not communicate itself.... Yea, grace is as it were the holy nature of the Spirit of God imparted to the soul.[84]

Such spiritual gifts are merely the temporary means to some more noble ends, notably, the spread of the Gospel, the diffusion of grace, and the promotion of holiness, which lasts into eternity.[85] Edwards's cessationist position further amplifies his ethical aspirations for the distinctiveness of the post-apostolic church.[86]

Love for Edwards promotes order, rather than chaos, in the church and in society. Watchful of spiritual danger or material dearth, the magistrate and the minister together secure protection and provisions for their community as expressions of charity and of course are in need of it for themselves as well.[87] A deferential society is presumed in such a model, whereby the duty of the flock is not merely to receive ministrations but to submit to the one offering them.[88] Remarkably, Edwards reminds his audience that the virtue of humility will "prevent a leveling behavior," as it discourages grasping at another's station:

---

83. Edwards, "Charity," *WJE* 8: 157. This sermonic thesis comes after the accumulation of positive examples of spiritually gifted believers from all dispensations, attesting the rhetorical skills of Edwards in leading his listeners toward a climax, only to pull the rug out from under their feet at the last.

84. Edwards, "Charity," *WJE* 8: 158.

85. Edwards, "Charity," *WJE* 8: 162, 166.

86. Michael A. G. Haykin, *Jonathan Edwards: The Holy Spirit in Revival: The Lasting Influence of the Holy Spirit in the Heart of Man*, Emmaus Series (Darlington: Evangelical Press, 2005), 59–73.

87. Edwards, "Charity," *WJE* 8: 261–62.

88. Edwards, "Charity," *WJE* 8: 136.

They who are under the influence of a humble spirit will not be opposite to giving to others the honor which is due to them. They will be willing that their superiors should be known and acknowledged in their place, and it will not seem hard to them. They will not desire that all should be upon a level; for they know it is best that some should be above others and should be honored and submitted to as such, and therefore they are willing to comply with it agreeable to those precepts.[89]

Though Edwards sets before his listeners and readers high moral demands with both intellectually taxing and personally challenging justifications, these sermons nevertheless exemplify moderating influences in the mid-eighteenth century. He is resolutely not an advocate for a church of sinless perfection, nor for one in which confession is disconnected from charity. In summary, the church militant ought not to consist of superior officers alone, for there would be no one to fight on the front line, nor, on the other hand, should the church relax recruitment standards in such a way that disciplined victory becomes unattainable. Love marks the way for the individual as for the fellowship, as the above exhortations show. Holiness is not to be understood in terms of liberation from the world, but in terms of our obligations within it.[90] The church in Edwards's view plays a key role in moral formation, just as the pursuit of love sustains the social plausibility of the pilgrim church. I concur with Danaher that in "Charity and Its Fruits," Edwards makes the transformed life of the church a central theme.[91]

The World of Love: The Church Triumphant

Such transformed life is constructed not just by philosophical or ethical conceptualities but also significantly through teleological vision. Edwards builds on assumptions concerning protology when he states that "[t]he love of God flows out towards Christ the Head, and through him to all his members, in whom they were beloved before the foundation of the world."[92] However, he goes beyond this to place discussion of love within eschatology when he suggests at the beginning of sermon fifteen, called "Heaven is a world of love," that the church militant on earth is "in an imperfect state, a kind of state of

---

89. Edwards, "Charity," *WJE* 8: 242.

90. Murray, *Jonathan Edwards*, 150–51.

91. Danaher, *Trinitarian Ethics*, 202, 235.

92. Edwards, "Charity," *WJE* 8: 373.

childhood in comparison with what it will be in the elder and latter ages of the church, when it will be in a state of manhood, or a perfect state in comparison with what it was in the first ages."[93] Edwards uses organic language to describe how the church matures, or is in progress, a sign of which is leaving behind gifts that properly belong to infancy.[94] Negatively, organic language also extends to inform us that in heaven, there is no "deformity of any kind,"[95] which would be a "monster, wherein many essential parts are wanting."[96] There is growth in the life of the church within this age (as gifts' usefulness is superseded), just as there is positive growth in the life of the church between this age and the next. The way of love and the world of love are continuous, an ecclesiologically unitary vision of the pilgrim church.[97]

Indeed, drawing from the assertion that love endures all things (1 Corinthians 13:7) and in order to teach us the nature of perseverance along the pilgrim way, Edwards makes the remarkable parallel between the presence of the Spirit in an individual's life and the presence of the people of God in the world:

> It is very much with grace in the heart of a Christian, as it is in the church of God in the world. It is God's post and it is but small, and great opposition is made against it by innumerable enemies.... So grace in the heart is like the church of Israel in Egypt, and in the Red Sea and the wilderness.... Thus as the gates of hell can never prevail against the church of Christ, so neither can they prevail against grace in the heart.[98]

Here we witness not just a movement from the church militant to the church triumphant, but we see also the mechanism for Edwards that connects the grace-bearing believer with the survival of the church in this world and for

---

93. Edwards, "Charity," *WJE* 8: 366.

94. Edwards, "Charity," *WJE* 8: 362.

95. Edwards, "Charity," *WJE* 8: 371.

96. Edwards, "Charity," *WJE* 8: 338.

97. Spohn makes clear the ways in which Edwards's approach to virtue is necessarily social, for Edwards does not fall prey to the mistake of bypassing "the world of social relations and institutions in the pursuit of the sacred," nor of using "spiritual practices instrumentally for personal benefit." See William C. Spohn, "Spirituality and its Discontents: Practices in Jonathan Edwards's *Charity and its Fruits*," *Journal of Religious Ethics* 31(2) (2003): 253–76, especially 271.

98. Edwards, "Charity," *WJE* 8: 342–43.

the next.[99] Astoundingly, the model by which to understand the church is the regenerate Christian. God sets up "Christ's kingdom in men's hearts,"[100] which will be perfected in the lives of individuals upon their death and in the "church of Christ collectively as a body."[101] The experience of grace working itself out in an individual's life begins a chain reaction that ignites God's work in the congregation. To defend God's engagement with the world in the philosophical context of deist attempts to remove him, Edwards attempted "to transport the dynamism revealed in saving grace from the inner sphere of the soul into the whole realm of history."[102] Edwards applies most moving imagery to persuade his audience that harmony in the coming world of love begins with the individual now, which from there permeates the world around:

> Every saint is as a flower in the garden of God, and holy love is the fragrancy and sweet odor which they all send forth, and with which they fill that paradise. Every saint there is as a note in a concert of music which sweetly harmonizes with every other note, and all together employed wholly in praising God and the Lamb.[103]

A similar progression is implicit in much of the structure of this sermon series. Though expounding love, Edwards repeatedly connects this one virtue to a list of others that find their supreme expression in charity. Love alone abides, but it is in his estimation not to be understood monistically. There is a plurality within the nature of love, for which the expressive word "concatenation" and the imagery of links in a chain is its distillation.[104]

There is one source of grace in the Spirit and one end toward which all graces tend. The pivotal experience of conversion is the point at which the Spirit joins the individual to the cosmic destination of love.[105] The singularity of conversion betokens a singularity of purpose. It is of great concern to

---

99. He makes this point in preaching later from Matthew 16: "'Tis with the church in the world, as 'tis with grace in the hearts of the saints." Jonathan Edwards, "812. Matthew 16:18 (March 1745/1746)," in *Sermons, Series II, 1746*, The Works of Jonathan Edwards Online 55 (Jonathan Edwards Center at Yale University, 2013), L. 14.v.

100. Edwards, "Charity," *WJE* 8: 360.

101. Edwards, "Charity," *WJE* 8: 359.

102. Zakai, *Jonathan Edwards's Philosophy of History*, 151.

103. Edwards, "Charity," *WJE* 8: 359, 386.

104. Edwards, "Charity," *WJE* 8: 327–28.

105. Edwards, "Charity," *WJE* 8: 332–33.

Edwards to demonstrate that all virtues must be engaged with all others holistically, allowing none expression without the concomitant presence of others of their kind, for no person can claim to honor God in their lives while selectively accentuating some virtues without others. Love brings order to diverse buddings of grace. Ramsay comments that a "beautiful symmetry and uniformity—the concatenation of all the graces—is the 'aesthetic' element in Jonathan Edwards's understanding of the Christian moral life."[106] Ramsay also argues that this whole series of sermons reflects a greater narrative arc, insofar as far as the idea of progress or growth in holiness of the individual and the idea of perfection or maturity in the life of the church are confirmed eschatologically throughout the preaching units as they tell the story of the work of God in the world. Redemption is the theme of this series, not finally moral psychology *tout court*. Edwards is at pains to situate his understanding of virtue on a broader theological canvas. The first sermons deal with charity in terms of its place within interpersonal relationships, while the latter sermons introduce into their titles the language of "grace" and the "divine." By inverting the traditional order of the tables of the law (placing duties toward humankind before our duties toward God), Edwards can both surprise his audience with a counterintuitive approach to ethics as well as highlight the goal toward which our ethical responsibilities tend. As 1 Corinthians 13 begins with activity that is without love, so the chapter ends with the fulfillment in Christ of all loving aspiration. Ramsay summarizes:

> We shall look at... some important moral progressions corresponding to the Christological-eschatological movement in the chapter.... From the beginning of the sermon series, the movement has been from God manward and returning to him. This is Edwards's master image or root metaphor.[107]

The way of love is a pilgrimage that finds its destination in the world of love, which is heaven. Reprising earlier Puritan rhetoric, Edwards exhorts his audience to press on toward that "glorious city of light and love... on the top of an high hill... and there is no arriving there without traveling uphill."[108] The view becomes better and better the higher a saint ascends. The convergence of individuals walking in love toward a common destination makes for a community

---

106. Edwards, "Charity," *WJE* 8: 331n3.

107. Paul Ramsay, "Editor's Introduction," in *Ethical Writings*, The Works of Jonathan Edwards 8, ed. P. Ramsay (New Haven: Yale University Press, 1989), 93.

108. Edwards, "Charity," *WJE* 8: 395.

overflowing in love, as Christ's love "flows out to his whole church there, and to every individual member of it."[109] As the Spirit perfects the church, so the Son unites the church, fitting it to be his bride.[110] The world of love is being rehearsed even now, as the church militant both within and without shapes its environment for good:

> [T]he ethos of the church is transformative of the surrounding soci-
> ety.... For Edwards, the church is not merely a vehicle for moral forma-
> tion... but establishes the *telos* for the moral life. That is to say, Edwards
> believes that the church's eschatological communion with the Trinity
> orders all our interpersonal relationships. To participate in the life of
> the church is to recognize that mutuality and self-giving are normative
> in all human relationships, for in the triune God, mutual love among
> persons is supreme.[111]

The church is the body of Christ, where mutual interdependence is exercised between members, where selfishness has no place, and where our horizontal responsibilities are encouraged. Elsewhere, the image of the body highlights not the horizontal but the vertical: it is the body of Christ who is its Head and from whom the church's life is derived.[112] Using theological vocabulary that unites the mundane with the mystical, Edwards provides another biblical avenue to strengthen the relationship between ethics and eschatology. The journey and the destination are cut from the same cloth, just as our oneness in Christ means for Christians that "all things shall be yours."[113] Edwards's preaching on love itself formed a vital strategy in repristinating Reformed theology in the eighteenth century and gifted to traditional presentations of redemption new emphases.[114] It awaits discussion in the next section of this chapter as to exactly what kind of experiences within redemptive history the pilgrim people of God ought to expect.

---

109. Edwards, "Charity," *WJE* 8: 374.

110. Edwards, "Charity," *WJE* 8: 368, 374, 371.

111. Danaher, *Trinitarian Ethics*, 237, 253–54.

112. Edwards, "Charity," *WJE* 8: 270. Edwards assembles a list of biblical references to the spiritual body in the application of sermon seven to illustrate this point.

113. Edwards, "Charity," *WJE* 8: 270.

114. Marsden, *A Life*, 191–92.

3.3 The Purposeful Church in A History of the Work of Redemption

From its opening line, it is clear that a guiding theme of Edwards's discourse, *A History of the Work of Redemption*, based on a sermon series of March to August 1739, is the doctrine of the church, for he begins with the hope that his preaching will "comfort the church under her sufferings and persecutions of her enemies."[115] Innovatively, he preaches this entire series under one single biblical banner, namely Isaiah 51:8: "For the moth shall eat them up like a garment, and the worm shall eat them like wool: but my righteousness shall be forever, and my salvation from generation to generation." While in the previous year, Edwards had constructed a whole sermon series by expounding 1 Corinthians 13 a verse at a time, here, the longer sequence of thirty sermons is based not on a chapter but on a single verse. The scope of this discourse, finally published posthumously in 1774,[116] is conceived on a more narrow footing but with a more expansive vision: to expound the purpose of the church in the world.

Purporting to recount the work of God "from the fall of man to the end of the world," as outlined repeatedly in the doctrinal heading of the sermons, this series describes in three overarching parts first of all the preparation for the incarnation in the nation of Israel, then the life and ministry of the Lord Jesus himself, concluding with the history of the people of God after the ascension until the last judgment. Edwards uses the language of redemption not merely as a synonym for the doctrine of the atonement but also to present the story of salvation history.[117] The "work of redemption" functions as shorthand for the outworkings of the "covenant of redemption" made pretemporally between the Father and the Son, achieved in time and space through the earthly ministry of Christ, and applied to human lives through the work of the Spirit.[118] Brown suggests that for Edwards, the terminology of the work of redemption "makes reference to the whole of God's work *ad extra*, and thus to the whole

---

115. Jonathan Edwards, *A History of the Work of Redemption*, The Works of Jonathan Edwards 9, ed. J. F. Wilson (New Haven: Yale University Press, 1989), 113.

116. Edwards's son, Jonathan Edwards Jr., presented this published edition to the printers with amendments to the original, which disguised its sermonic origins and pastoral intentions. There was little interest in publishing the work in revolutionary America, so it was taken up by John Erskine in Scotland and published in Edinburgh instead. See John F. Wilson, "Editor's Introduction," in *A History of the Work of Redemption*, The Works of Jonathan Edwards 9, ed. J. F. Wilson (New Haven: Yale University Press, 1989), 20–25.

117. Edwards, *WJE* 9: 117.

118. Edwards, *WJE* 9: 118.

of those doctrines relating to this work."[119] It is most significant that Edwards visualizes redemption on such a sweeping vista, for this situates his ecclesiology in this work as an essential feature of divine operations.

The church in this discourse, both local and universal, functions as the unifying thematic subject (indeed as the collision point between God's beneficence and Satan's malice) as well as the object of Edwards's apologetic attempts to define his theological program over and against that of his deist opponents. Edwards is reconfiguring a defense of divine engagement in the world using history and the church's place within it as his bulwark.[120] The church will be preserved by God "from generation to generation," while those who oppose God's design, in former days or even contemporaneously with Edwards, will perish, just as "a moth shall eat them up like a garment, and the worm shall eat them like wool." Despite their elevated tone, Edwards preached these sermons to his own congregation in Northampton, and by using the method of historical development to teach centrally important doctrines of Christian faith, he makes clear that these particular auditors are part of God's developing economy in the world. This chapter demonstrates, from the "Redemption" discourse, first the nature of the church's instrumentality, then its growth, and finally its purpose, with an eye to the philosophical challenges and local declension that Edwards witnessed.

The Instrumentality of the Church and the Doctrine of Redemption

When Edwards speaks of the church, he is making claims for God's ongoing commitment to, and involvement with, the material order. His schematic history of God's work in the world, carried by the language of redemption, is a sharp critique of deist thought in the early to mid-eighteenth century. Edwards insisted upon God's intervention in the world and not God's distance from the world, not universality of access to God but rather the particularity of access to God through events where God makes himself known. For deists, the power of rationality, or universal reason, was the "candle of the Lord" that illuminated insights gleaned from observation of the natural world—Christianity "either added nothing at all to 'natural religion' or contained foolish and false elements, and hence must be purged, reinterpreted or rejected."[121] In terms of their logic, deists applied deductive reasoning to the theological issues at hand

---

119. Brown, *Edwards and the Bible*, 172.

120. Brown, *Edwards and the Bible*, 164–66, 178.

121. Porter, *Enlightenment*, 112.

so as to bring order to ostensibly disparate religious convictions and practices. They asserted individual autonomy rather than traditional authority (whether it be the Scriptures, clergy, or ecclesiastical forms) and held that the "purpose of religion is morality."[122] Essentially, the self-evident truths of creation were ranked more highly than the suspect claims of revealed religion:

> God and true religion were thought to be absolutely invariable since the beginning of history. In this sense, deism was a-historical. Deists were adamant about the *static* nature of both God and religion because they rejected *particularity*.... For the deists, then, true religion has no history and little or no relation to culture. All religions connected to history are necessarily suspect and products of an arbitrary god who is not God. All changes in history are unrelated to religious or even philosophical truth.[123]

Edwards makes clear in this discourse that the threat posed by the deists is inimical to Christian faith.[124] He also asserts in sermon twenty-one that it is indeed a kind of particularity, that of the Gospel, that has led to the successes of the Christian religion within history generally, and to the triumphs of the church in the age of Constantine more notably.[125] For Edwards, God is presently active in the world, exercising divine power in historically contingent ways. Edwards moves beyond the facile contrast between the doctrine of redemption and the deists' emphasis on creation, for he actually appeals to the purpose of the creation even when subordinating it to the goal of redemption.[126] He takes the position that God expresses his glory penultimately through the world's creation, while the ultimate diffusion of his glory is planned for the divine work of redemption, which was, "if possible, even more fundamental than its [the world's] creation."[127] To make from the creation a "spouse and kingdom

---

122. McDermott, *Jonathan Edwards Confronts the Gods*, 18–22.

123. McDermott, *Jonathan Edwards Confronts the Gods*, 28–29 (emphasis mine).

124. Edwards, *WJE* 9: 432.

125. Edwards, *WJE* 9: 398–99.

126. For a similar point from a later sermon, see also Jonathan Edwards, "The Church's Marriage to Her Sons, and to Her God," in *Sermons and Discourses, 1743–1758*, The Works of Jonathan Edwards 25, ed. W. H. Kimnach (New Haven: Yale University Press, 2005), 187.

127. John F. Wilson, "History," in *The Princeton Companion to Jonathan Edwards*, ed. S. H. Lee (Princeton: Princeton University Press, 2005), 215.

for his Son" is an audacious desire, enabled through the trinitarian redemptive plan of God from the beginning of time:

> [T]he Work of Redemption is, as it were, the sum of God's works of providence. This shows us how much greater the Work of Redemption is than the work of creation, for I have several times observed before that the work of providence is greater than the work of creation because 'tis the end of it, as the use of an house is the end of the building of an house....This Work of Redemption is so much the greatest of all the works of God, that all other works are to be looked upon either as part of it, or appendages to it, or are some way reducible to it. And so all the decrees of God do some way or other belong to that eternal covenant of redemption that was between the Father and the Son before the foundation of the world; every decree of God is some way or other reducible to that covenant...for the Work of Redemption is the great subject of the whole Bible.[128]

While the work of redemption itself, according to Edwards's doctrine, is carried on from the "fall of man to the end of the world," Edwards is keen to nuance this with the explanation that there were "many things done in order to the Work of Redemption...before the world was created, yea from all eternity,"[129] though decrees to allow the fall or to pursue reprobation are not here made explicit. Here he stops short of espousing supralapsarianism *tout court*.

As Edwards describes such a work of redemption and the church's place within it in historically objective terms, he is subtly reshaping the Puritan approach. He of course still passionately echoes the Puritan concern for the subjective appropriation of grace in the life of an individual. "Charity and its Fruits," preached a year earlier, amply demonstrates this concern, as do several loci in the "Redemption" discourse, which draw a parallel between the soul's pilgrimage from conversion to glory and the progress of the church.[130] However, Edwards also demonstrates his Puritan, indeed premodern, historical sensibilities when he requires that the objective course of redemption history has meaning only in so far as it is provided through a prophetic voice from outside the creation. Prophets decipher the ambiguity of earthly reality.[131] Enlightened

---

128. Edwards, *WJE* 9: 513–14.

129. Edwards, *WJE* 9: 118. See also discussion of this in Edwards, "Misc." 1062, *WJE* 20: 430–43, where Edwards describes the work of the Trinity before the creation of the world in establishing the covenant of redemption.

130. For example, Edwards, *WJE* 9: 144.

131. See John F. Wilson, "Jonathan Edwards as Historian," *Church History* 46(1) (1977): 5–18, and William J. Scheick, *The Writings of Jonathan Edwards: Theme, Motif and Style* (College

thinkers of Edwards's day would insist that history ought only to be understood on its own terms, explained from within the observable world, disallowing any recourse to the transcendent to ascertain human or ecclesiological purpose.

The "Redemption" discourse is therefore distinctively new in terms of its concrete description of the historical connections between creation and redemption leading to the consummation of the world. Each stage builds upon the divine purpose embedded in previous historical achievement, giving to the overall shape an eschatological or cosmic trajectory. God's glory is the end for which God's creation and redemption are the means. Wilson highlights the importance:

> Edwards's argument was, so to speak, that if creation is a stage, the purpose of which is to permit the drama of redemption to be played out, the outcome of the drama (and thus the reason for creation) is God's self-glorification.[132]

In short, God's ordered relationship with the world can be understood in terms of deliberate and identifiable steps (at least in retrospect). While we have earlier seen that Edwards might better be described as a voluntarist with regard to conversion morphology, highlighting the freedom of God to work in surprising ways within the life of the individual,[133] when it comes to assessing the life of the church writ large, Edwards is just as likely to highlight the regularities and continuities to be found between design within history and in the church and so be described as an intellectualist. While the Spirit's work in the individual adheres to a minimum of stages, the church brings order to the Spirit's work inasmuch as it conforms to numerous successive dispensations of God.[134] As a consequence of the redemptive design being incorporated into the material creation, the church, as the redeemed part of the created order, occupies a dignified and exalted place.

Station: Texas A & M University Press, 1975), 65, for arguments concerning Edwards's historical method. Wilson critiques the views of both Peter Gay and Perry Miller, the former who makes of Edwards an anachronism and the latter who presents Edwards as modern without remainder. Neither position for Wilson can remain uncontested.

132. Wilson, "Editor's Introduction," *WJE* 9: 31–32.

133. Brand draws our attention to writers for whom Edwards's Augustinian and voluntarist heritage is essential to understanding his soteriology. See Brand, *Profile of the Last Puritan*, 111–24.

134. Edwards's first set of divisions creates three periods of history, namely the period before the incarnation, the period of Christ's humiliation, then the reign of Christ in heaven after his exaltation. Within this schema, the last dispensation is further subdivided into the era until the fall of Jerusalem, then until the conversion of the Empire under Constantine, then until the Fall of Antichrist at the Reformation, then until the Day of Judgment. These

The work of redemption is fundamentally a unifying work of God, despite the disparate historical contingencies it must inhabit. It must be recognized, however, that this unity is not the equivalent of universalism in which all are saved. For the church to be redeemed leaves others without such a redemption and leads to opposition for the people of God in the world. After all, the theme of the "Redemption" discourse is to provide comfort to the church in its dangerous pilgrimage and in its own battles with Satan. Not only does the leading text from Isaiah 51:8 imply the existence and eventual destruction of opposition, it is also expressed in more explicit terms in the first sermon: "the sufferings and the persecutions of her enemies," "the happiness of the church of God is set forth by comparing it with the contrary fate of his enemies that oppose her," "how shortlived the power and prosperity of the church's enemies is."[135] Indeed, such sufferings begin to define the church's experience in history.[136]

This is of great significance not only pastorally for Edwards's readers but also for his philosophy of history, which is driven most fundamentally by the redemption provided by God for the church since her fall and against her enemies. The contest within history between the forces of good and evil is the *sine qua non* of the whole discourse and the underlying and unifying reality of all history. McClymond locates such a narrative within the apocalyptic traditions of Christian thought.[137] God's activity to interpose is indeed fundamental to Edwards's conception of history, and the duality between good and evil is part of an apocalyptic worldview. However, Edwards's model is not one of occasional and spectacular divine intrusion, but rather continuous involvement with periodic recalibrations. The continuities between creation, redemption, and consummation suggest that instead of an apocalyptic model, a prophetic model better describes Edwards's philosophy of history in which God, through human instruments, provides necessary corrections and appeals to return to previously revealed ways. The church is not a defensive remnant but the victorious beneficiary of Christ's resurrection.[138]

Avihu Zakai is a most insightful commentator on Edwards's philosophy of history. He first wants to assert that it was a distinctive characteristic of

---

periodizations are structured for Edwards around different "comings of Christ." See Edwards, *WJE* 9: 351.

135. Edwards, *WJE* 9: 113.

136. Edwards, *WJE* 9: 453.

137. Michael J. McClymond, *Encounters with God: An Approach to the Theology of Jonathan Edwards* (New York: Oxford University Press, 1998), 70–71.

138. See, for example, Edwards, *WJE* 9: 360–61.

Protestant historiography more generally to locate eschatological and apocalyptic developments within the time and space continuum. The Reformers
had rejected the Augustinian framework of God's ultimate triumph beyond
history, which had rendered static the historical experience. With this denial,
Edwards would of course concur.[139] However, Zakai also asseverates that traditional Puritan eschatology, based on the model of the Exodus from Egypt
that appealed to apocalyptic rupture as the rationale for leaving England, had
been relativized in New England and was now conceived in more nuanced
terms. Edwards was distancing himself from more recent Protestant apocalyptic interpretation:

> Edwards inherited the quest to establish the closest possible link
> between prophecy and history. . . . Yet, in contrast to the Protestant
> assumption that the historical process is based ultimately on social,
> political, and ecclesiastical changes, such as the struggle against the
> Church of Rome, Edwards held that the principal source governing the
> historical process is God's redemptive plan.[140]

A battle within history between the people of God and all who oppose her
might be understood in apocalyptic terms; however, Edwards does not tie the
victory of God's people to cataclysmic intervention. Christ does not reign on
the earth in unmediated glory in the millennium.[141] Rather than a "tiny huddle
surrounded by a hostile mob,"[142] the church of God is a prosperous society,
though for a brief time possibly experiencing apostasy.[143] On the other hand,
Edwards does not go so far as to collapse God's will entirely into the historical process without remainder. He disavows a cyclical pattern of history that
in the end makes no progress. Such a position, "analogous to the life cycle of
the individual organism,"[144] would be to fail to acknowledge any millennial
structure in Edwards's thought.

With the church as case study, it becomes evident that Edwards bap-
tizes neither the abstract rationalism of the deists, which would permit of

---

139. Zakai, *Exile and Kingdom*, 22–24.

140. Zakai, *Jonathan Edwards's Philosophy of History*, 161–62.

141. Zakai, *Jonathan Edwards's Philosophy of History*, 269–70.

142. McClymond, *Encounters with God*, 71.

143. Edwards, *WJE* 9: 471–86.

144. Stow Persons, "The Cyclical Theory of History in Eighteenth Century America,"
American Quarterly 6(2) (1954): 147–63.

no historical particularity, nor the erratic or wholly arbitrary ministry of the enthusiasts, which tended toward the impossibility of determining historical order.[145] McClymond suggests that Edwards takes a mediating position, acknowledging both the continuities between creation and redemption and the possibility of the new in an individual's life. It may be characterized as a "graduated supernaturalism whose dominant characteristic was the blurring of any sharp line between the natural and the supernatural."[146] The church is theologically as well as practically situated to engender this collocation as an instrument of divine agency, with the disclaimer that such an instrumentality is not merely disposable or provisional, but rather substantial and permanent in God's plans.

Edwards has frequently been named the American Augustine,[147] and *A History of the Work of Redemption* certainly fulfills the role, similar to that of the *City of God* in the fifth century, of interpreting his own times, now in relation to the revivals, and answering objections to the claims of Christian faith in philosophically cogent ways. Both works describe the war in which believers are engaged in history. Edwards's discourse, however, does more than acknowledge the difficulties facing the people of God in their pilgrimage in this world, or allow for the usefulness of the church in waging that war. He makes a positive case to describe the progress that is made during their historical sojourn.[148] The verifiably real progress of the church is the theme of the next section of this chapter.

The Progress of the Church and the Use of Typology

The redeemed church is not just valiantly defending her toehold in a world opposed to the claims of Christ: she is actually making valiant though often unrecognized progress despite her adversaries. Edwards appropriates a typological strategy to demonstrate such progress and to deny the deist assumption that any change within the historical order must necessarily be degenerative. Typology in Christian history has provided cohesion in biblical interpretation and has brought order to literature commonly seen as unreliable because it is disparate in form and matter. It became an increasingly important

---

145. H. Richard Niebuhr, *The Kingdom of God in America*, first Wesleyan ed. (Middletown, CT: Wesleyan University Press, 1988), 55.

146. McClymond, *Encounters with God*, 110.

147. See, for example, Zakai, *Jonathan Edwards's Philosophy of History*, 334.

148. Marsden, *A Life*, 197.

methodology in several areas: to interpret difficult portions of Scripture, like the Song of Songs or the book of Revelation; to maintain the relevance of the Old Testament to the Puritans' New England situation, despite rejection of, for instance, the Old Testament sacrificial system;[149] and to allow a providential- ist view of history in the days after the closing of the New Testament canon.[150] When faced with persecution, it was most tempting through typological exe- gesis to connect present experience with Scriptural texts that admitted of a common shape to the adversity experienced, even if its details varied.[151] While redemption provided a unifying soteriology, typology provided a unifying epis- temology in Edwards's search for ecclesiological progress.

Typology is the hermeneutical strategy that connects an earlier event or achievement in history with one that comes after it, lending to the latter exem- plar some of the theological value that adhered to the earlier model. Unlike allegory, which takes a concrete historical instance and relates it to a suprahis- torical idea or concept, the structure of type (the earlier instance) and antitype (the latter instance) maintains historical checks and balances and disallows fanciful, perhaps Platonic, interpretation.[152] Puritans were not averse to seeking communication from God in historical events both within and without the bib- lical revelation: they simply had to establish a rigorous correspondence in the mind of the divine author between the parts to establish their case.[153] Edwards further grounds this hermeneutical device not just in the divine mind but also in the divine character. He maintains that an essential attribute of God is the desire to communicate his glory in creation and in history, wherefore phenom- ena in all the world can function as means of communication. In opposition to deist assumptions about the retreat of God from this world, Edwards is theo- logically predisposed to hear God "through many and diverse media."[154]

---

149. While typology might provide a case for historical development, appeal to the Old Testament at all for validation of New England's ecclesiastical settlement could have the opposite effect, namely to remind Puritans of decline from a primitivist purity of design and execution. See Bozeman, *To Live Ancient Lives*, 17. Edwards's ecclesiology is contrasted here with such a "first is best" mindset.

150. Mason I. Lowance, Jr., *The Language of Canaan: Metaphor and Symbol in New England from the Puritans to the Transcendentalists* (Cambridge: Harvard University Press, 1980), viii, 27, 35.

151. W. Reginald Ward, *Early Evangelicalism: A Global Intellectual History, 1670–1789* (Cambridge: University Press, 2006), 145.

152. See the excellent introduction to typology in McClymond, *The Theology of Jonathan Edwards*, 116–29.

153. Lowance, *Language of Canaan*, 4–5.

154. McDermott, *Jonathan Edwards Confronts the Gods*, 43, 225.

For Edwards, typology demonstrates both divine oversight of history and divine interpretation of history. Old Testament types, whether institutions, providences, or persons,[155] essentially point forward to, and teach about, Christ: the exodus from Egypt is "the greatest type of Christ's redemption of any providential event whatsoever," the details of Israel's legal code were together designed to show "that the whole nation by this law was as it were constituted in a typical state," the judges are understood as "types of the great redeemer and deliverer of his church," and supremely, David was presented as "the greatest personal type of Christ of all under the Old Testament."[156] To establish a typical relationship between historical events or institutions within the narrative of the Bible was relatively conventional, for Christological typology in the New Testament provided a "strong unifying tendency" between the testaments.[157] Such connections could be expressed either through propositional prophecy or figurative types:

> We observed before that the light that the church enjoyed from the fall of man till Christ came was like the light which we enjoy in the night, not the light of the sun directly but as reflected from the moon and stars, which light did foreshadow Christ to come, the sun of righteousness hereafter to arise. This light of the sun of righteousness to come they had chiefly two ways. One was by predictions of Christ to come whereby his coming was foretold and promised, and another was by types and shadows of Christ whereby his coming and redemption were prefigured.[158]

Edwards, however, more radically, is also prepared to see typical relationships between extracanonical historical events and the life of the church.[159] Somewhat predictably, the tabernacle is presented in sermon eight as the multivalent type for "the human nature of Christ, and of the church of Christ, and of heaven."[160] Remarkably, on the other hand, the parallel is drawn between

---

155. Edwards, *WJE* 9: 204.

156. Edwards, *WJE* 9: 175, 182, 196, 204.

157. McClymond, *Encounters with God*, 68. Note, for example, the recurrent use of the word τυπος in 1 Corinthians 10 to extract moral lessons from the Law.

158. Edwards, *WJE* 9: 136.

159. Edwards begins sermon twelve by allowing for confident interpretation of events in the period between the end of Old Testament prophecy and the coming of Christ, even without "Scripture history to guide us." See Edwards, *WJE* 9: 270.

160. Edwards, *WJE* 9: 224.

the conversion of the pagan Roman Empire under Constantine's leadership, a kind of "coming of Christ" as interpreted from Revelation 6:12–17, with the ultimate "coming of Christ" at the Last Judgment, working essentially from antitype back to type.[161] He also extravagantly describes the Constantinian achievement as "the greatest revolution and change in the face of things on the face of the earth that ever came to pass in the world since the flood."[162] Though noticeably lacking in the "Redemption" discourse, in his typology notebooks, Edwards also endorses "a system of types in nature,"[163] bordering on allegory, which would relate the contours of natural phenomena to spiritual lessons. In *Images of Divine Things*, he can imaginatively assert that ecclesiology can be drawn out of botany:

> 99....The church in different ages is lively represented by the growth and progress of a tree; and the church in the same age, in Christ its head and stock, is like a tree. The various changes of a tree in different seasons, and what comes to pass in its leaves, flowers and fruit in innumerable instances that might be mentioned, is a lively image of what is to be seen in the church....A tree also is many ways a lively image of a particular Christian, with regard to the new man, and is so spoken of in Scripture. *Corol.* Hence it may be argued that infants do belong to the church.[164]

In surrounding entries, Edwards extracts lessons for the prosperity of the church from the vicissitudes of daily weather patterns and teaches that the erect posture of human beings signifies "that he was made to have heaven in his eye."[165] Wilson sees this trajectory as a departure from conservative Puritan exegesis, thus allowing Edwards a more dynamic interpretation of history and Christian experience than was recently possible. Wilson's claim that "the discourse became as much a celebration of the God of nature as a hymn to the Lord of history" is, however, to overreach.[166] Observations on nature are distinctly not at the heart of the "Redemption" discourse.

---

161. Edwards, *WJE* 9: 351, 397.

162. Edwards, *WJE* 9: 396.

163. McDermott, *Jonathan Edwards Confronts the Gods*, 113.

164. Jonathan Edwards, *Typological Writings*, The Works of Jonathan Edwards 11, eds. Wallace E. Anderson, Mason I. Lowance Jr., and David H. Watters (New Haven: Yale University Press, 1993), 89.

165. Edwards, *WJE* 11: 88–89.

166. Wilson, "Editor's Introduction," *WJE* 9: 50.

One of the most pregnant uses of typology for ecclesiological purposes in this discourse is the portrayal of Christ as prophet, priest, and prince.[167] Those occupying these three mediatorial offices in the Old Testament had in common an anointing, which presaged the commissioning of Christ in his baptism for divine service. Immediately after the fall, the Son began his work mediating between the Father and sinful humanity: "He undertook hencefor-ward to teach mankind in the exercise of his prophetic office and to intercede for fallen man in the <exercise of the> priestly <office> and he took on him as it were the care and burden of the government of the church and of the world."[168] The priestly role is fulfilled through Christ's purchase of redemption and his pleading of the merits of his purchase before the throne of grace. The kingly role describes victory by God through Christ over his enemies and the distribution of blessings thereby won. The prophetic role, more important for us, suggests ecclesiological dynamism.

Christ as prophet reveals the Gospel, makes promises, predicts the future, inspires divine songs, makes clear the mind of God, and silences in the end the typical prophets when his own time for approach arrived. Christ allowed other kinds of teachers of philosophy in order that, by contrast with him, the limitations of human wisdom might be perceived.[169] The construction of successive stages of history, expounding the story of redemption in the world and using the language of types, lends itself to the privileging of the office of prophet to describe the work of Christ, for the historical development of the life and structures of the church requires continual explanation, as does the coordination of direct prediction with figural foretelling. Christ's priestly work of atonement may be chronologically the center of the history of the work of redemption, but Christ's prophetic work of revelation functions as the epis-temological web capturing the church's varying stages into a unified whole.

To present the church in such developmental terms, as making progress within the course of history, was significant for pastoral and apologetic reasons in Edwards's own day. It must be remembered that this discourse was, unlike similar compendia of church history, not written for academic purposes in the first instance.[170] Indeed, this series had as its first auditory the people of Northampton for whom these thirty sermons should locate New England in

---

167. Edwards, *WJE* 9: 218.

168. Edwards, *WJE* 9: 130. Words in angle brackets represent Edwards's own words, which appear in the original as interlinear additions.

169. Edwards, *WJE* 9: 137, 318, 358; 187, 358; 134, 137, 187, 315, 209, 269, 278.

170. See further Zakai, *Jonathan Edwards's Philosophy of History*, 235.

the progress of salvation history and function as a reality check given their recent but now waning experience of revival. The immediate goals of this subsequently misnamed "discourse" were to provide cosmic perspective on their mundane squabbles and to provide encouragement to persevere in their spiritual labors. One of the few explicit mentions of Northampton in this text places it at the end of a line of God's works throughout the world, making this western Massachusetts town tantamount to the climax of redemption history thus far.[171]

The tone of this remark does not inspire confidence that the townsfolk of Northampton (whose concerns, it appears, were growing more worldly) were eager to own the ongoing work of the Spirit. The recent separation of church meetinghouse from town meetinghouse did not bode well for integrated Christian living, dividing godly from secular affairs, as Northampton's growing regional status had necessitated larger spaces for both. Edwards's pulpit became a more exalted platform from which to exercise his expanding spiritual influence beyond the Connecticut River Valley, despite the very localized spiritual declension of church members and the pain it caused him. Even though Edwards situated motors to drive the history of world in revivals and not in a particular monarch or nation, Northampton clearly had a role to play in exemplifying God's purposes. Perry Miller senses such an aspiration: "[T]he book definitely embodies Edwards's time and place; it is the history of Northampton writ large."[172]

This discourse further reflects Edwards's historical location to the extent it reasserts classic Christian theism in the face of eighteenth-century deist denials of God's immanence in the created order. The deists' antagonism toward Christian claims to historical particularity was countered by Edwards in part by asserting the reality of divine redemptive intervention, but significantly also by asserting not just the reality of the redeemed people of God but also their development within history. Typology insists upon intentional progress.[173] Such dynamism is reflected further in the images that Edwards appoints to reinforce the framework of progress. He can write of the diurnal course of the sun in sermon nineteen as an image of gospel progress.[174] In a remarkable paragraph in sermon thirty, Edwards concatenates various images, all of which reinforce the dynamism of history and the relationship

---

171. Edwards, *WJE* 9: 436.

172. Miller, *Jonathan Edwards*, 315.

173. Edwards, *WJE* 9: 183–84.

174. Edwards, *WJE* 9: 367.

between its parts. The tropes of river, wheel, and chain, taken from nature and industry, militate against a static conception of time and its deist reflex that change necessitates deterioration:

> We began at the head of the stream of divine providence, and we have followed it and traced it through its various windings and turnings till we are come to the end of it, and we see where it issues: as it began in God, so it ends in God. God is the infinite ocean into which it empties itself. Providence is like a mighty wheel whose ring or circumference is so high that it is dreadful with the glory of the God of Israel above upon it.... We have seen the revolution of this wheel, and how that as it was from God so its return has been to God again. All the events of divine providence are like the links of a chain, the first link is from God and the last is to him.[175]

Deists wanted to level the epistemological playing field and give all human beings access to divine truth through the universalizing dictates of reason, making historical contingencies anathema. In their minds, this had become especially urgent with discoveries of new lands and new peoples, mediated through popular travel writings describing nations without Christian witness and led by pagan mystagogues. Despite his appeals to the *prisca theologia*, the contention that all peoples had some vestige of revealed truth available to them passed down from Noah and his sons, even if received in compromised form, Edwards still insisted on the overall positive growth of the church within history. History was Edwards's ally, not his adversary.[176] Edwards's respect for the essence of history reflects his commitment to the gradualness of God's work of redemption. God makes typological preparations for the comings of Christ in grace and in glory, which function as a pedagogical strategy, adapting God's communication to human capacity to understand.[177] As illustration, Edwards provides the story of preparations made for the coming of an important person to a town to suggest the emotional impact of steps and planning for a future event.[178] Stages of redemptive history ought to be expected as the norm:

---

175. Edwards, *WJE* 9: 517–18.

176. McDermott, *Jonathan Edwards Confronts the Gods*, 96, 108.

177. McDermott, *Jonathan Edwards Confronts the Gods*, 116–17.

178. Edwards, *WJE* 9: 292.

There is not reason from God's Word to think any other than that this great Work of God will be gradually wrought, though very swiftly, yet gradually....But this is a work that will be accomplished by means, by the preaching of the gospel, and the use of the ordinary means of grace, and so shall be gradually brought to pass....The Scriptures hold forth as though there should be several successive great and glorious events by which this glorious work shall be accomplished.[179]

Edwards's distance from personal preparationism contrariwise amplifies the kind of preparationism inherent in history.[180] When the parallels are made between the individual and the history of the world, then it is not the stages of conversion that are Edwards's interest, but instead the stages of the Christian's life in the church post-conversion that reflect and reinforce the gradualism of history.[181] Edwards is refashioning his Puritan patrimony. His focus is not on the complexity of Christian beginnings, but rather on the movement toward Christian ends. The introspective tendency of much previous Puritan thought is replaced by an expansive vision of the church's cosmic role. Conversions will take place until the end of time, so the work of redemption is to be understood cumulatively and as a corporate phenomenon:

And then will come the time when all the elect shall be gathered in; that work of conversion that has gone from the beginning of the church after the fall, through all these ages, shall be carried on no more. There shall never another soul be converted. Every one of those many millions, whose names were written in the book of life before the foundation of the world, shall be brought out; not one soul shall be left. And the mystical body of Christ, which has been growing ever since it first began in the days of Adam, will now be complete as to number of parts, having every one of its members; in this respect the Work of Redemption will be now finished.[182]

Types point to their antitypical fulfillment in Christ, the head of the church, and, by implication in Edwards's mind, types also point to the mystical body

179. Edwards, *WJE* 9: 458–59.

180. William J. Scheick makes this a central contention. See William J. Scheick, "The Grand Design: Jonathan Edwards' *History of the Work of Redemption*," in *Critical Essays on Jonathan Edwards*, ed. W. J. Scheick (Boston: G. K. Hall & Co., 1980), 183.

181. Edwards, *WJE* 9: 144.

182. Edwards, *WJE* 9: 492.

of Christ, which evermore completes Christ.[183] The very use of figural, more specifically typological, as opposed to propositional communication strategies was both a traditional and corporate literary conceit.[184] Just as the work of redemption is given Scriptural consistency in the use of typology, typology gives the church an essential role in the plans and purposes of God. What exactly that design is will be treated in what follows.

The Purpose of the Church and the Revivals of Piety

For Edwards, history is teleological. It is not just that history and the church located within it are dynamic, which could imply random or disorganized movement. The church instead progresses toward a particular and exalted goal. It is not just that, using the image of the wheel, history mechanistically turns or completes one or several revolutions (which in Edwards's day did not yet signify political upheaval but rather repetition and constancy). The "Redemption" discourse makes clear that the dynamism of the church in history has divinely appointed ends. God is not distant, nor is he impotent to change the course of history. God brings order to the creation[185] and demonstrates that order proleptically through the church, which gathers in the fruits of periodic revivals, themselves the engines of transformation. History has a unity, and the church provides evidence for the case, even if the progress of the church in the world is not easy to identify or does not always track a constantly upward trajectory.

The periodic revival of vital piety is central to Edwards's view of order in history, because such an occurrence presupposes the possibility of declension due to evil and sin and recognizes the need of a distinct work of God to overcome opposition or laxity. Cyclical spirituality furthermore has Scriptural warrant insofar as Old Testament narratives present the recurring rise and fall of Israel, draw on agricultural or seasonal imagery,[186] divide time into repeating patterns, for example the Sabbath day of rest or the year of Jubilee, or present miracles as concentrated within certain periods, and not always forthcoming. To insert surprising revivals into an already evolving work of divine redemption within history is to create a dynamism that is not innate but contingent

---

183. McDermott, *Jonathan Edwards Confronts the Gods*, 101.

184. John F. Wilson, "History, Redemption, and the Millennium," in *Jonathan Edwards and the American Experience*, eds. N. O. Hatch and H. S. Stout (New York: Oxford University Press, 1988), 138.

185. Scheick, *The Writings of Jonathan Edwards*, 50–53, 141.

186. Schmidt, *Holy Fairs*, 156.

upon the work of God, and to render unpredictable that same work. The life of the church is organic and unique, and not merely mechanistic or predictable. It is the Spirit that makes the difference.[187]

Furthermore, such growth is complicated through the presence of random evil. For example, Edwards outlines in sermon twenty various steps that God has enacted through the pouring out of the Spirit, whether it be on the day of Pentecost, in the mission to the Samaritans, in the city of Ephesus, or to the Gentiles, to achieve great numbers of converts.[188] Such growth is then met with opposition, as Satan, "seeing Christ's kingdom make such amazing progress such as never had been before, we may conclude he was filled with the greatest confusion and astonishment, and hell seemed to be effectively alarmed by it to make the most violent opposition against it."[189] This pattern would recur through history, with the pertinent illustration used often by Edwards of the darkness being heaviest immediately before the dawn.[190]

One can allow that overall redemptive progress is being made while at the same time acknowledging that this is not a steady achievement. The church may mark advances and suffer retreats if, at the end of the day, her forward line is better positioned for her next redemptive success.[191] Alongside the image of night and day, Edwards also uses the picture of a building that slowly rises to completion, though its construction may be intermittent:

> After this [the reign of Solomon] the glory of the Jewish church gradually declined more and more till Christ came, though not so [much] but that the Work of Redemption still went on; whatever failed or declined, God still carried on this work from age to age, this building was still advancing higher and higher.... And now the whole Work of Redemption is finished.... Now the topstone of the building is laid. In the progress of the discourse on this subject we have followed the

---

187. Edwards, *WJE* 9: 266.

188. Edwards, *WJE* 9: 371–86.

189. Edwards, *WJE* 9: 381.

190. Edwards, *WJE* 9: 229, 422.

191. Kenneth Scott Latourette, *A History of Christianity* (London: Eyre & Spottiswoode, 1954), 1471. Bosch suggests that Latourette has been the name most closely associated with this model in which the "pattern of expansion...had been like seven successive waves of an incoming tide. The crest of each wave was higher than the crest that had preceded it, and the trough of each wave receded less than the one before it." See David J. Bosch, *Transforming Mission: Paradigm Shifts in Theology of Mission*, American Society of Missiology Series (Maryknoll, NY: Orbis Books, 2003), 334.

church of God in all the great changes, all her tossings to and fro that [she] is subject to in all the storms and tempests through the many ages of the world, till at length we have seen an end to all these storms.[192]

Rather than it being an embarrassment for Edwards to acknowledge the vicissitudes of the life of the church, such a confession rather suits his overall purpose. The work of redemption is applied in the first instance to the experience of individuals, who face the crisis of conversion by imitating Christ in his death and resurrection. The church, too, reflects this spiritual shape, according to Edwards, insofar as its own journey in the world is constituted by the experience of judgment or conflict, with preservation and growth. Opposition to the church is cathartically written into its storyline. Although individuals may experience radical discontinuities leading to conversion, without predictable stages or expectations, and churches on the other hand experience more gradual growth or decline, both the individual and the church have in common what Davidson refers to as the model of afflictive progress. It is a psychological model writ large in history:

> The millennial perspective of New Englanders...focused not on a utopian model of social perfection but on a history which catalogues events, past and future, leading to the final triumph of Christ's kingdom. Preoccupation was not with the millennium itself (Edwards's *History of Redemption* devoted only four pages out of 220 to the subject) but with the pattern of God's actions within history which shaped the struggle between the Lamb and the beast. And the pattern which both consciously and unconsciously gave the drama its form was that of an individual's conversion.[193]

The church will triumph despite adversity. Sacred history has at its heart the work of redemption concentrated in periods of revival, which ecclesial life watches over and sustains until the consummation.[194] The reign of the church on earth through the saints during the millennium is not expansively

---

192. Edwards, *WJE* 9: 228, 508.

193. Davidson, *The Logic of Millennial Thought*, 216–17. See pp. 137–38 for further explanation of the connection between conversion, afflictive progress, and the millennial state of the church.

194. See comments on Zakai's views in R. Bryan Bademan, "The Edwards of History and the Edwards of Faith," *Reviews in American History* 34(2) (2006): 131–49, especially 137.

described by Edwards, for that would be to place the church in the driving seat. The unfortunate yet frequent association of Edwards with incipient American nationalism, generated by misreadings of *Some Thoughts Concerning the Present Revival* (1742)[195] and the place of the millennium in American history, finds no support in *A History of the Work of Redemption*.[196] The millennium is significant in Edwards's cause for hope but is not at the heart of Edwards's conception of history.

Of note as well is the fact that clerical ministry is not a prominent theme in the discourse. Ministry can be validated through appeals to ordination, learning, or charismatic gifting; however, none of these give authority to the church here, perhaps at least in part because clericalism had become such a contested theme in eighteenth-century debates over traditional authority. Sermon nineteen relates the origins of gospel ministry to Christ's commission to the apostles in Matthew 28 to preach to the nations, which exists as a model to all later ministers or elders. The role is one that facilitates the church's expansion.[197] Edwards briefly recognizes the role of councils of the church to bring order from both theological and organizational divisions.[198] Ministers are referenced in sermon twenty-seven to placard the harmony that will exist between them and their people in the future times of peace and love.[199] However, ministerial distinctives shall be relativized at that time:

A time of excellent order in the church discipline and government [shall] be settled in his church; all the world [shall then be] as one church, one orderly, regular, beautiful society, one body, all the members in beautiful proportion.[200]

His vision for the future of the church was not concerned with the prerogatives and privileges of the clerical caste, as this discourse makes plain, even if he does maintain that the pastor must answer to the Judge for the conduct of

---

195. Jonathan Edwards, "Some Thoughts Concerning the Revival," in *The Great Awakening*, The Works of Jonathan Edwards 4, ed. C. C. Goen (New Haven: Yale University Press, 1972), 353.

196. Gerald R. McDermott, *One Holy and Happy Society: The Public Theology of Jonathan Edwards* (University Park: Pennsylvania State University Press, 1992), 42–43.

197. Edwards, *WJE 9:* 364.

198. Edwards, *WJE 9:* 368.

199. Edwards, *WJE 9:* 483.

200. Edwards, *WJE 9:* 484.

his ministerial responsibilities.[201] Like his Puritan forebears, Edwards understood ministry as a conscious repudiation of sacramentally centered Roman
Catholicism and a kind of Protestantism that gave significant space to lay piety
and ministrations, especially at the beginning of the New England experiment,[202] but unlike his deist interlocutors, he would not have espoused the
position that clericalism was at the heart of social degeneration.[203] Ministerial
authority is rather harnessed by God for his purposes in revival.

Edwards's vision of the future of the church functions polemically and
modestly to demonstrate that order is part of the Christian interpretation
of history. While deists might assume historical entropy and the primitivist
necessity therefore of recapturing the pristine kernels of revelation implanted
in the creation, Edwards gives no credence to their assumptions. He succeeds
in formulating an account of history that allows for both diversity and unpredictability, with unity and purpose. He purports to provide a more satisfac-
tory explanation of the events of history than his philosophical adversaries.
Sermon thirty is infused with the language of teleology to draw together the
above themes:

> 'Tis with God's work of providence as it is with his work of creation: 'tis
> but one work.... God's works of providence ben't disunited and jum-
> bled, without connection or dependence. But all are united.[204]

The diversity of contributions toward the common aim can occasionally suggest that there is no design or end. This Edwards guards against, insofar as
he puts the case that any onlooker at a building site would be hard pressed
to accurately imagine the ultimate design of the project, though the archi-
tect has just such a plan, from which to work.[205] The church was bound to
triumph eventually in the coming millennial kingdom of Christ, though the
focus was not the local ecclesiastical tribe, but the divine universal perspective.[206] The contours of the church in the "Redemption" discourse are ever
expanding to correspond to the new order of the new creation. While Solomon

201. As I shall later show, Edwards's "Farewell Sermon" deals with this very issue of both
ministerial and congregational responsibility when Christ returns to judge.

202. McClymond, *Encounters with God*, 39, 82.

203. McDermott, *Jonathan Edwards Confronts the Gods*, 24.

204. Edwards, *WJE* 9: 519.

205. Edwards, *WJE* 9: 122–23.

206. Zakai, *Jonathan Edwards's Philosophy of History*, 247.

Stoddard could be content that a revival demonstrated God's pleasure with New England, his grandson had loftier visions of revival demonstrating the inevitable victory of God in the world.[207]

Though McClymond is cautious of Edwards's attempts to make providential history lie on an eschatologically taut Procrustean bed, he nevertheless concurs with Perry Miller that the unity of history is Edwards's philosophical aim in this discourse, with revival as the engine of history and the church as the ripe fruit of its progress.[208] Both deist ahistoricism and the suspicion of contamination of revelation in the course of history are impotent criticisms of theism in Edwards's apologia. The scandal of particularity that they prosecute finds itself without witnesses in the stand. Edwards's attempts to defend divine engagement with the world without rendering experience chaotic or arbitrary is the philosophical underpinning for *A History of the Work of Redemption*, as much as the ordering role of the church is its polemical center. Edwards adapts his Puritan patrimony by objectifying the work of redemption and highlighting historical process driven by periods of revival in which the church features prominently and purposefully.

3.4 The Structured Church in Some Thoughts Concerning the Revival

A short time following Whitefield's triumphant tour of the colonies in 1740 and Northampton's own experience of the flames of revival, Edwards preached a sermon subsequently entitled "Sinners in the Hands of an Angry God," at Enfield, Massachusetts (later Connecticut), in July 1741, while supplying the pulpit for a pastoral colleague. Though the awakening response, consisting of cries, faintings, and shrieks, marked Edwards himself as a revivalist of note, such notoriety was moderate compared with the ministry of James Davenport (1716–1757), whose itinerations and bizarre manifestations of the Spirit generated vociferous opposition and challenged traditional patterns of Christian experience and ministry in the New England.[209] Edwards the theologian,

---

207. Michael Crawford, *Seasons of Grace: Colonial New England's Revival Tradition in Its British Context* (New York: Oxford University Press, 1991), 134.

208. McClymond, *Encounters with God*, 104.

209. Though of excellent Puritan pedigree, Davenport's antics—for example, street-singing, overthrowing clerical privilege, and igniting a "bonfire of the vanities" in New London on March 6, 1743—polarized reaction to the nascent movement for revival. Singing in the streets appeared to cloud distinctions between public and ecclesiastical spheres.

jockeying psychologically for preeminence over Edwards the enthusiast, con-
demned the extreme antics of Davenport, and consequently Edwards positioned himself as the spokesman for the Great Awakening, both as practitioner
and theoretician. Edwards's own positive attitude toward the revivals plied a
mediating position between traditional ecclesial structures and movements of
extreme separatism.

Edwards's reflections on the revival, voiced in a lecture at the Yale
Commencement exercises in 1741 and published under the title "The
Distinguishing Marks," were subsequently presented to the printers in
1742, to be distributed in the form of a discourse known as "Some Thoughts
Concerning the Revival" and were made available to the public in 1743. In
Gura's words, Edwards in this writing wanted to win "support for the ongoing
awakening among those still confused by the events' untoward direction."[210]
Wholesale opposition, not just to the form but also to the content of the
revivals, was gaining ground. Edwards's metropolitan interlocutor, Charles
Chauncy (1705–1787) of Boston's First Church, preached against such revivalist frenzies in 1742, published later under the title "Enthusiasm Described
and Cautioned Against."[211] His own implacable disdain for the revivals pushed
Edwards increasingly into the middle ground. The revivals and their fruits
were splintering the clergy into a number of parties with varying ideological
responses.[212]

The purpose of Edwards's discourse is to correct any errors in interpreting
the movement for revival, irrespective of the origin of those misunderstandings, and in doing so to set up appreciation for structural innovations and to
prosper the "happy state of [God's] church on earth."[213] In his preface, Edwards
outlines a critical methodology, committing himself to accepting the truth of
a claim "wherever I see it, though held forth by a child or an enemy."[214] He
divides the work into five sections. In the first part, he nails his colors to the
mast and asserts that the revival is indeed to be received as a genuine work of

---

210. Philip F. Gura, *Jonathan Edwards: America's Evangelical* (New York: Hill & Wang, 2005), 124.

211. Goen, "Editor's Introduction," *WJE* 4: 56–65.

212. Kidd nuances the traditional categories of "Old Lights" and "New Lights" by examining the Great Awakening from the perspective of anti-revivalists, moderate evangelicals, and radical evangelicals. See Kidd, *The Great Awakening*, xiv.

213. Edwards, "Some Thoughts," *WJE* 4: 324.

214. Edwards, "Some Thoughts," *WJE* 4: 292. Edwards hereby avoids the "genetic fallacy," in which a truth-claim is assessed not by the content of the proposition but by the origin of the proposition itself.

God, adducing philosophical, scriptural and logical arguments for its authenticity. Notably, he also presents the case study of a significant believer, known to us as Sarah Edwards but never mentioned by name in the text, who successfully treads the fine line between extremes of Christian experience and becomes thereby a model to others.

Part two presents reasons why believers must not only recognize God's work in the revival but also advance that work, for "there is no such thing as being neuters."[215] Responsibilities of magistrates, ministers, and the laity are itemized. Next, in the third part, Edwards defends more specifically those promoters of revival who have experienced calumny, while in the fourth part, those selfsame revivalists are critiqued in order to salvage from the movement positive achievements of the Holy Spirit. The concluding section makes application of the foregoing analysis by suggesting ways to further prosper revivalist energy. Edwards wants to promote revival and social decorum.[216]

At heart, the discourse does not insist upon the separation of reason, will, and affections as the cause of disorder, but rather addresses misunderstandings of the revivals based "in the understanding, and not in the disposition."[217] Edwards makes clear from the outset that the revival must be judged not by looking *a priori* to its beginnings, instruments, or methods. The psychology of its proponents will always contain both noble and ignoble elements, and its means will be sullied by compromised motivations. Rather, he insists that the outcomes of the revival over time are a more substantial way of ascertaining the extent to which the Spirit of God has been part of the movement. He appeals to *a posteriori* evidence to adjudicate the case.[218] In so doing, he allows for the presence of disorder as a concomitant to the work of the Spirit, or at least he does not presume to dismiss the genuineness of the work merely on account of the presence of some evident disorder, which may be expressed in terms of gender, class, or race.[219] Edwards's own commitment to philosophical occasionalism provides space for secondary causation, even if this makes

---

215. Edwards, "Some Thoughts," *WJE* 4: 349.

216. Hall, *Contested Boundaries*, 93. Social decorum might not have been very different from obedience to the church.

217. Edwards, "Some Thoughts," *WJE* 4: 297; cf. 293.

218. Edwards, "Some Thoughts," *WJE* 4: 293. This position is summarized in Lambert, *Inventing the "Great Awakening,"* 189–90.

219. For examples of such disorder, see Erik R. Seeman, *Pious Persuasions: Laity and Clergy in Eighteenth-Century New England*, Early America: History, Context, Culture (Baltimore and London: Johns Hopkins University Press, 1999), 158, 172.

turbid the waters of propriety.[220] In short, one cannot argue "the nature of the cause from the nature of the effect, or vice versa."[221]

The church as it is presented in this discourse is described in relation to a narrow band of themes. Edwards does not address here in any detail the attributes of God in relation to the world, nor is there any sustained reflection on ecclesiastical polity, the sacraments, or questions of the morphology of conversion. This work does, however, contribute to our understanding of Edwards's ecclesiology as we see him address issues concerning the rise of itinerancy, the ministry of the laity, and the authority of the clergy, all modalities of divine operation in the context of the local congregation. The efficient cause of the church occupies our attention in this piece. New religious experience is acknowledged by Edwards, and, alongside this, new ecclesiastical forms are affirmed, but these are never simply the outcome of pragmatic pressures or social developments. Edwards is deliberately adapting structures to new theological insights.

The Rise of Itinerancy and the Fear of Social Disorder

One of the most significant challenges to both social and ecclesiastical order in the eighteenth century was the rise of itinerancy. While traveling preachers had been part of the Christian landscape since the days of the apostles, in the Middle Ages and in the early modern period, their role had been to itinerate where no settled parochial ministry was present.[222] Despite the growing oppositional character of Puritan aspirations during the reigns of James I and Charles I, the Puritans on new soil in North America still maintained the structure of established churches by recreating a parish-like system in order to maintain social as well as churchly authority.[223] By the time of George Whitefield's visit to America in 1740, however, new social and economic pressures had placed this system under great stress: migration toward the frontier, the pluralism of ethnic and denominational groupings, commercial exchange, and the development of communications all undercut the adequacy, or indeed the ability, of settled ministry to serve local interests.[224] Mobility fractured

---

220. Ultimately, Edwards ascribes efficient causation to God alone, but under the descriptor of "occasional" makes room for natural causation too.

221. Goen, "Editor's Introduction," *WJE* 4: 67.

222. Hall, *Contested Boundaries*, 17–23.

223. Hall, *Contested Boundaries*, 24.

224. Bonomi, *Under the Cope of Heaven*, 132.

inherited static models of authority.[225] The conceptual world of those living in times of rapid change was expanding, dealing to itinerancy a powerful and (for social conservatives) threatening hand, supporting an emerging dynamic social order. Focused on Whitefield,

> the new itinerancy...had broken out of its religious confines to make seemingly irreparable breaches in the local, deferential, patriarchal social order symbolized by the parish. Critics leapt to the defense of that traditional order by attacking itinerancy. In so doing, they elevated it to the status of a conceptual category.[226]

Whitefield and other itinerants further rubbed salt into the wound of nonitinerating clergy when they dared to suggest that many of those ministers, in whose parishes they preached, were not regenerate in the first place, necessitating their itinerancy and raising the thorny question of who was "better qualified to interpret the word of God."[227] Gilbert Tennent's sermon "The Danger of an Unconverted Ministry," delivered on March 8, 1740, concentrated the mind of his clerical brethren, though Whitefield had pioneered the breach.[228] Jones makes the salient point that the "Arminians warned of the dangers of an uneducated ministry; the evangelicals warned of the danger of an unconverted ministry."[229]

Furthermore, the itinerants preached importunately for the experience of new birth and the possibility of immediate assurance, something that Puritans of a previous generation had generally resisted. Such immediacy was in itself a threat to order, for in some eyes, it was viewed as antithetical to growth in obedience and commitment to social norms and was labeled "Antinomianism." It is reminiscent of the disorder in the period of early New England settlement when Anne Hutchinson forsook the established authorities of Bible and tradition and pursued instead immediate spiritual discernment as governing authority. This fear was not the preserve of one party alone:

> Both Arminian and Reformed opposers worried that by appearing to divorce the knowledge of a person's conversion from her or his outward

---

225. Hart, "Community of the Word," 38.

226. Hall, *Contested Boundaries*, 39.

227. Bonomi, *Under the Cope of Heaven*, 142–43.

228. Kidd, *The Great Awakening*, 116.

229. Jones, *Shattered Synthesis*, 117.

behavior, the doctrine of inward assurance undermined Christianity's role in the preservation of that person's place and the place of every other person within the deferential, elite-brokered social order.[230]

A rising internationalism among believers was both the observable means and the ultimate ends of such itinerancy, which "offered a new model of the church and its social world: a mobile, dynamic, expansive, potentially unbounded community held together voluntarily by a common spirit among individual members of every locale."[231]

Significantly, Edwards was a supporter of itinerancy in the context of the Great Awakening. In a letter drafted in the early phase of the revival, before writing "Some Thoughts," Edwards describes itinerants in positive though to some degree guarded terms, suggesting that they have been misunderstood.[232] Although Edwards was quick to distance the revived spirituality of his wife from the itinerant ministrations of George Whitefield,[233] he nevertheless speaks glowingly of Whitefield and his impact in the colonies: "Whenas, if we had but Mr. Whitefield's zeal and courage, what could we not do, with such a blessing as we might expect?"[234] A caveat is however offered. Though mightily used of God, it is the chief temptation of traveling preachers to succumb to arrogance,[235] which betokens the ultimate sinful subversion of godly order.[236] On the larger canvas, though itinerancy could undermine the standing order, Edwards is patient with expressions of disorder, knowing that there exist other means to constrain it. After a long litany of "errors and irregularities" attending this powerful work of the Spirit, he can aver that:

> [T]he end of the influences of God's Spirit is to make men spiritually knowing, wise to salvation, which is the most excellent wisdom; and he has also appointed means for our gaining such degrees of other knowledge as we need, to conduct ourselves regularly, which means should be carefully used: but the end of the influence of the Spirit of God is

---

230. Hall, *Contested Boundaries*, 54.

231. Hall, *Contested Boundaries*, 7.

232. Edwards, "To Deacon Lyman," *WJE* 4: 533–34.

233. Edwards, "Some Thoughts," *WJE* 4: 333.

234. Edwards, "Some Thoughts," *WJE* 4: 509.

235. Bonomi, *Under the Cope of Heaven*, 144.

236. Edwards, "Some Thoughts," *WJE* 4: 428.

not to increase men's natural capacities, nor has God obliged himself immediately to increase civil prudence in proportion to the degrees of spiritual light.[237]

Indeed, Edwards is so positive concerning this disruptive work of the Spirit that he ties it into a positive future for the world and the prosperity of the church. Millennial expectations for the people of God are nurtured in response to this "dawning" or "prelude" of that later work of God that "shall renew the world of mankind."[238] This loosening of the social order is affirmed and encouraged; in fact, it would be, in Edwards's mind, "dangerous . . . to forbear so to do."[239] Such cosmic perspective lends to the revivals an international frame of reference, transcending local contingencies and relationships of deference and replacing them with a "dynamic, expansive, potentially global religious orientation," in which Christians could experience "permeable boundaries and long-distance, affective ties."[240] Seeman notes contrariwise that the laity had little capacity to reflect eschatologically on events that they witnessed, though in Edwards's case, this could not be due to a deficit of pulpit exposition on the millennial themes.[241] Edwards's openness to itinerancy reflects a concomitant openness to a redefinition of order as the pastoral relationship between minister and people was redefined, as was the assumption of those listening when not in the socially controlled environment of a church building. However, Edwards's approval is not without qualification.

The Ministry of the Laity and the Challenge to Clerical Order

Tensions between clergy and laity were not swept away by the enthusiasm of the mid-century revivals either. Increasing clericalization had been part of New England life since the turn of the century, not least in Connecticut supported by the Saybrook Platform (1708). More recently, ministerial associations had

---

237. Edwards, "Some Thoughts," *WJE* 4: 323. I take it that the "civil prudence" spoken of equates to the appreciation of public order, which includes relationships of deference.

238. Edwards, "Some Thoughts," *WJE* 4: 353. The issue of America's role in this coming millennial reign of Christ is highly contested, though it appears to me to be salutary that it is because America is the "meanest, youngest and weakest part" that she fulfills such a vaunted position. See Edwards, "Some Thoughts," *WJE* 4: 356.

239. Edwards, "Some Thoughts," *WJE* 4: 358.

240. Hall, *Contested Boundaries*, 82, 103.

241. Seeman, *Pious Persuasions*, 151.

gained in authority, whether as part of the Anglicizing ethos of the era that tried to circumscribe lay congregational control in response to Enlightenment streams to rationalize social structures, or as a kind of professional development structure for clerical support and learning. Most notably, ordinations were no longer conducted by laymen, but rather fellow clergy from neighboring parishes performed the rite.[242] The clergy grew further away from the laity in terms of worldview as well, for the latter were more likely to interpret history providentially, reading off from historical events signs of God's pleasure or wrath.[243] Such divergences between the clergy and the laity were neither caused by the Great Awakening nor resolved by it, but were part of a larger cultural development that had been running its course through the first half of the eighteenth century.[244]

Edwards gives high status to lay ministry. He notes that "every Christian family is a little church, and the heads of it are its authoritative teachers and governors."[245] He praises those people—young and old, men and women— who have gathered together voluntarily to practice the spiritual disciplines on days other than the Sabbath.[246] Edwards even allows that, *in extremis*, women and children might exhort as a kind of warning or to express their own spiritual convictions, for example if one lies dying or has been struck by lightning![247] He also exhorts civil rulers to fulfill their own duties to God as part of their Christian obedience as laymen: they should take a lead for the rest of the community in expressing their own acknowledgement, indeed approval, of the work of revival that they witness. Edwards ennobles the work of civil magistracy when he chastises them for failures to strengthen the present work of the Spirit.[248] To illustrate his point, Edwards describes those situations when "a new king comes to the throne" or when "a new governor comes into a province" and the local authority shows deference.[249] The assumption here is that the revivals represent proleptically God's own coming to reign unopposed, in

---

242. Youngs, *God's Messengers*, 32.

243. Seeman, *Pious Persuasions*, 7.

244. The thesis of Seeman's book makes this very point well, pointing to reading habits, deathbed testimonies, the writing of personal histories, and attitudes toward the Lord's Supper to substantiate his claims that divergence of opinions between clergy and laity was endemic to the culture.

245. Edwards, "Some Thoughts," *WJE* 4: 487.

246. Edwards, "Some Thoughts," *WJE* 4: 519.

247. Edwards, "Some Thoughts," *WJE* 4: 486.

248. Edwards, "Some Thoughts," *WJE* 4: 372–73.

249. Edwards, "Some Thoughts," *WJE* 4: 370, 373.

consequence of which civil authorities must "manifest their loyalty, by some open and visible token of respect," lest they be "struck down" as the King passes.[250] The question of divine authority is conceived to be at the heart of the revivals from Edwards's perspective, highlighting not just ministerial accountability but the responsibilities of godly laity as well.

Beyond the magistracy, Edwards challenges "every living soul" to do as they are able to promote the work of the Spirit. Drawing on the account of building the tabernacle in the wilderness, Edwards reminds his readers that all contributed as they were able, some offering "gold or silver," while yet others brought "goats' hair."[251] He highlights the onus that lies on the very wealthy to give generously to the work of the Lord:

> If some of our rich men would give one-quarter of their estates to promote this work, they would act a little as if they were destined for the kingdom of heaven, and a little as rich men will act by and by, that shall be partakers of the spiritual wealth and glories of that kingdom.[252]

Edwards has a particularly strong word for those of his lay readers whose work was publishing, for they have an important role in helping or hindering the revival's spread. While some Boston publishers were great supporters of the work, others needed to be warned of their spiritual state:

> Those therefore that publish pamphlets to the disadvantage of this work, and tending either directly or indirectly to bring it under suspicion and to discourage or hinder it, would do well thoroughly to consider whether this be not indeed the work of God; and whether if it be, 'tis not likely that God will go forth as fire, to consume all that stands in his way, and so burn up those pamphlets; and whether there be not danger that the fire that is kindled in them, will scorch the authors.[253]

The Puritan assumption—that just as all are saved equally, so therefore all must serve with equal devotion—is in evidence here. All human activity could be distinguished as worship.[254]

250. Edwards, "Some Thoughts," *WJE* 4: 371.

251. Edwards, "Some Thoughts," *WJE* 4: 379.

252. Edwards, "Some Thoughts," *WJE* 4: 515.

253. Edwards, "Some Thoughts," *WJE* 4: 381.

254. Youngs, *God's Messengers*, 2–3.

Edwards even acknowledges that there is a case to be made for lay ministry of the Word, though this had proved divisive, with much "disputing, jangling, and contention."[255] He has no objection to someone preaching loudly, within earshot of a great number, nor even if such proclamation were to occur in the meetinghouse when the divine service has ended.[256] However, he insists that such be described as fraternal exhortation and that no one allows the impression to be received that authority is being claimed. His concern is not how people learn, but rather that both the attitude of the one teaching and the response of those being taught do not incite insubordination.[257] These guidelines seek to constrain lay ministry through interpretation of contextual factors. Such a nuanced and subjective rationale attests Edwards's limited permission-giving approach, responsive to new conditions, while at the same time preserving some degree of clerical privilege.[258]

A comparable situation is described when Edwards adjudicates the propriety of street-singing. He of course rejoices that spontaneous praise has erupted from God's people in response to the work of the Spirit, while demurring that such activity can be disruptive, or even harmful, if practiced in ways that fail to account for the slowness of some to embrace new forms. He does not suggest that street-singers wait until no objections are raised, but rather that the fruit not be picked "before 'tis ripe,"[259] demonstrating his proclivity to social gradualism. In the end, after due process both in respect of the congregation's fragility and his own theological reflection, he writes that "I cannot find any valid objection against it."[260]

His reasoning makes much of the distinction between what is private and what is public and concludes that an individual singing on the street would transgress Christ's command not to use piety to impress, but a group of worshippers making their way to church would not. The group extends public worship outside of the meetinghouse but compels none to participate, which would be the case if a private society were to behave in a similar fashion. Comparable to the practice of preaching outdoors, Edwards allows for the innovation of singing God's praises "in the open air, and not in a close place,"

---

255. Edwards, "Some Thoughts," *WJE* 4: 483.

256. Edwards, "Some Thoughts," *WJE* 4: 485–86.

257. Edwards, "Some Thoughts," *WJE* 4: 486.

258. McDermott, *One Holy and Happy Society*, 165.

259. Edwards, "Some Thoughts," *WJE* 4: 490.

260. Edwards, "Some Thoughts," *WJE* 4: 491.

"moving as well as standing still."[261] It is less clear to me how he can justify the practice of lay singing in relation to its results, while the practice of lay preaching, though attaining similar outcomes, is more suspect. The argument that the difference consists in the nature of the perception of the activity's threat to traditional authority is, while logically tenable, highly subjective and prone to misuse. It appears that the godly propriety of an activity was constituted less by its location, whether meetinghouse or street, or by the results of the words than by the particular traditional authority that activity threatened. To interpret the subtle distinctions, clergy were still needed.

The Work of the Clergy and the Appeal to Traditional Order

The revivals constituted a threat to the received order of New England towns and churches, but especially to the clergy who worked to stimulate revival and oversaw its results. The danger of formalism was combated by preaching to stir hearts and minds, leading to the connected danger of insubordination, exacerbating the tensions between laity and clergy already felt in the first half of the eighteenth century. The power of the laity in the Congregational model had been further encouraged through revivalist empowerment, against which some leaders would rail. The concern of the qualifications for ministry focus the questions concerning authority and order among those experiencing revival.

Edwards expounds his vision for the ordained ministry in "Some Thoughts" with reference to various metaphors for ministry. In one particularly concentrated passage, Edwards describes ministers as stewards, husbandmen, wise builders, architects, traders, merchants, fishermen, and soldiers, using Scriptural texts for support.[262] Chiefly, however, Edwards highlights the role of ambassadors or messengers of God, for it is this occupation that trades in words, as delegated from some higher authority, and secures clerical rights.[263] The authority of the ministerial caste is an extension of Christ's princely authority, just as the church is the anteroom for heavenly felicitude:

---

261. Edwards, "Some Thoughts," *WJE* 4: 492. It is noteworthy that part of Davenport's retractions concerned advocacy of singing outdoors. See Hall, *Contested Boundaries*, 96.

262. Edwards, "Some Thoughts," *WJE* 4: 445.

263. Hall, "The New England Background," 71. With this model, the clergy stand outside of the congregation. See the section in Chapter 4 on a "Farewell Sermon" for this view expanded.

Ministers are those, that the King of the church has appointed to have the charge of the gate at which his people enter into the kingdom of heaven, there to be entertained and satisfied with an eternal feast; ministers have the charge of the house of God, which is the gate of heaven.[264]

The authority of the gatekeeper therefore must have that kind of preparation or training that best accords with such a ministry, excluding "the admission of unlearned men to the work of the ministry, though they should be persons of extraordinary experience."[265]

The act of ordination itself is not made the basis of Edwards's appeal nor is gifting or godliness. In the above section, Edwards goes on to acknowledge that there may be some laymen who are indeed more gifted, or clergy who ought not to have been ordained after all for want of learning despite academic degrees. It is rather the power of education to make authority orderly rather than disruptive, due to its own gradual acquisition, that forms the basis of Edwards's argument. Such training ought to provide not just learning but formation in personal Christian godliness as well. Edwards's comments ought to be understood as an implicit critique of his experiences of Yale, where he had been student and tutor.[266] Youngs summarizes:

In sanctifying the position of men whose real qualification for the ministry was educational preparation, it was natural for the ministers to believe that God's movement in the world was rational and predictable.[267]

The ordering capacity of the ordained clergy was seen not just in their training but also in the liturgies, which it was their responsibility to conduct. Although

---

264. Edwards, "Some Thoughts," *WJE* 4: 377.

265. Edwards, "Some Thoughts," *WJE* 4: 456–57. See also Edwards's paraphrase of Zechariah 13:5, which stresses the gradual and natural means God employed to make a prophet. Edwards, "Some Thoughts," *WJE* 4: 434.

266. Edwards, "Some Thoughts," *WJE* 4: 511–12. At this point, Edwards echoes the appeal made by Philipp Jakob Spener (1635–1705), whose own "pious desires" included the provision of theological education by regenerate professors and attention to the moral as well as academic formation of students. See Philip Jacob Spener, *Pia Desideria*, Seminar Editions, trans. T. G. Tappert (Philadelphia: Fortress Press, 1964), 103–15. Edwards himself trained clergy by means of the apprenticeship model, when, for example, he took Samuel Hopkins into his home to share his ministry with him: McDermott, *One Holy and Happy Society*, 115.

267. Youngs, *God's Messengers*, 78–79.

Edwards does not in this treatise give much attention to the celebration of the Lord's Supper (an issue that was to occupy him more in the years ahead), after refusing to enter into the debate concerning the requisite "relation of grace" to be presented before the congregation, he does seem to advocate a consistent policy, such that once a person is admitted to the communion they ought not to be later rejected. He wants to protect against the dangers of a censorious spirit.[268] He does, however, express his commitment to the external worship of God as being a duty incumbent upon those who profess his name and encourages his readers to partake of the Lord's Supper more often than was at that time the custom. Interestingly, he describes the whole season of revival using language imported from the Communion, lending to the discrete and potentially disorderly events a unifying coordination through ministerial supervision.[269] Edwards is concerned about the lack of regard for the Lord's Supper. He sees it as a means by which individuals might express their devotion and by which the community might be brought together. However it is Seeman's contention that the communion was in the eighteenth century more prone to community disruption than community creation, suggesting already at the beginning of the 1740s a disconnection between Edwards and his people on the power of this rite.[270]

Clerical authority is again defended when Edwards comes to describe the habit of some to allow mutual censoring within the congregation. He chastises those who would maintain the "worthlessness of external order" or who deny that responsibility for judging within the congregation should be "reserved in the hands of particular persons, or consistories appointed thereto, but ought to be left at large for anybody that pleases to take it upon them, or that think themselves fit for it."[271] However, such an appeal to the necessary order within the local fellowship must be balanced by Edwards's later appeal to clergy and laity alike not to fall prey to a spirit of censoriousness, which is endemic in times of revival. Taking up the argument outlined in "Distinguishing Marks," he criticizes those who claimed to discern whether a particular clergyman was converted or not, no doubt in response to the preaching of Tennent and Whitefield on this topic.[272] Notably, it did not belong to the preaching of his venerable grandfather, Solomon Stoddard, to undertake such witch-hunts. It

---

268. Edwards, "Some Thoughts," *WJE* 4: 480, 481.

269. Edwards, "Some Thoughts," *WJE* 4: 522.

270. Seeman, *Pious Persuasions*, 81.

271. Edwards, "Some Thoughts," *WJE* 4: 455.

272. See Edwards, "Distinguishing Marks," *WJE* 4: 283–87.

is not that Edwards believed that all clergy were converted; rather it does not lie within the bailiwick of another minister to make such a judgment. He would himself not presume to make such a discerning claim: "I feel no disposition to treat any minister as if I supposed that he was finally rejected of God."[273]

The background argument that Edwards alludes to here establishes that a believer may not presume to have access into another's soul and thereby discriminate. Public charity insists that it is only by virtue of visible behavior that any distinction can be made between those claiming to follow Christ.[274] Clerical authority for Edwards, then, is a necessary attribute of ecclesiastical life, and at the same time it is limited in its capacity to make judgments to that which is visibly discerned, again treading a fine line between clergy's distinct powers and those common to all Christian believers.[275]

It appears to me that on balance, Edwards is not so much denying clerical authority or advancing the rights of the laymen in his church, but instead is positioning all human authority, clerical or lay, as subsidiary means of order- ing the work of the Spirit and in response to that surprising work of God. Although some scholars argue that the notion of revival was conceived by colo- nial clergy to revive moribund churches and thereby to aggrandize ministerial authority,[276] the overall intention of "Some Thoughts" is to allow for the rise of new practices and conventions without destroying the received order of the church. This is not so much the reactionary defense of Puritan polity or order as it is the creative adaptation of that order to new exigencies. God's new work requires both laity and clergy to accommodate revised structures of ministry, whether that means relinquishing authority or exercising it without readily discernible precedent. Ardor and order embrace.

---

273. Edwards, "Some Thoughts," *WJE* 4: 475, 476.

274. Edwards, "Distinguishing Marks," *WJE* 4: 286.

275. Edwards speaks strongly in "Misc." 689, one of the few written during the Connecticut River revivals, concerning the authority of ministers, as "officers of the church," to exer- cise a ministry of the keys. God is, of course, the head of the visible church but deputizes this authority to human leaders who search hearts provisionally and whose judgment is then accepted by God "on presumption of their sincerity and faithfulness." See Jonathan Edwards, "Misc." 689, in *The "Miscellanies" (Entry Nos. 501–832)*, The Works of Jonathan Edwards 18, ed. A. Chamberlain (New Haven: Yale University Press, 2000), 251–52. This is one of the few miscellanies furthermore written in the 1730s expressly to deal with the nature of the church.

276. Seeman, *Pious Persuasions*, 148.

3.5 *The Accountable Church in* The Treatise Concerning Religious Affections

Ava Chamberlain well notes that "Jonathan Edwards was a polemicist,"[277] writing not abstractly as a detached academic but in the cut and thrust of pastoral and revivalist challenges. Indeed, *The Treatise Concerning Religious Affections* (1746), which reads as a discourse on the nature of religious psychology and has spawned a multitude of commentaries on human anthropology and spiritual experience,[278] was originally conceived as a sermon series, preached in 1742–1743 in Northampton, and took aim at theological adversaries who would undermine the integrity of the revivals as a genuine work of God. It is true that although rationalist critics as well as enthusiastic exponents approached the revivals from differing perspectives, in Edwards's estimation, they could both inadvertently sponsor the same destructive ends: thwarting appreciation of the active involvement of God in human affairs. Edwards composes this now classic treatise on Christian experience to provide criteria for discerning true regeneration, establishing public accountability within the congregation and thereby sustaining the fruit of the revivals in corporate life. It was contested theories of psychology, which had the power to illuminate tensions within ecclesiology during the Great Awakening.[279]

Edwards built his case under the banner of 1 Peter 1:8. He expounded the nature of true religion as revealed through trials, which make it visible. True religion is also expressed in love and joy, which anticipate God's glory yet to be revealed.[280] Such confidence is ultimately based on "spiritual sight,"[281] for the passage assumes an eschatological context in which persecution teaches us to

---

277. Ava Chamberlain, "Self-Deception as a Theological Problem in Jonathan Edwards's 'Treatise concerning Religious Affections,'" *Church History* 63(4) (1994): 541–56.

278. See, for example, James Hoopes, "Jonathan Edwards's Religious Psychology," *Journal of American History* 69(4) (1983): 849–65, or Michael J. McClymond, "Spiritual Perception in Jonathan Edwards," *The Journal of Religion* 77(2) (1997): 195–216, or Miklos Vetö, "Spiritual Knowledge according to Jonathan Edwards," trans. Michael J. McClymond, *Calvin Theological Journal* 31(1) (1996): 161–81, or David R. Williams, "Horses, Pigeons, and the Therapy of Conversion: a Psychological Reading of Jonathan Edwards's Theology," *Harvard Theological Review* 74(4) (1981): 337–52.

279. Fiering, "Will and Intellect," 558. Fiering goes so far as to locate the central disagreement during the revivals as psychological and not theological.

280. Jonathan Edwards, *Religious Affections*, The Works of Jonathan Edwards 2, ed. John E. Smith (New Haven: Yale University Press, 1969), 93–96.

281. John E. Smith, "Editor's Introduction," in *Religious Affections*, The Works of Jonathan Edwards 2, ed. J. E. Smith (New Haven: Yale University Press, 1959), 12.

look beyond our present situation. Trials and their purifying temper provide assurance of salvation, for the resultant virtue is increasingly apparent and confirms the believer in their "true religion." Edwards's opening exposition on 1 Peter most poignantly concludes that "True religion, in great part, consists in holy affections."[282] His aim in this work is not to differentiate between the operations of the Spirit that are of a saving nature and those that are not, for this was his intention in the previous treatise, "Distinguishing Marks."[283] In *Religious Affections*, Edwards was originally not so much speaking to those outside the camp as to those within the church who were unsure how to assay their experience. He guides those who need to reassess where they stand *coram deo* by describing and critiquing experiences that may or may not give adequate insights into a person's spiritual state.[284] The issues addressed concern personal assurance and presumption, as much as external antagonism toward the faith. His own preface alerts us to this pastoral motivation:

> There is no question whatsoever, that is of greater importance to mankind, and that it more concerns every individual person to be well resolved in, than this, what are the distinguishing qualifications of those that are in favor with God, and entitled to his eternal rewards? Or, which comes to the same thing, What is the nature of true religion?[285]

Edwards's desire to ascertain "qualifications" and to establish "true religion" lead to pertinent ecclesiological implications in this work, for personal experience is held accountable to necessary social outcomes. No private religion is private without remainder. "True religion," in a Reformed framework, can allow for no human contribution to salvation, whether it be from the human subject

---

282. Edwards, *WJE* 2: 95. After this opening elucidation of 1 Peter 1:8, Edwards presents in Part II twelve signs, present in the revivals, which are no certain signs of grace, while in Part III he presents the positive case of twelve signs that do attest gracious affections, "their source, their nature and their results." See Stephen R. Holmes, *God of Grace and God of Glory: An Account of the Theology of Jonathan Edwards* (Edinburgh: T&T Clark, 2000), 176.

283. Jonathan Edwards, *Religious Affections*, 89. Such a distinction was intended to silence the detractors of the revivals, who regarded the whole as profoundly misguided.

284. It is most instructive to note that Edwards points to the revivals in Part I as having appeared in "the late extraordinary season." This temporal reference betokens his own emotional distance from the events, facing as he does the pastoral fact that "religious affections are grown out of credit." See Edwards, *WJE* 2: 119. Marsden sees the New Light threat as Edwards's focus here, while Cherry sees no difference between *Religious Affections* and preceding works in terms of reasons for composition. See Marsden, *A Life*, 285, and Cherry, *Theology*, 170.

285. Edwards, *WJE* 2: 84.

of election or from those charged with pastoral responsibility for the flock, but it does expect human consequences.[286] Edwards is at pains to use the personal experience of revival to underwrite the ecclesial expectation of renewal, even if, in the years immediately following the publication of the *Religious Affections*, such an unswerving commitment was to have momentous consequences for Edwards himself. Indeed, the risks of unmediated experience, for which Edwards had some sympathy, make all the more important the pursuant security the church provides.

Pure Experience: The Church and Beginnings

During the revivals, the experiential nature of the Spirit's work to save and to sanctify are scrupulously examined to discern whether and how they promote freedom and order, that is, how they subvert or support life in the church. Antinomian or extreme New Light attempts to locate conversion in direct inspiration of the Spirit without mediation of the Word were reviled by others as dangerously anarchic, and Arminian or Old Light attempts to position conversion in the intellect without reference to any power for godliness were similarly rejected as mere form.[287] Questions concerning Christian experience, its origins, and outcomes are profoundly ecclesiological because they beg questions concerning freedom and order, which are themselves structural concerns. One of the most foundational distinctives of Protestant ecclesiology is its determination to see the church and its order as a product of, and subservient to, the Word of divine initiative, which brings freedom, and not the progenitor of that freedom.[288] The Word

---

286. See McClymond, "Spiritual Perception in Jonathan Edwards," 201, where tensions within the Augustinian-Calvinist inheritance of Edwards are acknowledged.

287. William Breitenbach, "Piety *and* Moralism: Edwards and the New Divinity," in *Jonathan Edwards and the American Experience*, eds. N. O. Hatch and H. S. Stout (New York/ Oxford: Oxford University Press, 1988), 179–82. These concerns have been present in the writings of Edwards from his earliest years in Northampton. In his sermon "A Divine and Supernatural Light," preached in 1733, Edwards distances himself from both Antinomians and Old Light rationalists. He first of all defends the immediacy of the Spirit's work, appealing to the rights of the Creator to continue to be actively and intimately involved in the creation. He also defends the use of means, especially here the Word of God, while disclaiming that the Word is not a second cause, for "it don't operate by any natural force in it." He likewise makes clear that rationality has no power to create a new "sense of the heart." He avers: "Reason's work is to perceive truth, and not excellency." See Jonathan Edwards, "A Divine and Supernatural Light," in *Sermons and Discourses, 1730–1733*, The Works of Jonathan Edwards 17, ed. M. Valeri (New Haven: Yale University Press, 1999), 421, 416, 423, 422. Carr concludes that this sermon contained a "vision for renewal of the church." See Kevin C. Carr, "Jonathan Edwards and *A Divine and Supernatural Light*," *Puritan Reformed Journal* 2(2) (2010): 187–209, especially 207.

288. Veli-Matti Kärkkäinen, *An Introduction to Ecclesiology: Ecumenical, Historical and Global Perspectives* (Downers Grove, IL: IVP, 2002), 41.

precedes the Church. Historically, matters of faith (or responses to the Word) were the gravitational center of Reformation Protestantism, while matters of order (and the authority of the church) were given a more significant place in Roman Catholic conceptions of ecclesiastical exclusivity.[289]

Edwards is at pains first of all to defend the priority of unmediated experience of grace by expounding his Augustinian and voluntarist notion of the beginnings of religious affections in the soul, even when that appears to give too much ground to extremists.[290] He presents the regenerate person as unitary, without a hierarchy of faculties that had been common in previous systems of anthropology.[291] God's grace does not begin with one faculty and then proceed in stages to affect another, introducing intermediate experiences between God and the soul. Although different words are used in the Scriptures and in theological discourse to represent different features of human psychology, these in Edwards's estimation describe the intensity of the soul's relationship to the world rather than distinct powers:

> [T]he affections are no other, than the more vigorous and sensible exercises of the inclination and will of the soul.... The will, and the affections of the soul, are not two faculties; the affections are not essentially distinct from the will, nor do they differ from the mere actings of the will and inclination of the soul, but only in the liveliness and sensibleness of exercise.[292]

The fragmentation of the self by virtue of sin is overcome with the reordering work of the Holy Spirit.[293] The unity of soul with body is likewise affirmed,

---

289. John von Rohr, "*Extra Ecclesiam Nulla Salus*: An Early Congregational Version," *Church History* 36(2) (1967): 107–21. Von Rohr asserts that this contrast does not hold for the Congregationalism of the early seventeenth century, which inverted the traditional understanding and made matters of faith dependent on matters of order and polity. See especially 107; cf. 117.

290. This is in line with the trajectory of much spirituality in the seventeenth and eighteenth centuries, as noted by Geoffrey F. Nuttall, *The Holy Spirit in Puritan Faith and Experience* (Oxford: Basil Blackwell, 1947), 91–92.

291. It was assumed in Greek philosophy, for example, that reason's role was to make base animal passions submissive. See John E. Smith, "Religious Affections and the 'Sense of the Heart,'" in *The Princeton Companion to Jonathan Edwards*, ed. S. H. Lee (Princeton and Oxford: Princeton University Press, 2005), 104; Marsden, *A Life*, 281–82.

292. Edwards, *WJE* 2: 96, 97.

293. Roger Ward, "The Philosophical Structure of Jonathan Edwards's *Religious Affections*," *Christian Scholar's Review* 29(4) (2000): 745–68, especially 753, 758.

acknowledging the impact that each has on the other.[294] Such an approach to anthropology not only serves Edwards's immediate pastoral argument that preparationism may be inadequate to describe Christian beginnings but also disallows any notion that one part of human psychology might be isolated from the taint of sin, a theological platform "amenable to the very Arminianism that Edwards was seeking to refute."[295]

When Edwards does concede dual capacities within the soul, he does so by describing on the one hand doctrinal knowledge or speculative notions, which allow perception and judgment, and on the other inclinations or affections, which reflect attraction or repulsion toward the object being perceived.[296] Inclinations imply weighting and partiality, not neutrality, and make use of doctrinal knowledge or speculative notions. Such inclinations also give focus to their object and are not to be interpreted as distorting human understanding.[297] Using categories of relationship, attraction, or movement, which reminded of Newtonian ontology, Edwards defines religious affections as those "vigorous lively actings of the will or inclination," distinct from basic human reason or passions, which powerfully draw us toward an object or repel us.[298] And when it comes to the great matter of the Gospel, Edwards can see no place for disinterested assent or "weak, dull and lifeless wouldings, raising us but a little above a state of indifference," but only those responses "such as running, wrestling or agonizing for a great prize of crown" that attest the power and liveliness of true religion in personal experience.[299]

Edwards furthermore encourages the unmediated character of grace through repeated appeals to the sense of taste, particularly the taste of honey, as emblematic of immediate apprehension of divine or spiritual truth. No one is able adequately to convey the experience of tasting honey, no matter how much instruction a person has had concerning it.[300] The immediacy, perhaps intimacy, of putting something in one's mouth that the other senses of sight

---

294. Edwards, *WJE* 2: 98.

295. K. Scott Oliphint, "Jonathan Edwards on Apologetics: Reason and the Noetic Effects of Sin," in *The Legacy of Jonathan Edwards and the Evangelical Tradition*, eds. D. G. Hart, S. M. Lucas, and S. J. Nichols (Grand Rapids: Baker Academic, 2003), 135.

296. Smith avers that this taxonomy allows for distinction without opposition. See Smith, "Religious Affections and the 'Sense of the Heart,'" 105.

297. Smith, "Religious Affections and the 'Sense of the Heart,'" 104.

298. Edwards, *WJE* 2: 98.

299. Edwards, *WJE* 2: 99, 100. See also Smith, "Religious Affections and the 'Sense of the Heart,'" 107.

300. Edwards, *WJE* 2: 272.

or hearing or smelling would observe from a distance, is powerfully evocative in terms of its imagery and philosophical implications:

> I have shown that spiritual knowledge primarily consists in a taste or relish of the amiableness and beauty of that which is truly good and holy: this holy relish is a thing that discerns and distinguishes between good and evil, between holy and unholy, without being at the trouble of a train of reasoning.... He that has a rectified palate, knows what is good food, as soon as he tastes it, without the reasoning of a physician about it.... Thus a holy person is led by the Spirit...and judges what is right, as it were spontaneously, and of himself, without a particular deduction, by any other arguments than the beauty that is seen, and goodness that is tasted.[301]

A common trope in eighteenth-century moral discourse, Edwards goes on to cite an entry from the Chambers's *Cyclopedia* concerning taste to support his case.[302]

Immediacy was a contested category in theological debates surrounding the revivals for several reasons. For rationalists in the Aristotelian tradition like Charles Chauncy of the Old South Church in Boston, the dangers of anarchy arising from the decentering of reason as the ordering principle of religious psychology and of church life were immense. It is of course true that Edwards is critical of merely speculative notions, for as James reminds us, even the devils can believe (James 2:19). However, Edwards does not expect our experience to be at odds with our reason or to be expressed without reason's involvement; it is just that reason has no essential priority in the life of the soul. The affections in Edwards are "expressions of inclination through the mind," according to Smith.[303] Vetö notes that immediate apprehension of spiritual things does not negate critical awareness: "As the synthesis of an immediate sensation and an instantaneous judgment, the sense of the taste has an ethical and supernatural application."[304] Immediacy must also be disentangled from misconceptions concerning the potentially overpowering

---

301. Edwards, *WJE* 2: 281–82.

302. Edwards, *WJE* 2: 282–83.

303. Smith, "Editor's Introduction," *WJE* 2: 13. A similar point is made by Helen Westra as she summarizes Edwards's preaching in the 1730s and 1740s: Helen P. Westra, "Jonathan Edwards and "What Reason Teaches,'" *Journal of the Evangelical Theological Society* 34(4) (1991): 495–503; see especially 501 for interaction with the *Religious Affections*.

304. Vetö, "Spiritual Knowledge," 171.

collision of God's grace with human nature. Though there has been much discussion concerning the relationship between Edwards's "new sense" and those
five senses that human beings enjoy by virtue of their creation, the point here is
to demonstrate the ways in which grace for Edwards perfects nature rather than
annihilates it.[305] Hoopes usefully draws out the distinction that a new sense, but
not a new sensation, is given to the believer in conversion.[306] Conrad Cherry is
securely within this school of interpretation when he avers that:

> [N]ew faculties are not given in illumination, but a new basis is
> given to the mind from which the natural faculties operate in a new
> way.... Furthermore, the Spirit in illumination never becomes a human
> "possession" that is manageable by human mental powers.[307]

In McClymond's mind, Edwards wisely resorts to the conceptuality of participation to express distinction between the human and the divine role in spiritual
perception, without allowing absorption of the human into the divine or annihi-
lation of the human by the divine.[308]

Such a defense of immediacy not only distances Edwards from those churches
that preached rationalist interpretation of religious psychology, but it significantly
distances him as well from the intricate Puritan morphology of conversion, which
required ecclesiastical involvement throughout the fourfold process of conviction,
compunction, humiliation, and faith.[309] We note the denials regarding steps or

---

305. Edwards, *WJE* 2: 206. Edwards defends such immediacy, it should be recalled, as an
apologetic strategy against attacks of deism, but recognizes nevertheless that when grace
cooperates with nature as secondary causation, it does so because those means have no power
within themselves. See Smith, "Religious Affections and the 'Sense of the Heart,'" 108.

306. Hoopes, "Jonathan Edwards's Religious Psychology," 859. The argument outlining
a sense "discontinuous" with our five natural senses has been advocated by Paul Helm
and David Lyttle, among others, built upon a less nuanced interpretation of the putatively
Lockean phrase, "a new simple idea" (*WJE* 2: 205). McClymond acknowledges the verbal
similarity but suggests that Edwards is using this language and infusing it with new content,
and thereby presents the new sense as operative within the capacity of our natural five. There
is no sixth sense. See McClymond, "Spiritual Perception in Jonathan Edwards," 198–205.

307. Cherry, *Theology*, 30.

308. McClymond, "Spiritual Perception in Jonathan Edwards," 201. This coheres well
with the premise of Reg Ward that a defining feature of renewal movements of the seventeenth and eighteenth centuries is its anti-Aristotelianism, or the desire to subvert systems.
Scholastic theology, which was "orientated to Aristotle, moved the understanding only and
had no power to move the heart," while the second kind of theology "which had its seat in the
will implanted by God, is all experience, reality and practice." Ward, *Early Evangelicalism*, 13.

309. This breakdown was the particular nomenclature of Thomas Shepard, though its logic
was widespread, even when the vocabulary differed. See David Kobrin, "The Expansion of

stages in Edwards's description of public profession of the faith.[310] The *ordo salutis* inherited from his Puritan roots is critiqued, and thereby the seeds are sown for a new appreciation of the powers of individual ownership of the experience of conversion,[311] without oversight of the process by clergy, which had previously dominated. Indeed, the sovereignty of the Spirit of God to blow how he will relativizes any "ordinary" patterns. Conversion is nothing else than a "personal, revelatory experience" of grace, over which no traditional, familial, social or ecclesiastical authority has any control.[312] Stout sees in this development an instantiation of the democratizing of religious sentiment that accelerates after the Revolution. It is not just that negatively some social sectors lose control; Edwards's approach to religious affections also positively empowers others in significant ways:

> As long as the sources of true enthusiasm lay within the grasp of natural man, then the true enthusiast was the person of superior breeding and refined sensibilities. But if the source of true enthusiasm came from without—as Edwards insisted it did—then anyone was a potential candidate for remaking, and distinctions of learning or breeding lost their significance...he cut a doorway to an assertive lay piety that would open far wider than he ever imagined and that would permanently alter the relations between pastors and congregations in more democratic directions.[313]

Furthermore, the immediacy of the Spirit's work provided resources to define assurance in subjective terms. Like the seal used by princes to demonstrate ownership, so the Holy Spirit provides "clear evidence to the conscience, that the subject of it is the child of God," and is "enstamped in so fair and clear a manner, as to be plain to the eye of conscience."[314] Boldly, Edwards says that he allows for:

---

the Visible Church in New England: 1629–1650," *Church History* 36(2) (1967): 189–209, especially 192–93.

310. Edwards, *WJE* 2: 416.

311. Ward, "Philosophical Structure of *Religious Affections*," 763. The only possible pattern of progress toward the conversion of an individual, according to Edwards, has its parallel in the experience of the Hebrews after the Exodus: first terror, or convictions of conscience, then relief or joy, though even this sequence can be feigned. This argument constitutes the eighth negative sign of Part II. See Edwards, *WJE* 2: 151–63.

312. Ward, "Philosophical Structure of *Religious Affections*," 765.

313. Stout, *The New England Soul*, 207.

314. Edwards, *WJE* 2: 232, 233.

[I]ntuitive knowledge of the divinity of the things exhibited in the gospel…without any argument or deduction at all; but it is without any long chain of arguments; the argument is but one, and the evidence direct; the mind ascends to the truth of the gospel but by one step.[315]

Knowing our own adoption as children by our Heavenly Father is the privilege of all who have been saved and one that the Holy Spirit with the human spirit attests, not being able to be imitated by Satan. Edwards holds that the inner testimony of the Spirit is not one to produce revelations, but does produce the love of a child in place of the fear of the slave.[316] Edwards is not embarrassed by appeal to the inner testimony.[317] Although such a witness may not represent the "highest level of assurance," it nevertheless served an important role because "[i]t was both temporally immediate…and also functionally immediate…imparting to the saint the experience of being loved, and conveying the acceptance of sonship."[318] Cherry judiciously allows for distinct spheres, of which the inner must not be neglected:

Edwards does not deny that the Spirit of God works within the heart of a saint for the benefit of that saint's assurance; but he does maintain that when the heart is worked upon, the will is changed. When the will is changed, that change is discernible in practice wherein the willing has both an inside and an outside…the "signs of godliness" may be divided into those predominantly inward and those predominantly outward.[319]

---

315. Edwards, *WJE* 2: 298–99, and also *WJE* 2: 303.

316. Edwards, *WJE* 2: 238.

317. Murray, *Jonathan Edwards*, 265.

318. W. Ross Hastings, "Discerning the Spirit: Ambivalent Assurance in the Soteriology of Jonathan Edwards and Barthian Correctives," *Scottish Journal of Theology* 63(4) (2010): 437–55, especially 440. Hastings goes on to argue that the doctrine of assurance in Edwards is unstable, due to its pneumatological rather than Christological foundation, even when the useful corrective of social controls are introduced. Williams is surely right nevertheless to highlight the difference between Wesley and Edwards when it comes to discussion of inner testimony, for Edwards will not appeal to imagination alone, which can be replicated by the Devil. Garry J. Williams, "Enlightenment Epistemology and Eighteenth-Century Evangelical Doctrines of Assurance," in *The Emergence of Evangelicalism: Exploring Historical Continuities*, eds. M. A. G. Haykin and K. J. Stewart (Nottingham: Apollos, 2008), 361–63.

319. Cherry, *Theology*, 145.

Edwards's view on the immediacy of experience in salvation is, however, currently under review.[320] In reaction to the Bebbington thesis that assurance and therefore activism are the distinguishing features of evangelicalism as it broke away from Puritanism, several scholars are wanting to complicate the description of seventeenth-century Puritanism to allow for greater recognition of assurance toward the beginning of the Christian walk and early attempts at mission.[321] Conversely, Edwards is shown to be open to ongoing struggle to secure assurance, and his theological legacy is shown to generate structures for mission only slowly.[322] Despite these disclaimers and their underlying historiographical agenda that the continuities between Puritanism and evangelicalism are more substantial than their discontinuities, any nervousness on the part of these scholars concerning assurance of salvation is marginalized when we make room for Edwards's own ecclesiological framework, which creates theological continuity at a still deeper level.

God assures us of his favorable disposition in different ways. While Edwards's language of immediacy or directness quite literally speaks of God addressing the soul without intermediaries, it is not hard to see that his audience could misunderstand his intentions and assume him to say that as one begins the Christian life, so one goes on without order or structure. For Edwards, contrariwise, just as justification is by grace through faith, though issuing forth in works, so the immediacy of grace is for Edwards necessarily expressed in material ways. Edwards's depiction of conversion might marginalize the church's responsibility as a necessary agent of Christian beginnings, though he does not detract from the responsibility of the church as an instrument of Christian proclamation or personal maturation, as the next section will show. To magnify the immediacy and potential disorder of God in conversion is matched very quickly by the power of the church to bring order to Christian experience.

---

320. This topic functions as a *Leitmotif* in the recent compilation of essays discussing the merits of Bebbington's quadrilateral. See Michael A. G. Haykin and Kenneth J. Stewart, eds., *The Emergence of Evangelicalism: Exploring Historical Continuities* (Nottingham: Apollos, 2008).

321. John Coffey, "Puritanism, Evangelicalism and the Evangelical Protestant Tradition," in *The Emergence of Evangelicalism: Exploring Historical Continuities*, eds. M. A. G. Haykin and K. J. Stewart (Nottingham: Apollos, 2008), 252–77.

322. See Michael A. G. Haykin, "Evangelicalism and the Enlightenment: A Reassessment," in *The Emergence of Evangelicalism: Exploring Historical Continuities*, eds. M. A. G. Haykin and K. J. Stewart (Nottingham: Apollos, 2008), and Williams, "Enlightenment Epistemology," 345–74.

Proven Experience: The Church and Means

Edwards's defense of unitary anthropology and the affections that denote regenerate life were an implicit critique of nonexperimental Calvinism and the Puritan polity that supported it. There was however another, perhaps greater, fear in the New England psyche: namely, Antinomianism, or enthusiasm, which had bedeviled the colonies since the Hutchinson crisis of the 1630s.[323] Claims to direct illumination of the Spirit had occasionally led to social disorder, theological anarchy, and family breakdown. Worrying for those in positions of clerical authority, given the high esteem in which Edwards held such religious affections, was the possible implication that there was no place for a learned ministry among those who pursued such immediate and arbitrary experiences of grace.[324] Edwards squarely faces these objections in drafting *Religious Affections*.

The bulk of the *Religious Affections* is structured around two sets of twelve signs, the first set describing experiences that may not assuredly be signs of a regenerate life and the second set presenting attributes of the believer that most certainly do attest gracious affections, or true religion. The sign described in most detail is the twelfth in the second series, which places love as the most persuasive sign of a regenerate life. While arguments dealing with the subjective assurances of salvation appear intermittently throughout the treatise, it is salient to note that discussion concerning the objective signs of true religion form the very framework of the entire piece. Edwards is not here chiefly concerned with rationalists like Chauncy, but builds his entire case against those like Davenport who are satisfied with less than sustained moral transformation in the redeemed.[325] If it is irrefragable signs of the Spirit's presence that are contested, then it is visible tokens, public tests, proven experience, and objective criteria that Edwards will in turn demonstrate as necessary in the life of the regenerate.[326]

---

323. See David D. Hall, ed. *The Antinomian Controversy, 1636–1638: A Documentary History*, 2nd ed. (Durham: Duke University Press, 1990), 3–23.

324. Bainton, *Yale and the Ministry*, 34.

325. Chamberlain, "Self-Deception as a Theological Problem," 546. Other itinerants who pursued extravagant expression were Eleazar Wheelock, Samuel Buell, and Benjamin Pomeroy, to name the more prominent. See Marsden, *A Life*, 269.

326. McClymond notes the anti-Kantian perspective in Edwards's works, insofar as Edwards wants to ground objective reality not principally in the perception of the subject, but in God, who is the perceived object. However, more fundamentally, the construction of *objective reality* also differs between Edwards and Kant: for the former, God is at some level knowable, though for the latter, the noumenal world is forever inaccessible to human beings. See McClymond, "Spiritual Perception in Jonathan Edwards," 206; cf. Edwards, *WJE* 2: 240.

Edwards is not content with enthusiastic warmth of heart generated by the light of the Spirit if it is not consonant with the gift of Christian revelation previously given.[327] The Word of the Gospel is "as a glass, by which this light is conveyed to us,"[328] just as sunlight uses a magnifying glass to concentrate its rays to create a spark at close range to the kindling. This does not render the Spirit's work any less immediate, but rather the Spirit focuses the truth of the Word in the heart. Claims that an individual has received personal revelations or inspiration are particularly odious to teachers of Edwards's Reformed convictions, for they presuppose that the Spirit brings content as well as conviction. Using the nomenclature of Thomas Shepard (1605–1649), Edwards distinguishes between legal and evangelical hypocrites, meaning those believers who are deceived by the evidences of morality on the one hand or are deceived by the evidences of their own ecstatic experiences or discoveries on the other.[329] Subjective assurance is desirable but must be a correlate of an objective offer of salvation.[330]

Grace must be made visible as a valid way of testing true religious affections, for, Edwards writes, "grace is of the nature of light, and brings truth to view."[331] He makes the link between the subjective and objective facets of the impact of light when he asserts that

> Godliness is as it were a light that shines in the soul: Christ directs that this light should not only shine within, but that it should shine out before men, that they may see it. But which way shall this be? 'Tis by our good works.[332]

Smith perceptively remarks that such highlighting of activity is not what we may have expected in a treatise bearing the word affections in its title. Indeed, he asseverates that at this point, Edwards breaks from his own tradition by insisting that "Protestantism's sacred domain—the inner life—...be subjected to a public test." Though personal appropriation of grace through faith had become a Protestant slogan, and the Puritans had further internalized the faith when socio-political hurdles had impeded ongoing reform in

---

327. Edwards, *WJE* 2: 120, 266.

328. Edwards, "Divine and Supernatural Light," *WJE* 17: 416.

329. Edwards, *WJE* 2: 173.

330. Cherry, *Theology*, 155.

331. Edwards, *WJE* 2: 235.

332. Edwards, *WJE* 2: 407–08.

England,[333] here, Edwards takes "a large step in the direction of making action a center of attention," and all this without leaving himself open to the accusation of salvation by works.[334] McDermott rightly contextualizes the *Religious Affections* as a production of Edwards's despondency after the evident inadequacies of the revivals and has no hesitation in attributing that motive to their composition:

> Edwards has lost confidence in subjective forms of consciousness, which could be sources of self-deception. Now only publicly mani-fested Christian practice could be relied upon as a test of true religious experience.[335]

Noll succinctly sharpens our conclusion when he states that religious affec-tions make the church visible: "Edwards's ecclesiology reflected his belief that the effects of true grace were tangible, visible, and reliably discernible."[336] Religious affections have necessary ecclesiological entailments, for they can-not be explained with reference to subjective heat or private experience alone. Objective light must generate them, and public reception must welcome them, both of which the life of the church supports. Importantly, Edwards is relativizing the traditional means of grace to give religious affections a more determining role in the ecclesial life.

Religious affections, because their fruit is visible to public scrutiny, require furthermore public and moral appraisal. Indeed, this treatise at heart presents the evidential value of love in Christian experience and thereby demands "the complex and subtle language of character and moral assessment" when inves-tigating either first-person or third-person cases.[337] Edwards recognizes that the church is a mixed community, and its purity will always be a pious desire as much as a present reality and therefore falling within the bailiwick of cor-porate scrutiny. Individual human capacity to determine one's own spiritual state is limited, but determining that of others is more difficult still.[338] The

---

333. See Charles L. Cohen, *God's Caress: The Psychology of Puritan Religious Experience* (Oxford: Oxford University Press, 1986), 272, and Brauer, "Conversion," especially 239.

334. Smith, "Editor's Introduction," *WJE* 2: 42–43.

335. McDermott, *One Holy and Happy Society*, 113.

336. Noll, *America's God*, 45.

337. Wayne Proudfoot, "Perception and Love in *Religious Affections*," in *Jonathan Edwards's Writings: Text, Context, Interpretation*, ed. S. J. Stein (Bloomington and Indianapolis: Indiana University Press, 1996), 125, 132. Proudfoot goes further to suggest that third-person moral appraisal, exemplified in Edwards, is a vital methodology in religious psychology.

338. Cherry, *Theology*, 157.

Antinomian enthusiasts were prone to conflate assurance with the act of belief itself, which built in no checks and balances, nor did it adequately allow for the possibility of self-deception as an outworking of sin. Edwards wants to distinguish faith from assurance, and he can achieve this by relativizing the evidential value of experiences connected with conversion in order to highlight the evidential value of experiences connected to moral development:

> The Scripture represents faith, as that by which men are brought into a good estate; and therefore it can't be the same thing, as believing that they are already in a good estate. To suppose that faith consists in persons believing that they are in a good estate, is in effect the same thing, as to suppose that faith consists in a person's believing that he has faith, or in believing that he believes.[339]

Evaluation of Christian practice has more potential for objective verification than mere appraisal of Christian sentiment, whether one's own or someone else's. As Chamberlain suggests, Edwards affirms external tests not only to critique the claims of the enthusiasts but also to provide surer knowledge:

> In *Religious Affections*, therefore, he both insisted upon the centrality of the affections in the religious life and rejected immediate experience as a solution to the epistemological problem concerning the nature and means of assurance. To minimize the potential for self-deception, he advocated a life of persevering Christian practice as the only sound foundation on which to build a hope of salvation.[340]

The church therefore plays an important role for Edwards in prosecuting such measures as are designed to prove religious affections. It is not just the inquiry into relations of grace whereby the church can exercise its judgment of charity, but more generally, it is empowered to provide outside affirmation and encouragement to those who doubt. Edwards affirms as well the role of the sacraments when he asserts "that they should be, as it were, exhibited to our view, in sensible representations...the more to affect us with them."[341] Similarly, the "duty

---

339. Edwards, *WJE* 2: 178.

340. Chamberlain, "Self-Deception as a Theological Problem," 555.

341. Edwards, *WJE* 2: 115. Nuttall furthermore presents a range of Puritan authors who affirm the ordinances as Scripturally mandated instruments of the Spirit's work, recognizing also Puritan hesitation toward material helps. Nuttall, *Holy Spirit*, 91. Chamberlain reminds us that it was a peculiarity of Antinomian perfectionism to deny the efficacy of the

of singing praises to God" fulfills the function of prompting our affections. The Ministry of the Word expressed through preaching was also designed to be different from the use of books or commentaries so as primarily and affectively to impress upon human hearts the application of the Word,[342] and to convince sinners of the misery of their state before God and the remedy of their sickness through Christ.[343] This ministry in turn was the preserve of the ordained and not open to laymen, even those of otherwise godly disposition.[344] These ecclesiological helps could sustain the Christian's affective discipleship, which had been part of New England ecclesiology since its founding.[345]

Indeed, part of the church's role was to confirm wavering assurance in its members, even if judgments made were done so conditionally. Edwards does not want to arrogate to himself or to any of the clerical caste the irrefragable right of indubitable discernment. He maintains that God alone can definitively separate the sheep from the goats.[346] In the meantime, the church is given the task not of declaring without error who is regenerate, but of building confidence in their election:

And the nature of the covenant of grace, and God's declared ends in the appointment and constitution of things in that covenant, do plainly show it to be God's design to make ample provision for the saints

---

ordinances, for immediacy would disdain the use of means: Chamberlain, "Self-Deception as a Theological Problem," 551.

342. Marsden, *A Life*, 282.

343. Edwards, *WJE* 2: 115. Interestingly, in this description of means, there is no scrutiny of how it is that the Spirit avails himself of such means for affectional ends. The link between the Word and the Spirit is not so tight that Edwards can't distinguish affections that "arise on *occasion* of the Scripture, and not *properly come from* the Scripture, as the genuine fruit of the Scripture, and by a right use of it; but from an abuse of it." Edwards, *WJE* 2: 143. He does not posit an *ex opere operato* impact of preaching. Conversely, preaching is not the only means, argues Ward, that can be used by God to bring a sinner to comprehend the condition of his soul: Ward, "Philosophical Structure of *Religious Affections*," 764.

344. Edwards, "To Moses Lyman," *WJE* 16: 101–03.

345. Kobrin, "The Expansion of the Visible Church in New England," 190, 195. In earlier times, the church provided support for the *completion* of the process of salvation (given the regnant conversion morphology of the 1630s and 1640s). In Edwards's day, it was no less true that the church was given to improve the spiritual confidence of its members, though now conversion was more often understood as a compressed movement with the church providing *confirmation* of the salvation attained.

346. Edwards, *WJE* 2: 193. Whether Edwards relinquishes the judgment of charity assumed here in the later crisis around his dismissal will be dealt with in Chapter 4 in the section on the *Humble Inquiry*.

having an assured hope of eternal life, while living here upon earth. For so are all things ordered and contrived in that covenant.[347]

Edwards, in this eleventh sign of no certain grace, is attempting to disconnect the affections from the necessity to produce assurance. He is rebuking pride that grows out of strong affections. He is suggesting that the remedy for wavering confidence is not strong or violent emotion, but rather is the regular and orderly ministrations of the church or covenant.[348] Assurance is for all but will not necessarily be present in all evenly or immediately. Antinomian claims to private validation of spiritual graces are denied.

Significantly, Edwards both affirms the centrality of religious affections to Christian experience and relativizes their subjective reality in the life of the church. Religious affections are a coordinating category for the individual, drawing together all faculties toward the one end of love for God and neighbor, yet they are inadequate without reference to further criteria to establish assurance for life in the world. Religious affections may be experienced as an intensive crisis, yet their outworkings need to be cultivated gradually and extensively and with due consideration of means. Religious affections are not merely for the individual's assurance, but their expression and validation do function as positive witnesses both to the individual and the church at large.

Purposeful Experience: The Church and Ends

Religious affections, in Edwards's estimation, are a sign of regenerate life, which requires however external attestation for the assurance of those who believe. Such affections bring critique to both Arminians, who stressed rationality in Christian experience, and to Antinomians, whose immediate apprehension of the Spirit did not necessarily coordinate with moral transformation. The affections are furthermore an implicit challenge to the immediate audience of these sermons or arguments, namely the lax who were seated Sunday after Sunday in the meetinghouse in Northampton, who may have agreed with Edwards's critique of excessive enthusiasm and speculative preaching, but who nevertheless were not engaged with Edwards's program for social

---

347. Edwards, *WJE* 2: 168, 169.

348. As we shall have reason to pursue later, Tracy interprets such ministerial interventions as essentially motivated by desire for control and is skeptical of the role of the clergy to appraise moral development. See Tracy, *Jonathan Edwards, Pastor*, 144, 173.

transformation.[349] Edwards, albeit more obliquely, addresses public concerns in this treatise, not merely privatistic piety.

Edwards is of the conviction that true religious affections must necessarily be expressed in public ways, for their nature is to move toward their object, namely, other human beings or God. Indeed, one of the marks that distinguishes true from counterfeit piety is its capacity to act in the interest of the object without any benefit accruing to the subject of the affections. He recognizes that in appearance, a disinterested action and a self-seeking one can look similar, but he nevertheless prizes the true expression of affective faith:

> [N]ow the divine excellency and glory of God, and Jesus Christ, the Word of God, the works of God, and the ways of God, etc. is the primary reason, why a true saint loves these things; and not any supposed interest that he has in them, or any conceived benefit that he has received from them, or shall receive from them, or any such imagined relation which they bear to his interest, that self-love can properly be said to be the first foundation of his love to these things.[350]

Furthermore, such love becomes the steady practice of true believers in such a way that a life of strenuous activity in the world results.[351] Action in turn provides a kind of confidence in the soul of the believer that one is of the elect.[352] Edwards reminds his audience of the practical significance of that kind of ministry, which served the physical needs of others and which was exemplified in the active and compassionate life of Christ.[353]

The place that Edwards assigns to exertion in Christian experience has often been contested. Cohen makes much of the dynamic of activism within Puritan spirituality generally, in which great anxiety is met by great relief from

---

349. William K. B. Stoever, "The Godly Will's Discerning: Shepard, Edwards, and the Identification of True Godliness," in *Jonathan Edwards's Writings: Text, Context, Interpretation*, ed. S. J. Stein (Bloomington and Indianapolis: Indiana University Press, 1996), 96. We encounter instances within *Religious Affections* of applications directed toward very particular social situations, for example, the use of fine apparel or ornamentation. Edwards, *WJE* 2: 335. David Hall purports to see references to the "Bad Book Affair" as another example of social declension lying behind Edwards's remonstrations. See David D. Hall, "Editor's Introduction," in *Ecclesiastical Writings*, The Works of Jonathan Edwards 12, ed. D. D. Hall (New Haven: Yale University Press, 1994), 58.

350. Edwards, *WJE* 2: 240.

351. Edwards, *WJE* 2: 398.

352. Edwards, *WJE* 2: 195.

353. Edwards, *WJE* 2: 369.

great action (though he is justly critical of details of Max Weber's analysis of Calvinist activism). He asserts that activism is a correlate of conversion, even if works righteousness is formally denied by Puritan teachers.[354] Smith is most adamant that piety is not to be divorced from practice in understanding Edwards's ethics:

> Religion, much as it concerns the heart in Edwards' view, is not to be confined to an internal feeling or state of mind. Religion, though it is ultimately an intangible relationship between the individual and God, must express itself objectively and thus assume public shape...the entire social order must ultimately be affected.[355]

Heimert energetically states that the "*Religious Affections*...was an exhortation to Edwards' readers to be up and doing, and to the ministers of the colonies to urge their people on their way."[356] Hall reiterates the importance of recognizing that Edwards's writings of the 1740s, due to disappointment with the revivals, have a public reflex: Edwards wants the movement of the Spirit to have a longer, lasting impact on social forms. Bebbington sees Edwards's doctrine of assurance being responsible for a keen activism in the nascent evangelical movement.[357] Writings coming after *Religious Affections* are an application of the dynamic activism embodied in that seminal work of 1746.[358]

From a broader theological perspective, we ought not to be surprised that Edwards's piety is not quietistic but has its expression in the world of social or ecclesiological forms. His theology of conversion absorbs much of the crisis-oriented themes of the New Testament, leaving the process-oriented material its due application in matters of church and eschatology. The

---

354. Cohen, *God's Caress*, 22, 109–10, 272.

355. John E. Smith, "Jonathan Edwards: Piety and Practice in the American Character," *The Journal of Religion* 54(2) (1974): 166–80, 176.

356. Alan Heimert, *Religion and the American Mind: From the Great Awakening to the Revolution*, The Jonathan Edwards Classic Studies Series (Eugene, OR: Wipf and Stock, 2006), 132.

357. David W. Bebbington, *Evangelicalism in Modern Britain: A History from the 1730s to the 1980s* (London: Unwin Hyman, 1989), 47.

358. Richard Hall surveys the attitude of commentators toward Edwards's depiction of piety and practice. Although there have been a number of writers who portray Edwards as quietistic (for example, Mead, Alexis, and De Jong), Hall, along with Heimert and Smith, sees the social reflex latent in Edwards's conception of religious affections. See Richard A. S. Hall, *The Neglected Northampton Texts of Jonathan Edwards: Edwards on Society and Politics*, Studies in American Religion 52 (Lewiston, NY: Edwin Mellen Press, 1990), 25–28, 58, 150.

immediacy of conversion crisis needs the gradualness of church life to provide orientation and direction. The growing tendency among reform-minded believers in the seventeenth century to adjourn the return of the Lord, or to expect it not immediately but in the middle distance, funded both the immediacy of apocalyptic presentations of conversion and openness to worldly commitments while waiting for the parousia. Though the authority of many among the clergy had benefited from preaching the imminent return of Christ, providing as it did urgency and points of leverage over the congregation, to preach the expectation of a longer-range return empowered the laity to see their place and responsibility within the historical order, not least as this was expressed in adjudicating the affections of those seeking admission.[359] The outcome of the revival of true religion might be disorderly and apparently antisocial in the short term, but Edwards's own belief in the ultimately stable purposes of God in history made from these affections an essential ingredient in the reconstitution of the present order. The exercise of affections would have an impact on both individuals and society.[360]

Whether such lofty expectations of social transformation were realistic will better be understood with reference to the reaction of the parishioners of Northampton to Edwards's espousal of this notion of the affections. Though he is already flagging here the relative unimportance of precise order or method in recounting one's conversion experience,[361] there is nonetheless still the requirement that an account be publicly rendered:

> I am far from saying that it is not requisite that persons should give any sort of account of their experiences to their brethren. For persons to profess those things wherein the essence of Christianity lies, is the same thing as to profess that they experience those things.[362]

He wants to emphasize as well that to be able to give a formal relation of grace is relativized by the ability of those around to testify to the presence of love in the named person.[363] A church comprising an expectation of converted saints

---

359. Ward traces this development back to the influence of Spener's eschatology. See Ward, *Early Evangelicalism*, 31–33.

360. Stout, *The New England Soul*, 204. See as well Ward, "Philosophical Structure of *Religious Affections*," 761, where he connects the exercise of the fruit of the Spirit with the saint's desire for harmony, perfection, or completion in the external world.

361. McClymond, *Encounters with God*, 42.

362. Edwards, *WJE* 2: 416.

363. Edwards, *WJE* 2: 418, 420.

is necessarily more demanding than a congregation of the nurtured, though any judgment arrived at after the relation of grace is necessarily provisional, for no one can ascertain with absolute precision the state of another's soul.[364] This determination contains both the high hope of genuine transformed lives and the gritty realism that our best efforts at appraising are still only our best efforts. In all likelihood, the denizens of Northampton heard the former hope loudly and had little time for clerical disclaimers. The appeal to religious affections was evidently received as an appeal to lift their game, one that they almost instinctively chose to resist, itself reflecting an attitude of confidence in ecclesiological if not pneumatological status.[365] Though several years would pass before Edwards's dismissal, the contours of his theological approach to pastoral expectations were clearly now open to scrutiny. The purpose of the church would be a matter of dispute between pastor and people.

---

364. Edwards, *WJE* 2: 420.

365. See Stoever, "The Godly Will's Discerning," 96.

4

Ordered Ecclesiological Visions (1747–1758)

4.1 The Church's Millennial Hope in An Humble Attempt

EDWARDS RECOGNIZED THAT the second half of the 1740s was a difficult time for the church, of which he was a leader. He devoted himself therefore to formulating a renewed vision, theologically defined and concretely applied, of the place of the church in the world. Disappointments from local revivals and their ensuing pastoral and experiential dilemmas were displaced by new aspirations for the global expansion of the Kingdom of Christ. Richard Hall argues that Edwards's writings of the later 1740s demonstrate a new social agenda, which broke open ecclesiological concerns with greater determination.[1] It is my contention that Edwards's doctrine of the church lies at the heart of the treatise calling believers to united prayer, published in 1748, under the laborious title *An Humble Attempt to Promote Explicit Agreement and Visible Union of God's People in Extraordinary Prayer for the Revival of Religion and the Advancement of Christ's Kingdom on Earth, Pursuant to Scripture Promises and Prophecies Concerning the Last Time.*[2] The very first sentence demonstrates Edwards's intentions: "In this chapter we have a prophecy of a future glorious advancement of the church of God."[3]

---

1. Robert Hall notes the relative ignorance of the writings of Edwards from the late 1740s despite their value in understanding Edwards's ecclesiological and social agenda, and their importance in an ecclesiological vision larger than the church in Northampton, which has disappointed him. See Hall, *Neglected Northampton Texts*, 46, 58, 63.

2. Edwards, "Humble Attempt," *WJE* 5: 308.

3. Edwards, "Humble Attempt," *WJE* 5: 312.

Combined efforts in corporate prayer were in themselves the embodiment of new kinds of Christian union.⁴ Of course, Puritans had previously
been great exponents of the life of prayer, either through manuals of piety
or through personal exhortation,⁵ but now, Christian leaders began to challenge
those in their care to meet for "extraordinary prayer" at times and in places other
than during the Sunday gathering or in household groupings. Such calls to prayer
reflected a broader impatience with the state of the church in the mid-eighteenth
century.⁶ Edwards's appeal to constitute a movement of prayer meetings in New
England, in connection with Concerts of Prayer elsewhere, is just such an example of encouragement for new ecclesial models of the church. His own unique
contribution to this movement is to be found in his steps of logic between ener-
gized prayer and the expansion of the Kingdom, which give significant signposts
to his ecclesiological vision: the theological connections between missions, the
millennium, and the ministerial role in this *Humble Attempt* give us insight into
the ways Edwards was reconceiving human agency and historical contingency
for the sake of the church's impact in the world.

Edwards as Ecclesial Entrepreneur

A certain "Memorial" had been sent by "a number of ministers" from Scotland
outlining their hopes and rationale for an international prayer meeting.⁷
Though the call to concerted prayer did not originate with Edwards, he included
within the *Humble Attempt* a summary of this background to his own request,
presented the Memorial substantially as it was printed in *The Christian Monthly
History* and reprinted in *Historical Collections*, and added his own theological
motivations.⁸ The Memorial sets out the hope that ministers will encourage
their parishioners to meet every week for a prayer concert, either on Saturday
night or Sunday morning, and further on the first Tuesday of each quarter, with

---

4. Crawford, *Seasons of Grace*, 229.

5. Haykin, *Holy Spirit in Revival*, 137–38.

6. Count Ludwig von Zinzendorf, for example, had promoted prayer through his Order of
the Grain of Mustard Seed, which was expressed in the round-the-clock and 100-years-long
prayer meeting on his estate in Upper Lusatia. Praying Societies in the Scottish lowlands
had been constituted, which had a significant bearing on the development of associate pres-
byteries and revival there in the 1730s. John Wesley himself used Edwards's treatise, albeit
expurgated of Calvinist coloration, to encourage his Methodists to pray. In less organized
ways, children had *spontaneously* devoted themselves to prayer as well, both on the estates
of the Moravians and also among children in Silesia. See Ward, *The Protestant Evangelical
Awakening*, 127.

7. Edwards, "Humble Attempt," *WJE* 5: 320

8. Edwards, "Humble Attempt," *WJE* 5: 321–28.

due acknowledgement that circumstances in different places may necessitate changes to this schedule.⁹ The invitation is open to all who have "at heart the interest of vital Christianity and the power of godliness,"¹⁰ irrespective of their denominational or party background. The proposal was ecumenically inclusive and designed to heal divisions resulting from the earlier revivals.¹¹

Edwards longed for the latter-day glory of the church of God that would sweep over the world.¹² Taking as his primary text the prophecy of Zechariah 8:20–22 concerning the future "accession of Gentile nations to the church of God,"¹³ Edwards expounded this vision by highlighting how it might be achieved through the practice of prayer: vast numbers of nations will come together to pray intentionally that God might bestow his presence and blessing on their common life. He argued that believers have a "duty of prayer," at heart a thirsting for God himself, which will be expressed among many nations when they join together in a "visible union...explicit agreement, a joint resolution," performed with willing alacrity, which brings great honor to God.¹⁴ The inflow of the nations is further supported by appeal to Isaiah 60:2–4, where the light of God in this world acts centripetally to draw together those who were previously in darkness.¹⁵ The treatise is replete with Scriptural references, often from the Old Testament, outlining the ways in which God will fulfill glorious promises as yet only partially realized. It is not just that Edwards is encouraging people to pray; he is also encouraging his readers to pray with the particular hope that their praying will bring a consummation to God's work in history.

Indeed, it is Edwards's use of apocalyptic in justifying prayer, missions, and revival that makes his work so distinct. The Boston sponsors for this treatise (Joseph Sewall, Thomas Prince, John Webb, Thomas Foxcroft, and Joshua Gee) provide a preface that not only affirmed the intentions of Edwards but

---

9. The proposal was made that this prayer movement be continued for seven years, perhaps longer, building on an earlier network for prayer begun in 1744. Such precise recommendations made Edwards vulnerable to the accusation of pharisaicism, which demanded works of piety beyond those prescribed by the law. He responds to such accusations in Part III of the treatise and thereby gives us some insight into the suspicion aroused by the introduction of new means for the sake of the church's advance.

10. Edwards, "Humble Attempt," *WJE* 5: 326.

11. Hall, *Neglected Northampton Texts*, 57.

12. Using another frame of reference from Isaiah 11:9, Edwards awaits the moment when the knowledge of God will be known everywhere, just as "the waters cover the sea." Edwards, "Humble Attempt," *WJE* 5: 332.

13. Edwards, "Humble Attempt," *WJE* 5: 312.

14. Edwards, "Humble Attempt," *WJE* 5: 314, 316, 317, 318, 319, 320.

15. Edwards, "Humble Attempt," *WJE* 5: 313.

also drew attention to the novelty of some of his views on prophecy and the Kingdom.[16] Edwards attempts to call people to pray and calls them to pray in earnest for the revival of religion on the basis of an eschatological timetable, albeit with some reservations on the part of his backers. Even after his dismissal from the Northampton church, Edwards still maintained the value of the Concert of Prayer as a means of encouraging revival.[17]

Edwards as Ecclesial Internationalist

It would be too easy to isolate the cooling of revivalist sentiment in New England and to begin to question whether there had been a Great Awakening at all. Recent historiography on the period has moved beyond the particularities of New England to suggest that the context of Edwards's thought must be painted more broadly,[18] paying due respect to its regional and international commonalities.[19] Significantly, the prayer movement, of which Edwards is a sponsor, highlights a most remarkable feature of the eighteenth-century revivals: namely how they were either established, coordinated, or encouraged through a network of correspondence, not just within Europe or within North America, but between them as well,[20] with their results published and circulated widely. Indeed, the Memorial inserted into the *Humble Attempt* argues that private correspondence requesting support for the Concert of Prayer will prove an effective adjunct strategy alongside the Memorial itself.[21]

The culture of letter writing, described from time to time as "the republic of letters," crossed denominational as well as geographical boundaries. George Whitefield, an Anglican Calvinist who became a focal point of the revivals in North America as well as in England, Scotland, and Wales, used correspondence to publicize his campaigns. John Guyse and Isaac Watts, both Dissenting ministers in Northamptonshire in Old England, learned of events in America through correspondence and encouraged the publication of

---

16. Edwards, "Humble Attempt," *WJE* 5: 310.

17. Jonathan Edwards, "To the Reverend John Erskine, July 5, 1750," in *Letters and Personal Writings*, The Works of Jonathan Edwards 16, ed. G. S. Claghorn (New Haven: Yale University Press, 1998), 350.

18. O'Brien, "Transatlantic Community of Saints," 832.

19. For Kidd's recent historical defense of the "Great Awakening" in relation to the writing of Jon Butler, see the opening discussion in Chapter 3, Section 3.1 of this book.

20. Ward, *Awakening*, 2. It has been estimated that August Hermann Francke of Halle in Prussia had around five thousand correspondents!

21. Edwards, "Humble Attempt," *WJE* 5: 327.

Edwards's works in London. Edwards requested news of the revivals among the Dutch Reformed in the Netherlands from his Presbyterian correspondent in Scotland, likely to be John McLaurin of Glasgow.[22] The correspondence not only existed between clergy, but laymen of different denominations also promoted the revival through their own money and letters.[23] The *Humble Attempt* reflects more than the importance of a prayer meeting. Its organization reinforced relationships beyond denominational or regional associations:

> The new community created by international correspondence was, in part a continuation of the seventeenth-century Puritan letter-writing community, but its spirit of evangelism marked a point of departure.[24]

Indeed, while constructing this treatise, Edwards's family was playing host to a great example of healthy revivalist piety, David Brainerd, whose moderate success ministering among the indigenous Indian populations at the Forks of the Delaware and along the Susquehanna River[25] was an eloquent testimony to transatlantic networking described in a letter by Edwards to a Scottish correspondent:

> Besides those things that have a favorable aspect on the interest of religion in these parts, among the English, and other inhabitants of European extract, Mr. Brainerd, a missionary employed by The Society in Scotland for Propagating Christian Knowledge, to preach to the Indians, has lately had more success than ever.[26]

While some older interpretations of this treatise give prominence to a vision of a great American future,[27] Edwards's internationalism militates against any narrowly sectarian millenarianism.

---

22. Edwards, "Letter to a Correspondent in Scotland," *WJE* 5: 444.

23. O'Brien, "Transatlantic Community of Saints," 819.

24. O'Brien, "Transatlantic Community of Saints," 820.

25. Ward, *The Protestant Evangelical Awakening*, 292.

26. Edwards, "Letter to a Correspondent in Scotland," *WJE* 5: 449.

27. Heimert, *Religion and the American Mind*, 156–58.

Edwards as Ecclesial Millennialist

Edwards believed that prayer changes history. As his supporters pointed out in their preface,[28] the link between prayer and the glory of the latter days of the church was integral to the vision of Zechariah 8:20–22, with which he began the *Humble Attempt*. Edwards went on to expound another apocalyptic passage from the book of Revelation, which testified to the impact of prayer on the course of history.[29] Furthermore, Edwards appeals to the Lord's Prayer in Luke 11, which expressly links the activity of praying for the Kingdom to come on earth as it is in heaven with the pouring out of the Spirit, for the paragraph following the Lord's Prayer promises the Holy Spirit to those who ask. The various petitions of the prayer, which Jesus gave us as a model, are then effectively the equivalent of asking for the greatest of God's blessings, his Spirit himself.[30] Prayer that encourages the pouring out of the Spirit changes the course of history, not infrequently for Edwards through revival.[31]

Although a renewed commitment to prayer coupled with the pouring out of the Spirit are highlighted as means used by God to enlarge and strengthen his people, the paradigm that Edwards used to summarize the result of this activity is the millennial Kingdom of Christ, drawing from the timetable of Revelation. Such speculation was not new to Edwards, as it had been common to Puritan eschatology in the century before him.[32] However, Edwards takes those leading Puritan categories to build his own eschatological edifice in new ways.

Central to Edwards's interpretation of Revelation is the identity of the Pope with the Antichrist, a parallel constant since the Reformation.[33] Since the Protestant cause had grown since the sixteenth century, and the defenders of vital religion had not experienced the bleakness of days like those before the sixteenth century,[34] Edwards appealed most persistently to the accounts in

---

28. Edwards, "Humble Attempt," *WJE* 5: 310–11.

29. Edwards, "Humble Attempt," *WJE* 5: 353.

30. Marsden, *A Life*, 335. Hall points out how the blessing of the Spirit is an outworking of covenant promises. Hall, *Neglected Northampton Texts*, 87.

31. Crawford, *Seasons of Grace*, 229. See also Edwards, "Humble Attempt," *WJE* 5: 348, and Thomas S. Kidd, " 'The Very Vital Breath of Christianity': Prayer and Revival in Provincial New England," *Fides et Historia* 36(2) (2004): 19–33.

32. Crawford points out the millennial commitments of Cotton Mather as motivation for concerted prayer. See Crawford, *Seasons of Grace*, 229.

33. Edwards, "Humble Attempt," *WJE* 5: 381.

34. Withrow, "A Future of Hope: Jonathan Edwards and Millennial Expectations," especially 90–92.

Revelation 11 (the slaying of the witnesses) and Revelation 16 (the timing of the pouring out of the vials, in modern translations "bowls") of the triumphs of the Antichrist,[35] which he argued must refer to the period before the ministry of Luther and Calvin.[36] This position allowed Edwards to promote the Concert of Prayer with the positive expectation of glorious days for the church, and not with foreboding that prayer for revival would exacerbate the suffering of the church under the terrors of the Antichrist's impending rule. Prayer was ecclesiologically motivated.

Though Edwards pinpoints the decisive blow against the Antichrist in the ministry of the Reformers, he nevertheless acknowledges that the complete destruction of the Antichrist will only come gradually, through the patient proclamation of the Gospel attending the persistent prayers of the saints in the course of history. Just as the Exodus of the people of God from Egypt and the entry into the Promised Land involved stages,[37] so Edwards argued that it would be in vain to await an apocalyptic intervention of God to inaugurate the millennial reign of Christ:

> As the power of Antichrist, and the corruption of the apostate church, rose not at once, but by several notable steps and degrees; so it will in the like manner fall: and that divers steps and seasons of destruction to the spiritual Babylon, and revival and advancement of the true church, are prophesied of under one. Though it be true, that there is some particular event, that prevails above all others in the intention of the prophecy, some one remarkable season of the destruction of the Church of Rome and papal power and corruption, and advancement of true religion, that the prophecies have a principal respect to.[38]

Often supported by international perspectives garnered through correspondence, political events in Europe and North America provided important background to the thought of Edwards in the *Humble Attempt* and further encouraged millennial speculation. The frequent military encounters between England and France in the eighteenth century in the Caribbean, India, the South Pacific, Europe, and North America betokened a larger issue in Puritan

---

35. Withrow, "A Future of Hope: Jonathan Edwards and Millennial Expectations," 79.

36. This is at odds with the opinions of Moses Lowman (1680–1752), whose *Paraphrase and Notes on the Revelation*, 1st ed. (1737) had been such an important model in Edwards's earlier reflections.

37. Edwards, "Humble Attempt," *WJE* 5: 384.

38. Edwards, "Humble Attempt," *WJE* 5: 407–08.

minds concerning the suprahistorical battle between Christ and Satan, given concrete expression in English Protestantism and French Roman Catholicism. The urgency with which Edwards called his people to prayer must be read against the urgency generated through military conflict very close to home. Edwards experienced in his own family the results of French mobilization in Canada, where his father was sent as chaplain to the English troops.[39] Later French incursions into New England created the need for his home in Stockbridge to be palisaded and drove many Indians as refugees into Massachusetts. There had even been a recent reassertion of Roman Catholic claims to rule in the United Kingdom, which agitated Edwards.[40]

Many of these threats to the Protestant character of New England were in time averted. In fact, the English in North America had witnessed some extraordinary turnarounds in their military fortunes. However, rather than these victories dampening the apocalyptic fervor of New Englanders, Edwards chief among them, the connection between these military feats and prayer actually incited still further confidence in the mighty works of God in history.[41] Indeed, the prospect of Antichrist's gradual demise encouraged concrete speculation about the gradual advance of Christ's Kingdom in the world.[42] This schema encouraged adventurous missionary enterprise. It also defended the justice of God in a Calvinist worldview, as it allowed for the total number of the elect to be greater than those who are damned, given that the population of the world, like that of New England, was growing exponentially and that the vast majority of people who would ever live and be converted were yet to be born.[43] The steady progress of the purposes of God would in time incorporate many peoples as yet untouched by the Gospel:

> Would it not be a great thing, to be accomplished in one half century, that religion, in the power and purity of it, should so prevail, as to gain conquest over all those many things that stand in opposition to it among Protestants...? And if in another, it should go on so to prevail, as to get the victory over all the opposition and strength of the kingdom of Antichrist...? And if in a third half century, it should prevail and subdue the greater part of the Mahometan world, and bring in the

---

39. Stein, "Editor's Introduction," *WJE* 5: 9.

40. Edwards, "Letter to a Correspondent," *WJE* 5: 459–60.

41. Edwards, "Humble Attempt," *WJE* 5: 362.

42. Marsden, *A Life*, 337.

43. Edwards, "Humble Attempt," *WJE* 5: 343.

Jewish nation...? And then in the next whole century, the whole heathen world should be enlightened and converted to the Christian faith, throughout all parts of Africa, Asia, America and Terra Australis.[44]

It is the understanding of Edwards in this treatise that though Christ is Lord of history, his reign is exercised essentially through the church and extended through the church's expansion. The millennium is the climax to the history of the church that witnesses Christ's rule with minimal opposition in the world, with the saints in heaven as co-rulers through the church militant on earth.[45] Such a framework requires a church polity, with membership increasingly restricted to those who are unambiguously regenerate. Edwards highlighted the continuities of the historical process, and offered hope within history to his readers, when he expounded the relationship between the Kingdom of God and the kingdoms of this world, over both of which Christ reigns.[46]

Though this treatise discusses prayer, the means of revival, and the millennium, and answers at length possible objections to Edwards's understanding, at its heart, Edwards is actually writing about the church, its place in history, and hope for its expansion, providing Scriptural support for such millennial hopes. If Edwards's postmillennialism refers to the Kingdom's coming as "emergent rather than supervenient upon history," then it is the church that becomes the center of the world's future.[47]

Edwards as Ecclesial Optimist

Although Edwards the optimist looks forward to greater days for the church on earth, he nonetheless has great regard in this treatise for the visible, perhaps mixed, church in daily experience. He spoke highly of the "gospel ordinances" as means of grace,[48] valued the fellowship of God's people beyond the local congregation by promoting the "welfare and happiness of the whole body of Christ,"[49] and stressed the continuity between the Old and the New

---

44. Edwards, "Humble Attempt," *WJE* 5: 411.

45. Reiner Smolinski, "Apocalypticism in Colonial North America," in *The Encyclopedia of Apocalypticism*, Apocalypticism in the Modern Period and the Contemporary Age, ed. S. J. Stein, vol. 3 (New York: Continuum, 2003), 59.

46. Edwards, "Humble Attempt," *WJE* 5: 330.

47. Hall, *Neglected Northampton Texts*, 101.

48. Edwards, "Humble Attempt," *WJE* 5: 322.

49. Edwards, "Humble Attempt," *WJE* 5: 366.

Testaments by describing the whole nation of the Jews in Esther's day as
"the church of God."[50] Like many Puritan supporters of the Christendom
model of church-state relations before him, Edwards is prepared to affirm the
Constantinian revolution of the fourth century as providentially engineered.[51]
Despite this providential engineering, he does, however, recognize the need
for God to address the decrepitude of the old church by reviving it in order to
bless the world.[52]

Most significantly, these blessings for the church are focused on the conceptuality of "union," which becomes a *Leitmotif* within Edwards's ecclesiology. Unity is the "peculiar beauty of the church of Christ."[53] Derivatively,
the essentially personal and invisible union, which believers enjoy with God
through the Spirit, is to be prized.[54] However, the union that Edwards particularly highlights in this treatise is a visible union among the regenerate, with
participation in the Concert of Prayer as a valued expression and an example of the "social embodiment" of revived piety.[55] Such explicit agreement in
prayer is seen by Edwards as "one of the most beautiful and happy things
on earth, which indeed makes earth most like heaven"[56] and indeed brings
heaven to earth.[57] In an extraordinary section in Part III (Objection II, Answer
2), Edwards uses cognates of the word "visible" twenty-six times to promote
his argument that a universal movement of God's Spirit can be visibly manifested through the prayers of God's people offered at one and the same time,
though the gathering of God's people in one place is not possible.[58] Union
among professing Christians is somehow inadequate without such concrete,
visible expression:

---

50. Edwards, "Humble Attempt," *WJE* 5: 367.

51. Edwards, "Humble Attempt," *WJE* 5: 400, 402.

52. Edwards, "Humble Attempt," *WJE* 5: 321.

53. Edwards, "Humble Attempt," *WJE* 5: 365.

54. Edwards, "Humble Attempt," *WJE* 5: 315.

55. Hall, *Neglected Northampton Texts*, 58. See also James Carse, *Jonathan Edwards and the Visibility of God* (New York: Scribner's, 1967), 149, where Carse argues that the church was, for Edwards, "the most apparent good for the world."

56. Edwards, "Humble Attempt," *WJE* 5: 365.

57. Crawford, *Seasons of Grace*, 230.

58. Edwards wrote to a Glasgow correspondent making this aspiration specific: "though we dwell at a great distance, one from another here in this world, yet that we may meet together often at the *throne of grace here*, and have a joyful meeting and eternal co-habitation before the *throne of grace hereafter*." Edwards, "To the Reverend John MacLaurin," *WJE* 16: 207.

As 'tis the glory of the church of Christ, that she, in all her members, however dispersed, is thus one, one holy society, one city, one family, one body; so it is very desirable, that this union should be manifested, and become visible; and so, that her distant members should act as one, in those things that concern the common interest of the whole body, and in those duties and exercises wherein they have to do with their common Lord and Head, as seeking of him the common prosperity.[59]

This union is embedded deeply in the knowing capacity of those participating. The harmony perceived in such a gathering for united prayer could inspire further attempts at beautiful union.[60] Though sense perception is regularly presented positively by Edwards, here he nevertheless grounds this prayerful expression of unity in an ontologically realist perception of the mind:

> The encouragement or help that one that joins with an assembly in worshiping God, has in his worship, by others being united with him, is not merely by anything that he immediately perceives by sight, or any other of the external senses (for union in worship is not a thing objected to the external senses), but by the notice or knowledge the mind has of that union, or the satisfaction the understanding has that others, at that time, have their minds engaged with him the same service.[61]

Later in the treatise, the practical significance of visibility becomes increasingly evident. Preparation for the coming of Christ in his Kingdom (as distinct from his coming in his "public ministry, in the days of his flesh"[62]) will be attended by "the distinguishing between true religion and its false appearances, the detecting and exploding errors and corrupt principles, and the reforming the wicked lives of professors, which have been the chief stumbling blocks and obstacles that have hitherto hindered the progress of true religion."[63] Though Edwards is arguing gently for *ecclesiolae in ecclesiam*, he works hard to defend his proposal against the claims of the Old Light conservatives that his own views of the revival are tending toward separatism. The Concert of Prayer fulfills the function of the *collegia pietatis* in other schemes for the revival of the

---

59. Edwards, "Humble Attempt," *WJE* 5: 365.

60. Heimert, *Religion and the American Mind*, 115–16.

61. Edwards, "Humble Attempt," *WJE* 5: 374–75.

62. Edwards, "Humble Attempt," *WJE* 5: 426.

63. Edwards, "Humble Attempt," *WJE* 5: 426.

church,[64] which are made not by "separatists or schismatics," nor do they lead to "wildness or extravagance in matters of religion."[65]

It is, however, true that Edwards's use of the word "visible" is somewhat of an innovation and could lead to confusion. Though Puritans before him made the distinction between the visible church (those who professed the creeds and participated in the sacraments, without scandalous living) and the invisible church (the elect known only to God mingling with those who are not elect during regular worship), Edwards applies the language of visibility to those who make themselves distinct from those mere professors, who are not necessarily regenerate. True members of Christ's body are described, in this appeal at least, as visible, not invisible. With renewed confidence in the work of God within history, renewed emphasis on regeneration and "vital Christianity and the power of godliness,"[66] and consequently the role of members of the church to be the means through which Christ's Kingdom is seen as glorious in the world, it is no wonder that Edwards's chief goal in writing the *Humble Attempt* is to promote the visible unity of the true church of God:

> There is a repeated use of the language of glory, and a repeated stress on not just on [sic] unity, but on its visibility. Edwards's great vision of these concerts of prayer is that the Church will be united and be seen to be united, and that is what God will use in part to answer the prayers of the Church, as others see this glorious unity and are drawn to God as a result…unity, in the rich sense of communal consent, is essential to the very being of the Church. Equally, if God is to be glorified by this unity, it must be seen, and so the Church's necessary unity must be visible unity.[67]

This combination flags a new stage in ecclesiology. While the sixteenth-century reformers built their doctrine of church, somewhat polemically, on the twin foundations of the faithful preaching of the Word and due administration of the sacraments, Edwards moves beyond this most clerical definition by presenting the fruits of regeneration expressed in visible unity as aspirationally required in the true church as well.[68] In proposing a Concert of Prayer, in negotiation with

---

64. Edwards furthermore makes an implicit case in the *Humble Attempt* for the distinction between "pious and civil society," which is based on a conception of the former involving a form of beauty and therefore of consent. See Hall, *Neglected Northampton Texts*, 317–18.

65. Edwards, "Humble Attempt," *WJE* 5: 377, 433.

66. Edwards, "Humble Attempt," *WJE* 5: 326.

67. Holmes, *God of Grace and God of Glory*, 193–94.

68. Calvin advises against presuming to be able to distinguish between the visible and the invisible church. See Calvin, *Institutes*, IV/1/ii, or IV/1/vii.

other ministers, he is of course still making the minister's authority central to the revival of the church.[69] At another level, however, he is leveling the ground on which both clergy and laity together stand and, in McDermott's estimation, applied the Great Commission in new ways, with high regard for praying and "only marginal place to preaching as the stimulus which prompts outpourings of the Holy Spirit upon the earth."[70] A common meeting, outside of the time assigned for regular prayer, preaching, and sacraments, tends to the equality of those participating.[71]

A more organic model of church is on view. An apparently administrative appeal to participate in a prayer meeting has provided a window into Edwards's openness to innovate, his international credentials, his millennial expectations, and his break with more traditional Puritan categories of ecclesiology. For Edwards, the church of God ought increasingly to demonstrate visibly its universal reach, along with purity of lives and unity of faith, characteristics that reflect the being of God himself. The traditional marks of the church in the Apostles' Creed as catholic and holy are given new experiential loading. God uses concrete means to achieve his work in the world and validates those means visibly through the work of his Spirit. The piety encouraged in the *Humble Attempt* begins to redefine the purity and unity of the church. Crawford summarizes:

> Just as salvation comes to individual souls through the means administered by the church, so too the redemption of the world comes through the community of the saved.[72]

4.2 The Church's Missiological Challenge in The Life of Brainerd

The Life of Brainerd (1749) is an edited compilation by Edwards of the diary and journal of the eighteenth-century missionary to the North American Indians, David Brainerd (1718–1747). It is a series of highly introspective, often depressing, yet always provocative entries by a man orphaned in his youth, suffering

---

69. Edwards, "Humble Attempt," *WJE* 5: 435.

70. Gerald R. McDermott, "Missions and Native Americans," in *The Princeton Companion to Jonathan Edwards*, ed. S. H. Lee (Princeton: Princeton University Press, 2005), 259.

71. Edwards, "Humble Attempt," *WJE* 5: 366.

72. Crawford, *Seasons of Grace*, 231.

from the physical effects of tuberculosis as well as the misguided remedies of eighteenth-century medicine,[73] but who nevertheless perseveres in his task of bringing the Gospel to indigenous peoples and sees some eighty converted. Brainerd's own youthful earnestness (he died at the age of twenty-nine)—and the belief that a revival of religion among the indigenous peoples would accelerate the coming of the millennium and the return of Christ—motivated his mission.[74] He almost accidentally pioneered a new way of ministering by living "on terms set by the life of a society other than one's own," which we would know as cross-cultural mission.[75]

Starting with Brainerd's ambiguous place in the Christendom model of ministry and his experiences *in extremis*, it is my contention in this section that *The Life of Brainerd* not only presents Brainerd's private reflections on his own cross-cultural endeavors but also, through polemical drafting, provides Edwards's own commentary on the inadequacies of the Christendom model of ecclesial life and strategies for repristinating the relationship between the church and its social setting.[76] The liminal position of New England society brings into clear relief the changing fortunes of the Puritan project at the perimeter of the British dominions and raises questions concerning the adequacy of territorial assumptions in ministry.[77] New impulses for understanding the church and its mission were generated not at the center of

---

73. An example of such a misguided remedy was the advice that riding horseback over uneven ground could cure consumption by acting as an expectorant for coughing up blood!

74. Norman Pettit, "Editor's Introduction," in *The Life of Brainerd*, The Works of Jonathan Edwards 7, ed. N. Pettit (New Haven: Yale University Press, 1985), 1–2.

75. Andrew F. Walls, "Missions and Historical Memory: Jonathan Edwards and David Brainerd," in *Jonathan Edwards at Home and Abroad: Historical Memories, Cultural Movements, Global Horizons*, ed. D. W. Kling and D. A. Sweeney (Columbia: University of South Carolina Press, 2003), 256.

76. As examples of his editing, Edwards has left out altogether some of Brainerd's most private thoughts and sifted Brainerd's entries through his own theological grid. Edwards added commentary to explain events, changed particular words, and bookended the material first with his own "Author's Preface," then with "Some Further Remains of the Rev. Mr. David Brainerd," "An Appendix containing some Reflections and Observations on the Preceding Memoirs of Mr. Brainerd," and "A Sermon Preached on the Day of the Funeral of the Rev. Mr. David Brainerd." The Yale edition then includes some correspondence related to Brainerd's ministry. Jonathan Edwards, *The Life of Brainerd*, The Works of Jonathan Edwards 7, ed. N. Pettit (New Haven: Yale University Press, 1985). The interplay between Brainerd's example and Edwards's commentary is in evidence on the title page when we contrast the heading "Account of the Life" in *large* print with the explanation in *smaller* print: "Chiefly taken from his [Brainerd's] own Diary and other private writings, written for his own use." This work is distinctly Edwardsean, though at first it was Brainerd and not Edwards who was regarded as the most important contributor to its content. For a reproduction of the title page, see Edwards, *WJE* 7: vii.

77. See Andrew F. Walls, "The Eighteenth-Century Protestant Missionary Awakening in Its European Context," in *Christian Missions and the Enlightenment*, ed. B. Stanley (Grand

Empire, but at its periphery, through cohabitation of a land with non-Christian peoples. *The Life of Brainerd* opens doors for understanding the life and ministry of the church in mid-eighteenth-century New England and gives recognition to Edwards's concern for new forms to defend received faith.

The Limits of Territorial Christianity and Brainerd's Vocation

David Brainerd aspired to a settled pastoral ministry, the model for which was an accepted feature of New England life: one man, one church, one geographically defined ministry. The shape of such a pastoral charge was integral to the bigger conceptuality of Christendom, which "consisted of contiguous territory ruled according to the law of Christ by Christian princes subject to the King of kings, with no public place for idolatry, or blasphemy, or heresy."[78] The Roman Catholic world had exemplified such a crusading, or Christendom, model of extra-European Christian expansion in the sixteenth century,[79] which through the Jesuit order and the maritime experience of Portugal in particular had successfully prosecuted a missiological agenda, for example, Francis Xavier's endeavors in the East Indies, Japan, and China.[80] Imperial expansion was an apt compatriot with territorial Christianity.

In New England, the theocratic ideal was a variation on this Christendom theme, although for the first time in a millennium, Christians were living as neighbors with unbelievers, not having to cross oceans to minister among them. The earlier established "crusading" model of engagement with non-European peoples gradually gave way to a more missionary model of interaction and reciprocity.[81] With an attractional model of ministry as essential to the founding rhetoric of the "city on a hill," the strategy to win American

---

Rapids: Eerdmans, 2001); Carpenter, "New England Puritans," 520–21; and Ward, *The Protestant Evangelical Awakening*, 78, who builds the case for resistance to imperial assimilation in Silesia or Moravia as factors contributing to revivals there. Suggestively, Sweeney sees in the early eighteenth century a transgression of "the ethnic, geographical, and confessional zoning system that had long divided the citizens of Western Christendom—for the sake of promoting revival and conversion cooperatively." See Douglas A. Sweeney, "Evangelical Tradition in America," in *The Cambridge Companion to Jonathan Edwards*, ed. S. J. Stein (Cambridge: University Press, 2007), 217.

78. Walls, "Missions and Historical Memory," 248.

79. Walls, "Missions and Historical Memory," 249.

80. Walls, "The Eighteenth-Century Protestant Missionary Awakening," 27.

81. John B. Carpenter, "Puritan Missions as Globalization," *Fides et Historia* 31(2) (1999): 103–23, especially 107.

Indians to the cause of Christ was unlike the received imperial model, which assumed military conquest. Though not mandated in the New England vision of the Christian society, nevertheless skirmishes and battles with the indigenous tribes and clans of the Northeast did regretfully eventuate: the King Philip's War (1675–1676) between the settlers and the Indians led by the Wampanoag chief Metacom, also known as Philip, made, for all practical purposes, the evangelistic mission of the Massachusetts colonists impossible.

Brainerd's early vocation was however interrupted by his expulsion from Yale in 1741–1742 due to attendance at a revival meeting and to the private indiscretion of comparing a graceless chair with a graceless tutor. The college was determined to make an example of his enthusiasm and to stop revivalist fervor in its tracks. The college's attitude in turn fueled revivalist resentment toward the clerical establishment, for which it stood, and toward its understanding of the ministerial role.[82] Brainerd re-routed his vocation and became a preacher to Indians of Kaunaumeek, New York; Crossweeksung, New Jersey; and Susquehanna, Pennsylvania. Without the imprimatur of the established church hierarchy, he was strengthened in his ministry aspiration by the model of John Eliot ("Apostle to the Indians"), who in the seventeenth century had established fourteen "Praying Towns" to provide protection, catechism, and economic security for the Native American population.[83]

Territorial Christianity functions as the key to grasp the significance to ecclesiology of Brainerd's ministry among the indigenous population. Competing spheres of Christian influence brought different experiences to the Indians contacted or converted by Europeans. It was not just that the Indians had to decide for the folk religion of the powwow or the Christian Gospel; they also had to decide between the rival claimants to Christian hegemony—the French Roman Catholic missionaries, traders and soldiers west of the Appalachians navigating south on the Mississippi, and the European Protestant (including English and Puritan) colonizers, landholders, and educators along the Atlantic coastal plain.[84] Not surprisingly, these encounters

---

82. Joseph Conforti, "Jonathan Edwards's Most Popular Work: The *Life of David Brainerd* and Nineteenth-Century Evangelical Culture," *Church History* 54(2) (1985): 188–201, especially 188.

83. Richard W. Cogley, "John Eliot's Puritan Ministry," *Fides et Historia* 31(1) (1999): 1–18.

84. These Indian contacts were often located in the dense and uninviting forests, mountains, and foothills of the Appalachian chain, forming the border between English and French spheres of influence, which between 1756 and 1763 would explode into colonial fighting known as the Seven Years' War (to the Europeans) or the French and Indian Wars (to the Americans). From a European perspective, winning the Indians was strategic militarily, as James Fenimore Cooper's *The Last of the Mohicans* makes so clear.

generated moral dilemmas: entrepreneurs were encouraged to speak the Gospel as they traveled to find new markets or to source furs, food, and labor, presenting a conflict of interests to both those offering and those receiving their ministrations. Bringing "civilization to the natives" might offer new economic and educational opportunities, but more often could destroy traditional cultures and languages, disperse tribes from their ancestral lands, and introduce disease, vice, and anomie into village life. Brainerd ministered among Indians who had already been affected by colonial pressures.

However, there was more to the attempts to bring the Gospel to the indigenous peoples of America than imperial motivation. Theological factors shaped the encounter as well. When the Puritans made efforts to preach the problem of human sinfulness and its solution in redemption only through the name of Christ, they were treating Indians with dignity and equality. Not to preach sin and salvation in this way would have been to deny that Indians were of the same stuff as the remainder of the human race.[85] The conversion of Indians demonstrated God's acceptance of them and the propriety of the revivals themselves.[86] Though there was the belief among some Christians that North American Indians had been trapped by the Devil in a continent as yet unreached by the Gospel, this did not obviate their need as men and women made in the image of God to hear Christian proclamation on the same basis and terms as the English themselves had heard it when still living in pagan darkness.[87] Puritan assumptions concerning the dignity of the native population were often at odds with those of political ideologies.

Alongside preaching, Puritans also expected that the Indians should be treated as equals by including them under the laws of the land and its economic system, though not at the expense of their language and survival. In the minds of the English, encouraging the Indians to pursue a vocation would be a way to help them avoid mischief and to inculcate discipline for the sake of sanctification.[88] Brainerd's model of living among the Indians but not expecting the Indians to settle in the midst of Europeans attests to his desire to affirm a distinct method of Christian outreach. Encouraging a township to grow around his own cottage equated with the belief that to receive civilization in the European cities was not necessary preparation for Christian conversion:

---

85. Rachel Wheeler, "'Friends to Your Souls': Jonathan Edwards' Indian Pastorate and the Doctrine of Original Sin," *Church History* 72(4) (2003): 736–65, especially 759, where reference is made to the doctrine of original sin as guarantor of spiritual equality.

86. Ward, *The Protestant Evangelical Awakening*, 272.

87. Carpenter, "New England Puritans," 521.

88. Carpenter, "New England Puritans," 524.

December 31 [1746]…The Indians are now gathered together from all quarters to this place, and have built them little cottages, so that more than twenty families live within a quarter of a mile of me. A very convenient situation in regard both of public and private instruction.[89]

This was not evangelism by absorption into white culture, but separation from both traditional and European forms for the sake of spiritual independence. The Christendom model was inadequate insofar as it would use coercion to deny Indians any ongoing cultural or linguistic distinctives and expect clear allegiance to one European system or another. Brainerd rather used persuasion, expressed through an interpreter named Moses Tinda, to pursue the cause of Christ in his part-sedentary, part-itinerating ministry. Brainerd's ministry at the edge of the known world was reshaping pastoral vocation.

Brainerd's remunerative network was also innovative. Structures that had been created to serve different social settings were redefined and their modus operandi reconfigured. For example, organizations like the Society in Scotland for Propagating Christian Knowledge (organized in 1701 and chartered by Queen Anne in 1709) or the Society in London for Propagating the Gospel in New England and Parts, which were originally incorporated to support a traditional model of parochial ministry, were now raising money for Brainerd's work outside of the parochial structure. His contractual association with these societies in the broader church creates a transatlantic layer of responsibility, yet his distance from accountability highlights to all intents and purposes his individual autonomy. His outreach among the Indians of the Six Nations was neither territorially constrained nor clerically defined, but was internationally inspired and underwritten. The Life of Brainerd was promptly translated into German, and was published first by Fresenius and then by Steinmetz as tokens of its appeal beyond British borders.[90]

His personal support network is another striking feature of Brainerd's diary. The number of friends and ministerial colleagues with whom he remains in contact, or with whom he stays and seeks the opportunity of recuperation in his many sicknesses, is prodigious. He frequently returns to New York, Long Island, or Boston to consult with his sponsors, to seek aid, and to refresh his ailing body and spirit. Indeed, Pettit, in his introduction to the Yale edition of Brainerd, enumerates these figures under the headings "Family," "Evangelists," "Adversaries," "Friends," "Associates," and "Confidants."[91] It is

---

89. Edwards, WJE 7: 350–51.

90. Ward, The Protestant Evangelical Awakening, 275.

91. Pettit, "Editor's Introduction," 32–71.

a dizzying constellation. It is not just that Brainerd seeks their company but also covets their prayers, both while he is with them and when he is away. Edwards's *Humble Attempt,* published a year earlier, had described the links between prayer, revival, and mission that Brainerd now exemplifies as an appropriate preparation and support of missionaries in the field. New means for new opportunities were accepted.[92] Edwards sees these convergences as something worthy of emulation and broadens the purpose of the church to include missionary expectation:

> I think we have reason to hope that the wonderful things which God wrought among them by him are but a forerunner of something yet much more glorious and extensive of that kind; and thus may justly be an encouragement to well-disposed charitable persons to "honor the Lord with their substance" [Prov. 3:9] by contributing as they are able, to promote the spreading of the Gospel among them; and this also may incite and encourage gentlemen who are incorporated and entrusted with the care and disposal of those liberal benefactions which have already been made by pious persons to that end; and likewise the missionaries themselves that are or may be employed; and it may be of direction unto both as to the proper qualifications of missionaries and the proper measure to be taken in order to their success.[93]

Such renewal in structures was decidedly, however, not an end in itself, but a means to the arrival of the millennial Kingdom. The conversion of the Indians was the most proximate step toward the defeat of the Antichrist and all that held back the coming of the Kingdom. Christendom was not just inadequate to modern conditions, but it also inadequately subserved a more cosmic ideal. Marsden suggests that their eschatology was even intended to have an impact upon political structures in order to prosper the coming Kingdom.[94]

However, despite the fact that the colonization of New England had at least in part been driven by the missiological desire to evangelize the indigenous population and to provide a model to Old England of a Christian Commonwealth, early attempts at mission among the North American Indians had not been

---

92. Hindmarsh suggests that just as roads enabled mission in the early church, and the printing press multiplied the effects of the Reformation, so the Awakenings appropriated new methods, focused in individual agency. Bruce Hindmarsh, "Is Evangelical Ecclesiology an Oxymoron? A Historical Perspective," in *Evangelical Ecclesiology: Reality or Illusion?*, ed. J. G. Stackhouse Jr. (Grand Rapids: Baker Academic, 2003), 29.

93. Edwards, *WJE* 7: 533.

94. Marsden, *A Life*, 334, 338.

spectacularly successful. Though John Eliot may have seen greater fruit for his labors than many of his contemporaries laboring among Europeans, his was the exception that proved the rule. As Carpenter points out:

> Like most Protestants, the Puritans had not developed the church struc-
> tures to carry out mission.... Though they had the highest percentage
> of clergy to populace in the European world, they were handicapped by
> their assumption that a true minister must have a church.... It is easy
> to look back and assume that Protestants should have intuitively known
> how to organize missions structures and go about the work; but in real-
> ity, the lessons we take for granted today had to be hard won.[95]

However, a new stage in missions was dawning. The use of various and innovative means to reach the heathen was later to be emphasized by William
Carey in his tract of 1792, though such a strategy had previously been pioneered, for example, in the exertions of the German Pietists in the Tranquebar
mission in South India and by Brainerd himself. He exemplifies the value of
creative modeling and the need for renewal of church life in a distinct and
emerging New World ecclesiological context.

The Reversion to Totalizing Christianity and Brainerd's Piety

Nominal Christian commitment, often a partner with territorial Christianity,
was something that the Puritans could not abide and was, of course, part of
the reason for early migrations to New England to set up a new "model of
charity," in the words of Winthrop. Although their assumptions did not focus
on the need to crusade and conquer, they were nevertheless people of their
own time who perpetuated the Christendom model of church-state codepen-
dency to create a godly Commonwealth ordered through covenantal gearing.
They were, as Walls asserts, "totalitarian Christians, those for whom the religious imperatives overcame the economic and political."[96] Each part of social
life was connected to every other part, even when the church in the middle of
community experience was conceived congregationally and not with presby-
teral or episcopal coordination. Carpenter makes the point:

95. Carpenter, "New England Puritans," 520–21.

96. Walls, "Missions and Historical Memory," 249.

Mission for the Puritans required far more than a few missionaries; it demanded the transplantation of a whole social system. For Puritans, since missions was [sic] the extension of God's rule…it was more than church planting and certainly far more than individual conversions. They envisioned, since they assumed all people were made in the image of God, a united civil-ecclesial community. Of course, their holistic approach to mission opens up the Puritans to criticism for using religion for political ends.[97]

Brainerd's more traditional social assumptions and his acceptance of Reformed patterns can be seen where he catechizes his Indian converts. He has high standards and great hopes for the Indians, their Christian obedience, and sacramental observance. As quoted in his *Journal*, from which Edwards excerpts material regarded as significant to include in the *Life*, Brainerd writes: "Saturday, August 24 [1745]…Spent the forenoon in discoursing to some of the Indians, in order to their receiving the ordinance of baptism…April 7 [1746]. Discoursed to my people at evening from 1 Cor. 11:23–26. And endeavored to open to them the institution, nature, and ends of the Lord's Supper, as well as the qualifications and preparations necessary to the right participation of that ordinance."[98] Brainerd's expectation of Indian converts was not unlike what he would have desired for Anglo-American believers generally.[99] As Wall summarizes:

Not surprisingly, the early Protestant movement, which was principally evangelical in character, initially brought to the non-Western world the same message and the same methods that it brought to the nominally Christian world which produced evangelical radicalism. And it expected the responses (and evangelicals had plenty of experience within Christendom of hostile or indifferent response) to be along the same lines.[100]

---

97. Carpenter, "Puritan Missions as Globalization," 110.

98. Edwards, *WJE* 7: 317, 381.

99. It is easy to draw attention to the blind spots of the Puritans in their attitudes to *the Indians*, but perhaps less easy to acknowledge our own prejudices toward *the Puritans*: "To assume that their [seventeenth-century Puritans'] behavior toward Native Americans was simply motivated by hypocrisy, cynicism, and greed is to fail to take on board the historical and cultural context, the structure of belief, which they inhabited—in other words, to be as blinkered in relation to them as they in turn were in relation to the Native Americans." See Richard Francis, *Judge Sewall's Apology: The Salem Witch Trials and the Forming of an American Conscience* (New York: Harper Perennial, 2005), 16–17.

100. Walls, "Missions and Historical Memory," 258.

It is important to understand, however, that the essential narrative arc of *Brainerd* is driven not by external events but by internal reactions to the conditions of life and mission that he faces. This work presents a model of piety, not so much a program of ecclesiastical reform or a platform for church growth. The disinterested benevolence that became the hallmark of virtue for Christians engaged in mission in the nineteenth century can at times appear here like self-absorbed malevolence with introspection rather than inculturation the theme. The progress of his own godly character becomes for Brainerd an important source of assurance of salvation. Edwards alerts us in his "Appendix" to the way that Brainerd prized personal piety above ecstatic or revivalist experiences:

> I find no one instance of a strong impression on his imagination through his whole life: no instance of a strongly impressed idea of any external glory or brightness, of any bodily form or shape, any beautiful majestic countenance: no imaginary sight of Christ hanging on the cross with blood streaming from his wounds; or seated in heaven on a bright throne with angels and saints bowing before him; or with a countenance smiling on him; or arms open to embrace him.... But the way he was satisfied of his own good estate, even to the entire abolishing of fear, was by feeling within himself the lively actings of a holy temper and heavenly disposition, the vigorous exercises of that divine love which casts out fear: This was the way he had full satisfaction soon after his conversion.... And we find no other way of satisfaction through his whole life afterward.[101]

In setting up Brainerd as the prototype of regenerate piety in this way, Edwards wants to challenge nominal faith and a myopic vision of the Kingdom of Christ in its European guise, and not in the first instance to create a hero of someone who incidentally labors among Indians. Edwards presents Brainerd as a man of great perseverance despite incapacity, prayer despite doubt, and self-sacrifice despite meager resources. Brainerd embodied a generic evangelical piety.[102] Such character is the necessary ingredient to all renewal and

---

101. Edwards, *WJE* 7: 503–04. Distance from "blood and wounds" spirituality creates a contrast with the Moravians, especially Zinzendorf, for whom this particularly vivid imagery served regenerative ends. Their christomonistic mysticism demonstrated an aversion to doctrinal precisionism, Enlightenment categories, and engagement with structural reform. Edwards wants to maintain Brainerd's distance from this type of spirituality. Ward, *The Protestant Evangelical Awakening*, 116–59.

102. Sweeney, "Evangelical Traditions," 223.

reform among the clergy and within the church.[103] Mission was regarded as the essential outworking of revived character and religious affections, which was Edwards's polemical intention in publishing these reflections:

> For Edwards, who made that [Brainerd's] life known to the world, it was primarily a demonstration of the true character, authentic experience, and proper doctrine of a Christian minister.... For Wesley...it [the expurgated version of *The Life*] was valuable not because it would call people to the mission field, but because it would teach them devotion and acceptance of harsh conditions in their service in England. For Wesley and Edwards alike, what we would call the cross-cultural aspect of Brainerd's work was coincidental.[104]

Brainerd is a potent sign that the revivals are neither moralistic nor enthusiastic, but doctrinal and affective. His zeal "ran off neither into pharisaism on the one hand nor antinomianism on the other."[105] Such a model of piety has not merely an impact on those who have not heard the Gospel, but also serves to validate a theological agenda embedded in Western theological debates and offers a plausibility structure for Edwards's own conception of religious affections:

> His [Brainerd's] conversion was plainly founded in a clear, strong conviction, and undoubting persuasion, of the truth of those things appertaining to these doctrines which Arminians most object against, and which his own mind had contended most about.... And if his conversion was any real conversion, or anything besides a mere whim, and if the religion of his life was anything else but a series of freaks of a whimsical mind, then this one grand principle, on which depends the whole difference between Calvinists and Arminians, is undeniable, viz., that the grace or virtue of truly good men not only differs from the virtue of others in degree, but even in nature and kind.[106]

---

103. Edwards, *WJE* 7: 520, 530.

104. Walls, "Missions and Historical Memory," 256.

105. Ward, *Early Evangelicalism*, 144.

106. Jonathan Edwards, "An Appendix Containing some Reflections and Observations on the Preceding Memoirs of Mr. Brainerd," in *The Life of David Brainerd*, The Works of Jonathan Edwards 7, ed. N. Pettit (New Haven: Yale University Press, 1985), 522–23.

It is a commonplace to see the theological distinctive of the eighteenth-century revivals in their commitment to regeneration and the experience of sanctification. Although a divine forensic declaration has no necessary visible outcome, the organic nature of the new birth must surely be witnessed through human senses. Indeed, *Brainerd* becomes the concrete and visible expression of the very principles that *Religious Affections* teaches more abstractly.[107] Edwards's final prayer in the "Appendix" makes not just of Brainerd's circumstances, but of his individual example as well, a means to inspire future mission and revival.[108]

This theological agenda itself spawned a social vision, for Brainerd's piety confirmed orthodoxy and order, with a dynamic center. The key to the renewal of the church, both doctrinally and structurally, and the extension of God's rule, in America as elsewhere, was the conversionist piety of its leadership. Conservative Calvinism may have inadvertently discouraged exertion in the conversion of unbelievers or the awakening of the nominal, but Edwards wants to defend theological anti-Arminianism while at the same time espousing evangelistic enterprise. For him, the sovereignty of God is the basis for mission, not its enemy.[109] God would achieve his own ends with the aid of new material means,[110] but those ends did not lead to the disembowelment of Christianized society, but rather to the radical recentering of such society in the personal piety of its representatives. This church did not yet prosper "on others' terms," but the fracture of Puritan social consensus in the revivals was nevertheless a harbinger of a world in which the church in New England would no longer occupy a privileged position.

The juxtaposition of missionary endeavors and autobiographical expression in the person and writings of Brainerd, as they are transmitted to us through the hand of Edwards, makes the point clear. We see from outside the paradigm more distinctly than from within that Edwards's agenda is to repristinate the local church through personal spiritual renewal in order to shape the world for Christ. The territorially defined church is relativized without being marginalized. The church grows comfortable with a missionary edge, though missiological considerations do not yet drive ecclesiology. The ministry

---

107. Marsden, *A Life*, 331.

108. Edwards, *WJE* 7: 541.

109. Carpenter, "New England Puritans," 527. The distinction between natural and moral ability, which empowers for mission, is a theme in Edwards's later writing. See Edwards, *WJE* 1: 156–59.

110. Carpenter, "Puritan Missions as Globalization," 119.

of David Brainerd provides an opportunity for us to approach missiology as a prism through which eighteenth-century ecclesiology can be reconstructed.

4.3 The Church's Visible Union in An Humble Inquiry

At the end of the 1740s, Edwards undertook a massive review of the nature of the Lord's Supper as it was experienced and practiced in his congregation in Northampton. He wanted to expose assumptions concerning this ordinance tenaciously held by Solomon Stoddard and his supporters, both in Northampton and in surrounding towns in western Massachusetts, who had essentially practiced a policy of open communion, disbarring from the sacrament only those who were notorious sinners. Edwards prompted a reconsideration of deeper contentions concerning the relationship between corporate and personal covenants, which in turn revisited the trajectory of New England theology, both sacramental and otherwise, and brought to the surface simmering pastoral tensions between him and his people.[111] In some minds in Northampton, being a citizen of a nation covenanted to God required participation in the Lord's Supper, irrespective of the presence of heightened religious sensibilities, such were the interlocking assumptions concerning public and personal covenants and God's expectations of all of life.

The discourse that provoked the debate is *An Humble Inquiry into the Rules of the Word of God, Concerning the Qualifications Requisite to a Complete Standing and Full Communion in the Visible Christian Church.*[112] Here, Edwards wants to retrieve rules concerning admission to the sacrament from the Scriptures rather than from the Congregational Way,[113] and to revise grandfather Stoddard's practice by admitting to full communion only those who are "in profession, and in the eye of the church's Christian judgment, godly or gracious persons."[114] Edwards would thereby create a distinction between groups within the local church, some confessedly in full communion and

---

111. See Ava Chamberlain, "'We Have Procured One Rattlesnake': Jonathan Edwards and American Social History" (paper presented at the American Society of Church History Conference, Seattle, Washington, January 2005), 11, where Chamberlain outlines the growing importance of social history in understanding events like Edwards's dismissal.

112. Hereafter referred to in the text as the *Humble Inquiry*. The first part of the discourse is a summary of the position being argued. The second part comprises eleven subpoints, elaborating on the thesis. The third part answers objections being raised against his views.

113. Hall, "Editor's Introduction," *WJE* 12: 68.

114. Jonathan Edwards, *Ecclesiastical Writings*, The Works of Jonathan Edwards 12, ed. D. D. Hall (New Haven: Yale University Press, 1994), 174.

others not.[115] This is a high-stakes maneuver that ultimately resulted in his dismissal from the church after twenty-three years of service. The reason this particular dispute had such dire outcomes has been a persistent question in colonial American history, with an extraordinary variety of explanations.

It is of course true that Edwards handled a number of presenting pastoral issues in maladroit fashion in the years immediately preceding the dismissal. The intrusive Edwards has been described, who in 1744 mishandled the "Bad Book Affair." He not only named publicly those youths in the church who consulted a chapbook's midwifery diagrams (an eighteenth-century version of seeking out pornography) and used the information gained to deride young women, but he also named without any qualification those who were witnesses but not participants in the episode. This, not surprisingly, infuriated families of good reputation in the town.[116] Ava Chamberlain has outlined these arguments to provide background to Edwards's surprising dismissal, presenting someone not entirely comfortable with recently renegotiated boundaries of sexual propriety.[117]

Simmering resentment surfaced when Edwards finally presented to the eldership of Northampton his desire to revisit communion qualifications, but only after salary negotiations had been finalized and subsequent to the death on June 19, 1748, of Colonel John Stoddard, an erstwhile supporter of Edwards but also a fierce advocate of Solomon Stoddard's more inclusive policies on worthy participation in the Supper.[118] Clumsy responses by Edwards to actual incidents of sexual immorality were similarly incendiary: in 1749, after a council had been convened to hear the matter, despite Edwards's instruction, neither Lieutenant Elisha Hawley nor Thomas Wait would marry the women they had deflowered, respectively Martha Root and Jemima Miller. Edwards's authority was thereby challenged by some leading Northampton clans, the Hawleys and the Pomeroys, of whom a daughter was later to marry Lieutenant Hawley![119] Some measure of pastoral ineptitude made turbid the

115. Edwards acknowledges the widespread practice of admitting "to baptism on lower terms than to the Lord's Supper," although he confesses that regarding change to the criteria for baptism, "there is scarce any hope of it." See Edwards, "To Thomas Foxcroft," *WJE* 16: 283.

116. Sweeney, "The Church," 183–84.

117. Ava Chamberlain, "Edwards and Social Issues," in *The Cambridge Companion to Jonathan Edwards*, ed. S. J. Stein (Cambridge: University Press, 2007), especially 338.

118. Strange, "Visible Sainthood," see especially 127, 131.

119. Murray, *Jonathan Edwards*, 316.

waters of pastoral relations in Northampton and further confirmed for many (men in particular) Edwards's intrusive style.[120]

Edwards is furthermore occasionally portrayed as socially hostile, for it is argued he had a long-running vendetta with the Williams clan, a wealthy and influential New England family for whom tightening communion requirements represented an attack on their liberal or Arminian principles. This approach was advanced by Sereno Edwards Dwight (Jonathan's great-grandson) in the nineteenth century and more recently by Perry Miller, David Hall, and Edwards Davidson.[121] Another theory presents the naïve Edwards as a victim of growing capitalist and democratic forces, which Edwards was unprepared to face. Self-assured exponents of the free market would broach no ministerial impediments to their reckless greed.[122] Captain Ephraim Williams wrote scathingly of Edwards: "I am sorry that a head so full of divinity should be so empty of politics."[123] Ola Winslow popularized this theory in the 1940s. Coupled with this position were Edwards's ongoing grievances concerning "settlement" or remuneration throughout the 1740s, which were frequently viewed by townsfolk as greedy and unrealistic, though such conflicts were not limited to Edwards and his relationship with the church in Northampton.[124]

Nor is the portrayal of the frightened Edwards adequate.[125] This interpretation supposes that Edwards, when backed into a corner, reverted to type and exercised an outmoded authoritarian leadership style better suited to the seventeenth century than the increasingly democratic structures of

---

120. The details of pastoral breakdown in the parish are examined in detail in Tracy, *Jonathan Edwards, Pastor*, 147–70, and in Marsden, *A Life*, 341–74. Minkema lays great weight on the demographic factors contributing to poisoned pastoral relationships and consequently the dismissal. Kenneth P. Minkema, "Old Age and Religion in the Writings and Life of Jonathan Edwards," *Church History* 70(4) (2001): 674–704.

121. Hall, "Editor's Introduction," 84–85. A similar sentiment is expressed by Edward H. Davidson, *Jonathan Edwards: The Narrative of a Puritan Mind* (Cambridge: Harvard University Press, 1968), 127.

122. This model of interpretation is most famously expressed in the writings of Perry Miller; see Miller, *Jonathan Edwards*, 218.

123. Wilson H. Kimnach, "Preface to the Period," in *Sermons and Discourses, 1743–1758*, The Works of Jonathan Edwards 25, ed. W. H. Kimnach (New Haven: Yale University Press, 2006), 28n2.

124. James W. Schmotter, "Ministerial Careers in Eighteenth-Century New England: The Social Context, 1700–1760," *Journal of Social History* 9(2) (1975): 249–67, especially 256.

125. For further espousal of this interpretation, see Tracy, *Jonathan Edwards, Pastor*, 108–11, 183–88; R. David Rightmire, "The Sacramental Theology of Jonathan Edwards in the Context of Controversy," *Fides et Historia* 21(1) (1989): 50–60, especially 53; Scheick, *The Writings of Jonathan Edwards*, 50.

eighteenth-century ministry. Although it is true that Edwards was a keen
observer of human religious psychology and that he was also undoubtedly
exasperated by the spiritual recalcitrance of members of his own congregation
and might justifiably be critiqued for dogged determination in an issue without consideration of long-term outcomes, he was not, most assuredly, merely
reactionary. He was not without theological principles, nor was he unaware of
the limitations of the New England Way as he had inherited it. The positive
theological concerns of Edwards and his ownership of innovation during the
revivals, as highlighted in this book, give us reason to pause before we accuse
him of changing the criteria for taking communion out of merely reactionary
motives.

   This chapter has as its aim not so much to reconstruct the reasons for
Edwards's dismissal, which were multifarious, as to analyze the theological
contours of his sacramental thought as they were expressed at this critical
juncture, paying particular attention to their ramifications for, or their being
framed by, his broader ecclesiology.[126] His *Humble Inquiry* is the centerpiece
of this investigation, though reference will also be made here to the later
"Misrepresentations Corrected" and his "Narrative" of the controversy.[127] Even
if his revised sacramental views had not led to his separation from the parish,
they would nevertheless be instructive for understanding theological conditions on the ground in eighteenth-century Massachusetts. Relations within
the parish were deteriorating so quickly that Edwards might well have been
dismissed by members of the congregation appealing to some other provocation, even if he had not changed his mind concerning qualifications for
complete standing and full communion.[128] His ecclesiological beliefs are in
sharpest relief in this controversy and form a natural outlet to streams of ecclesiological thought previously adumbrated.

---

126. Some of these factors are summarized in Marsden, *A Life*, 69–371.

127. These texts can be found in Edwards, *WJE* 12.

128. It appears that the actual content of his views was of little practical concern to his
church. Indeed, Edwards makes repeated reference to the fact that his parishioners were
not prepared to read his *Humble Inquiry*, and when he finally presented some weekday lectures on the contention at hand, few denizens of Northampton came, the lecture being at
least half full of "strangers," or those from out of town, presently visiting Northampton for
a meeting of the court. See Jonathan Edwards, "Narrative of Communion Controversy," in
Ecclesiastical Writings, The Works of Jonathan Edwards 12, ed. D. D. Hall (New Haven: Yale
University Press, 1994), 598. McDermott sees the communion controversy as the "formal" though not "material" grounds for his dismissal. McDermott, *One Holy and Happy
Society*, 167.

Suspicion of Separatism: Rejection of the Pure Church

Present from the beginning of the New England experiment was the dream of the pure church.[129] Though the settlers of the Massachusetts Bay Colony were not themselves committed to a disestablished church that would maintain its purity through separation from the coercion of civil society, the colony at Plymouth, having been planted ten years earlier in 1620, did espouse a covenant that renounced state support and affirmed the power of the congregation to adjudicate in all matters of dispute. Such a desire for freedom from state control and the purity of the fellowship were coordinate beliefs, for freedom provided them with the capacity to choose pure fellowship and a pure ministry.[130] Significantly, ideological support for separatism came from the marginalia printed alongside the text of the Scriptures in the Geneva Bible and used widely by Christians, and especially those dissenting, in Britain.[131] Other settlers in Massachusetts, more concerned to establish social order in a chaotic New World, brought with them the Authorized Version, without marginalia but with the imprimatur of the monarch and the assumption that their errand in this wilderness was to create a civilization founded on Scriptural blueprint, which would in time reform the polity of Britain, toward whom they had only temporarily turned their backs.

The majority church in Massachusetts, centered in Boston, was concerned for purity, but was not prepared to define the nature of the church in terms of its subjective holiness. It tended instead toward a Calvinist conception of the church's responsibility to provide for the community pastorally, rather than the Anabaptist position, which saw the church's life as a gift almost exclusively to the redeemed.[132] English Puritans had struggled in the course of the seventeenth century to hold together both conceptions of the church; the fragility of the synthesis led to imminent instability under New World conditions. The Antinomian Crisis of the late 1630s was an attempt from within the Boston establishment to create a pure church through appeal to spiritual sensation or subjective illumination as arbiter of membership. The crisis that ensued, treated elsewhere in this book, left a permanent mark on the psyche of New

---

129. George M. Marsden, *A Short Life of Jonathan Edwards*, Library of Religious Biography (Grand Rapids: Eerdmans, 2008), 36.

130. David D. Hall, *The Faithful Shepherd: A History of New England Ministry in the Seventeenth Century* (Chapel Hill: University of North Carolina Press, 1972), 39.

131. Harry S. Stout, "Word and Order in Colonial New England," in *The Bible in America: Essays in Cultural History*, eds. N. O. Hatch and M. A. Noll (New York: Oxford University Press, 1982), 25–26.

132. Hall, "Editor's Introduction," *WJE* 12: 21. See also Hall, *Neglected Northampton Texts*, 212.

World settlers for whom the preservation of external order—under constant threat from nature, the indigenous population, wars between European powers, and theological disputation—was a reflexive desire and its achievement a mark of progress.

The Congregational Way, exemplified in the New World, held the settled order of the gathered church to be of first importance in the polity of New England churches. Though historically it was the Roman Catholic Church that preached true faith as dependent on true order and Protestant denominations that had inverted the sequence, von Rohr regrets the development of something unusual among Congregationalists:

> [I]n the dissenting movement in England in the late sixteenth and early seventeenth centuries a new Protestant pattern emerged. Church order again assumed a role of significance, even of centrality, as the commands of the Lord were understood to prescribe a particular form of ecclesiastical life and also of worship.... It is only within the order which the Lord has prescribed that can arise the faith and continued faithfulness requisite for salvation. There is no question but that for these separatists the forms of ecclesiastical organization and government were no mere *adiaphora*, but were *fundamenta* in relation to God's plans for men's temporal and eternal destiny.[133]

Even though the New England churches had to make adjustments and modifications to their Congregational Way—by defining it more precisely in the Cambridge Platform (1648),[134] by allowing for a more inclusive membership in the so-called Half-Way Covenant (1662), or by acknowledging the merits of associational councils, particularly of the clergy, in the Saybrook Platform (1708)—order remained a vital principle to guarantee the propriety of salvation, even when it was not precisely separatism of the Plymouth variety being demanded.

Jonathan Edwards was adamant that his attempts to regulate access to the Lord's Supper, by expecting prospective communicants to offer a profession of their faith rather than a relation of spiritual experience,[135] was not motivated by a desire to create a pure or separatistic church, though this was the accusation leveled against him. He distances himself from such notions in the "Author's

---

133. von Rohr, "*Extra Ecclesiam Nulla Salus*," especially 107, 117.

134. Such a process of clarification was part of the work of the Westminster Assembly as well.

135. Hall, "Editor's Introduction," *WJE* 12: 61.

Preface" to the *Humble Inquiry*.[136] His requirement of a profession of faith did not assume irrefragable claims to assurance based on internal illumination, nor did it deny any contribution of ministerial means for affirmation.[137] Of the two sample professions Edwards includes in "Misrepresentations Corrected," the first makes reference to baptism and covenant and obedience to the commandments of God, while the second omits reference to baptism and covenant, but repeats the singular importance of complying with the commandments and serving God "with my body and my spirit."[138] Implicit in these professions is a denial of enthusiastic separatism that is generated by Antinomianism, disobedience, and lawlessness, just as these professions also refute the necessity of immediate and intense feelings of assurance, given that each begins with the phrase "I hope, I [do] truly find..."[139] Though writing "Misrepresentations Corrected" in 1752, long after the dispute was determined and he had been dismissed, he argued that at stake in his challenge to reform

---

136. Edwards, *WJE* 12: 170–71.

137. Jamieson describes the conundrum faced by Edwards in the 1730s concerning the criteria adduced for passing judgment on the spiritual experiences claimed by revivalists. John F. Jamieson, "Jonathan Edwards's Change of Position on Stoddardeanism," *Harvard Theological Review* 74(1) (1981): 79–99, especially 89.

138. Such a profession of faith described generically the experience of grace in one's life, while the earlier expectation of a narrative of grace differed insofar as it presented an orderly account of the progress of grace leading to conversion. Edwards promotes neither formal doctrinal assent nor the narrative of grace as sufficient to permit complete membership: both potentially excused the believer from present engagement with God. See Strange, "Visible Sainthood," especially 109. The revised statement, a modest declaration when compared to the text of the 1742 covenant renewal (see Edwards, "Letter to the Rev. Thomas Prince," especially 550–54), can be found in Edwards, "Misrepresentations Corrected," *WJE* 12: 361.

139. Edwards, "Misrepresentations Corrected," *WJE* 12: 361. See also Strange, "Visible Sainthood," 134–35, for more on Edwards's interactions with separatists on the nature of assurance. An example of separatist claims to certain knowledge of a saint's spiritual status is given through the words of Ebenezer Frothingham, a minister in Middletown, Connecticut, as cited in Hall, "Editor's Introduction," *WJE* 9: 47. Edwards's refusal to countenance experience of stages of conversion as essential to profession left him open to the accusation that he, like separatists, saw the appropriation of grace as sudden and disorderly rather than as gradual and orderly, though the very case Edwards makes for distinction between partial and complete standing within the church reimposes the majority position in New England that assumed the church's role in aiding spiritual assurance and godly growth. See further Kobrin, "The Expansion of the Visible Church in New England," 193–94. Furthermore, highlighting the sacraments in a definition of the church was unlikely to be held by a Separatist. E. Brooks Holifield, *The Covenant Sealed: The Development of Puritan Sacramental Theology in Old and New England, 1570–1720* (Eugene, OR: Wipf and Stock, 1974), 64. Any early unintentional antinomianism in Edwards's thought was later corrected. Robert W. Caldwell, *Communion in the Spirit: The Holy Spirit as the Bond of Union in the Theology of Jonathan Edwards*, Studies in Evangelical History and Thought (Milton Keynes, UK: Paternoster Press, 2006), 141.

requirements for communion was not the manner of profession or the precise formulation of words, but instead the matter that was owned, namely gracious affections in the heart:

> The controversy was, *Whether there was any need of making a credible profession of godliness, in order to persons' being admitted to full communion; whether they must profess saving faith, or whether a profession of common faith were not sufficient; whether persons must be esteemed truly godly, and must be taken in under that notion, or whether if they appeared morally sincere, that were not sufficient?* ... It was wholly concerning the *matter* of profession, or the *thing* to be exhibited and made evident or visible; and not about the *manner* of professing, and the *degree* of evidence.[140]

At heart in the contentions concerning requirements for full communion is an understanding of the theological relationship between grace and nature, a fragile connection at best in separatist thinking. Edwards maintained that the secret workings of grace in the heart must have their outward and visible expression in lifestyle and community, that is, in the regular patterns of natural life. Edwards was suspicious of the pride generated by separatist certainties growing out of their claimed clarity of personal experience.[141] Separatists' rejection of the national covenant in order to highlight the purity of a voluntary church covenant was a denial of the responsibility "even if only indirectly and incidentally, for the religious life of the larger part of the community."[142] The separatist agenda was at odds with the hegemonic and long-practiced Puritan and Christendom model. Purity was secured in the separatists' model at the expense of social stability, a position Edwards rejected.

Protest against Formalism: Critique of the National Church

Edwards's revised position on communion inadvertently appeared to connect him to Antinomians and separatists, which he energetically repudiated. It was, however, not inadvertent that Edwards distanced himself from the practices of

---

140. Edwards, "Misrepresentations Corrected," *WJE* 12: 355–56, 357 (emphasis in original).

141. Christopher Grasso, "Misrepresentations Corrected: Jonathan Edwards and the Regulation of Religious Discourse," in *Jonathan Edwards's Writings: Text, Context, Interpretation*, ed. S. J. Stein (Bloomington/Indianapolis: Indiana University Press, 1996), 26.

142. Kobrin, "The Expansion of the Visible Church in New England," 190.

sacramental theology in Northampton, which he had inherited from Solomon Stoddard. Despite misgivings and the pain of public disagreement with Stoddard's legacy, Edwards protested his right to subject all church traditions to the scrutiny of Scripture through his preaching and writing.[143] In undertaking this inquiry, he not only critiqued local conditions but also drew attention to larger national concerns, particularly the headway being made in New England theology and pulpits by Arminian moralism, which, underscored by popular religion, may well have secured stability in the Commonwealth but more perniciously also weakened the distinctives of the local church. Although a pure church may not be sociologically viable, a merely formal church could not be theologically plausible.

Provocative to his peers, Stoddard had abolished the necessity of a narrative of grace, opening participation in the Lord's Supper to all who were morally sincere, who gave assent to the doctrines of the church, and who were not notorious sinners. In Stoddard's estimation, the Lord's Supper functioned in a way commensurate with evangelistic preaching, namely, to bring sinners to faith and to establish them in godliness.[144] It had a converting function. In his opinion, it was not possible to determine with any degree of certainty who were among the elect and who were not.[145] His position drew animosity from the Mathers of Boston, among others, who frequently maligned Stoddard's motivations for introducing a new conception of membership. He was not merely acquiescing to the demands of the lax, who, under the provisions of the Half-Way Covenant, could own the covenant of baptism for themselves or their children without attesting to the work of God in their heart. He was more importantly acknowledging the spiritual confusion of many would-be communicants who, due to heightened scrupulosity, refused to take the Lord's Supper for fear of inviting judgment on themselves should they prove not to be of the elect. Stoddard "was indeed attempting to remove existing barriers to membership, but he was also criticizing the laxity, as well as the rigor, of prevailing New England practices."[146] It was however easy to impute to him overriding concern not so much for the church's purity as for the moral order of the community in which the church was located: "For Stoddard, the sacraments attested the temporal prosperity of a national Church rather than merely the spiritual blessings of a select community of regenerate saints . . . thus making

---

143. Edwards, *WJE* 12: 167–71.

144. The precise year of Stoddard's innovation is not known. Strange, "Visible Sainthood," 114.

145. Hall, "Editor's Introduction," *WJE* 12: 39.

146. Holifield, *The Covenant Sealed*, 210.

it seem as if the sacrament sealed a social contract rather than a spiritual covenant."[147] It was widely held that to maintain the integrity of a community established through covenantal obligations based in the churches, those selfsame churches had to accept more adherents into their midst, even if their own distinctives were compromised.[148]

Both Stoddard and Edwards preached for conversions, and neither man demurred against the priority of grace in the process of salvation.[149] It was, however, a lingering fear for Edwards that to take a position of extreme inclusivism on the sacraments was to aid and abet even unwittingly the growth of Arminian sentiment among the churches.[150] After his dismissal and removal to Stockbridge, Edwards wrote a letter to the church in Northampton to be appended to the tract "Misrepresentations Corrected." In it, he reminded his former parishioners (perhaps in his own mind still imagined to be under his charge) that to embrace the views of his interlocutor, Solomon Williams, minister of Lebanon, Connecticut, was not merely to reject his own sacramental theology but more ominously to reject as well Stoddard's views of the nature of saving faith (which both Edwards and Stoddard agreed upon).[151] Edwards warned against evacuating Stoddard's position of Gospel content. Oliver Crisp summarizes somewhat tersely: "The Stoddardean conception of the sacrament would then be a sort of forerunner to the rather crass postmodern notion of 'belonging, before believing.' "[152]

At first glance, Stoddard's practice in Northampton, continued by Edwards after him until repudiated in 1749, does appear inclusive and democratic, with Edwards's revised position as reactionary and aristocratic. In the older model, no degrees of access to the life of the church are maintained for those fulfilling the most moderate criteria, with epistemological modesty being applied in any case for judging. An objective definition of the church is assumed in which the settled presence of means of grace determines the possibility of access to God, not the purity of life witnessed in those who believe. Equality among parishioners is purportedly displayed.

---

147. Holifield, *The Covenant Sealed*, 217.

148. Strange, "Visible Sainthood," 113.

149. Hall, *The Faithful Shepherd*, 257.

150. Strange, "Visible Sainthood," 126.

151. Edwards, "Misrepresentations Corrected," *WJE* 12: 502–03.

152. Oliver D. Crisp, "Jonathan Edwards and the Closing of the Table: Must the Eucharist be Open to All?" *Ecclesiology* 5(1) (2009): 48–68, especially 66.

It is however a misleading representation, for the history of Puritanism in both the Old World and the New frequently oscillated between understanding the ministry as a prophetic calling to the redeemed people of God and a sacer-dotal calling that magnified the authority of the clergy and their role not only among the redeemed but also in the wider community. Stoddard may have leveled distinctions among the laity, but he reinforced his own authority and the authority of the ministerial caste as distinct from the laity: "Stoddard not only overthrew the concept of the gathered church; in repudiating the church covenant he also repudiated the congregational doctrine that the power of the keys belonged to the entire church."[153] Stoddard was effectively Presbyterian and not Congregational in his application of the rights of the clergy[154] and was known ironically as the Pope of the Connecticut River Valley for the imposing place he occupied in the local imagination. Democratic sentiment could easily be interpreted as anarchical, necessitating, for example, Stoddard's reflexive attempts to preserve and protect order. Inclusiveness with regard to the sacra-ments might justify claims to increased clerical oversight.

Just as Edwards is critical of the view of the separatists that the spiritual state of a church member can be determined with certainty, so is he criti-cal of the converse position espoused by those advocating a national church, that it is impossible to search into human souls and discover the workings of grace there. Edwards has more confidence in the powers of the congregation to determine the signs of spiritual life than Stoddard.[155] He does recognize that certainty is not attainable, but is nevertheless content with the possibility of a positive judgment:

> I mean a positive judgment, founded on some positive appearance, or visibility, some outward manifestations that ordinarily render the thing probable. There is a difference between suspending our judgment, or forbearing to condemn, or having some hope that possibly the thing may be so, and so hoping the best; and a positive judgment in favor of a person.... Though we can't know a man believes that Jesus is the Messiah, yet we expect some positive manifestation or visibility of it,

---

153. Hall, *The Faithful Shepherd*, 210.

154. Hall, *The Faithful Shepherd*, 206.

155. While his disputants would asseverate that Edwards was claiming the right to judge the state of an individual's heart, it would be more accurate to suggest that the minister together with full members of the congregation in Edwards's model had responsibility for a positive assessment of the presence of gracious affections in the heart. The issue at stake was not the distinction between the clergy and the laity as much as it was the distinction between the saved and the unsaved. See McDermott, *One Holy and Happy Society*, 170.

to be a ground of our charitable judgment....I say "in the eye of the church's Christian judgment," because 'tis properly a visibility to the eye of public charity, and not of a private judgment, that gives a person a right to be received as a visible saint by the public.[156]

The judgment of charity had become commonplace in the churches of western Massachusetts, such that the onus for any modification fell to Edwards to demonstrate.[157] He still intuitively reached for the language of charity to make his case, while articulating a position distinct from Stoddard or his own more immediate disputant, Solomon Williams.

It was also not enough in Edwards's view to make the easy parallel between the Old Testament theocracy, which was inclusive of all the Hebrews, and the church order of New England. Although, he suggests, Stoddard did indeed apply criteria established for the Passover to the Lord's Supper,[158] he points out the dangers from the Old Testament Scriptures themselves of ways in which the "covenanting or swearing into the name of the Lord degenerated into a matter of mere form and ceremony; even as subscribing religious articles seems to have done with the Church of England; and as, 'tis to be feared, owning the covenant, as 'tis called, has too much done in New England."[159] Interestingly, Edwards can use typology to justify his own approach to the God-drenched symbols of nature, but in the matter of the constitution of the church, he is much more coy.[160] In other places, Edwards makes abundantly clear that, unlike the Old Testament dispensation, the church should be understood as the congregation and not the broader community, and that the meeting of the church ought not to have the "affairs of civil societies" falling within its bailiwick.[161] He shifted the debate toward New Testament conceptualities.

Such reconsideration of the relationship between the covenanted people of New England and the people of God under the Old Testament has led Grasso to aver that the communion controversy in Northampton was much more than a debate concerning a sacrament and called into question the very ideological

---

156. Edwards, *WJE* 12: 178–79.

157. Baird Tipson, "Invisible Saints: The 'Judgment of Charity' in the Early New England Churches," *Church History* 44(4) (1975): 460–71, especially 471.

158. Edwards, *WJE* 12: 276.

159. Edwards, *WJE* 12: 213.

160. Edwards, *WJE* 12: 279.

161. Edwards, *WJE* 12: 271, 519.

underpinnings of the Puritan experiment in the New World.[162] Edwards does indeed balk at collapsing grace into nature or assuming that God's work in the church is indistinguishable from his work in the world. Edwards wants to reassert their theological distinction, a perspective he feared to be lost through an inherited and impaired policy of communion and a rising tide of enlightened anthropology washing up on the shores of New England in the form of Arminian heresy.[163]

Incorporation of Revivalism: Repristination of the Mixed Church

It is my contention that Edwards did not advocate a pure church, nor one in which the clergy ruled aristocratically without congregational consent.[164] Edwards neither dismisses the language of covenant as applied to church or nation, nor does he build his ecclesiology monomaniacally upon such a core concept.[165] Instead, we see in the discourses and letters penned around the time of the communion controversy between 1749 and 1752 an approach to the doctrine of the church that manages delicately the tensions embedded within the Puritan constitution between the Reformed/comprehensive and Anabaptist/separatist streams of polity. New challenges, generated from within the revivals and provoking reconsideration of the state of the church, gave Edwards the opportunity to work creatively with his patrimony to repristinate an ossified church.[166]

Edwards's ecclesiological standpoint attempts to hold together both objective (ministry and means of grace) and subjective (affections and godliness)

---

162. Grasso, "Misrepresentations Corrected," 20–21.

163. Grasso, "Misrepresentations Corrected," 32.

164. Edwards repeatedly argues that the pastor is not a "searcher of hearts" among his congregation. See, for example, Edwards, *WJE* 12: 312, 370, 394.

165. Although earlier twentieth-century interpreters of Edwards had assumed his rejection of covenant terminology altogether, especially in his teaching on social ethics and the place of New England in God's providential purposes, more recently the case has been made winsomely that Edwards held to covenant conceptualities, even if the language of covenant was muted. See the summary of this debate in Noll, *America's God*, 44–50. McDermott nuances Edwards's understanding of the national covenant, however, as "neither tribalist nor provincial." See McDermott, *One Holy and Happy Society*, 34.

166. The language of "repristination" draws together the features of an enduring model with desire for contemporary adaptation or refreshment and is not being used in a more confessional sense to describe the process of reclaiming a theological position from the past without any acknowledgement of present debates or concerns.

elements, as had been the assumption before the Great Awakening.[167] As with other theological debates that appeal to the notion of distinction without separation, so also in ecclesiology Edwards wants to connect the objective nature of God's consistent and regular offer of grace in the church with the subjective vicissitudes of an individual's regenerate life. To shape this synthesis, he turns to the language of communion as a bridging category, for this term suggests subjective participation in God without allowing for objective absorption into God.[168] It is Danaher's argument that the language of communion demonstrates Edwards's Puritan heritage while repristinating it in a new context:

> Edwards still implicitly maintained two central concepts of Puritan covenant theology, the covenant of redemption and covenant of grace. The difference was that while seventeenth-century Puritans put covenant in the foreground and communion in the background, Edwards did the opposite.[169]

Though Danaher draws his evidence from the sermonic corpus alongside the discourses of the communion controversy, in both cases he reflects upon the blending of the old and the new in Edwards's thought. Edwards's view of communion is moreover a blending of positions deriving from Zwingli and Calvin, namely a memorial and a means of grace.[170] For instance, Edwards joins these together:

> [I]n the minister's offering the sacramental bread and wine to the communicants, Christ presents himself to the believing communicants...and by these outward signs confirms and seals his sincere engagements to be their Savior and food, and to impart to them all the benefits of his propitiation and salvation.[171]

Both Crisp and Caldwell likewise detect, lying behind the presenting debate concerning qualifications for communion, a metaphysical commitment by Edwards to the notion of union. Whether phrased as "metaphysically real

---

167. Brauer, "Conversion," especially 240.

168. This was central to Edwards's thought. See McDermott, *One Holy and Happy Society*, 73; Cherry, *Theology*, 88.

169. Danaher, "By Sensible Signs Represented," especially 269.

170. Danaher, "By Sensible Signs Represented," 262, 265.

171. Edwards, *WJE* 12: 256.

union" or as "invisible spiritual union," the Lord's Supper confirms and enables a participation in Christ and his benefits.[172] Although the language of covenant suggests an external or legal feature of the union, Edwards qualifies its substance through proposition and illustration:

> For the covenant, to be owned or professed, is God's covenant, which he has revealed as the method of our spiritual union with him, and our acceptance as the objects of his eternal favor.... The transaction of that covenant is that of espousals to Christ; on our part, it is giving our souls to Christ as his spouse: there is no one thing, that the covenant of grace is so often compared to in Scripture, as the marriage covenant.... There are some duties of worship, that imply a profession of God's covenant: whose very nature and design is an exhibition of those vital active principles and inward exercises, wherein consists the condition of the covenant of grace, or that union of soul to God, which is the union between Christ and his spouse, entered into by an inward hearty consenting to that covenant.[173]

Such an understanding of union between the creature and the Creator, reappropriating the teaching of Calvin, assumes a purity of confession and an integrity connecting heart and mouth and life, but it reaches beyond the conceptualities of purity. The purpose for which the church has been formed is not purity *tout court* but rather union with God, of which subjective purity is an attestation.[174] Edwards broadens the conceptualities to reeducate his contemporaries. The language of covenant can highlight moral obligations expressed in obedience and purity. That same language, when pressed into service, can also highlight not just the possibility of human beings falling short but also the proximity to God that can be experienced and union with God that can be enjoyed by virtue of the covenant:

> But the union, cleaving, or joining of that covenant is saving faith, the grand condition of the covenant of Christ, by which we are in Christ: this is what brings us into the Lord. For a person explicitly or professedly to enter into the union or relation of the covenant of grace

---

172. Crisp, "Closing of the Table?," 58; Caldwell, *Communion in the Spirit*, 163.

173. Edwards, *WJE* 12: 205, 301.

174. The Apostle Paul makes a similar case: God makes the church ready for Christ, through washing and cleansing, so that she might be presented to him as the bride on the last day (see Ephesians 5:25–32).

with Christ, is the same as professedly to do that which on our part is the uniting act, and that is the act of faith. To profess the covenant of grace is to profess the covenant, not as a spectator, but as one immediately concerned in the affair.[175]

Edwards is not rejecting the language of covenant but refreshes it to give priority to an experience of grace leading to intimate and immediate union with God, which the more traditional assumptions concerning covenant might have disguised.[176] Indeed, Danaher sees in this framework one of the chief innovations in Edwards's thought. While Edwards's forebears spoke of the sacrament of the Lord's Supper in terms of sealing a covenant formally adopted, itself a soteriological assumption, by contrast, the language of union and communion bespeaks something more ontological and therefore more teleological. We experience salvation through a new way of knowing for a new way of being.[177]

In this, as in other similar cases, Edwards is attempting to make explicit the relationship between the sign and the thing signified, or between the lexical label and its existential thrust, a relationship that had been incrementally sundered due to the sociological contingencies of the New World.[178] Acerbically, he exposes the incoherence of Solomon Williams's position on the sacraments in "Misrepresentations Corrected":

> These sacramental actions all allow to be significant actions: they are a signification and profession of something: they are not actions without a meaning. . . . To say, that these significant actions are appointed to be a profession of something, but not to be a profession of the things they are appointed to signify, is as unreasonable as to say, that certain sounds or words are appointed to be a profession of something, but not to be a profession of the things signified by those words.[179]

---

175. Edwards, *WJE* 12: 206.

176. Torrance suggests that a benefit of the language of "union with Christ" comes with faith being interpreted in noncontractual terms. See James B. Torrance, "Covenant or Contract? A Study of the Theological Background of Worship in Seventeenth-Century Scotland," *Scottish Journal of Theology* 23(1) (1970): 51–76, and especially 63.

177. Danaher, "By Sensible Signs Represented," 287.

178. At one point, Edwards suggests that the whole controversy centers on words used with double meanings, often intentionally. Edwards, "Misrepresentations Corrected," *WJE* 12: 389.

179. Edwards, "Misrepresentations Corrected," *WJE* 12: 452–53 (italics in original).

If union as a theme in Christian theology—made possible by the Spirit and witnessed in the nature of the triune Godhead and in the incarnation of the Son—is to have its essential application to the individual believer, then communion in the Lord's Supper is "a concentration of what normally occurs in the course of the Christian's spiritual experiences.... The Lord's Supper for Edwards, thus powerfully weaves together and makes visible everything that is spiritually transacted in the Christian life."[180] Edwards's focus is not on the sacrament as converting (the headline position of Stoddard), nor on the sacrament as covenant seal,[181] but the sacrament as opportunity for communion with the Lord, both in the present and proleptically of the future. Edwards's revised policy of admission to the Lord's Supper is more concerned with avoiding hypocritical inclusion than accidental exclusion, for the stakes are high when the issue at stake is participation in the Lord.[182]

The language of communion, based as it is on spatial imagery of proximity or the personal imagery of intimacy, has funded extensive discussion of the eschatological implications of the *Humble Inquiry*. Heimert connects Edwards's desire for a purified congregation to future millennial hopes, with the contemporary church as a type of the future antitype. Boldly he declares that the "*Humble Inquiry* was clearly cast in an eschatological framework."[183] Carse, more poetically, sees Edwards calling for "the church to be a community of men who clearly understand their office in the world to be the vanguard, the first legion, in the long journey toward the ultimate society."[184] Richard Hall introduces his fine work on Edwards's writings of the late 1740s by asserting that the *Humble Inquiry* presents "the visible church as the earthly paradigm of a pious society and the prototype of millennial society."[185] The urgent desire for ecclesiastical reform of a worldly church is easily and logically projected onto the wider canvas of the heavenly purity of the church, or rather that future perfection gives hope to all earthly undertakings. Unbelievably, however, in none of these commentators do we find any quotation from the *Humble Inquiry* to support their case, and indeed after extensive scrutiny, nor

---

180. Caldwell, *Communion in the Spirit*, 164.

181. Rightmire expands on the nature of the seal as assurance of authenticity. See Rightmire, "The Sacramental Theology of Jonathan Edwards," 57.

182. Holifield, *The Covenant Sealed*, 229. See also Edwards's own position, advocating caution rather than indiscriminate welcome. Edwards, *WJE* 12: 310, 312.

183. Heimert, *Religion and the American Mind*, 125–26.

184. Carse, *Jonathan Edwards and the Visibility of God*, 149.

185. Hall, *Neglected Northampton Texts*, 59.

did I find any substantial eschatological material in these writings. Edwards's intentions are altogether different.

Of course, Edwards does acknowledge the existence of the coming Kingdom and interprets the wedding garment expected of those invited to the feast as their appropriation of saving grace.[186] He uses the language of glory and Kingdom and makes reference to self-examination to avoid heaping judgment upon oneself when discussing 1 Corinthians 11.[187] What he expressly does not do is make the pitch that he is enjoining a more rigorous expectation of purity upon the church to anticipate its eschatological future. This may be due to the stress in this discourse on the covenant of grace in the life of the individual, rather than the covenant of redemption as a plan for entire world order.[188] These documents certainly have a more practical and polemical flavor because they were written in the heat of debate as policy papers and not delivered in the first instance as pastorally driven sermons.[189] Danaher maintains that Edwards is putting forward an essentially negative case to deny sacramental access to some, and so starts out wrong-footed if he attempts to expound positive reasons for the practice of exclusion.[190] My reflection on this unusual omission draws upon the legal and combative demands of the situation in which Edwards personally finds himself, the recent substantive exploration of eschatology in the *Humble Attempt,* and most importantly the very present import of communing with the Lord. The Lord's Supper is not just a picture of the heavenly banquet that yet awaits us, nor is it merely a seal of a previously ratified covenant, but the birthright of the believer to enjoy Christ and his benefits now. Communion as the theme of these writings suggests a living experience of the Lord to savor and to protect and a useful practice to conjoin objective and subjective, Reformed and Anabaptist, notions of the church.

Avoidance of the language of eschatology and deliberate reconnection of the language and experience of covenant for the individual do not, however, in Edwards's mind totally neglect social forms nor inevitably lead to social discord.[191]

---

186. Edwards, "Misrepresentations Corrected," *WJE* 12: 468–69.

187. Edwards, *WJE* 12: 258–62.

188. McDermott suggests that often in New England, the language of eschatology was reserved for crises of magnitude and large-scale social critique rather than for everyday events. McDermott, *One Holy and Happy Society,* 44, 91.

189. Rightmire, "The Sacramental Theology of Jonathan Edwards," 54.

190. Danaher, "By Sensible Signs Represented," 262.

191. Indeed, there are frequent and striking usages of the language of "lawful" and its cognates in the "Misrepresentations Corrected." The absence of eschatology makes room for

The covenant providing stability for the nation is attenuated, but the union with God, which the covenant of grace protects, assumes a framework, motivation, and power for social engagement in the very world we encounter. Epistemological assurance underwrites this treatise. Voluntary ownership of the covenant by presenting one's profession to the scrutiny of the congregation can encourage consciously active and deliberate engagement with the community around.[192] Even if the order of society is not foremost in mind, a believer can contribute to its order not through coercion but through contrition, which itself is a way of reordering our desires, the better to honor God's intentions for the creation.[193] Even without explicit eschatological reflection, the mixed church in Edwards's depiction would not be reducible to the present order of the world, nor would it stand entirely outside of it, but it would act as a "spiritual preservative that protected the wider society from ruin and decay."[194] The mixed church that Edwards espouses here allows for a dynamic conception of the church as it must continually adjust itself to internal tensions, even when not eschatologically framed.

Reformed and Radical: Dynamism of the Evangelical Church

With a larger taxonomy in mind, Edwards's view of the church can be described as pastoral in that it incorporates dynamic protest toward the received structures of ministry, such protest germinated in the revivals, while at the same time he expresses appreciation of traditional means of grace and recognition of the social reality of the church. A prophetic model, drawing on the experience of the Anabaptists, presents the minister outside of the culture located within the pure church and speaking into the world with words of judgment. This stream of Puritan polity was incubated in a world of Laudian persecution, but finding themselves in the majority position in New England, such ministerial defiance had to be channeled increasingly toward concern for the whole community's

---

other ordering conceptualities. See, for example, Edwards, "Misrepresentations Corrected," 385, 474, *inter alia.*

192. Lambert makes the useful point that a public account of experienced grace tends to objectivize that which was previously subjective alone. See Lambert, *Inventing the "Great Awakening,"* 50.

193. Patricia Caldwell sees in the history of the conversion narrative in the New World a mechanism by which a centralized moral order might be established. See Caldwell, *Puritan Conversion Narrative,* 20, 35, 135–62. Charles Cohen acknowledges that such narratives could bind communities in mutual regard. Cohen, *God's Caress,* 161.

194. Danaher, "By Sensible Signs Represented," 287.

survival.[195] Edwards is on occasions prepared, wearing the mantle of a prophet, to speak out against social vice and maintain a critical distance from the regnant political groupings of his day.[196]

The priestly model, on the other hand, assumed that clerical authority has wide powers in the church and responsibilities within the broader community. Such a hierarchical and potentially static model was funded from a more Reformed view of the ministry, which acknowledged the interdependence of the church with the ministry of the magistracy and made space for the church's comprehension of the community.[197] Edwards has no hesitation in affirming some hierarchical authority for the clergy and gives it disciplinary capacity within the church in the contentions around the qualifications for communion. His approach to the sacraments is not overly sacerdotal, however, for he does regard the ministry of the Word and the priesthood of all believers highly, as the context within which to understand sacramental concerns. Neither the prophetic nor the priestly option was pursued by Edwards exclusively.

Edwards takes a position concerning the nature of the church that is neither Antinomian nor Arminian, and likewise overturns both Stoddardeanism and the Half-Way Covenant from which Stoddardeanism grew.[198] However, he is not merely reasserting the values of the Congregational Way before 1662, for he is hesitant concerning the national covenant and gives space to those honoring the covenant of grace with their own voluntary profession. Indeed, he envisions a church that has a distinct form in the world and that is yet also dynamically responsive to the concrete contingencies of the world in which it exists. His ecclesiology is elliptical, taking shape around the twin foci of Word and Spirit,[199] and is thereby classically orthodox in the Western

---

195. Hall, *The Faithful Shepherd*, 271.

196. See McDermott, *One Holy and Happy Society*, chaps. 3 and 4. Carse likewise presents Edwards as a prophet: Carse, *Jonathan Edwards and the Visibility of God*, 148.

197. Hall, *The Faithful Shepherd*, 19. The language of prophetic and priestly dimensions of ministry is often applied with sociological rather than strictly theological overtones. Interestingly, Hall contrasts the prophetic with the sacerdotal and suggests that the Reformed position lies between them and ought to be described as pastoral, though the hierarchical element is more often in Protestant writing referred to as the priestly than the sacerdotal. See also Martin E. Marty, "Two Kinds of Two Kinds of Civil Religion," in *American Civil Religion*, eds. D. G. Jones and R. E. Richey (San Francisco: Mellen Research University Press, 1990), and Davidson, *The Logic of Millennial Thought*, 10, where Davidson recognizes that ministry has traditionally appealed to both priestly and prophetic, that is comforting and challenging, categories of validation.

198. Strange, "Visible Sainthood," 126, 137.

199. Rightmire, "The Sacramental Theology of Jonathan Edwards," 55–56.

tradition, neither beholden to form nor driven by content without expression in human lives. Edwards's evangelical view of the Lord's Supper is theologically integral, therefore, to the renewed church of which he dreamed,[200] in which orderly ministrations connect to extraordinary works of God's Spirit to reorder lives and communities from below. The church is for Edwards the place where God's promise, presence, and purpose are most clearly and predictably experienced and in which Christian believers render their prayers and praise unto God.

> The critical matter was not Edwards's theology of God, humanity, or salvation; it was rather what he held about the nature of the church and the relationship of the church to society that created a substantially new context for the writing of theology. . . . As displayed sharply in *Humble Inquiry* and *Misrepresentations Corrected*, the covenant for Edwards no longer served as an all-embracing theological rationale. To make the covenant more powerful for the church, Edwards was willing to relinquish its all-purpose functions for society. It was precisely this move that also spelled the dissolution of Puritan theology as the all-purpose guardian of thought.[201]

The pervasive theory of the frightened Edwards, which accounts for his dismissal by describing a man who was not only naïve to new social forces but also reactionary, attempting to turn back the clock and reestablish a seventeenth-century model in which the pastor represented aristocratic checks and balances against the "democratic" forces of Congregationalism, is simply inadequate.[202] Patricia Tracy has eloquently prosecuted this case, arguing that "Edwards's fundamental problem was that he was much more like Stoddard (and his authoritarianism) than the Northampton of 1750 was like the Northampton of 1700."[203] To argue that Edwards reverted to type when under pressure and tried to impose an outmoded model of leadership on an

---

200. Just as this sacrament had been of paramount importance to the revivals of religion in Scotland earlier. See Schmidt, *Holy Fairs*, 49.

201. Noll, *America's God*, 44, 48. Noll here echoes earlier scholarship, which argued that Edwards surrendered the language of covenant in its social application. This position has been critiqued by Stout, among others. Stout, "Puritans and Edwards," 288.

202. "The Cambridge Platform," in *Creeds of the Churches: A Reader in Christian Doctrine from the Bible to the Present*, ed. J. H. Leith (Louisville: John Knox, 1982), Chapter X/3, 393.

203. Tracy, *Jonathan Edwards, Pastor*, 188.

unsuspecting congregation does not deal with the theological themes in his life and writing.

Edwards wants to reform an ossified Puritan ecclesiology without shaking all social norms. He gets behind the assumptions of national covenant and—in the terms of the theology of union with God, a central platform in Calvin's thinking and subsequent Reformed faith—repristinates expectations of Christian life and thinking. He is radical insofar as he goes back to the roots of the movement and does not just reapply more recent New England forms. His own reflections on his dismissal and its aftermath in the "Farewell Sermon" make abundantly clear, as we shall see in the next section, that the prophetic Edwards is a more sustainable model of reasons for espousing ecclesiological reform.

4.4 The Church's Prophetic Ministry in "A Farewell Sermon"

Only nine days after the formal separation of pastor and people, on June 22, Edwards rose to address the congregation of Northampton in what he entitled "A Farewell Sermon." It was to be a significant statement of Edwards's self-understanding in ministry and the nature of the church that he served. Not surprisingly, therefore, this was the last sermon published during his lifetime and was written not as a series of headings or "pick up lines," as Kimnach so evocatively suggests, but as a full text. While Edwards had more recently composed his sermons using two columns on a page, this sermon broke that pattern and was drafted with a single column. This was to be an unusually significant preachment for Edwards, for his congregation, and for posterity. While in one sense the sermon is a release for both pastor and people, Edwards stayed on for almost another year in Northampton to preach many other sermons until the church had settled another pastor and Edwards had decided on another position.

In another way, this sermon is not really a farewell at all, for the substantive theme of the address was the reassembling of both pastor and people before the judgment seat of Christ at his second coming, for the Lord to adjudicate with justice the case brought against Edwards by the congregation. The text for the sermon was 2 Corinthians 1:14: "As also ye have acknowledged us in part, that we are your rejoicing, even as ye also are ours, in the day of the Lord Jesus." Edwards builds upon the verse, and indeed upon the theme of conflict between the Apostle Paul and the Corinthian believers, to establish the doctrine or the thematic parameters of the sermon: "Ministers and the people that have been under their care, must meet one another, before Christ's tribunal, at the day of judgment."[204] In the first section of the sermon, Edwards outlines the reasons for and nature of that meeting, giving particular emphasis to the responsibility of ministers to prepare their people for the Great Assize and the responsibility of the people to heed the warnings of their teachers. In the Application section, Edwards provides some "reflections" and "some advice suitable to our present circumstances" by addressing particular groups within the congregation serially.[205] He addresses "professors of godliness," those in a "graceless condition," those under "some awakenings," then the youth, and lastly the children. He concludes with more general warnings to maintain family order and social cohesion, to avoid Arminian heresy and prayerlessness, and to "take great care with regard to the settlement of a minister."[206] He does all this with precision in choice of words, suspenseful arrangement of ideas, and restrained emotional engagement. His final moving sentences resonate with the mood of the Apostle at the end of 2 Corinthians.[207] Edwards writes: "Having briefly mentioned these important articles of advice, nothing remains; but that I now take my leave of you, and bid you all, farewell." Perhaps more ominously, he adds: "And let us all remember, and never forget our future solemn meeting, on that great day of the Lord; the day of infallible decision, and of the everlasting and unalterable sentence, Amen."[208] The die had been cast. The eschatological accountability of the church and its members was in view.

When a Minister Is More than a Pastor: Themes of the Sermon

The Objective Character of Ministerial Authority

For the purposes of our investigation, one of the most significant features of this sermon is the way in which it avoids the details of the communion controversy in Northampton altogether and gives valuable insights into the

---

204. Jonathan Edwards, "A Farewell Sermon Preached at the First Precinct in Northampton, after the People's Public Rejection of their Minister...on June 22, 1750," in *Sermons and Discourses, 1743–1758*, The Works of Jonathan Edwards 25, ed. W. H. Kimnach (New Haven: Yale University Press, 2006), 463.

205. Edwards, "Farewell Sermon," *WJE* 25: 474.

206. Edwards, "Farewell Sermon," *WJE* 25: 487.

207. Edwards, "Farewell Sermon," *WJE* 25: 485.

208. Edwards, "Farewell Sermon," *WJE* 25: 488.

deeper ideas concerning the nature of ministry, which generated the crisis, at least from Edwards's perspective.[209] He stands back from the questions of qualifications for communion and presents instead the divine qualifications for the ministry. He does not speak of academic preparation for ordination, a substantial theme in the early eighteenth century, because professional concerns and competition had seen the ministry downgraded in social utility with a corresponding loss of clerical prestige.[210] Nor does he make mention of charismatic gifting or enthusiastical marks for validation of authority.[211] It is instead the objective call and value of the ministry that he highlights. He is set over and against the congregation insofar as the minister is answerable to Christ alone for his service:

> Ministers are sent forth by Christ to their people on his business, are his servants and messengers; and when they have finished their service, they must return to their master to give him an account of what they have done, and of the entertainment they have had in performing their ministry.[212]

The minister in some sense stands outside the congregation, speaking into its life and concerns, representing the will and ways of God. In the course of the early eighteenth century, ordinations in New England were increasingly shaped liturgically to highlight the professional caste being entered, rather than to acknowledge the role of the laity in the ministerial call.[213] Christ's ambassador provides objective, perhaps institutional, weight when engaged in disputes. The increased authority and energy of the laity as a result of the earlier revivals is not here highlighted insofar as the clergy stand ultimately under dominical authorization, despite the activity or achievements of the congregation.[214]

---

209. Marsden, *A Life*, 361.

210. Youngs, *God's Messengers*, 11–17, 121, 127–28, and Schmotter, "Ministerial Careers in Eighteenth-Century New England," especially 249.

211. These options for validating ministry are explored further in Holifield, *God's Ambassadors*, 1–9.

212. Edwards, "Farewell Sermon," *WJE* 25:470, 473.

213. James W. Schmotter, "The Irony of Clerical Professionalism: New England's Congregational Ministers and the Great Awakening," *American Quarterly* 31(2) (1979): 148–68, especially 155.

214. MacGregor makes the point that Calvin himself held this position (*Institutes* IV/iii/1) as a strategy to defend God's own sovereignty. See Geddes MacGregor, *Corpus Christi: The Nature of the Church According to the Reformed Tradition* (London: Macmillan, 1959), 57.

Adding further provocation to the argument that the minister stands out-side the congregation, Edwards uses the image of light to reinforce his case. He asserts, for example, that ministers "are represented in Scripture as lights set up in the churches," in order to "enlighten and awaken the consciences of sinners."[215] In this way, the minister reflects something of the final day, when "the infallible Judge, the infinite fountain of light, truth and justice, will judge between the contending parties."[216] With allusion to the churches of Revelation 2 and 3, Edwards wishes for the people of Northampton a new minister who will be "truly a burning and shining light set up in this candlestick…and [for the people of Northampton to] be willing to rejoice in his light."[217] There was a time when the whole Bible Commonwealth of Massachusetts Bay Colony was described as a light on a hill, and later whole churches were referred to as New Lights (pro-revival) or Old Lights (dismissive of revival), but now it was the minister alone who was the mediate source of light for the congregation and the world, a staggering claim.[218] Consequently, the progress of the church in the history of the world was no longer equated with the progress of light, as had been an earlier assumption. When Christ returns to judge the living and the dead, it will be not as a triumph at high noon, when the sun has reached its apex, but more somberly, Christ will appear at the dawning of the day, for "the darkness of the night vanishes at the appearance of the rising sun."[219] An embattled minister adapts common cultural currency to his particular situation.

The Local Identification of the Pastor and the People

However, tantalizingly, the distinction of the pastor from the congregation is not all Edwards has to say concerning ministerial vocation. Indeed, the whole sermon has as its premise the fact that this disappointing "separation" between pastor and people is only temporary, for the bonds that unite them are stronger than some provisional and local legal verdict. There will be an

---

215. Edwards, "Farewell Sermon," *WJE* 25: 466, 467.

216. Edwards, "Farewell Sermon," *WJE* 25: 471.

217. Edwards, "Farewell Sermon," *WJE* 25: 488.

218. Helen P. Westra, "Divinity's Design: Edwards and the History of the Work of Revival," in *Edwards in our Time: Jonathan Edwards and the Shaping of American Religion*, eds. S. H. Lee and A. C. Guelzo (Grand Rapids: Eerdmans, 1999), 153. A further example of the minister being described as the congregation's light is the central motif in the following: See Jonathan Edwards, "Sons of Oil, Heavenly Lights," in *Sermons and Discourses, 1743–1758*, The Works of Jonathan Edwards 25, ed. W. H. Kimnach (New Haven: Yale University Press, 2005), 257–74.

219. Edwards, "Farewell Sermon," *WJE* 25: 466.

accounting for their conduct, one toward the other, at the Judgment, when separation or dissolution of the relationship is final. Edwards is realistic in speaking of separation in this world:

> Thus ministers and people, between whom there has been the greatest mutual regard and strictest union…may never have any more to do one with another in this world. But if it be so, there is one meeting more that they must have, and that is in the last great day of accounts.[220]

In another section, Edwards repeatedly and sonorously notes the "mutual concerns of ministers and their people,"[221] counting himself alongside them. Indeed, such mutual concerns are "in many respects, of much greater moment than the temporal concerns of the greatest earthly monarchs, and their kingdoms or empires."[222] He points out just how much he has suffered on their behalf, not standing aloof from their lives but devoting himself to their welfare: "I have found the work of the ministry among you to be a great work indeed, a work of exceeding care, labor and difficulty: many have been the heavy burdens that I have borne in it, which my strength has been very unequal to."[223] The nature of the connection between pastor and people is further exemplified when Edwards draws upon familial imagery to express love and duty. He is their "spiritual father," and the people of Northampton are his "spiritual children."[224] Even allowing for puerile rebellion or parental negligence, such bonds are not easily severed.

The Adoption of a Prophetic Framework for Ministry

Edwards, therefore, finds himself in an unenviable position. He labors within the congregation as a servant in the Master's vineyard, arriving early and staying late with inadequate recompense. However, he also labors as someone sent on a mission to represent a landowner from a faraway land, to warn the tenants of the vineyard of their presumption and complacency and the danger they face unless they bear fruit. He stands with the people and against the people. No wonder Edwards takes up the story of the prophet Jeremiah to describe and summarize his own ministry.[225]

---

220. Edwards, "Farewell Sermon," *WJE* 25: 463.

221. Edwards, "Farewell Sermon," *WJE* 25: 473–74.

222. Edwards, "Farewell Sermon," *WJE* 25: 473.

223. Edwards, "Farewell Sermon," *WJE* 25: 475.

224. Edwards, "Farewell Sermon," *WJE* 25: 479.

225. Edwards, "Farewell Sermon," *WJE* 25: 475.

Edwards has preached as Jeremiah did with little or no results. He has preached to revive the nation, but they would not listen. He has been spurned, which plunged him into "an abyss of trouble and sorrow,"[226] not unlike the man of sorrows whom Jeremiah prefigures and Edwards follows. Remarkably, his own labors endured for twenty-three years, just as Jeremiah says his own did (Jeremiah 25:3). In fact, Edwards had originally planned to preach his farewell sermon from that very text but changed his mind and decided to use the words of the Apostle Paul (to the same ends). Edwards is effectively locating his own ministry as a continuance of the ministry of the prophets, in identifying with the people and yet exposing and challenging their sins.[227] David Hall argues that being a divine ambassador is at the heart of the prophetic calling.[228] Though Edwards had been accused by his adversaries in Northampton of the arrogance of seeing into others' souls and thereby denying to some the opportunity for communion, it is more accurate to suggest that Edwards was dismissed for speaking to resistant souls and challenging them to reconsider their relation to the Lord.

One further corollary is to be noted. Though a revivalist sensibility would normally stress the individual in his or her relation to God, the whole tenor of this sermon and its imagery highlights the corporate nature of reality. It will be the church alongside the minister who together face the light of the judgment. It is the minster as prophet who calls the congregation to prepare for that day. Moreover, Edwards sees the family as more foundational even than the church in inculcating piety in the believers. No one is simply an individual:

> We have had great disputes how the church ought to be regulated; and indeed the subject of these disputes was of great importance: but the due regulation of your families is of no less, and in some respects, of much greater importance. Every Christian family ought to be as it were a little church.... And family education and order are some of the chief of the means of grace.[229]

The particular application of the doctrine section of the sermon to various groups within the congregation, defined using spiritual or other demographic

---

226. Edwards, "Farewell Sermon," *WJE* 25: 477.

227. John E. Johnson, "The Prophetic Office as Paradigm for Pastoral Ministry," *Trinity Journal* 21(1) (2000): 61–81.

228. Hall, *The Faithful Shepherd*, 6, 49, 270.

229. Edwards, "Farewell Sermon," *WJE* 25: 484.

criteria, substantiates further the social nature of reality in Edwards's mind. Richard Hall suggests that Edwards is at odds with the atomism and mechanicism of much of eighteenth-century thought at this point.[230] Preaching with regard to the developmental needs of such groups as children or youth assumes social distinctions but also social solidarity; either way, social concerns are evident.[231] The social reality of the church is affirmed.[232]

Edwards's approach to congregational life might thus be read as conservative social engineering, denying the individualizing impetus present in the revivals as well as in much Enlightenment philosophy. When he reasserts expectations of filial piety or ministerial authority, it can sound like heavy-handed reaction or corporatist conformity. In this regard, it must be pointed out that while conserving the orders of creation, Edwards stands at the same time ready to transgress them, being fully aware of the dynamism, perhaps even instability, of the present order of things and arrogating to himself the function of further destabilization. If the people of Northampton had kicked against the providential ordering of their world by ignoring the warnings of the minister or failing to own their spiritual responsibilities as parents,[233] so would the pastor disturb the temporal order to introduce the priorities of the coming world. He recognized that the times are changing:

> We live in a world of change, where nothing is certain or stable; and where a little time, a few revolutions of the sun, brings to pass strange things, surprising alterations, in particular persons, in families, in towns and churches, in countries and nations.[234]

He therefore recognizes his responsibility to inveigle his way into the life of families and address the spiritual concerns of the youth or the children, cutting out the mediate authority of parents or guardians. He acknowledged that this world is "preparatory, mutable" and that the day of judgment would contrariwise "fix" our everlasting state, so he intervenes.[235] He has directly warned

---

230. Hall, *Neglected Northampton Texts*, 287, 289.

231. Minkema, "Old Age and Religion in the Writings and Life of Jonathan Edwards," especially 703.

232. Indeed, it was illegal in Massachusetts in Edwards's day for an adult to live alone! See Chamberlain, "Edwards and Social Issues," 334.

233. Scheick, *The Writings of Jonathan Edwards*, 117.

234. Edwards, "Farewell Sermon," *WJE* 25: 463.

235. Edwards, "Farewell Sermon," *WJE* 25: 465, 474.

against "frolicking (as it is called) and some other liberties commonly taken by young people" and has not overlooked the children: "I have endeavored to do the part of the faithful shepherd, in feeding the lambs as well as the sheep...you know, dear children, how I have instructed you, and warned you from time to time."[236] Social or ecclesiastical order is contingent, until the Lord returns.

Perhaps he was unwise in expecting too much of the revivals to produce a harvest among youth and children. Perhaps he failed to expect Christian nurture through the creation good of family order. The reconstitution of rules governing complete membership, or who could take communion, likewise planed against the grain of family life, for to deny to some the ordinance of communion was potentially to deny to their progeny the right to be baptized, as Minkema suggests.[237] Edwards may have lacked the capacity to foresee some of the consequences of his actions. He may have been overly optimistic. However, appealing to the social and theological location of the prophets of Israel, he demonstrates his commitment to a form of social dynamism within the church, which can aptly be described as prophetic ecclesiology.[238] His own role has prophetic parallels, and the relationship of the church to its broader community furthermore owns the tension of being engaged though distinct. Even when the revivals are being institutionalized and their initial fervor is dissipating, the prophetic Edwards has hope that his suffering will be generative of greater transformation.[239]

When a Church Is More Than a Structure: Aspirations for Transformation

For Edwards, the church is unquestionably a social institution, both in terms of its corporate concerns as well as its material composition. It has a distinct form within the world and is dynamically responsive to the concrete contingencies of the world. The church has a social location—it is a visible

236. Edwards, "Farewell Sermon," *WJE* 25: 483.

237. Minkema, "Old Age and Religion in the Writings and Life of Jonathan Edwards," 697–99.

238. Marty, in tracing the development of civil religion in America, contrasts the priestly and the prophetic modes and situates Edwards clearly within the latter. See Marty, "Two Kinds," 147.

239. Kimnach, "Preface," *WJE* 25: 17.

community.[240] However, Edwards suffers the humiliation of "separation," itself a spatially freighted term, because of his attempts to create some distance between this visible church in Northampton and the wider community through limiting participation in the Lord's Supper. The church here wasn't visible enough! Indeed much of the reality of the church in this world is veiled and requires the penetrating gaze of God to strip back all dissembling and bring to light "every specious pretense, every cavil, and all false reasoning."[241] Edwards does not here aspire to citizenship in the invisible church, but rather to life in the more visible church. The ultimate destination for believers is the beatific vision of God, to enjoy: "[T]he most immediate sensible presence of this great God, Savior and Judge, appearing in the most plain, visible and open manner, with great glory, with all his holy angels, before them and the whole world."[242]

Justice will be done and will be seen to be done, for the purpose of that day is to make plain God's righteous judgments for minister and people alike.[243] Though Edwards was wedded to the importance of the visible church, his ecclesiology was nevertheless aspirational and cognizant of an eschatological horizon, even though the revivalist and millennial themes so evident in earlier writings are muted here. Edwards's ecclesiology in his "Farewell Sermon" honors the orderly processes of the created order, while holding out for extraordinary transformation in the congregation's life, if not in the now, then certainly in the not yet. Edwards is an advocate of prophetic ecclesiology, which is prepared to destabilize the church to create a distinction from the world and which nevertheless recognizes the visible reality of the church within this world and refuses to give in to a static conception of the structures of ministry as if beholden to present forms. The dynamism of the church is a function of the interaction between the promise, presence, and purpose of God, inasmuch as God's gift of ministry represents these marks of ecclesial life. The church is an expression not just of pastoral or apocalyptic functions but of prophetic aspirations too.

---

240. Edwards, "Farewell Sermon," *WJE* 25: 477.

241. Edwards, "Farewell Sermon," *WJE* 25: 476.

242. Edwards, "Farewell Sermon," *WJE* 25: 469.

243. Edwards, "Farewell Sermon," *WJE* 25: 472.

4.5 The Church's Cosmic Context in the Stockbridge Treatises

The Stockbridge Period: Edwards's Ecclesiological Context

It would be wrong to assume that in leaving Northampton with his family for life at the Stockbridge mission station, Edwards was turning his back on any interest in revivals or commitment to the church. It is true that during this period (1751–1758) Edwards wrote works that bear a philosophical cast, works for which he is best remembered, like *Freedom of the Will*, *Original Sin*, *The End for Which God Created the World*, and *True Virtue*, but he was not employed in Stockbridge as a philosopher in residence or as an academic at all. He even resisted the invitation in 1757 to leave his missionary post in western Massachusetts to take up the position as third president of the College of New Jersey, later to be known as Princeton, for he did not consider himself suited to the life of institutional leader and scholar.[244] Indeed, his position in Stockbridge was formally a church minister and not a freelance missioner, whose sociological role was yet to be developed. Edwards led regular Sunday services, catechized the youth, and in time, also acted as principal of boarding schools for Indian boys and girls, though his schedule did allow him time to write. Edwards's ministry in Stockbridge was essentially pastoral and not academic.[245]

Furthermore, the context of this ministry of Edwards was persistently revivalist. The mission in Stockbridge had been established as recently as 1734–1735 as a result of the revivals in the Connecticut River Valley, and the negotiations for the mission's foundation had involved Edwards from the earliest phase of planning.[246] He preached at Stockbridge for conversions and worked to see men and women of the local Mahican tribe declare their confession of faith before the congregation, something that he had attempted at Northampton with disastrous consequences.[247] It must be said as well that Edwards took up

---

244. See Jonathan Edwards, "To the Trustees of the College of New Jersey, October 19, 1757," in *Letters and Personal Writings*, The Works of Jonathan Edwards 16, ed. G. S. Claghorn (New Haven: Yale University Press, 1998), 725–30.

245. His pastoral heart at Stockbridge can further be gleaned from a letter to Sir William Pepperrell, in which he advises that his progressive pedagogy includes the education of girls as well as boys, and the style of learning is not merely rote but Socratic. Edwards, "To Sir William Pepperrell," *WJE* 16: 406–14.

246. Rachel Wheeler, "Edwards as Missionary," in *The Cambridge Companion to Jonathan Edwards*, ed. S. J. Stein (Cambridge: Cambridge University Press, 2007), 197.

247. Wheeler, "Edwards as Missionary," 204.

the position in Stockbridge not because no other jobs were forthcoming: in correspondence with John Erskine, he had been alerted to ministerial positions in Scotland,[248] and two "comfortable pulpits in New England" had also been offered.[249] Edwards took the job as missionary to the Indians rather to give expression to his own optimistic, internationalist, and revivalist mindset.[250] This was a positive decision to make good on the failures of much of the Puritan project to reach the Indians with the Gospel of Christ, though it was a positive engagement with enormous personal and familial costs: the Williams family, well represented in Stockbridge as they had been in Northampton only forty miles away, continued to cause Edwards much grief through their obstreperous opposition to his programs and leadership.[251] Three of Edwards's daughters decided that marriage and life elsewhere were preferable to moving to the frontier![252]

It should be acknowledged that Edwards's ministry at Stockbridge was also colored by the imperialist context in which he lived: he was no neutral observer in writing or preaching. His service on the frontier was overshadowed by the French and Indian War between 1756 and 1763, in which British imperial aspirations clashed with French territorial expansion in North America, with many northeastern Indian tribes being forced to decide which master to serve in order to better resist assimilation or at least to choose the lesser of two evils. The Stockbridge mission played its part in defense of the Dominions to the extent Indians were taking refuge there, were sending their children to its school, were learning England's civilizing ways, and were potentially learning Protestant principles of faith. Edwards stoutly defended Indian rights over and against the rapacious land-grabbing of European settlers in the region.[253] He educated Indian youth when he was granted the right to be principal of

---

248. See "To the Reverend John Erskine, July 5, 1750," in Jonathan Edwards, *Letters and Personal Writings*, The Works of Jonathan Edwards 16, ed. G. S. Claghorn (New Haven: Yale University Press, 1998), 355–56.

249. McDermott, "Missions and Native Americans," 265.

250. McDermott, "Missions and Native Americans," 258, 260–61.

251. Wheeler, "Edwards as Missionary," 198–99.

252. Stephen J. Nichols, "Last of the Mohican Missionaries: Jonathan Edwards at Stockbridge," in *The Legacy of Jonathan Edwards: American Religion and the Evangelical Tradition*, eds. D. G. Hart, S. M. Lucas, and S. J. Nichols (Grand Rapids: Baker, 2003), 52n14, where Nichols quotes from Minkema.

253. McDermott, "Missions and Native Americans," 266–67, and Rachel Wheeler, "Lessons from Stockbridge: Jonathan Edwards and the Stockbridge Indians," in *Jonathan Edwards at 300: Essays on the Tercentenary of His Birth*, eds. H. S. Stout, K. P. Minkema, and C. J. D. Maskell (Lanham, MD: University Press of America, 2005), 133.

the schools and taught English to them to empower Indian negotiations over contracts and title deeds.[254] He argued that all nations were equal in the eyes of God. Most tellingly, Edwards and his family did not live on Prospect Hill, above the township, but chose to live among the Indians near the river, to express their solidarity with those they served.[255]

Despite his belief that Indians were no worse than the English in matters of sin and no less able to be saved through faith in Christ,[256] Edwards's unwitting complicity in the imperial project is highlighted by Rachel Wheeler, who argues that deliberate incorporation into the church as the results of revival is more in evidence in New England than in the Middle Colonies: the civilizing framework of Edwards's ministry is demonstrated with the requirement of a public confession of faith, which (though adapted for Indian usage) betrays larger institutional and therefore cultural commitments.[257] The larger arc of her argument suggests that the philosophical works written during this period could not be ideologically neutral or theology conceived without any historical pressures influencing their conception, but were conditioned by the power dynamics in which they were drafted.[258]

Though with initial demurring, Edwards did finally acquiesce and take the job as college president. Interestingly, he had at first argued that to take such a job would be to deny himself time to write his grand theological project. Eventually, other factors encouraged his acceptance of the offer, not least his sense that revivals could only be sustained with like-minded leaders in the churches, and Harvard and Yale were no longer sympathetic to the cause of the New Lights in pastoral leadership.[259] Edwards's ecclesiological commitment to the health of Congregational life and to the importance of revivals (rather than human agency) to motor history were at the forefront of Edwards's mind in Stockbridge as they

---

254. Edwards speaks of the empowering advantages of Indian children learning English. Edwards, "To Sir William Pepperrell," *WJE* 16: 413.

255. Nichols, "Last of the Mohican Missionaries," 53.

256. Jonathan Edwards, *Original Sin*, The Works of Jonathan Edwards 3, ed. J. E. Smith (New Haven: Yale University Press, 1970), 183, 194. See also Wheeler, "'Friends to Your Souls': Jonathan Edwards' Indian Pastorate and the Doctrine of Original Sin," especially 739, 765.

257. Wheeler, "Lessons from Stockbridge," 135–36.

258. Wheeler, "Lessons from Stockbridge," 138. Cohen accounts for attraction to the new birth, furthermore, as a means of power to resist social change or ecclesiastical interference. See Cohen, *God's Caress*, 272.

259. Marsden, *A Short Life of Jonathan Edwards*, 131.

had been in Northampton.[260] The following brief introduction to the Stockbridge treatises seeks to draw together theological themes that demonstrate the presence of ecclesiological concerns for Edwards in this period, many of which we have encountered in our earlier investigation.

The Stockbridge Content Part I: Edwards's Codas on Ecclesiological Revivalism

When we look at the first two treatises written during this period, *Freedom of the Will* (1754) and *Original Sin* (written in 1757 and published in 1758), we see both philosophical interests and revivalist concerns. It has recently been suggested that at heart, these two discourses are actually codas on the revivals,[261] for both works re-engage with the incapacity of human beings to bring about their own salvation and the necessity of radical dependence on God and reception of the work of Christ to experience conversion and new life.[262] They explicitly address the ongoing theological dispute with the so-called Arminians, who would ennoble human contributions to salvation and who would reconfigure human capacity to undertake preparation for salvation. Edwards's restatement of Reformed doctrine during the Stockbridge period had polemical as well as pastoral and academic intent: Arminianism was perceived to promote an anti-revivalist mindset.[263] Both these works have the Arminian threat in the crosshairs.[264]

Looking in greater detail at *Freedom of the Will*, we see Edwards build a case that human beings are still morally responsible for their decisions and actions, even when it has been established that their will is impotent to do anything other than follow whatever appears to be at that moment the greatest good: "the will always is as the greatest apparent good is."[265] Indeed, the will is merely an instrument that does not of its own power choose, but is rather inclined to follow the dictates of the mind or soul: "the will always follows the last dictate of the understanding."[266] The will is free insofar as there is no

---

260. Zakai, "Jonathan Edwards, the Enlightenment, and the Formation of Protestant Tradition in America," 189.

261. Ward, "Philosophical Structure of *Religious Affections*," especially 746.

262. Zakai, "Jonathan Edwards, the Enlightenment, and the Formation of Protestant Tradition in America," 194–95.

263. James P. Byrd, *Jonathan Edwards for Armchair Theologians* (Louisville: Westminster John Knox, 2008), 82.

264. Edwards, *WJE* 3: 375.

265. Edwards, *WJE* 1: 142.

266. Edwards, *WJE* 1: 148.

impediment to it acting on the strongest desire of the person, though it is never self-determining: "For the will itself is not an agent that has a will: the power of choosing, itself, has not a power of choosing."[267] It is never neutral or indifferent in the process of volition. To isolate a self-determining will is for Edwards both psychologically and philosophically untenable. Instead, Edwards advances a unitary conception of human psychology, replacing the theory of a manifold faculty psychology so prominent until now among Puritans.[268]

Significantly, to downgrade the centrality of the human will in defining culpability and freedom is to open a door to other explanations of moral agency, involving necessity and contingence. Essentially, Edwards works backward to defend the priority of the divine will as the ultimate theory of causation, expressed through predestination, though he is careful to do this without implying that God is capricious in his dealings with the human race, or that human beings have no moral responsibility in this world: our "virtuousness or viciousness…consists not in the origin or cause of these things, but in the nature of them."[269] Edwards takes a compatibilist position on the relationship between divine sovereignty and human freedom.[270] To support this contention, Edwards argues strenuously that God's will, arbitrium, is not arbitrary, but is constrained by his own wisdom:

> 'Tis the glory and greatness of the divine sovereignty, that God's will is determined by his own infinite all-sufficient wisdom in everything; and in nothing at all is either directed by any inferior wisdom, or by no wisdom; whereby it would become senseless arbitrariness, determining and acting without reason, design or end.[271]

Edwards essentially began this work to defend the revivals and the freedom of God to draw people to faith in Christ without any moral contribution, but has ended by asserting that God's activity in human lives is not without design. Extreme voluntarism cannot be attributed to Edwards's view of God.[272]

---

267. Edwards, *WJE* 1: 163.

268. According to Haroutunian, this helps Edwards to escape the accusation of psychological determinism. See Joseph Haroutunian, *Piety versus Moralism: The Passing of New England Theology from Edwards to Taylor* (Eugene, OR: Wipf and Stock, 1932), 222.

269. Edwards, *WJE* 1: 337.

270. Allen C. Guelzo, "The Return of the Will: Jonathan Edwards and the Possibilities of Free Will," in *Edwards in Our Time: Jonathan Edwards and the Shaping of American Religion*, eds. S. H. Lee and A. C. Guelzo (Grand Rapids: Eerdmans, 1999), 94.

271. Edwards, *WJE* 1: 380.

272. Paul Ramsay, "Editor's Introduction," in *Freedom of the Will*, The Works of Jonathan Edwards 1, ed. P. Ramsay (New Haven: Yale University Press, 1957), 111.

Edwards himself concisely states: "as God designedly orders his own conduct, and its connected consequences, it must necessarily be, that he designedly orders all things."[273] The application of these sentiments to our inquiry into Edwards's ecclesiology affirms our contention that though he had revivalist aspirations that would break down order through God's immediate action, these are tempered by the constraints of purpose and design, of which the nurturing life of the local congregation is the chief means.[274]

A complementary line of argument is present in the later volume, *Original Sin*. To hold to the truth of human solidarity in the imputation of the sin of Adam, and concomitantly the righteousness of God in holding us accountable for it, Edwards defends significant features of the Reformed account of biblical faith in dispute with Arminianism. Edwards makes a traditional appeal to the radical dependence of creatures on their Creator. He does so, however, by expounding the notion of "continuous creation," or the divine capacity to uphold the creation at every moment, doing so without any secondary causation, and by arguing that God chooses to regard the human race as organically unitive.[275] The universe is radically discontinuous from moment to moment, and yet the descendants of Adam and Eve are fundamentally united in sinful solidarity. A potentially destabilizing espousal of radical contingence is shored up by commitment to ordered union. His Augustinian framework is viewed through Lockean lenses.[276] The imputation of the sin of Adam to his progeny is justifiable given Edwards's account of corporate identity. We are one with Adam in sin and guilt.[277]

Furthermore, our oneness with Adam is necessarily established through "God's sovereign constitution,"[278] the "continued immediate efficiency of

---

273. Edwards, *WJE* 1: 432.

274. Significantly, these themes converge in "Misc." 1263, written between 1753 and 1754, where Edwards acknowledges the ruptures of conversion that are set alongside the less remarkable influences of God that humans "ordinarily...are the subjects of in the course of their lives." The church is clearly the product of the "arbitrary operations" of God, but this is only established most clearly when Edwards traces her origins back to the "foundation laid and when it was as it were formed and established." Jonathan Edwards, "Misc." 1263, in *The "Miscellanies" (Entry Nos. 1153–1360)*, The Works of Jonathan Edwards 23, ed. D. A. Sweeney (New Haven: Yale University Press, 2004), 211, 209.

275. Edwards, *WJE* 3: 402. See also Oliver Crisp, *Jonathan Edwards and the Metaphysics of Sin* (Aldershot, UK: Ashgate, 2005), especially 130–35, for a critique of Edwards's position.

276. Crisp, *Metaphysics of Sin*, 98.

277. Edwards, *WJE* 3: 389.

278. Edwards, *WJE* 3: 404 (italics in original).

God,"[279] and the "law of the Supreme Author and Disposer of the universe."[280] He explains how such an arbitrary constitution does not make for a universe without design:

> And there is no identity or oneness in the case, but what depends on the arbitrary constitution of the Creator; who by his wise sovereign establishment so unites these successive new effects, that he treats them as one, by communicating to them like properties, relations, and circumstances; and so, leads us to regard and treat them as one. When I call this an arbitrary constitution, I mean, that it is a constitution which depends on nothing but the divine will; which divine will depends on nothing but the divine wisdom. In this sense, the whole course of nature, with all that belongs to it, all its laws and methods, and constancy and regularity, continuance and proceeding, is an arbitrary constitution.... And I am persuaded, no solid reason can be given, why God...may not establish a constitution whereby the natural posterity of Adam, proceeding from him, much as the buds and branches from the stock or root of a tree, should be treated as one with him, for the derivation, either of righteousness and communion in rewards, or of the loss of righteousness and consequent corruption and guilt.[281]

Enlightenment assumptions, which frequently define the individual over and against the community of which he or she is a part,[282] are here at odds with Edwards's appeal to the corporate solidarity of the race insofar as he is an advocate for God's desire to bring together that which is otherwise prone to dissolution.[283] Edwards salvages here a place for a "communion in rewards" as a potent allusion to the nature of the church that he elsewhere describes as a "new man" or as "represented as one holy person," for example, "servant of God," "daughter of God," or "spouse of Christ."[284] When Edwards defends divine designs for human solidarity or unity, he is at the same time laying the

---

279. Edwards, *WJE* 3: 401.

280. Edwards, *WJE* 3: 397.

281. Edwards, *WJE* 3: 402–04, 405.

282. It must be acknowledged, however, that there were some significant leaders of the Anglophone Enlightenment who appreciated the social context and solidarity of individual experience, for example, David Hume, Thomas Reid, or Thomas Jefferson.

283. Holmes, *God of Grace and God of Glory*, 229.

284. Edwards, *WJE* 3: 368.

foundation for an ecclesiological vision, of which oneness or communion is the primary gift.

The Stockbridge Content Part II: Edwards's Reflections on Ecclesiological Design

Published jointly and posthumously in 1765, the *Two Dissertations*, comprising *Concerning the End for Which God Created the World* and *The Nature of True Virtue*, in that order, pick up themes from Edwards's earlier writings concerning divine glory, human self-interest, and a defense of the importance of sanctification to Christian assurance. Although the two former treatises above deal with issues generated by soteriological debates, these latter works now under consideration are motivated by cosmological and philosophical concerns. The relationship between the Creator and the creaturely world, or in other terms, the connection between the spiritual and the material, are here discussed. In *Concerning the End for Which God Created*, the supposition that the glory of God is the purpose of the universe raises the question as to the place of the world and its history in that grand design. In *True Virtue*, the relationship between the moral achievements of unregenerate human beings and their pursuit of virtue without the aid of God, becomes a factor in our understanding of common grace and the created order. The earlier treatises assumed the distinction between Christian and non-Christian. These *Two Dissertations* instead draw our attention to the common ground. The church is no Platonic society, existing ethereally and elsewhere, but has rather a substantial footprint in the world we know.

Though origins and causation had been a major theme of *Freedom of the Will* and *Original Sin*, in *Concerning the End for Which God Created*, Edwards outlines his understanding of consequences and consummation by distinguishing between inferior and chief ends and subordinate and ultimate ends.[285] Such fine distinctions, apart from signaling philosophical perspicuity, allow Edwards to relate theological themes, such as the divine will, human responsibility, cosmic order, historical sequence, and eternal progression, by reconciling hierarchy and mutability. Such teleology is not without academic precedent, but its application to the realm of redemption is, according to Edwards, not readily comprehensible to human reasoning without divine illumination.[286]

---

285. Edwards, "Concerning the End for Which God Created," *WJE* 8: 405–06. As noted, we might differentiate such language by speaking of means, instruments, and ends.

286. Edwards, "Concerning the End for Which God Created," *WJE* 8: 419–20.

In short, the mystery of God is to declare the glory of God through the created order, not least the church, without necessitating the conclusion that God is self-centered nor that God is in need of the creation or the church for his own fulfillment. Making use of John 17, Edwards summarizes his case through the example of Christ, who "sought the glory of God as his highest and last end; and that therefore...this was God's last end in the creation of the world."[287] All subsidiary ends are finally coordinated and united. God both seeks his own glory and communicates his glory to human beings:

> God is their good. Their excellency and happiness is nothing but the emanation and expression of God's glory: God in seeking their glory and happiness, seeks himself: and in seeking himself, i.e. himself diffused and expressed (which he delights in, as he delights in his own beauty and fullness), he seeks their glory and happiness.[288]

Remarkably for the eighteenth century, in which portraiture and statuary of leading Enlightenment philosophers were fashioned with the innovation of smiles on their faces, Edwards here, as elsewhere, reclaims happiness for Christian believers.[289]

The process of diffusing glory and reclaiming it, enabling the happiness of both Creator and creature, entails a further corollary. Human beings participate in the diffused life of God and asymptotically progress toward greater union with God, both in this world and in the heavenly realm as well.[290] Edwards compacts these conceptualities and processes under the banner of "fullness," a term appearing in Pauline material (for instance Ephesians 1:22–23) to describe the relationship of Christ the Head with his Body, the Church.[291] Christ dwells with and so fills his people, just as God had once filled the Temple with his brilliant glory. Because God's people acknowledge Christ as Head over all things for the sake of the church, the language of "fullness" is particularly apt to trace the arc of God's will for the whole creation, which necessarily focuses on God's will for the church. Edwards combines the spatial

---

287. Edwards, "Concerning the End for Which God Created," *WJE* 8: 484.

288. Edwards, "Concerning the End for Which God Created," *WJE* 8: 459.

289. George M. Marsden, "Challenging the Presumptions of the Age: The Two Dissertations," in *The Legacy of Jonathan Edwards: American Religion and the Evangelical Tradition*, eds. D. G. Hart, S. M. Lucas, and S. J. Nichols (Grand Rapid: Baker Academic, 2003), 102.

290. Edwards, "Concerning the End for Which God Created," *WJE* 8: 533–34.

291. Edwards, "Concerning the End for Which God Created," *WJE* 8: 439.

image of fullness with the physical properties of light to position the church within God's cosmic plans:

> In the creature's knowing, esteeming, loving, rejoicing in, and praising God, the glory of God is both exhibited and acknowledged; his fullness is received and returned. Here is both an emanation and remanation. The refulgence shines upon and into the creature, and is reflected back to the luminary. The beams of glory come from God, and are something of God, and are refunded back again to their original. So that the whole is of God, and in God, and to God; and God is the beginning, middle and end in this affair.[292]

The language of fullness and light is elsewhere expressed in terms of union with God and conformity to God, as the destiny of the elect in the divine economy is lauded. Having just appealed to Trinitarian logic, Edwards writes:

> In this view, those elect creatures which must be looked upon as the end of all the rest of the creation…must be viewed as being, as it were, one with God. They were respected as brought home to him, united with him, centering most perfectly in him, and as it were swallowed up in him: so that his respect to them finally coincides and becomes one and the same with respect to himself. The interest of the creature is, as it were, God's own interest, in proportion to the degree of their relation and union to God.[293]

Edwards is so enthusiastic in his vision that he must three times in this short paragraph check his theologizing with the refrain "as it were," to caution both himself and his readers against facile understandings of mystical absorption into the Godhead.[294] However, in the end, the union of Christ with his church is explicitly named as "unspeakably more perfect and exalted" than any human analogy can suggest.[295]

It has become evident that Edwards holds together two significant theological motifs in *Concerning the End for Which God Created*. First of all, he assumes that the created universe can be read morally with reference to glory,

---

292. Edwards, "Concerning the End for Which God Created," *WJE* 8: 531 (italics in original).

293. Edwards, "Concerning the End for Which God Created," *WJE* 8: 443.

294. McDermott, *One Holy and Happy Society*, 73, 99.

295. Edwards, "Concerning the End for Which God Created," *WJE* 8: 535.

excellency, and happiness, and thereby locates himself in an essentially medi-eval world of divine enchantment with the creation, which was in eclipse. That is, the cosmos can be described, *pace* Newton, in ways nonmathematical.[296] On the other hand, Edwards depicts the universe as essentially relational and thereby locates himself in a more modern conceptual framework, which allows for mutability, instability, and potentiality, making unambiguous moral readings of the created order more difficult.[297] Holmes rightly points out that it is not his theocentrism that is so remarkable, but it is rather his commit-ment to the "dynamic life of God, that is so central to Edwards."[298] The church, as the focus of God's work in the world, exists in this tension, a community of moral discourse that is open to the vicissitudes of history, a community sub-ject to the pressures of contingency, which also runs a commentary allowing interpretation of God's necessary purposes for the cosmos.[299]

In Edwards's estimation, God cannot be described by referring to his will alone, or his understanding alone. God acts without consulting created intel-ligent beings, yet acts not capriciously but according to his own mind's design. Conversely, the church is always subject to its Master and yet grows dynami-cally toward union with its Master. The church is always the Body, and never the Head, and yet it is organically and necessarily united to the Head, to allude to the language of the Apostle once again. Edwards's ecclesiology is consis-tently theological yet never merely mechanistic nor without reference to the chances and changes of concrete reality.

It is at this point that I offer a corrective to the important pioneering essay by Thomas Schafer, written in 1955, which has remained a standard in under-standing Edwards's ecclesiology for many years. Schafer pulls together various threads in Edwards's writings, most importantly the Miscellanies, which are, in his estimation, germane to his doctrine of the church.[300] His argument is essentially that Edwards has been misread, inasmuch as he has been treated as a separatist and therefore has been presented as belonging to the revivalist wing of the American church. Schafer takes exception to this view and writes

---

296. Holmes, *God of Grace and God of Glory*, 77.

297. Marsden, *A Short Life of Jonathan Edwards*, 129.

298. Holmes, *God of Grace and God of Glory*, 245.

299. Edwards, "Concerning the End for Which God Created," *WJE* 8: 449.

300. Schafer, "Conception of the Church," especially 52. Schafer also recognizes here that to discuss the church, "its nature, its unity, its form, and its destiny" would require a more substantial work, taking into account the whole opus of Edwards, a challenge that I have taken seriously in this book.

"with the hope of correcting in some measure the general impression of his ecclesiology as revivalist."[301] Not surprising, Schafer deliberately begins his piece with *Concerning the End for Which God Created* and expounds Edwards's ecclesiology, highlighting the nature of creation, the decrees, the fall, and Trinitarian process, all ontologically and cosmologically loaded loci.[302] To provide another source of support for his contention, Schafer investigates the soteriological themes of covenants, faith, union with Christ, excellence, and virtue; and he acknowledges Edwards's commitment to the universality and visibility of the church embodied in "higher and higher unities."[303] Schafer's method predisposes him to discover in Edwards a theologically robust ecclesiology from above that is generated by systematic considerations.

However, it is my belief that Schafer goes too far by concluding that Edwards has "strengthened the classical Protestant conception of the church"[304] (without actually defining what this might be) and fails to make reference to the ways in which Edwards might have repristinated such a Protestant view, or indeed how Edwards has destabilized in some sense that same view. Granted, popular approaches to Edwards highlight his evangelistic concern, alongside his predestinarian mindset, marginalizing in both instances his ecclesiology (something my argument has sought to rebut), but this is not to deny that his revivalist concerns did influence his assumptions about the church's life and worship. His "theological and philosophical realism" is not to be sundered from his avowed voluntarism, in which God reserves the right to break into this world apart from regularly constituted means.[305] Schafer makes no space for us to adduce from Edwards's writings and practice an ecclesiology from below.

Even when Schafer speaks of the dynamism of the church in history, he is quick to point out that such dynamism has never jeopardized the "perpetuity" of the church, and indeed more tellingly he asseverates that "the divine glory and the union of the elect in Christ have a static, timeless quality about them."[306] He quite rightly wants to argue that Edwards is trying to minimize the distinction between the visible and the invisible church, but overstates his case when he asserts that because Edwards denounced separatism, he must also

---

301. Schafer, "Conception of the Church," 52.

302. Schafer, "Conception of the Church," 52–53.

303. Schafer, "Conception of the Church," 55–56, 57.

304. Schafer, "Conception of the Church," 62.

305. Schafer, "Conception of the Church," 62.

306. Schafer, "Conception of the Church," 56 (italics mine).

have actively worked against the development of "self-consciously converted *ecclesiolae* within the ecclesia."[307] We have seen that through prayer meetings, youth meetings, voluntary attendance at open-air revivals, or catechism classes, Edwards could encourage intense exercises in piety without falling prey to separatist sentiments. On occasions, Schafer takes single sentences as Edwards's final mind, without due consideration of their place in Edwards's tumultuous ministerial career nor the provisional nature of many of the Miscellanies.[308] Edwards's "ecumenical concerns" (clearly the language of the twentieth century) do not just arise out of his "Biblical ecclesiology and eschatology," much as Schafer might wish, but out of the painful and serious redefinition of unity as a consequence of the revivals, which he experienced firsthand.[309] Though Sweeney is correct to point out that Schafer values the extraordinarily rich and rare ontological basis for Edwards's ecclesiology, it must be added that Schafer is silent on the more phenomenologically formative features of the same.[310] It seems to me that Schafer has prosecuted a case for a certain understanding of Edwards's ecclesiology that marginalizes a more nuanced vision of the church, which it has been the burden of this book to establish.

Finally, it is worth observing that Edwards's last treatise, *The Nature of True Virtue*, parallels the arguments in *Concerning the End for Which God Created*, though remarkably it does so without any interaction with biblical material. It is among the purest of Edwards's philosophical writings.[311] Here, Edwards engages with the dominant philosophical trend of his age, the project to justify universal moral norms without reference to Christian dogma, showing himself to be in the mainstream of British Enlightenment debate.[312] He is keen to affirm virtuous action, even if motivated by private interest, acknowledging the outcomes of God's gift of common grace, especially in regulating society.[313] He insists, however, that true virtue

---

307. Schafer, "Conception of the Church," 60 (italics in original).

308. See Holmes, *God of Grace and God of Glory*, 141, for frustration at such a methodology.

309. Schafer, "Conception of the Church," 62.

310. Sweeney, "The Church," 169.

311. The safe assumption has been that the second dissertation is dependent on the first, which frames the eschatology of the second, but does so without drawing out a comprehensive set of corollaries.

312. Marsden, "Challenging the Presumptions of the Age," 107–08. See also Norman Fiering, *Jonathan Edwards's Moral Thought in Its British Context* (Chapel Hill: University of North Carolina Press, 1981).

313. Marsden, "Challenging the Presumptions of the Age," 110–11.

most essentially consists in benevolence to Being in general. Or perhaps to speak more accurately, it is that consent, propensity and union
of heart to Being in general, that is immediately exercised in general
good will....And consequently, that no affection whatever to any creature...which is not dependent on, nor subordinate to a propensity or
union of the heart to God, the Supreme and Infinite Being, can be of
the nature of true virtue.[314]

Just as a musical phrase can sound harmonious when performed on its own
and can sound discordant when inserted into a passage of music in a different
key or tempo, so also virtue needs to be appreciated in relation to the larger
moral, or theological, symphony of God's will and design.[315]

The beauty of moral harmony is ultimately sensed in an interpersonal reality
when one is related to God as to the "lawful sovereign."[316] Edwards here carefully asserts that this Lord, or sovereign, does not govern according to whimsy
or caprice, but rather rules with regard to order, design, or lawfulness. Again, we
see the deliberate collocation of his theological voluntarism and epistemological
idealism in its eighteenth-century guise.[317] Though this treatise has the least of
any of his works concerning the doctrine of the church, we are reminded that at
the end of his productive ministry, any explanation of the moral life of Christian
believers must be depicted on a larger theological canvas, remembering that
experiences of Christian fellowship are themselves personal, provisional, and
yet ultimately public, and grounded in the divine character and works.[318] As
Ramsay avers, "*True Virtue* should first be read as Edwards' ethics of creation."[319]
This vision of the essence of the moral life for Edwards is necessarily connected
to a vision of moral transformation. We hold that Edwards's understanding of
true virtue has revivalist and social implications.

---

314. Jonathan Edwards, "Dissertation II: The Nature of True Virtue," in *Ethical Writings*, The
Works of Jonathan Edwards 8, ed. J. E. Smith (New Haven: Yale University Press, 1989), 540,
556–57.

315. Edwards, "The Nature of True Virtue," *WJE* 8: 540.

316. Edwards, "The Nature of True Virtue," *WJE* 8: 555.

317. However, a small qualification is in order. Edwards's epistemology has, in addition,
some voluntaristic elements insofar as he rejects regnant faculty psychology, which distinguishes constituent parts of human anthropology, and instead brings together understanding and affections *with the will* in an intricate way.

318. It would therefore be too much to conclude with McDermott that, in the end, the
regenerate heart is at the center of Edwards's vision of the social or ecclesiastical order. See
McDermott, *One Holy and Happy Society*, 153.

319. Ramsay, "Editor's Introduction," *WJE* 1: 34.

5

Ordered Ecclesiological Life

5.1   The Worshipping Church Expressing Its Praise

What We Do Alongside What We Say

THE STUDY OF ecclesiology can be ordered around topics in systematic theology, structured around offices and orders in ministry, or viewed through the lens of the importance for the believer of regular participation in sermon, sacraments, supplications, and song.[1] Indeed, what we do phenomenologically week by week when we gather as God's people says something about our deepest beliefs. We assent to certain practices and patterns, which in turn form our further expectations of corporate ecclesiastical life, which, if our responsibility is as clergy, we shape for the perceived common good of the people. Puritans in New England had exalted expectations of Sunday worship, its purity, and its purpose. Disencumbered from frivolous and anti-Scriptural liturgical and structural forms of the established Church of England, their New World freedom was most spectacularly demonstrated and enjoyed in worship. Their vision for a godly Commonwealth found its epicenter and example in the ordinances that were observed in public worship.[2] The length of the services, sometimes three hours on Sunday mornings and the same again on Sunday afternoons, attests to the significance they attached to these meetings. Worship provided a focus not just for their edification but also for

---

1. Brian Wren, *Praying Twice: The Music and Words of Congregational Song* (Louisville: Westminster John Knox, 2000), 93.

2. Hambrick-Stowe points out that the exact number of ordinances was never precisely defined in New England. Charles E. Hambrick-Stowe, *The Practice of Piety: Puritan Devotional Disciplines in Seventeenth-Century New England* (Chapel Hill: The University of North Carolina Press, 1982), 93. The category would, however, likely at least include the ministry of the Word, sacraments, prayer, and observing the Sabbath. Edwards includes "public singing of God's praises" as an ordinance "instituted by Christ to be observed in the Christian church." See Edwards, "Singing Lecture Sermon," 137.

their whole life.[3] By tracing longitudinally throughout the career of Edwards practices in the worshipping church that he oversaw, this chapter, consisting of three sections, will serve as a summary of themes in this book, provide instantiated expression of priorities in Edwards's ministry, and demonstrate the ways in which Edwards's espoused ecclesiology functioned operationally throughout his life.

Meeting Each Sunday for Worship in Puritan New England

The Puritans' hermeneutical approach—known as the regulative principle, which allowed only those practices in worship that had positive Scriptural warrant—created an unadorned and sparse, perhaps uncluttered, experience in worship and is commonly recognized as a Puritan distinctive.[4] Taking their lead from the Westminster Directory, a simple selection of predictable elements created a focused service, or at least one in which human traditions were removed.[5] A Puritan service, then, which it appears Edwards did little to reconfigure, began with a call to worship and then a pastoral prayer, as instructed by the Apostle Paul (1 Timothy 2:1–2, 8), and proceeded to a Scriptural reading or two in *lectio continua* format, to which was adjoined a critical commentary and the praying of a psalm from *The Bay Psalm Book*.[6] It was one of the wonders of early New England settlement that this new psalter was compiled within ten years of arrival and testified to the essentially devotional character of Puritanism and to the restorationist aims of the New England project in which the desire to recover "divine rule and pattern" were preeminent.[7] Of

---

3. Harry S. Stout, "Liturgy, Literacy, and Worship in Puritan Anglo-America, 1560–1679," in *By the Vision of Another World: Worship in American History*, ed. J. D. Bratt (Grand Rapids: Eerdmans, 2012), 11.

4. Walter McConnell, "Facing New Paradigms in Worship: Learning New Lessons from Old Masters," *Evangelical Review of Theology* 29(4) (2005): 331–46, especially 334.

5. See further: Douglas A. Sweeney, *Jonathan Edwards and the Ministry of the Word: A Model of Faith and Thought* (Downers Grove, IL: IVP Academic, 2009), 58–59.

6. For extra detail, see Sweeney, *Jonathan Edwards and the Ministry of the Word*, 57–59.

7. The full title of the work was *The Whole Book of Psalms Faithfully Translated into English Meter*, and it was known colloquially as the *Bay Psalm Book* of 1640. Interestingly, the reading that included interpretative commentary was dropped in many places, perhaps because of insufficiency of funds to pay for the office of teacher (as distinct from pastor). See John von Rohr, *The Shaping of American Congregationalism, 1620–1957* (Cleveland: Pilgrim Press, 1992), 165–66. Also see Hambrick-Stowe, *Practice of Piety*, 113, and Theodore Dwight Bozeman, *To Live Ancient Lives: The Primitivist Dimension in Puritanism* (Chapel Hill: University of North Carolina Press, 1988), 148–50.

course, metrical psalm-singing by the congregation had been a staple of worship in the Reformed tradition both on the European mainland and in Britain, using the editions of Sternhold and Hopkins (1562) and then Tate and Brady (1696), though a new psalter was deemed appropriate in a new world.[8]

The sermon of one to two hours duration, which involved exposition of Scripture and exhortation toward obedience and had greater weight in the service than any earlier readings, followed the psalm and prayers of confession and intercession. After preaching, there was a further time of prayer, then an opportunity for the Lord's Supper (aspirationally each month).[9] Weekly prophesyings, whereby parishioners, either clerical or lay, were given permission to present their own thoughts on a Scriptural text or to bring some comfort or challenge to the community (1 Corinthians 14:26–33) had originally been a part of New England worship, but was discontinued after the Antinomian Controversy.[10] A dismissal signaled the conclusion of the service.[11] The

---

8. It must be remembered that although we may find psalmody restrictive as the only medium of praise, from the Reformation forward, any participation by members of a congregation had been a radical departure from singing restricted to priest and choir alone. See McConnell, "Facing New Paradigms in Worship," 341. Psalm-singing with each individual proceeding at a rate different from those sitting together in the pew had been interpreted as providing devotional freedom. See Ola Elizabeth Winslow, *Jonathan Edwards 1703–1758: A Biography* (New York: Macmillan, 1941), 107.

9. Care was taken to separate unbelievers, or "members of the congregation," from believers, or "the church," on occasions of communion. Edwards managed the frequency of once every eight weeks, though he aspired to weekly observance. Jonathan Edwards, "To the Reverend John Erskine, November 15, 1750," in *Letters and Personal Writings*, The Works of Jonathan Edwards 16, ed. G. S. Claghorn (New Haven: Yale University Press, 1998), 366. John Cotton aspired to its celebration at least monthly. See Doug Adams, *Meeting House to Camp Meeting: Toward a History of American Free Church Worship from 1620 to 1835* (Saratoga: Modern Liturgy Resource Publications, 1981), 31–33, and Michael J. McClymond and Gerald R. McDermott, *The Theology of Jonathan Edwards* (New York: Oxford University Press, 2011), 487, 488.

10. David D. Hall, *Worlds of Wonder, Days of Judgment: Popular Religious Belief in Early New England* (Cambridge: Harvard University Press, 1989), 64. Women were empowered to speak in this setting of prophesyings, though not to ask questions, which was reserved for the domestic setting to obey apostolic injunction (1 Corinthians 14:35).

11. Edwards, perhaps surprisingly, refers to the use of 2 Corinthians 13:14, known as The Grace in Anglican liturgical formulation, as a form of dismissal from the public assembly, in Jonathan Edwards, "Christians have Communion with Christ," in *Sermons on the Lord's Supper*, ed. D. Kistler (Orlando: The Northampton Press, 2007), 138. Apparently, some in the congregation in Northampton were leaving church before the dismissal had been declared: "another thing is going out of the house before the blessing is pronounced—if it be a proper thing that a blessing should be pronounced, then certainly 'tis proper that the Congregation should attend it and that in a sol[emn] manner." See Jonathan Edwards, "452. Unpublished Sermon on Haggai 2:7–9 (Dec. 1737)" (accessed from the Jonathan Edwards Center at Yale University, 2011), L. 24r.

afternoon meeting had a similar format, except that the prophesyings had been replaced by interrogation of those seeking membership, relations of grace, and baptisms instead of celebration of the Lord's Supper. A psalm might conclude the time together followed by a benediction. In some towns, there might also be a midweek service, which was essentially a psalm, a reading, and its exposition. Edwards later persuaded the congregation at Northampton to take up a weekly collection for the poor of the parish as well.[12] These elements together betoken regularity, consistency, and reinforcement of boundaries, which further created their own kind of ritual expectations, even if the language of ritual was not a lexicographical commonplace.[13]

What is more surprising in Puritan worship, and rarely recognized today, was the variety of players who had roles or participants with responsibilities in the weekly meeting. Different voices were heard in readings, exposition, and prophesyings. Sometimes, a number of clergy were together responsible for the preaching, making it a team commitment. Winiarski makes this point concerning the arrangements for a variety of preachers, including Edwards, at Enfield in July 1741, and suggests thereby that Edwards was originally a more radical exponent of the New Light cause than is sometimes assumed.[14] Commonly around the table for celebrations of the Lord's Supper sat the board of elders who were engaged in distributing the bread and the wine.[15] Before the service or even during it while the leader of the intercessions made his way to the front, parishioners could hand along a note with items for prayer.[16] In the afternoon meeting, the process for

12. Ted Rivera, *Jonathan Edwards on Worship: Public and Private Devotion to God* (Eugene, OR: Pickwick Publications, 2010), 67.

13. E. Brooks Holifield, "Peace, Conflict, and Ritual in Puritan Congregations," *The Journal of Interdisciplinary History* 23(3) (1993): 551–70, especially 553–55. Stout rightly points out the ways in which Puritans rejected liturgical ritual of the Laudian kind, insofar as they replaced traditional "inherited ceremonial forms" by modern "ideological consensus," built around texts, literacy, and history as the "bearer of the sacred." Despite this, repeated communal patterns generate embodied worldviews known as ritual even when Scripture and its exposition are at the center of the worship experience. See Stout, "Liturgy, Literacy, and Worship," 14, 18.

14. Douglas L. Winiarski, "Jonathan Edwards, Enthusiast? Radical Revivalism and the Great Awakening in the Connecticut Valley," *Church History* 74(4) (2005): 683–739, especially 700–03. Thomas Kidd suggests that Edwards may have been playing to the audience in Enfield and used his skills as a wordsmith rather than unrestrained "performative tactics" to make his mark. See Thomas S. Kidd, *The Great Awakening: The Roots of Evangelical Christianity in Colonial America* (New Haven: Yale University Press, 2007), 104–05.

15. Philip D. Zimmerman, "The Lord's Supper in Early New England: The Setting and the Service," in *New England Meeting House and Church: 1630–1850*, The Dublin Seminar for New England Folklife: Annual Proceedings, 1979 eds. P. Benes and J. M. Benes (Boston: Boston University, 1980), 128.

16. For example, such a "prayer bill" is referred to in Jonathan Edwards, "A Faithful Narrative," in *The Great Awakening*, The Works of Jonathan Edwards 4, ed. C. C. Goen (New

receiving new members involved a variety of leaders from the congregation asking questions or affirming answers. Even the architectural layout of the building with its family boxed pews acknowledged multiple actors and different centers of attention, for not all rows faced the pulpit at the front.[17] The highly participatory character of Puritan worship is obscured by the interposition of practices generated by Presbyterian polity or Anglican clericalism in the eighteenth century and Charles Finney's revivalism in the nineteenth century, which further changed the nature of free church worship, making it cumulatively more clerical, addressed to the will, and ultimately less participatory. Doug Adams alerts us to the myopia:

> From the landing of the Mayflower through the American Revolution, the majority of free church clergy probably spent more time interacting with worshippers around the communion table than they did preaching from pulpits.... Adopted for [nineteenth century] revival circumstances, the "new means" posited the preacher on a stage as the central focus in a worship service devised to convert the people in the congregation who were not yet eligible to commune or give substantial shape to the preaching and praying.[18]

Puritan worship in New England until the Great Awakening, though allowing for some minor differences between regions, was an essentially homogenous expression of Scriptural precedents and community values, with several people and their voices participating.[19] It was the question of hymnody composed

---

Haven: Yale University Press, 1972), 205. Submitting prayer bills was open to all in the parish, not just members in full standing, making the practice very democratic. Additionally, the bills could be delivered to the minister, attached to the door of the meetinghouse, or placed into boxes designed for them. This was a common practice, but few, possibly just 189, have survived. For detail about the practice, its use, and misuse, see Douglas L. Winiarski, "The Newbury Prayer Bill Hoax: Devotion and Deception in New England's Era of Great Awakenings," *The Massachusetts Historical Review* 14 (2012): 53–86, especially 55–61. Some movement during the service was however declared unwelcome by Edwards; there appeared to be some "going to & fro about the meeting" for social reasons. See Edwards, "452. Unpublished Sermon on Haggai 2:7–9 (Dec. 1737)," L. 23r–24r.

17. Originally, men and women sat apart on either side of the central aisle, with seating arranged according to the size of the contribution made toward the building's erection. In time, pews with backs were constructed. Children were assigned seats in the gallery until they were brought into family boxes. See von Rohr, *Shaping of American Congregationalism*, 236.

18. Adams, *Meeting House to Camp Meeting*, 13, 14.

19. The nature of debates between Solomon Stoddard in Northampton and the Mathers in Boston concerning the nature of the Lord's Supper is perhaps the most dramatic instance of a breach in the walls of Puritan agreement on worship. See Adams, *Meeting House to Camp Meeting*, 85–86. The stability of liturgical practice is attested in Zimmerman, "The Lord's Supper in Early New England," 132.

by contemporaries, known as "human composures," without the imprimatur of sacred writ, that exercised Edwards in his own developing understanding of the practice of worship (some time before controversy over qualifications for communion erupted), and to which he was one of the earliest in New England to give ground. Marini argues that although much of Puritan liturgical expression remained stable, contentious debates over music, singing, and psalmody were an early harbinger of change long before the revivals erupted.[20]

Praying Each Sunday with Psalms and Hymns

Worship is the Christian's conscious participation in and enjoyment of her place in the divine drama of cosmic redemption, an expression of our communion with the Lord.[21] Edwards grounds such claims for worship in his theological project, which at its heart attempted to provide a teleological account of the nature of religious experience and Christian virtue in a world that was abandoning theistic assumptions.[22] His own theory of consent to being, evident throughout his writings, was an essentially dynamic and relational strategy in which goodness and beauty were related within a theistic worldview to maximize the growth toward human happiness or flourishing.[23] Indeed, the future of the world would be the fitting praise by all the creation of the Godhead, whose own life had overflowed toward the creature and was returned to him in an unending cycle.[24] Fittingly, therefore, music or harmony is a pervasive metaphor used by Edwards to give an account of the beauty of God's plans and of our unity within them. When regenerate believers sing to the Lord a new song, their vocal praise is the evidence of congregational unity and internal

---

20. Stephen A. Marini, "Rehearsal for Revival: Sacred Singing and the Great Awakening in America," in *Sacred Sound: Music in Religious Thought and Practice*, ed. J. Irwin (Chico: Scholars Press, 1983), 71, 86–87. Even the version of the psalms to be used in public worship was contested.

21. Jonathan Edwards, "They Sing a New Song," in *Sermons and Discourses, 1739–1742*, The Works of Jonathan Edwards 22, eds. H. S. Stout, N. O. Hatch, and K. P. Farley (New Haven: Yale University Press, 2003), 240. Minkema says (in the foreword to Rivera, *Jonathan Edwards on Worship*, ix): "For Edwards, worship and praise were ways of participating in the beauty of God, enjoying union with God as a member of the body of Christ."

22. Jonathan Edwards, "Dissertation II: The Nature of True Virtue," in *Ethical Writings*, The Works of Jonathan Edwards 8, ed. J. E. Smith (New Haven: Yale University Press, 1989).

23. Phil C. Zylla, *Virtue as Consent to Being: A Pastoral-Theological Perspective on Jonathan Edwards's Construct of Virtue*, McMaster Ministry Studies Series (Eugene, OR: Pickwick Publications, 2011), 47, 54, 74.

24. Rivera, *Jonathan Edwards on Worship*, 18.

harmony, for God has worked at "tuning the heart."[25] Christ's voice has been a melodious influence within a discordant or rebellious soul.[26] The conceptualities of music apply not only to personal religious experience or to congregational unity, but to the very fabric of the destiny of the created order as well.[27]

Although medieval assumptions concerning music attached it to knowledge, intellect, and rationality, in the Enlightenment, it was reconceived to excite and sustain passions.[28] For Edwards, music under such new conditions could contribute to an experience of transcendence in a world increasingly disenchanted[29] and bring some measure of experiential order to passions potentially disparate.[30] Human voice and song are creation goods that are sequestered by God as means of grace.[31] It may be surprising, therefore, to discover that for the first fifteen years of Edwards's ministry in Northampton, the only musical expression during public worship was sung metrical psalmody. The practice of lining out a psalm, or having the leader of song (known as the precentor) sing a line and then wait for the repetition of the line by a congregation, many of whom could not read or did not own hymnbooks, had long since been abandoned in Northampton, but it was still encountered elsewhere in New England.[32] It was labeled as "Usual" or "Customary" singing and enabled "the religious devotion of the individual singer."[33]

Contrariwise, in Northampton, it was singing the psalms, rewritten in a type of poetic meter understood and appreciated by English-speaking

---

25. Edwards, "They Sing a New Song," *WJE* 22: 236. See also Holifield, "Peace, Conflict, and Ritual," 555–56.

26. Edwards, "They Sing a New Song," *WJE* 22: 244.

27. Edwards, "Charity," *WJE* 8: 386.

28. Paul Westermeyer, *Te Deum: The Church and Music: A Textbook, a Reference, a History, an Essay* (Minneapolis: Fortress, 1998), 119.

29. Marini argues that for evangelicals, hymn-singing has been a "ritual mode" and a "primary vehicle of transcendence." See Stephen Marini, "Hymnody as History: Early Evangelical Hymns and the Recovery of American Popular Religion," *Church History* 71(2) (2002): 273–306, especially 273.

30. In Westermeyer, *Te Deum*, 30, Walter Brueggeman is reported to expound this function of praise.

31. Hambrick-Stowe, *Practice of Piety*, 113. Later in his ministry, music could serve equally well as part of the revised curriculum and as an educational strategy for the Indian schools in Stockbridge. See Edwards, "To Sir William Pepperrell," *WJE* 16: 411.

32. Harry Eskew and Hugh T. McElrath, *Sing with Understanding: An Introduction to Christian Hymnology*, 2nd, rev., and expanded ed. (Nashville: Church Street Press, 1995), 221.

33. Marini, "Rehearsal for Revival," 73. Modern musicologists see in this practice the distinct advantages generated by folk traditions.

Europeans and described as "Regular," that was the liturgical practice under Edwards's leadership until 1742.[34] This involved singing in parts, which required some musical skill and appreciation of beauty in performance, and allowed the distinct contribution of women's voices to be heard, reinforcing the unity in diversity of congregational participants.[35] Those identifying as noncommunicant members of the fellowship could participate in the singing of psalms, which were often viewed as a converting ordinance, generating less brouhaha than Stoddard's same approach to the Lord's Supper.[36] Regular singing "democratized Congregationalist psalmody and brought women their first significant liturgical role,"[37] but this was more usually attained in metropolitan centers than in rural and conservative parishes. Northampton, being in the prosperous Connecticut River Valley, experienced a tension between social progressivism and theological conservatism under Edwards's leadership, reflecting its rural location yet urbane pretensions.[38]

The so-called "Little Awakening" of 1734–35 had witnessed enlivened singing of psalms according to Edwards,[39] but his disappointment with the sustaining of the revival after 1740–41 induced further openness to reform.[40] When

---

34. It was significant that this psalmody was metrical, to distinguish it from Roman Catholic or Anglican chant.

35. David W. Music, "Jonathan Edwards and the Theology and Practice of Congregational Song in Puritan New England," *Studies in Puritan American Spirituality* 8 (2004): 103–33, especially 120–21. This practice is related in Edwards, "Faithful Narrative," *WJE* 4: 151, where he praises the congregation's singing even before the revivals further increased its beauty.

36. Hambrick-Stowe, *Practice of Piety*, 113. For some leaders in New England, singing psalms was expected even of the unregenerate or noncommunicant members as part of their human duty to worship God alone. See Marini, "Rehearsal for Revival," 78.

37. Marini, "Rehearsal for Revival," 76, 85.

38. Marini, "Rehearsal for Revival," 77–79. Edwards explains to Benjamin Colman in 1744 how he had two years previously begun in the congregation the new practice of singing Watts's hymns to complement psalmody and the opposition that it engendered. Edwards, "To the Reverend Benjamin Colman," *WJE* 16: 144.

39. Edwards, "Faithful Narrative," *WJE* 4: 151. See Sweeney, *Jonathan Edwards and the Ministry of the Word*, 109–12, for an account of hymn-singing in the revivals.

40. It appears likely that singing the psalms could also no longer adequately express contemporary corporate concerns, nor was it easy for a singer to maintain the device that he or she was to be identified with the people of Israel in a growing "pluralistic, popular culture." See Madeleine Forell Marshall and Janet Todd, *English Congregational Hymns in the Eighteenth Century* (Lexington: University of Kentucky Press, 1982), 152, 153–54. While Christological interpretation of the psalms had been traditionally upheld, the advantage of hymns was their ability to make this kind of interpretation explicit. Much interpretation of the Old Testament, including the Psalter, had become increasingly individualized as a matter of course. Adams, *Meeting House to Camp Meeting*, 120. Edwards notes the limitations of psalms. Edwards, "Some Thoughts," *WJE* 4: 405–07.

eventually the singing of humanly composed hymns was introduced into Northampton worship in 1742, it was while Edwards was away preaching and was done by a layman in the congregation without Edwards's prior permission.[41] Although an apparently abrupt innovation, the importance of deliberate training in singing had been acknowledged by Edwards in a Thanksgiving sermon as early as 1734, in which he encouraged parents to make efforts to teach their children to sing.[42] He later gave support to the introduction of singing schools to New England, the first of which was to appear in 1721,[43] when he presented a lecture at the conclusion of just such a time of training on June 17, 1736, and strengthened his challenge to teach singing, for "singing is an art" and "a duty for Christian parents to take care that their children be taught to sing as that they be taught to read."[44] Long before the introduction of formal hymnody to the church, Edwards saw the contribution that practiced music-making could offer to the cause of revival:

> What special and extraordinary cause God has given us in this town to employ ourselves in this holy exercise. God and Christ have been wonderfully amongst us. . . . This is a duty of divine worship that has of late been remarkably blessed. . . . And this ought to be looked on as a divine signification to us to endeavor constantly and diligently to wait on God for this duty.[45]

It was the introduction of the hymns of Isaac Watts (1674–1748) to the worship of New England and especially to the repertoire of Northampton that is of such signal consequence. Puritan commitment to worship prescribed by Scripture struggled long with the propriety of hymn composition, which was initially intended merely to supplement psalmody, though its power to displace psalmody was later confirmed.[46] The possibility of contributing anything to pure worship was regarded as ludicrous, and the dangers of deviating

---

41. See Edwards, "To the Reverend Benjamin Colman," *WJE* 16: 144–45.

42. See this encouragement to parents and the place of singing in the purposes of God in Jonathan Edwards, "Praise One of the Chief Employments of Heaven," in *Altogether Lovely: Jonathan Edwards on the Glory and Excellency of Jesus Christ*, ed. D. Kistler (Morgan, PA: Soli Deo Gloria Publications, 1997), 231. The manuscript of this sermon, preached on November 7, 1734, and based on Revelation 14:2, is not extant.

43. Music, "Edwards and Congregational Song," especially 106.

44. Edwards, "Singing Lecture Sermon," 143, 144.

45. Edwards, "Singing Lecture Sermon," 145.

46. Music, "Edwards and Congregational Song," 126–27.

from Scriptural precedent were recognized. Edwards, however, would point out that there are songs in the book of Revelation that are not psalms, and yet when offered with a true heart and directed toward worship of the Lamb, make profound spiritual melody.[47] It was his view that any worship practices were liable to engender presumption, even those with Scriptural precedent.[48] His greatest concern was not the free composition of lyrics, but hypocritical performance of religious duties. Indeed, Edwards suggested that because parishioners could comfortably say amen to the *ex tempore* formulations of prayers led by the preacher or elder, which was in substance no different from hymnwriters' composed words (which actually had the advantage of reflection and timely deliberation), they should be able to receive hymns devised by human wit as well.[49]

Watts's hymns, then, were an extraordinary boon for the revivals of the eighteenth century, even if they were composed some years earlier.[50] They are characterized by a series of stanzas, each with its own leading vision or moment, which together constrain the singer to progress through a series of encounters with the God of whom they speak and with other singers joined in praise. Chiefly, they take psalms or other Scriptural passages and versify them in ways conducive to congregational singing and in the light of contemporary speech and thought-forms.[51] Their patterned construction is designed to impress the singer with divine truth and to elicit emotional response within those bounds.[52] Whereas later hymns by Charles Wesley (1707–1788) had a less sequential structure and allowed for already-existing emotion to be released, Watts's hymns reflect the sensibilities of an earlier era and the settled ministry of an Independent pastor who did not have the freedoms arising from

---

47. Edwards, "They Sing a New Song," *WJE* 22: 242.

48. Edwards points out that even singing psalms as an outward act of worship can be hypocritical. See Edwards, "Mercy Not Sacrifice," *WJE* 22: 117–18.

49. Music, "Edwards and Congregational Song," 123–24. Calvin had taken the view that singing is a subset of prayer. See Westermeyer, *Te Deum*, 155.

50. See Eskew and McElrath, *Sing with Understanding*, 242–44. Watts published his first collection of verse in 1706, entitled *Horae Lyricae*, and his most significant compendium of hymns in 1707, called *Hymns and Spiritual Songs*. See Marshall and Todd, *English Congregational Hymns*, 29–31. These works had been published in New England from early in the century. Music, "Edwards and Congregational Song," 127.

51. Watts incorporated the insights of modern science into his hymnody as well, describing the circulation of blood or the shape of the earth as round. Particular references to British constitutional arrangements in his hymns were amended after the American Revolution. See Wren, *Praying Twice*, 156, 308.

52. Marshall and Todd, *English Congregational Hymns*, 148; Wren, *Praying Twice*, 185.

itinerating in the fields. His assume greater concentration on the part of the singers and inculcate more intentionally Reformed doctrinal positions. Edwards does have occasion to question the theological integrity of Watts's hymns, but is apparently ultimately satisfied that they will not lead his people astray. Even if singing a Watts hymn happened only infrequently (on those Sundays when a third hymn was sung in the afternoon service during the summer months), the innovation was nevertheless a momentous develop-ment in eighteenth-century terms.[53]

The introduction of Watts's hymns to Northampton was an excellent fit with Edwards's ecclesiology.[54] His dynamic and innovative approach to the place of the church in the divine work of redemption had its counterpoint in Watts's hymns, where the dramatic impact of new lyrical expression was housed within more predictable poetic forms. Watts does not set himself the task of provoking experiences of God, which had heretofore been unknown, but rather to valorize and voice "familiar devotional states."[55] For the Augustan mood of early eighteenth-century England, Watts's sometimes shocking imag-ery, intended to disturb the complacent and indifferent[56] and to create aware-ness of the gulf between the human and the divine, suited Edwards's agenda of reviving a church seemingly inured to the supernatural and to the Calvinist beliefs that presupposed it.[57] Watts's hymns form a bridge between "the spiritual self-consciousness of the Puritans" and "contemporary psychology," between flight from the world and education of it.[58] Just as Edwards took a mediating position between the rationalists and the enthusiasts, so he adopted the hymns of Watts that express through poetry rather than prose, somewhere

---

53. See Edwards, "To the Reverend Benjamin Colman," *WJE* 16: 144–45, for the polemical context of his inquiry. Music, "Edwards and Congregational Song," 124–25, 126.

54. Marini intriguingly points out how little explicit ecclesiology appears in the most popu-lar hymnody of the eighteenth and nineteenth centuries, while at the same time the prac-tice of singing creates ecclesiological expectations and experiences. He resolves the issue by suggesting that in the movement's attempts to be evangelically ecumenical, contentious choruses or phraseology concerning the church were avoided. See Marini, "Hymnody as History," 282, 283.

55. Marshall and Todd, *English Congregational Hymns*, 10.

56. Marshall and Todd, *English Congregational Hymns*, 149.

57. Marshall and Todd, *English Congregational Hymns*, 26. Appealing to the work of Peter Williams, Marini suggests that just such a framework is essential to the future development of the movement: "popular American Protestantism has been characterized by hierophany, the dramatic intrusion of the sacred into the profane. The heart of early American evangeli-calism was spiritual regeneration, the hierophanic transformation of the soul by the sover-eign power of God." See Marini, "Hymnody as History," 302.

58. Marshall and Todd, *English Congregational Hymns*, 30, 32–34.

between "traditionalism" and "radical modernity," such a transitional literary strategy for his age.[59]

Though speaking about eighteenth-century epistolary conventions, Bruce Hindmarsh could equally well be addressing the questions of hymns when he suggests that their genius consists in their being both constrained and free, permitting predictable patterns of piety alongside opportunity for emotional engagement or formal convention studded with innovative language, metaphor, and identity-creation. Revivalist sentiment nests within metrical expressions of piety,[60] to enable Christians to occupy "a linguistic middle ground between biblical text and theological propositions."[61] Watts's hymns achieved an extraordinarily unifying victory by proving sufficiently "regular" to the cultural elite and sufficiently affecting to the revivalists.[62]

It is also instructive to examine Edwards's approach to hymn-singing in contexts other than regular Sunday worship. Though it is true that he accommodated innovations like street-singing[63]—given the examples from the Scriptures of extraordinary instances of praise outside the Temple, and he justified their practice through appeal to the necessity of new wineskins to contain new wine—his openness was not without limits.[64] His rebuke of James Davenport for street-singing in New London, Connecticut, demonstrated his social conservatism, even when he stretched himself all that he could to appropriate new forms.[65] Thomas Kidd argues that Edwards eventually settled into a moderate form of New Light practice, advocating "reverence and solemnity,"[66] even if his earlier assertions were bolder and connected him to more extreme

---

59. Marshall and Todd, *English Congregational Hymns*, 59.

60. Bruce Hindmarsh, *John Newton and the English Evangelical Tradition: Between the Conversions of Wesley and Wilberforce* (Grand Rapids: Eerdmans, 1996), 32, 246–47.

61. Marini, "Hymnody as History," 287.

62. Marini, "Rehearsal for Revival," 83–85.

63. Edwards writes that he "cannot find any valid objection against it." Edwards, "Some Thoughts," *WJE* 4: 491.

64. Edwards took a position contrary to Charles Chauncy of Boston's First Church who opposed hymn-singing as a pastime performed "through the streets and in ferry boats," as quoted in Westermeyer, *Te Deum*, 252.

65. Von Rohr reminds us of contemporary reaction to Davenport, describing him as "a madman just broke from his chains" or to his followers as "a company of mad Bacchanalians after a mad frolic," which gives perspective to Edwards's own more moderate opposition. See von Rohr, *Shaping of American Congregationalism*, 188.

66. Edwards, "Some Thoughts," *WJE* 4: 489. Propriety in praise functions as an expression of concern for the dignity of God's name (Exodus 20:7), even while the Holy Spirit is responsible for new song.

separatism.[67] Even Edwards's staggered introduction of hymn-singing within church betrays his cautious approach to liturgical reform for the sake of those believers for whom such change is unsettling. Care must be taken, however, not to hear a blanket rejection of music and song: Edwards and many of his parishioners enjoyed music-making in their own homes as an adjunct to private devotions, and Edwards used the psalms in this way too.[68] The development of Edwards's nuanced views on regenerate affections are ultimately reconcilable with his moderate approach to congregational song.[69]

Waiting Each Sunday for Heavenly Rest

One of the most bracing of social transformations adopted by the Puritans was to reconstitute the notion of sacred time. The traditional cycle of the Western church had reenacted annually the career of Christ, beginning with the approach to his incarnation during Advent, his birth and circumcision, appearance to the magi, preparing for his crucifixion and resurrection in Lent, moving thereafter toward his ascension and the pouring out of the Spirit at Pentecost. Roman Catholic tradition had added moments from the life of Christ connected to the ministry of his mother, Mary. This broad approach was overturned when the yearly liturgical calendar was rejected in favor of a weekly cycle of remembrance in Puritan spirituality. The Christian life of arduous spiritual combat necessitated more frequent cycles of ritual to empower renewal,[70] creating a shorter penitential cycle that made more sense of daily experience.[71] The seventh day achieved a connection between the theological

---

67. It has recently been argued that Edwards moved ground on attitudes toward extreme expressions of revivalist energy, becoming more conservative in relation to lay exhorting and street-singing over time. See Kidd, *The Great Awakening*, 120, 138–55, for a nuanced reckoning of Edwards amid the social questions of excitement, itinerancy, and assurance. See Winiarski, "Jonathan Edwards, Enthusiast? Radical Revivalism and the Great Awakening in the Connecticut Valley," 691, and especially 727–28 for evidence of Edwards's earlier radicalism, in which it appears that he fostered "[v]iolent somatic outbursts, spiritual pride, uncharitable censoriousness, lay exhorting, dreams, trances, and visions," and admitted ninety-seven new communicants to the Lord's Table without interrogation. He would later inhibit the practice of lay exhorting. See Edwards, "To Moses Lyman," *WJE* 16: 102–03.

68. Edwards, "Diary," *WJE* 16: 766, 781, written in 1723.

69. Marini, "Rehearsal for Revival," 83, 86.

70. Hall, *Worlds of Wonder*, 167. See also Theodore Dwight Bozeman, *The Precisianist Strain: Disciplinary Religion and Antinomian Backlash in Puritanism to 1638* (Omohundro Institute of Early American History and Culture; Chapel Hill and London: University of North Carolina Press, 2004), 97.

71. Jane Kamensky, *Governing the Tongue: The Politics of Speech in Early New England* (New York/Oxford: Oxford University Press, 1997), 131–32.

themes of creation, redemption, and ultimate rest, and of repeated beginnings and ends. The celebration of the sacraments on the Sabbath reinforced this understanding of life as a peripatetic pilgrimage requiring frequent resources for the road.[72] A ritual cycle of seven days allowed colonists to keep short accounts with God, "limiting the danger of God's judgment," while affirming social order where few traditional structures existed.[73] For Puritans, no time was any more sacred than the present time, in which God makes his gracious offer of salvation (2 Corinthians 6:2). For Edwards, maintaining the Sabbath meant that "the face of religion is kept up in the world" and is "a day of salvation; 'tis a time wherein God especially loves to be sought and loves to be found."[74]

While it proved difficult to sustain the rejection of an annual cycle, given the powerfully impacting experience of seasons in an agricultural world,[75] the Puritans nevertheless reconceived time and connected it more profoundly with the coming reign of Christ than the earthly career of Christ. Daily labor was dignified by drawing it more deliberately into the eschatological pattern of work and rest.[76] Edwards praised the wisdom of God who had decreed the seven-day cycle for human benefit and theological instruction.[77] Observance of the Sabbath (rather than observance of holy days reflecting the lives of saints) became the primary measure of progress on which work was limited and praise and edification were expanded.[78] The primitivist dimension to Puritan faith, reaching back to the Old Testament for models of social life, had its reflex in sabbatarian commitments, but the forward-looking millennialism of the Puritan project easily put down deep roots in the weekly cycle. It was important to be able to mark progress, praise providence, and expect heaven,

---

72. Hambrick-Stowe, *Practice of Piety*, 96–97, 123–24.

73. Hall, *Worlds of Wonder*, 212.

74. Jonathan Edwards, "The Perpetuity and Change of the Sabbath," in *Sermons and Discourses, 1730–1733*, Works of Jonathan Edwards 17, ed. M. Valeri (New Haven: Yale University Press, 1999), 244, 245.

75. Hambrick-Stowe, *Practice of Piety*, 101.

76. Indeed, observing a weekly Sabbath kept men away from work or taverns, and instead at home with their families, contributing to the public good. See Marilyn J. Westerkamp, *Women and Religion in Early America, 1600–1850: The Puritan and Evangelical Traditions*, Christianity and Society in the Modern World (London and New York: Routledge, 1999), 157.

77. Edwards, "Perpetuity and Change of the Sabbath," *WJE* 17: 226, 233.

78. Stout further suggests that sabbatarian spirituality exemplifies Puritan commitment not to received traditional authority but to commandment and law as validating sacrality. Stout, "Liturgy, Literacy, and Worship," 31.

not merely to review foundations.[79] Even the inclusion of worship on days of Thanksgiving, Elections, or Fasting, outside of the hebdomadal cycle, could be made to fit the eschatological shape of civic life, for these days too acknowledged "danger, yet deliverance."[80] A revivalist pattern, growing to full flower in the nineteenth century, was germinated perhaps unwittingly in the Puritan model of smaller units of sacred time.[81]

Edwards's understanding of praise maintained this perspective. He understood the life of the church to reflect the priorities of a pilgrim people whose destination is heavenly felicity, and believed that the Sabbath exercises equip us for the journey. Our praise in church is therefore proleptic of our praise in heaven when our ultimate Sabbath rest involves not idleness but the work of worship.[82] Ultimately, all of our singing on earth is preparation for eternal praise, when we shall see God "in his transcendent glory and divine excellence."[83] Edwards uses the concept of praise to relativize the experience of the church militant and triumphant: "Let it be considered that the church on earth is the same society with those saints who are praising God in heaven. There is not one church of Christ in heaven and another here upon earth....We ought now to begin that work which we intend shall be the work of another world; for this life is given us on purpose that therein we might prepare for a future life."[84] Even when relativized, our life below stands as a door to another world through our praise: "to have the presence of Christ...in an house of God...becomes a place through which and by means of which men enter into heaven as a gate is that through which men enter into a city."[85] Our present participation in the worship of the heavenly church is yet another pointer to the nature of our communion with Christ and other believers in Edwards's operational ecclesiology.

---

79. Hall, *Worlds of Wonder*, 58–59.

80. Hall, *Worlds of Wonder*, 166.

81. Eskew and McElrath, *Sing with Understanding*, 242–46.

82. See Music, "Edwards and Congregational Song," 109, and Edwards, "They Sing a New Song," *WJE* 22: 241.

83. Music, "Edwards and Congregational Song," 109–10.

84. See Edwards, "Praise One of the Chief Employments of Heaven," 223, 225.

85. Edwards, "452. Unpublished Sermon on Haggai 2:7–9 (Dec. 1737)," L. 11r.

5.2 The Distinctive Church Submitting to Discipline

The Puritan experiment in the New World was more than a Calvinist adventure in pure doctrine. At heart, it was founded on a pious vision for pure worship, which was constrained by pure congregational life. The Cambridge Platform of 1648 begins with an expansive definition of discipline that would secure such purity: "Ecclesiastical Polity or Church Government, or discipline is nothing else, but that Form and order that is to be observed in the Church of Christ upon earth, both for the Constitution of it, and all the Administrations that therein are to be performed."[86] Discipline as an organizational achievement was itself related to discipline as a psychological stabilizer in the early modern period, with its "population growth, expanding poverty, and dread of disorder." In turn, discipline provided new identity "by redefining relationships, by valuing the comradeship and exclusiveness brought by membership in an intensive subculture," leading to a "new basis for interpersonal trust and community."[87] As Bozeman has so cogently argued:

> The reconstruction of identity through purity, conflict, and antithesis seems logical and likely enough, given the power of ascetic ideals in historic Western Christianity, given the important function that "the adversary" served in the age, and given as well the known tendency of early modern Europeans, especially those involved in religious controversy, to see unbridgeable contrariety as a basic principle of reality. To find strenuous battle with sin and sinners a stabilizer in shifting times was to expand upon an eminently available option.[88]

Though the precise constitutional arrangements defending discipline in Massachusetts were significantly different from those in England (for it was laymen in full membership of the church and not elite ecclesiastical courts who exercised jurisdiction over covenant breaches), in both places, the practice was still taken seriously.[89] New World assumptions made the pursuit of

---

86. "The Cambridge Platform," in *Creeds of the Churches: A Reader in Christian Doctrine from the Bible to the Present*, ed. J. H. Leith (Louisville: John Knox, 1982), 386.

87. Bozeman, *The Precisianist Strain*, 51, 59.

88. Bozeman, *The Precisianist Strain*, 60.

89. David C. Brown, "The Keys of the Kingdom: Excommunication in Colonial Massachusetts," *New England Quarterly* 67(4) (1994): 531–66, especially 540–41, 547. See also Emil Oberholzer Jr, *Delinquent Saints: Disciplinary Action in the Early Congregational Churches of Massachusetts*, Columbia University Studies in the Social Sciences 590 (New York: AMS Press, 1968), 31.

discipline—expressed through the steps of censure, admonition, and ultimately excommunication—a powerful precipitant of purity and therefore
liberty in both theological and sociological terms. Though under ideological
revision, concern for these practices extended into the eighteenth century and
Edwards's ministry as well.[90]

Processes of Purity: The Mechanics of Discipline

From the end of the seventeenth century, excommunication had been severely
challenged. The establishment of the Dominion of New England after 1684
with more intrusive royal control and the pursuant royal charter of 1691 guar-
anteeing religious toleration to all Protestants were signs of seismic shifts in
New England polity.[91] It is often assumed, therefore, that excommunication
fell into complete desuetude, accelerated by the madness of the Salem witch
trials in 1692,[92] and that Edwards demonstrated his reactionary personality by
reinstituting congregational discipline in the 1730s after the death of Solomon
Stoddard, known for his policy of "open communion" and abandonment of
excommunication in the first church of Northampton. Brown speaks of "discipline's decline," its "extinction," and disappearance.[93] However, this conclusion may be premature. Holifield notes that between 1690 and 1729, 159
ecclesiastical trials are recorded among seven congregations.[94] In churches
affected by the Great Awakening, discipline in the form of confessions and
censures was widely practiced between the 1720s and 1740s. Even though
Northampton prosecuted comparatively few occurrences in the same period,[95]
disciplinary process was still more frequently undertaken than earlier and in
comparison with the more lax disciplinary culture of the eastern counties of

---

90. Edwards sees the ministry of censure as an appointed ordinance securing right worship: "the setting apart of certain officers in the church[,] the appointed ways of discipline[,]
public confession of scandals and admonition and excommunication...are ordinances."
Jonathan Edwards, "222. Ezekiel 23:37–39 [July–August 1731]," in *Sermons, Series II, 1731–
1732, The Works of Jonathan Edwards Online* 46 (The Jonathan Edwards Center at Yale
University), L. 2r.

91. Holifield, "Peace, Conflict, and Ritual," 568.

92. It should be noted, however, that the witch trials were conducted "not by the churches
but by the judicial branch of the civil government." See Oberholzer, *Delinquent Saints*,
13, 70–71.

93. Brown, "The Keys of the Kingdom," 562.

94. Holifield, "Peace, Conflict, and Ritual," 556–57. The tables provided by Oberholzer are
extraordinarily useful in substantiating such claims.

95. Oberholzer, *Delinquent Saints*, table X, 261.

Massachusetts in these same years.[96] The ultimate demise of discipline in Northampton is rather to be traced from the 1820s.[97]

Edwards provides an excellent insight into the dynamics of excommunication as a form of discipline from his earliest writings. In his New York period, sometime between October 1722 and April 1724, Edwards penned a miscellany regarding excommunication in which he highlighted its nature as a last resort that confirms the obstinacy of the sinner. Alluding to the responsibility of the clergy to retain or remit sins (conflating the language of John 20:23 and Matthew 16:19), Edwards granted to the ministry the objective authority of the keys, though in the next breath relativized that same authority by insisting that any procedure must be conducted justly and thereby establish not the whim of the cleric but the ultimate judgment of God: "What man doth is only for himself, to keep himself free from sin; but the punishment is Christ's, who is the sole head of the church."[98] In a later miscellany composed between July 1729 and August 1731 in Northampton, Edwards reasserted the validity of excommunication and its competency as due process with proper means to reflect the mind of God.[99] It would ordinarily "mark out men as being in a damnable condition, as if it made them so."[100] He makes a similar point in a sermon on Acts 8:22 from this period, adding that recognition of one's own sins is not necessarily required before the church proceeds with its censure.[101] It cannot be maintained that Edwards was prompted to form his mind on the value of excommunication after the failures of later awakening.

It was, however, at the end of the 1730s that Edwards's views on discipline were pastorally tested, with the waning of the Connecticut River Revival and the construction of the new meetinghouse in which status-conscious families

---

96. Oberholzer, *Delinquent Saints*, 48, 153.

97. Oberholzer, *Delinquent Saints*, table XI, 262.

98. Jonathan Edwards, "Misc." *q*, in *The "Miscellanies" (Entry Nos. a–z, aa–zz, 1–500)*, The Works of Jonathan Edwards 13, ed. T. A. Schafer (New Haven: Yale University Press, 1994), 172.

99. He writes, for example, that "in administering church censures, he [the pastor] acts as the apostle expresses in the person of Christ (2 Cor. 2:10)." See Edwards, "222. Ezekiel 23:37–39 [July–August 1731]," L4.r.

100. Edwards, "Misc." 485, *WJE* 13: 527.

101. Jonathan Edwards, "182. Acts 8:22 [Fall 1730–Spring 1731]," in *Sermons, Series II, 1729–1731*, The Works of Jonathan Edwards Online 45 (Jonathan Edwards Center at Yale University), L. 10r. Proceeding with discipline without having confronted the sinner privately was a pastoral process available to the clergy if the consequences of the sin were already of public concern. See Ava Chamberlain, "Bad Books and Bad Boys: The Transformation of Gender in Eighteenth-Century Northampton, Massachusetts," *New England Quarterly* 75(2) (2002): 179–203, especially 195–96.

asserted their social rank, bringing to a head for him new spiritual concerns.[102] It was in this mix that the recidivist drunkenness of a certain Mrs. Bridgman had been brought to his attention, as a consequence of which he decided to preach a sermon of censure in July 1738 from the text of Deuteronomy 29:18–21, concerning the hypocrisy of pretending to have inner peace when outward behavior belies that reality. The doctrine of the sermon is "[t]hat those that go on in the sin of drunkenness under the light of God's word are in the way to bring God's fearful wrath and a most amazing destruction upon themselves."[103] The timely application of the sermon is first of all addressed to any in the congregation "here present" who need to be warned to be honest about their own addiction.[104] Additionally, Edwards directs particular words to Mrs. Bridgman, who is "required to stand forth and distinguish herself," recognizing that she has lived under the means of grace and has previously been admonished privately and publicly for her contumacy.[105] Edwards warned her "in the name of Jesus Christ the great head of the church and judge of the quick and dead and in his presence and in the presence of the holy angels . . . to forsake this wicked practice and to be thorough and final in your reformation." If she would not comply, Edwards averred that "I do now this day in the name of God solemnly denounce unto you that God will not spare you."[106] Others in the community were warned of their own responsibility not to provide her with alcohol.[107] Sadly, this first step of censure was not enough.

Edwards found it necessary to preach a follow-up sermon on July 22, 1739, now published under the title "The Means and Ends of Excommunication," which outlines his justification to proceed with the first excommunication in Northampton since 1711. Though not named in the sermon itself, Mrs. Bridgman is clearly the catalyst. With appeal to 1 Corinthians 5:11, Edwards outlined a theological rationale for the punishment of excommunication, which consisted of the denial of the privileges of membership in the

---

102. George M. Marsden, *Jonathan Edwards: A Life* (New Haven: Yale University Press, 2003), 186, 189.

103. Jonathan Edwards, "482. Deuteronomy 29:18–21 (July 1738)," in *Sermons, Series II, 1738, and Undated, 1734–1738*, The Works of Jonathan Edwards Online 53 (Jonathan Edwards Center at Yale University, 2008), L. 2v.

104. Edwards, "482. Deuteronomy 29:18–21 (July 1738)," *WJEO* 53, L. 9v.

105. Edwards, "482. Deuteronomy 29:18–21 (July 1738)," *WJEO* 53, L. 11r–12r.

106. Edwards, "482. Deuteronomy 29:18–21 (July 1738)," *WJEO* 53, L. 12r–12v.

107. Edwards, "482. Deuteronomy 29:18–21 (July 1738)," *WJEO* 53, L. 14r.

fellowship in order to seek the correction and recovery of the penitent.[108] It is "at God's sovereign disposal whether it [the process of excommunication] shall be for a person's humbling or their dreadful and eternal destruction, as it always is one or the other."[109] Central to Edwards's argument is the nature of excommunication from the church as privative, which itself suggests that the greatest privileges known to the Christian are to be enjoyed corporately.[110] The excommunicate is cut off "first, from the charity of the church; second, brotherly society; third, fellowship of the church in worship; fourth, internal privileges of visible Christians."[111] High-handed sin in the fellowship required drastic measures: "like a physician's cutting off a diseased member from the body.... When a member of the visible church is guilty of scandal, a stumbling block is laid before others."[112] Discipline of this order assumed both the sanctity of the congregation with its ordinances and the distinction between liturgical and social exclusion,[113] for Edwards spends much of the rest of the sermon outlining how much social contact those excommunicated might still expect, an issue to be discussed in the next section.

A number of other cases of discipline, sometimes climaxing with excommunication, occupied Edwards in the 1740s, though he may not have dedicated much time to write about their details, and the situation might have arisen outside his parish. Edwards oversaw the excommunication of Samuel Danks for the sin of fornication in June 1743.[114] In Westfield, in February 1743,

---

108. In these terms, excommunication was understood medicinally, a process for restoring a penitent to spiritual health. See Elisabeth Vodola, *Excommunication in the Middle Ages* (Berkeley: University of California Press, 1986), 138, and Brown, "The Keys of the Kingdom," 545.

109. Jonathan Edwards, "The Means and Ends of Excommunication," in *Sermons and Discourses, 1739–1742*, The Works of Jonathan Edwards 22, eds. H. S. Stout, N. O. Hatch, and K. P. Farley (New Haven: Yale University Press, 2003), 70.

110. Vodola, *Excommunication in the Middle Ages*, 12, 191. In this regard, Edwards was fully consistent with the trajectory of Christian tradition, even before the Reformation. Edwards refers to the painful reality of excommunication as denial of fellowship. Edwards, "Misc." qq, *WJE* 13: 189. Elsewhere, he makes clear that even to "turn our backs upon it,"—that is, to fail to partake of the Lord's Supper—is a sin and casts a "visible contempt on the ordinance" and on "the future glory of [the] saints that it is a representation of." Jonathan Edwards, "287. Luke 22:30 (June 1733)," in *Sermons, Series II, 1733*, The Works of Jonathan Edwards Online 48 (The Jonathan Edwards Center at Yale University), L. 5r.

111. Edwards, "The Means and Ends of Excommunication," *WJE* 22: 71.

112. Edwards, "The Means and Ends of Excommunication," *WJE* 22: 71.

113. Vodola, *Excommunication in the Middle Ages*, 8.

114. Chamberlain, "Bad Books and Bad Boys," 199.

he acted as a consultant in the case of Bathsheba Kingsley, who was ultimately admonished to fulfill her duties in the home instead of

> almost perpetually wandering about from house to house and very frequently to other towns under a notion of doing Christ's work and delivering his messages... often disobeying her husband's commands in going abroad... and taking her husband's horse to go away to other towns contrary to his mind.... Mrs. Kingsley has of late almost wholly cast off that modest, shamefacedness and sobriety, and meekness, diligence and submission that becomes a Christian woman in her place.[115]

Her husband was also reproved and encouraged to take better care of his wife, given the reference to her emotional frailty encoded in the description of her "weak vapory habit of body" and her "continual tumult like the sea in a storm being destitute of that peace and rest in God that other Christians enjoy."[116] Her itinerant prophesyings and mystical revelations were to be channeled but not stifled, although on another occasion, he sternly rebuked Moses Lyman for a similar expression of charismatic license. Edwards was involved in the excommunication of Thomas Wait for fornication and denial of paternity in February 1747, though he recognized Wait's right to appeal the censure.[117]

Most notorious of all is the affair of 1744, in which Edwards clumsily reproved some youth (probably around their mid-twenties) who had misapplied the graphics of an early manual in midwifery to mock some girls in Northampton. As Chamberlain so memorably puts it: "The bad book affair was primarily about sex, sex and speech, reading and talking about sex."[118] As with Mrs. Kingsley, this is not in the first instance a case of excommunication, but rather an attempt to uncover the perpetrators of the sin in order that they might be warned and censured. Though the process might have been clear in Edwards's mind, the execution of it appears not to have been.[119] Several of

---

115. Jonathan Edwards and Members of Ecclesiastical Council, "Advice to Mr. and Mrs. Kingsley, February 17, 1743," in *Church and Pastoral Documents*, The Works of Jonathan Edwards Online 39 (The Jonathan Edwards Center at Yale University), L. 2r.

116. Edwards and Council, "Advice to Mr. and Mrs. Kingsley," *WJEO* 39, L. 2r–2v.

117. Jonathan Edwards, "To the Reverend Robert Breck," in *Letters and Personal Writings*, The Works of Jonathan Edwards 16, ed. G. S. Claghorn (New Haven: Yale University Press, 1998), 222.

118. Chamberlain, "Bad Books and Bad Boys," 180.

119. There is some debate as to precisely what the error of judgment was that Edwards is said to have committed. See Chamberlain, "Bad Books and Bad Boys," 180.

the youth called out belonged to established and influential families in the town, which precipitated a crisis of confidence among the leaders of society in their pastor. It also appears that Edwards's own frustration with the youth colored his responses, for those very young adults about whom he had written so glowingly just a few years earlier in the revivals when they had shown such spiritual promise were now rebellious. Although Chamberlain interprets Edwards to represent "Puritan traditionalism" here,[120] this understanding must be moderated by recent positive feminist surveys of the incident, as we will see in a later section. Edwards is mindful of the status of the women involved, reflecting his openness to changing sexual mores.[121]

The final case to be examined in this section is the difficult account of the adulterous relationship between Martha Root and Lieutenant Elisha Hawley. The process of establishing Hawley's guilt proceeded in a publicly responsible way, though the acrimony between Edwards and the Hawleys, related to him through his mother's sister, undoubtedly intensified Edwards's emotional engagement. Both Elisha and his brother Joseph Jr., who was to represent him in the ensuing legal proceedings, were sons of Joseph Sr., who had committed suicide in a depressive incident in 1734 when doubting his own salvation during the first wave of revival preached by his nephew Jonathan.[122] It was not so much the eventual excommunication of Hawley in August 1748 that generated division as much as it was Edwards's subsequent insistence that Hawley demonstrate his contrition by marrying Martha, who had borne him twins out of wedlock (though only one son lived). Despite the fact that Hawley had expressed his repentance in May 1748 through the gift of £155 as a civil settlement, and Martha's family did not want her to marry Hawley in any case, Edwards persisted and lost the cause. At the same time that this case was being played out, the more encompassing crisis of Edwards's revision of the rules for full membership was generating bitter and combative partisanship. Patricia Tracy draws together these incidents as mutually reinforcing evidence of Edwards's ministerial heavy-handedness.[123] Her assumptions are substantially taken up by Kish Sklar.[124] Irrespective of the nature of moral obligation,

120. Chamberlain, "Bad Books and Bad Boys," 181.

121. Marsden, *A Life*, 295.

122. Kathryn Kish Sklar, "Culture Versus Economics: A Case of Fornication in Northampton in the 1740s," *University of Michigan Papers in Women's Studies* 3(1) (1978): 35–56, especially 50.

123. Patricia J. Tracy, *Jonathan Edwards, Pastor: Religion and Society in Eighteenth-Century Northampton*, The Jonathan Edwards Classic Studies Series (Eugene, OR: Wipf and Stock, 2006), 185, 190.

124. Kish Sklar, "Culture Versus Economics," 49.

because this incident displayed fewer crisp lines of procedural clarity than the others, easy resolution through civil sanctions was impeded. Ecclesiastical discipline under changing social and moral conditions was exposing tensions within Edwards's approach.

Ethics of Love: The Limits of Discipline

Edwards had to some degree justified his theological and procedural approach to discipline through preaching and writing on the topic. The mechanics of discipline had been well illuminated, even when his own pastoral method had been found wanting. Perhaps more important than the necessary deliberations on his own immediate clerical authority, Edwards has also faced questions relating to broader clerical spheres of influence in society and less definable lines of accountability in the same debates. In Massachusetts, because of the distinct categories of full communicant and outsider, the task of excommunication fell to the church alone (unlike in Old England), as it was only full members who could be thus disciplined: it had become "a wholly spiritual punishment."[125] For those outside the reach of clerical authority, moral suasion would be the only legitimate path. With this in mind, one of the most intriguing themes in the sermon "The Means and Ends of Excommunication" is how much attention Edwards gives to the ethics of love and how much he expects of his congregation in terms of their own nuanced appreciation of love as expressed in interactions with those being disciplined outside of church. Discipline may well be objectively defined at its center, but very quickly it becomes subjectively loaded at the periphery—and Edwards is not blind to this complexity.

In Massachusetts, excommunication from the church did not impair legal or political rights, for it was a spiritual and not social punishment.[126] Excommunication was not executed by the state, as it had been traditionally in Europe.[127] In New England, minor excommunication, that is separation from communion of the saints or from communion in the Lord's Supper, was practiced, and not major excommunication, separation from society.[128] Edwards affirms as much in the sermon when he advises the auditory:

---

125. Brown, "The Keys of the Kingdom," 540, 554.

126. Kish Sklar, "Culture Versus Economics," 43. In the medieval world, the excommunication of princes by popes had significant social ramifications, to which Edwards refers. Jonathan Edwards, *A History of the Work of Redemption*, The Works of Jonathan Edwards 9 (New Haven: Yale University Press, 1989), 413.

127. Brown, "The Keys of the Kingdom," 556.

128. Vodola, *Excommunication in the Middle Ages*, 36, 54.

Duties of natural or civil relation are still to be performed towards [them]. Excommunication don't release children from obligations of duty to parents, nor parents from parental affection and care towards children; nor are husbands and wives released from duties proper to their relations, and so of brothers and sisters and other domestic relations.[129]

Monica Fitzgerald has argued that this favorable attitude toward ongoing civic responsibilities for the excommunicate contributed to the gendering of Puritan discipline insofar as men, already more likely to be defined through their social roles outside the home, were less socially affected after their trial.[130] We have yet to observe to what degree Edwards transgressed normative expectations of gender in matters of church discipline.

The recognition of the complexity of social interactions is highlighted by Edwards in other ways in this sermon. His appeal to the ethical distinction between "love of benevolence" and "love of complacence"—perhaps not surprising after having recently preached the series now known as *Charity and its Fruits*, which expounded the nature of love—is nonetheless nuanced and in contrast to the stark legal language of "punishment," "destruction," "correction," or "enemies" that occurs a page or so earlier.[131] Edwards intends for us to understand that good will can be expressed toward someone without this necessarily being joined to a "delight in the company one of another."[132] We must excommunicate "as an act of benevolence or good will" while at the same time regarding those so punished as "objects of displicency and abhorrence."[133] The following illustration assuming emotional intelligence demonstrates the theoretical possibility of such ethical distinction: we may still speak with those so punished on the street, but not invite them into our home or eat with them at a common meal.[134] Practically speaking, however, the inevitable overlap of spheres of social engagement in small-town New England and the attempt to offer fine-grained philosophical distinction between types of love applied in a

129. Edwards, "The Means and Ends of Excommunication," *WJE* 22:75. It is not clear if Edwards knew this to be an injunction promulgated by the medieval Pope Gregory VII in 1078! See Brown, "The Keys of the Kingdom," 552.

130. Monica D. Fitzgerald, "Drunkards, Fornicators, and a Great Hen Squabble: Censure Practices and the Gendering of Puritanism," *Church History* 80(1) (2011): 40–75, especially 41.

131. Edwards, "The Means and Ends of Excommunication," *WJE* 22: 70, 72.

132. Edwards, "The Means and Ends of Excommunication," *WJE* 22: 73.

133. Edwards, "The Means and Ends of Excommunication," *WJE* 22: 72.

134. Edwards, "The Means and Ends of Excommunication," *WJE* 22: 73.

town riven by visceral resentments and familial animosities, would likely be insufficient to make his policy on discipline workable in the long run. Eating and drinking and the life of the tavern could easily overwhelm the impact of discipline at society's edges.[135] Edwards is not unaware of the very real psychological and moral challenges that his vision presents.

This is in evidence in the sermon as Edwards builds in epistemological disclaimers concerning the authority of the disciplinary agenda.[136] Edwards uses the language of visibility no fewer than fifty-two times to buttress his caution concerning the propriety of claiming to know another's heart.[137] Furthermore, using visible intermediate agency as a strategy for justifying purification of God's church, Edwards can distance himself from subjective caprice and acknowledge the contingency of any decisions taken.[138] To apply the ordinance of excommunication is to use means for others' good, and indeed the devil can be made an instrument of the divine purpose to chastise their apostasy.[139] Such hedging is evident when he writes: "They that are excommunicated are in a sense cast out of God's sight...."[140] Certainly the theme of visibility comes to its climax in the later parts of the sermon when Edwards speaks of "God's face," "smiles of providence," and "God's countenance," to personalize either the punishment for sin or the reward for confession. The jurisprudential elements in discipline have been relativized to make room for a vision of personal pilgrimage away from or toward God. Although physical banishment to the land of Nod was neither a geographical nor constitutional option in colonial Massachusetts, existential banishment at distance from the normal paths

---

135. Edwards, "The Means and Ends of Excommunication," *WJE* 22: 65–66.

136. An earlier sermon from 1735, reproached in 1752, provides a similar caution in the art of censuring: "what is in the heart is not visible nor is it the business of the public to pry into it but they are to look upon these [people] as of the church." See Jonathan Edwards, "358. Ephesians 5:25–27 (1735/1752)," in *Sermons, Series II, 1735*, The Works of Jonathan Edwards Online 50 (Jonathan Edwards Center at Yale University), L. 3v.

137. Edwards makes reference to visible criteria both in welcoming and removing members: "So that nothing is left to the church as their rule with respect to admission or exclusion of members, but those things that are visible to the eye of the public, and not those things that appear to the private opinions of men." See Jonathan Edwards, *Sermons by Jonathan Edwards on the Matthean Parables, Volume 1: True and False Christians (On the Parable of the Wise and Foolish Virgins)* (Eugene, OR: Cascade Books, 2012), 70. See also Edwards, "The Means and Ends of Excommunication," *WJE* 22: 78.

138. Edwards is committed to making a distinction between the church and the world to defend the integrity of the saints, as the entire disciplinary agenda embodies, even when epistemological concessions are made.

139. Edwards, "The Means and Ends of Excommunication," *WJE* 22: 74, 77, 79.

140. Edwards, "The Means and Ends of Excommunication," *WJE* 22: 76–77.

of covenant blessing was severe enough, though not always easy to define legally.[141]

Trials of Liberty: The Trajectory of Discipline

The pursuit of religious enthusiasm in eighteenth-century America was a contested phenomenon with partisan premonitions of community impact coming from all quarters. Some held that the awakenings would challenge "custom and convention, obedience and morality." Others saw these developments as remarkable opportunities: "God in America was working outside the accustomed forms."[142] The Great Awakening concerned the application of the new birth to individuals' lives, but the impact of this could not be limited to individuals alone. Broader social concerns for discipline interacted with the particular contingencies of ecclesiastical discipline in the midst of pressures toward new expressions of liberty. Even if excommunication in Massachusetts was of the minor variety, the ritual dimensions of any disciplinary process could produce profound pastoral and social corollaries, especially in labile social surrounds. Inevitably, when a church undertook with due seriousness the process of excommunicating a member, the boundaries of the group were revised, the reach of the authority of its leaders was established afresh, and the norms of behavior for a new situation were defined. Discipline may ultimately have had the stabilizing function of reassurance, but the ritual process itself raised questions about the integrity and limits of the group and the freedom of the individuals within it, and so provoked some measure of instability or fear before attempts at harmonious reintegration.[143]

Monica Fitzgerald, in her article on Puritan processes of censure, helpfully introduces us to the sociology of Victor Turner, in which cultural rituals are atomized into the four steps of "breach of social norms, crisis, adjustments or redress, and reintegration or permanent breach." This has its own analog in the life of the church: "the sin, calling the sinner to confess, the confession to the congregation, and acceptance or excommunication."[144] While she hesitates as a feminist to endorse entirely Turner's model, she nonetheless upholds the idea that a transgressor can be pushed to the limit and then encouraged to

---

141. Edwards, "The Means and Ends of Excommunication," *WJE* 22: 77.

142. David S. Lovejoy, *Religious Enthusiasm in the New World: Heresy to Revolution* (Cambridge: Harvard University Press, 1985), 196, 179.

143. Hall, *Worlds of Wonder*, 137.

144. Fitzgerald, "Censure Practices and the Gendering of Puritanism," 50.

turn around and return to a known community setting. This demonstrates a process of stretching, reversal, and ultimately social plasticity, which can produce, even unwittingly, a new social shape. Though excommunication might sit more comfortably in a hierarchical, perhaps patriarchal, world of predetermined authority structures, it nevertheless can be hijacked by latent social forces to serve a more dynamic social environment and outcomes. People may have "valued rites that restored moral order to the body politic," but those self-same rites may have restored order and at the same time have inverted intended meanings: an execution of a martyr could suggest either the power of the sword or the power of persevering example.[145]

Edwards finds himself sponsoring the possibility of social inversion in the wake of the Great Awakening of the 1740s, using the natural world as his illustration. In commenting on Psalm 19, he writes: "That the sun shall rise in the West [is] contrary to the course of this world, or the course of things in the old heavens and earth. The course of God's providence shall in that day be so wonderfully altered in many respects, that God will as it were change the course of nature."[146] Edwards's preparedness to minimize the value of preparation for the reception of grace had become a socially transgressive strategy to empower the laity,[147] and not insignificantly to empower women, who could develop their own relationship with the divine without clerical mediation.[148] Though Hall draws our attention to the "lay tribalism" that ultimately led to Edwards's dismissal,[149] it is worth pointing out that it was principally the lay women of the parish who remained supportive of their pastor to the end.[150] Edwards overturned the expected order when he set up a young girl, Phebe Bartlet, as a model of piety in *A Faithful Narrative*. The theme of social inversion had also been part of the Bad Book Affair from the outset: Timothy Root had referred to the offending midwifery manual as the "young folks' bible," which in a Puritan setting was to turn the world of authority upside down![151] Even Edwards's own practice of censuring women for drunkenness and men

145. Hall, *Worlds of Wonder*, 185, 186.

146. Jonathan Edwards, "Some Thoughts Concerning the Revival," in *The Great Awakening*, The Works of Jonathan Edwards 4; ed. C. C. Goen (New Haven: Yale University Press, 1972), 357.

147. Hall, *Worlds of Wonder*, 244.

148. Westerkamp, *Women and Religion in Early America*, 21.

149. Hall, *Worlds of Wonder*, 156.

150. Edwards, "To the Reverend John Erskine," *WJE* 16: 364.

151. Chamberlain, "Bad Books and Bad Boys," 190.

for fornication was out of step with his own context.[152] It is certainly easy to decry Edwards's disciplinary practice as reactionary or controlling, but it must also be acknowledged that Edwards's practice could function transgressively and transformatively. To work for the confession of sin and restitution of wrong will not necessarily return relationships or ecclesiological vision to the place it was before. Having touched a set of relationships will change that set of relationships, and indeed it might also affect the fortunes of the one in charge of the process. His discipline was certainly intended as purgative and curative, but in the end, it was also transformative, for it involved the fresh negotiation of social expectations.

Edwards's growing appropriation of discipline in the life of the local church during the 1740s runs up against the assumption that Edwards should be situated squarely within the New Light box, for his commitment to discipline places him in opposition to the radical enthusiasts who threw off traditional authority and against what is seen as the inevitable flow of history toward more individual freedom and the overthrow of arbitrary hegemony.[153] While the seventeenth-century Puritan consensus had understood freedom to be the corollary of purity,[154] in the eighteenth century, new conceptions of liberty called into question this relationship, assuming church discipline to be not the origin of freedom, but its enemy. In this later unstable period, Edwards's pursuit of purity may have assumed a certain objective relationship between pastor and people, but unintentionally resulted in the dynamic recalibration of the private and the public in social life, giving shape to the "emergent ethic of privacy."[155] The early paradox in New England between "respect for personal freedom and a need for external discipline" reaches a new kind of resolution after the revivals in Northampton.[156] It is clear that the discipline Edwards

---

152. See, for example, Fitzgerald, "Censure Practices and the Gendering of Puritanism," 66, 79.

153. For arguments detailing the nature of the debate, see Lovejoy, *Religious Enthusiasm,* especially chaps. 10 and 11; Clarence C. Goen, *Revivalism and Separatism in New England, 1740–1800: Strict Congregationalists and Separate Baptists in the Great Awakening* (Middletown, CT: Wesleyan University Press, 1987); Kidd, *The Great Awakening,* especially chaps. 18 and 19. Interestingly, Joseph Hawley Jr., who defended his brother's freedoms against Edwards's actions during the church investigation, later went on to fight as an officer in the revolutionary wars. See Kish Sklar, "Culture Versus Economics," 44, 48.

154. David D. Hall, *The Faithful Shepherd: A History of New England Ministry in the Seventeenth Century* (Chapel Hill: University of North Carolina Press, 1972), 39.

155. Chamberlain, "Bad Books and Bad Boys," 201–02.

156. Kai T. Erikson, *Wayward Puritans: A Study in the Sociology of Deviance* (Needham Heights, MA: Macmillan, 1966), 53.

promotes in congregational life is more than just a commitment to expunging sin, but entails a more nuanced renegotiation of social roles and the ethical integrity of an alternative model of social life.

5.3 *The Dynamic Church Shaping Its Polity*

Far from being a merely organizational tool, the process by which a church decides to structure its common life reflects something quite profound concerning its values, aspirations, and social position.[157] An elder may rule in the local congregation, but the relationship of that position to others serving in that church or beyond, social assumptions of hierarchy, methods by which that person receives validation for their role, or connections to sacramental ministry all make the seemingly innocuous requirement of elders in the church (Titus 1:5) to be a rather more complex theological reality. Debates in colonial America concerning polity were further loaded with anxieties generated by Laudian persecution of dissent, the primitivist worldview of Puritans, failures of the English Commonwealth, and subsequent Anglicization in North America given the revocation of the Massachusetts charter and the English Toleration Act of 1689. Ward has so succinctly reminded us that the parish in New England was a "social ideal."[158] The aim of this section is to outline the ways in which Edwards adapted the Congregational Way to fit better his emerging ecclesiology under eighteenth-century conditions, which in turn provides significant background to his later dismissal from Northampton.

Primitivism and the Congregational Way: Edwards's Espoused Appreciation

The Reformed tradition of polity emerging from sixteenth-century Switzerland had been identified by its plurality of ministries and ministers, honoring the vocational contributions of the laity and espousing the permanence of the structures witnessed in the New Testament.[159] With breathtaking audacity,

---

157. See Chad Owen Brand and R. Stanton Norman, "Introduction: Is Polity that Important?" in *Perspectives on Church Government: Five Views on Church Polity*, eds. C. O. Brand and R. S. Norman (Nashville: Broadman & Holman, 2004), 5: "As the church corporately submits herself to the Lordship of Christ, the process, expression, and structure of her submission can be designated church polity."

158. W. Reginald Ward, *The Protestant Evangelical Awakening* (Cambridge: Cambridge University Press, 1992), 277.

159. Elsie Anne McKee, "The Offices of Elders and Deacons in the Classical Reformed Tradition," in *Major Themes in the Reformed Tradition*, ed. D. K. McKim (Grand Rapids: Eerdmans, 1992), 344–45.

Calvin drew the unordained into team ministry with him and created a purified structure that coordinated ministries addressing physical needs, community standards, and spiritual discipline.[160] While not elevating polity to the
esse of the church (by hesitating to make discipline embodying the structural
interaction between leadership and membership a true mark of the church),
he nevertheless believed that the New Testament outlines a polity that secures
the *bene esse* of the local congregation. The objectively verifiable purity of
local church polity became a feature of those adopting, at least notionally, the
Genevan model. It may have been difficult to replicate this model everywhere,
not least in the Kingdoms of Scotland and England, but the example of an
alternative to episcopacy was nevertheless powerfully enticing. Both Pilgrims
and Puritans brought with them to the New World expectations of purity in
polity from which emerged the concrete proposals of the Cambridge Platform
in 1648, known popularly as the Congregational Way, which itself defended the
twin goals of congregational autonomy and democratic decision making, and
together would secure the freedom of the faithful. Against external threats, a
pure fellowship was attained, as like-minded members covenanted together.

At heart, the earliest majority ecclesiological position in Massachusetts
attempted to recover and implement a fixed model of church structure that was
anchored in the Scriptural, more especially Old Testament, vision for the people of God. This retrieval program assumed an epistemology that drew upon
identification with and imitation of a pristine primordium, which was generated by the motivation of dissent from developed, according to some opinions
invented, forms,[161] and which took definitive shape only after arrival in New
England.[162] The concept of covenant, which would play such a significant role
in Reformed soteriological debates, played another role in New England insofar as it provided a mechanism for continual return to beginnings with the
desire thereby to see new waves of ecclesiological renewal.[163] Such a vision was
also embedded within New England civil law, for the Pentateuch and Moses's

160. Thomas F. Torrance, "Eldership in the Reformed Church," in *Gospel, Church,
and Ministry: Thomas F. Torrance Collected Studies I*, ed. J. Stein (Eugene, OR: Pickwick
Publications, 2012), 184–85.

161. Theodore Dwight Bozeman, *To Live Ancient Lives*, 16–17, 39; Richard T. Hughes and C.
Leonard Allen, *Illusions of Innocence: Protestant Primitivism in America, 1630–1875* (Chicago
and London: University of Chicago Press, 1988), 13. It should be noted, however, that the New
England project increasingly drew on primordial precedents not for dissent but for order.

162. Theodore Dwight Bozeman, "Biblical Primitivism: An Approach to New England
Puritanism," in *The American Quest for the Primitive Church*, ed. R. T. Hughes (Urbana and
Chicago: University of Illinois Press, 1988), 26–27.

163. Bozeman, *To Live Ancient Lives*, 290.

commands for the social structure of Israel were received as directly applicable to the Puritans' own exodus and plantation in the promised land.[164] Of course, to leap back into the Golden Age of Moses and to draw contemporary implications from that encounter required extraordinary energy and imagination, rather than educated or even sanctified reason, drawing on a different Puritan discourse. By contrast, appeal to the adiaphora of the Church of England, and notably the writings of Richard Hooker (1554–1600) to justify episcopacy, felt like rationally justified compromise.[165]

Edwards's understanding of church polity is readily understood as Congregational. In a carefully crafted early miscellany, he acknowledges the broader category of the people of God, but wants particularly to highlight the significance of the local congregation as a narrower definition of the church because meeting for weekly worship secures visibility for the people of God. Edwards writes in a miscellany: "And by a particular true church must be meant a society of men that are visibly God's people...and that are indeed joined together in the Christian holy public worship."[166] In an unpublished sermon, he wrote: "The design of public worship, is to put open honor on God in the sight of the world, not only to honor him in the sight of the worshipping society that is present."[167] In the words of McDermott and McClymond: "Local assemblies had received from Christ himself a full power to exercise authority in church life, sacraments, and jurisdiction over their members."[168]

The sermon, "Deacons to care for the body, ministers for the soul," preached at an ordination service for deacons in August 1739, gives one of the clearest outlines in Edwards's writings on the nature of local church offices.[169] Even if external circumstances should change, or extraordinary gifts should lapse, there nevertheless remains by the appointment of Christ the ordinary offices "namely, these two of bishops and deacons," of which "the former respects the souls of

---

164. Hughes and Allen, *Illusions of Innocence*, 43–46.

165. Bozeman, *To Live Ancient Lives*, 33, 58.

166. Jonathan Edwards, "Misc." 339, in *The "Miscellanies" (Entry Nos. a–z. aa–zz, 1–500)*, The Works of Jonathan Edwards 13, ed. T. A. Schafer (New Haven: Yale University Press, 1994), 414.

167. Jonathan Edwards, "842. Unpublished Sermon on Ecclesiastes 5:1 (Oct. 1746)" (accessed from the Jonathan Edwards Center at Yale University, 2011), L. 4r–4v.

168. McClymond and McDermott, *Theology of Jonathan Edwards*, 461.

169. Jonathan Edwards, "Deacons to Care for the Body, Ministers for the Soul," in *The Salvation of Souls: Nine Previously Unpublished Sermons on the Call of the Ministry and the Gospel by Jonathan Edwards*, eds. R. A. Bailey and G. A. Wills (Wheaton, IL: Crossway Books, 2002).

men, and the latter their bodies."[170] The focus of the responsibility of the elder (used synonymously with bishop) lay in "prophesying, teaching, exhorting, and ruling,"[171] or more suggestively to make sure, as a steward of the household, that "every one may have his portion of meat in due season in spiritual respects."[172] The deacon had responsibility on the Lord's day for the collection of charitable contributions as part of the "public service of the Christian church" and in deliberate parallel with the physical reality of coming together on that same day "to break bread."[173] The ruling elder as a *lay* officer fell into desuetude in the course of the eighteenth century,[174] but it appears that Edwards regarded himself in this way, given the centrality of the ministry of the Word to his pastoral labors. The deacon's role did not deteriorate in the same way, but functioned as an "intermediary between the minister and the congregation."[175] The great importance of the role of deacons is identified by the nature of ordination to the diaconate itself: "the solemnity of an ordination argues some Great Business requiring the exercise of Great care & precedence & faithfulness."[176] Responsibility falls to the church to "choose and appoint" the deacons, drawing on the model of procedure in Acts 6.[177] Furthermore, there is a fixity in Edwards's view of the office of deacon or elder in the church when he states, for example, in an unpublished sermon of June 14, 1739, that "we have no hint of its being but temporary."[178]

---

170. Edwards, "Deacons to Care for the Body," 100.

171. Edwards, "Deacons to Care for the Body," 96, 97.

172. Edwards, "Deacons to Care for the Body," 101.

173. Jonathan Edwards, "Misc." 1055, in *The "Miscellanies" (Entry Nos. 833–1152)*, The Works of Jonathan Edwards 20, ed. A. P. Pauw (New Haven: Yale University Press, 2002), 394.

174. J. William T. Youngs, *God's Messengers: Religious Leadership in Colonial New England, 1700–1750* (Baltimore: The Johns Hopkins University Press, 1976), 96–97.

175. Youngs, *God's Messengers*, 96.

176. Jonathan Edwards, "512. Acts 6:1–3 (June 1739)," in *Sermons, Series II, 1739*, The Works of Jonathan Edwards Online 54 (Jonathan Edwards Center at Yale University), L. 8v.

177. Edwards, "512. Acts 6:1–3 (June 1739)," *WJEO* 54, L. 10r. It is of some interest that of the three deacons who were ordained in 1739 and whose authority Edwards was keen to affirm, Ebenezer Pomeroy Jr. and Noah Cook were later to orchestrate the moves to dismiss Edwards from his Northampton charge. See Amy Plantinga Pauw, "Editor's Introduction," in *The "Miscellanies" (Entry Nos. 833–1152)*, The Works of Jonathan Edwards 20, ed. A. P. Pauw (New Haven: Yale University Press, 2002), 3.

178. Edwards, "512. Acts 6:1–3 (June 1739)," *WJEO* 54, L. 10v. The fixed arrangement is further witnessed in the same place: "The main business of a deacon, by Christ's appointment, is to take care of the distribution of the church's charity for the outward supply of those that need."

Fixity undergirding division of labor between the spiritual and the physical might suggest an early guiding Platonic ontology.

Edwards defends his Congregationalist credentials during the infamous Breck affair, emerging in 1733–34 but dragging on at least until 1737, in which Northampton's neighboring parish of Springfield called Robert Breck as minister, without consulting the Hampshire Association and despite Breck's growing reputation for turpid orthodoxy. While commitment to any ecclesiastical association might be regarded as a fall from pure Congregationalism, the argument mounted by Edwards and his cobelligerents focused on the illegal involvement of parishes of eastern Massachusetts in the affairs of a church so far removed from them, and thereby their failure to recognize local (albeit associational) authority guaranteed in the Cambridge Platform. Edwards writes:

> You suppose that what we plead for is directly contrary to congregational principles, in that it renders the government of our churches not congregational but classical... but it seems plain to us that the [Cambridge] Synod had no thought of setting aside neighbor churches.... We have from the beginning till now, always managed our ecclesiastical affairs within ourselves; 'tis the way which the county from its infancy has gone on, by the practical agreement of all, and the way in which our peace has ever been maintained.[179]

Acknowledgement of some level of associational identity did not invalidate congregational autonomy: a church may freely enter into any association so long as no authority is foist upon it from outside.[180] Ironically, it is an appeal to the theological results of the trans-local council meeting at Cambridge that forms the basis of Edwards's critique of trans-local interference. In writing to Colonel John Pynchon and other local clergy in 1735 about the meddling of Boston churches, Edwards avers that "we cannot but testify against it as an irregular and disorderly proceeding, and we cannot in conscience concur to such an ordination, and must say that Mr. Breck's conduct in this affair is very surprising to us."[181] Appealing to the language of freedom and tyranny

---

179. Jonathan Edwards, "A Letter to the Author of the Pamphlet Called an Answer to the Hampshire Narrative," in *Ecclesiastical Writings*, The Works of Jonathan Edwards 12; ed. D. D. Hall (New Haven: Yale University Press, 1994), 108–09.

180. Edwards, "Letter to the Author," *WJE* 12: 112.

181. Jonathan Edwards, "To Col. John Pynchon, August 14, 1735," in *Letters and Personal Writings*, The Works of Jonathan Edwards 16, ed. G. S. Claghorn (New Haven: Yale University Press, 1998), 62.

and order and confusion, Edwards provides limits for the type of synodical government proposed.[182] This incident demonstrates Edwards's own frustrations with the unwieldiness of Massachusetts polity early in his ministry, even before the disorderliness arising from later revivals.

Interestingly, Edwards addresses the nature of eldership within a brief miscellany that concerns the issue of church discipline. "Miscellany" No. 948, composed sometime between 1742 and 1743 when the renewal of the Northampton covenant and instances of censure and excommunication in the parish were again practiced, advances the typological case that "[e]lders of Christian churches answer much to the elders of the particular cities of Israel," for "the whole Jewish nation represented the whole church of God, and were a type of the Christian church, so the particular cities and towns seem to represent particular churches *in some respects.*" An ostensibly primitivist argument, though noteworthy, are the qualifiers (here in italics) that draw back from complete identification. Furthermore, though the "elders of the cities seemed to have been like the selectmen of our towns here in New England," Edwards reminded himself that the "priests were superior to them in judgment."[183] In leadership, he allowed for an aristocratic, ecclesiastical superiority that could exist over elders, offset to some degree by the democratic impulse to elect representatives, which was ultimately consistent with the Cambridge Platform: "This Government of the church, is a mixed government...in respect of the Presbytery and power committed to them, it is an Aristocracy....The power granted by Christ unto the body of the church and Brotherhood, is a prerogative...in choosing their own officers, whether elders or deacons."[184] Elders have broad though not necessarily final authority, for their power of office is necessarily derived from a power of privilege, which inheres in the congregation as an inalienable gift from Christ.[185] A delicate dance of accountability is being performed, which highlights overlapping spheres rather than strict demarcations.

Presbyterian Polity: Edwards's Operational Commitment

Edwards's public move toward Presbyterian polity was exacerbated by the revivals, though certainly not caused by them. Practically speaking, the Cambridge

---

182. Edwards, "Letter to the Author," *WJE* 12: 109, 134, 148–50.

183. Edwards, "Misc." 948, *WJE* 20: 204.

184. "The Cambridge Platform," 393.

185. Edwards, "Letter to the Author," *WJE* 12: 124.

Platform of 1648 in Massachusetts[186] and the Saybrook Platform of 1708 in Connecticut,[187] alongside more informal arrangements,[188] had provided consociational models of church government long before Edwards struggled with discipline and order as a consequence of the awakenings. Stoddard's epithet as Pope of the Connecticut Valley suggests charismatic yet regional authority. Edwards had worked after graduating in a Presbyterian congregation in New York from 1722 to 1723, which was for him an extraordinarily positive and affirming experience of ministry and of family, though as a breakaway house church, it may have felt more like a congregation with independent rather than associational aspirations. Growing clericalism in the colonies reflected a desire to receive ministerial validation not merely through the traditional channels of education and call but also through ordination by peers, which encoded new social status.[189] Attacks on the worthiness of ministers in the course of the revivals, especially their credentials as regenerate believers, further emboldened the recalibration of clerical authority.[190] The entrenchment of ministerial associations reflected "the self-consciousness of an honored group and...a perception of threat" and "an implicit assertion of the 'rational authority' of the ministry: a declaration of collective expertise that promised more efficient administration of the churches."[191] Edwards defends the propriety of synods for just such ends in a miscellany of 1723.[192] The theological issue for Edwards in this entry was not so much whether clergy should confer, but whether their conclusions could be enforced by a magistrate as binding on a local congregation. Significantly, defending the role of the civil magistrate increased in the course of Edwards's career.[193]

---

186. Bozeman, *To Live Ancient Lives*, 318.

187. Youngs, *God's Messengers*, 69.

188. McClymond and McDermott, *Theology of Jonathan Edwards*, 461.

189. Youngs, *God's Messengers*, 64, 66. Edwards makes comment on the propriety of being consulted in the ordination of nearby clergy: "Especially does the [affair] of the settlement of a minister concern neighbouring ministers as they are to be fellow Labourers & fellow helpers in the same Great work." See Jonathan Edwards, "591. Acts 14:23 (Jan. 1741)," in *Sermons, Series II, January–June 1741*, The Works of Jonathan Edwards Online 57 (Jonathan Edwards Center at Yale University), L. 3v.

190. E. Brooks Holifield, *God's Ambassadors: A History of the Christian Clergy in America*, Pulpit & Pew (Grand Rapids: Eerdmans, 2007), 94–95.

191. Holifield, *God's Ambassadors*, 72–73.

192. Jonathan Edwards, "Misc." *rr*, in *The "Miscellanies" (Entry Nos. a–z, aa–zz, 1–500)*, The Works of Jonathan Edwards 13, ed. T. A. Schafer (New Haven: Yale University Press, 1994), 189.

193. Gerald R. McDermott, *One Holy and Happy Society: The Public Theology of Jonathan Edwards* (University Park: Pennsylvania State University Press, 1992), 129n34.

The ultimate clarity of Edwards's views is evident in a four-part sermon series he delivered in June 1748, based on Deuteronomy 1:13–18, with the doctrine, "'Tis the mind of God that not a mixed multitude but only select persons of distinguished ability and integrity are fit for the business of judging causes."[194] Taking up the example of Moses and his leadership, but appealing to other Scriptural traditions as well, Edwards argues that the authority of a local congregation must function subordinately to the authority of an appointed leader, because "a mix'd multitude of young & old wise & unwise was not fit."[195] The language of wisdom appears dozens of times in the first part of the series. He appeals to the example of common sailors who are not "fit to steer the ship and govern it,"[196] just as it would be inappropriate to put "a naked sword into the hand of a child."[197] More substantially, Edwards fears that congregations who are entrusted with judging causes create "confusion, as it sets up those to rule over others to whom they ought to be subject, it in many cases sets servants to judging their masters and mistresses to whom the Scripture everywhere requires of 'em subjection."[198] Furthermore, to prosecute a case fairly necessitates great labor in research and understanding and capacity for verbal exchange and debate, which is not always widely possible.[199] In the second sermon of the series, Edwards boldly states that instead of congregational meetings producing healing for the "diseases and wounds of the church," "our way of managing church discipline has been the greatest wound…worse than all the scandals."[200] In the same paragraph, he refers suggestively to contentions like "quareling [sic] with their minister" and "quarrelling with one another." He muses wistfully that a church should instead be known for its beauty, and order, and peace.[201]

To make his case, Edwards did not, as we might have expected, merely call in a primitivist model and argue for reform based on primordial precedent. His growing frustration with the polity of Congregationalism provoked

---

194. Jonathan Edwards, "898. Deuteronomy 1:13–18 (June 1748)," in *Sermons, Series II, 1748*, The Works of Jonathan Edwards Online 66 (Jonathan Edwards Center at Yale University), L. 2v.

195. Edwards, "898. Deuteronomy 1:13–18 (June 1748)," *WJEO* 66: L. 4r.

196. Edwards, "898. Deuteronomy 1:13–18 (June 1748)," *WJEO* 66: L. 9r.

197. Edwards, "898. Deuteronomy 1:13–18 (June 1748)," *WJEO* 66: L. 8v.

198. Edwards, "898. Deuteronomy 1:13–18 (June 1748)," *WJEO* 66: L. 9r.

199. Edwards, "898. Deuteronomy 1:13–18 (June 1748)," *WJEO* 66: L. 8v.

200. Edwards, "898. Deuteronomy 1:13–18 (June 1748)," *WJEO* 66: L. 21r.

201. Edwards, "898. Deuteronomy 1:13–18 (June 1748)," *WJEO* 66: L. 21r.

him to acknowledge other kinds of authority when formulating church government. He appealed to the "light of nature," to which "the common sense and practice of all nations and ages" agree.[202] Judging causes depends not on ignorance, but "expects a rational service," which doesn't follow the crowd but is capable of independent analysis.[203] He can begin paragraphs with the apparently objective claim that "Experience shews...."[204] Metonomy is used over a number of pages to argue that the Scriptures may sound as if they are referring to the whole congregation, but actually intend us to understand only the part: "many need not be understood of a greatmultitude [sic] but only of a plurality."[205] In setting up a model for a more nuanced congregational polity, Edwards is not embarrassed in using reason, with the Scriptures, to outline the blueprint. A traditional Puritan, inoculated against "human invention," could not have proceeded in this way.[206] It must be acknowledged that Edwards does not see his model as definitively new, though the possible objection of novelty is one he seeks to forestall. Many churches in Scotland, Holland, Geneva, Switzerland, and France—not to mention Presbyterian churches in New York and in New Jersey—had adopted similar structures. He reminds his listeners that blind commitment to the "tradition of our forefathers" and their Congregational Way would itself be disobedient and unscriptural, for reformation always requires the searing light of biblical witness to expose ossified ways, even in New England.[207]

Edwards is here suggesting that a new model of congregational life is needed. Such a vision does not consist in the precise details of ancient Israel's life being replicated nor congregational meetings having the last word. Instead he espouses a polity for which the foundation is to be located in a body of elders (to which both Old and New Testament witness), who, importantly, are set apart by the congregation to act as its representatives, to some degree thereby functioning as paternal oversight and independent authority, who are thereby given responsibility to judge causes in the church:

> The business of these fathers of the people is to assist the minister to act with him not to act above him nor to act without him nor is he to

---

202. Edwards, "898. Deuteronomy 1:13–18 (June 1748)," *WJEO* 66: L. 24r.

203. Edwards, "898. Deuteronomy 1:13–18 (June 1748)," *WJEO* 66: L. 9r.

204. Edwards, "898. Deuteronomy 1:13–18 (June 1748)," *WJEO* 66: L. 19v.

205. Edwards, "898. Deuteronomy 1:13–18 (June 1748)," *WJEO* 66: L. 38r.

206. Bozeman, *To Live Ancient Lives*, 17–18.

207. Edwards, "898. Deuteronomy 1:13–18 (June 1748)," *WJEO* 66: L. 50v.

act without them, but there is no church act without the concurrence of both.[208]

He suggests that they would function much like the agents of the people who are elected to the House of Commons, who in that space do not function as deputies second-guessing the mind of the electorate and relaying their opinions, but as representatives finding "concurrence" with the mind of the King, though not enjoying equality with his status. Elders hold an office in the church, though the proposal embedded in this sermon makes plain that elders, by making their business "to assist the minister," are not on equal footing with the minister. A view of eldership is emerging that requires deep renegotiation of inherited roles, built on greater distinct spheres of authority and therefore requiring greater trust.

Most telling, therefore, in this explanation of roles is the language of checks and balances by which the potentially usurping authority of both minister and eldership is understandably circumscribed. The final sermon in the sequence spells out further the reason for insisting on checks and balances: "to take care of their liberties, and prevent the tyranny of superiour officers...and be a balance to the power of the kings and peers."[209] Centralizing political authority has its parallel in emboldened ministerial claims. Not only is this language reminiscent of later revolutionary potency, but it also works within the conceptual range of contract rather than covenant, the former assuming breach, which must be forestalled, rather than the latter assuming trust, which must be maintained. The apparent failure of the 1742 process of covenant renewal in Northampton perhaps highlighted the impotency of received polity to generate and manage change.[210] At its most innocuous, Edwards's model is merely clarifying lines of accountability in the local church. More provocatively, his model could be understood to shift radically the locus of power from the assembled congregation to its agents, who are investing in a common interest beyond the boundaries of the local congregation for which

---

208. Edwards, "898. Deuteronomy 1:13–18 (June 1748)," *WJEO* 66: L. 24r.

209. Edwards, "898. Deuteronomy 1:13–18 (June 1748)," *WJEO* 66: L. 50v.

210. Interestingly, in preaching on covenant renewal, Edwards highlights the benefits of solidarity within the congregation, which is confirmed by covenant rather than repaired. In speaking to the issue of the merit of public covenant-making, he writes: "'Tis for the good of a people, as it is a great restraint. [It] puts 'em in mind of their duty and obligation. [It is] a means of hearty self-dedication to God, makes their bonds the stronger and so restrains the conscience." Jonathan Edwards, "Renewing our Covenant with God," in *Sermons and Discourses, 1739–1742*, The Works of Jonathan Edwards 22, ed. H. S. Stout (New Haven: Yale University Press), 516.

they are demanding increased trust and perversely thereby generating a culture of suspicion. Edwards sits, perhaps uncomfortably, between a "Country"
party ideology that affirmed both republican virtue and the accountability of
elected officials, and "Court" party assumptions, which suggest that magistrates ought not to be beholden to popular will.[211] This was a common tension
in the eighteenth century, and one that Edwards himself was to exemplify.[212]

Edwards preached this sermon series in the period immediately before
his ultimate dismissal, in the midst of emerging local tensions between him
and his congregation. He recognizes that there are great "controversies...in
the wor[l]d about Church government," caused by "that dismal confusion that
hitherto we have gone on in by which satan [sic] has had so great advantages
against us."[213] The Congregational Way is thereby discredited, and, not surprisingly, some who are chary of the instability of their tradition have returned to
the Church of England.[214] To espouse both in principle and in practice a variant
of Presbyterian polity[215] could be to deny to some the privileges of membership
that they had heretofore enjoyed. If the church is founded by divine initiative,
the privileges of belonging to this divine institution are a function of acceptance of the covenant of grace, and not by a covenant generated through local
solidarity. He writes that "[w]e have no right or claim by nature to any one gospel privileges [sic], and therefore no right to any church privilege," which "are
not to be sought for in nature." Though this series of sermons does not formally interact with sacramental theology and qualifications for membership,
which were the presenting challenges in Edwards's last years in Northampton,
more substantial issues concerning justifications for the authority of membership are raised, and ultimate questions of unity are not entirely absent. Agents
in the British Parliament, whose privileged authority is from below by virtue
of common interest with those they represent, nonetheless find themselves to
be members of a new body with its own sense of solidarity and sovereignty.

---

211. See McDermott, *One Holy and Happy Society*, especially 117–19. McDermott sees
Edwards as better representing the "Country" party in colonial politics insofar as Edwards
rejects the notion that wealth or property is of itself the best predictor of worthiness to serve
in public office, and affirms that political authority must be scrutinized, not merely accepted.
Although this argument has great merit, it does not necessarily require that popular will be
the last word in ecclesiastical or civil life.

212. Youngs, *God's Messengers*, 139.

213. Edwards, "898. Deuteronomy 1:13–18 (June 1748)," *WJEO* 66: L. 38r.

214. Edwards, "898. Deuteronomy 1:13–18 (June 1748)," *WJEO* 66: L. 50v.

215. Presbyterianism in the American colonies could be divided into four different
types. See D. G. Hart and John R. Muether, *Seeking a Better Country: 300 Years of American
Presbyterianism* (Phillipsburg: Presbyterian & Reformed, 2007), 40–42.

Famously, Edwards's journey to Presbyterian polity was expressed most clearly in a letter to the Reverend John Erskine, written in the days immediately after he preached his "Farewell Sermon" in Northampton. There was now no longer any reason to be bashful:

> As to my subscribing to the substance of the Westminster Confession, there would be no difficulty: and as to the Presbyterian government, I have long been perfectly out of conceit with our unsettled, independent, confused way of church government in this land. And the Presbyterian way has ever appeared to me most agreeable to the Word of God, and the reason and nature of things, though I cannot say that I think that the Presbyterian government of the Church of Scotland is so perfect that it can't in some respects be mended.[216]

Earlier in this letter, Edwards reported how he had secured representation from parishes distant from Northampton, men who were not related or directly implicated in the affair of his dismissal, though insistence on the propriety of this arrangement was in contrast to the rules of engagement that he insisted upon in the Breck case, and confirmed his associational sympathies. Such a trajectory is further traveled in this same correspondence when he affirms the ministry of the Archbishop of Canterbury, Thomas Herring, and praises the labors of those who have seen conversions and baptisms in the Russian Empire.[217] Presbyterian polity, while intimating possible international scope, functions for Edwards as a desirable tool of order for which he provides lofty metaphysical justification:

> And the ministry in general, or the whole number of faithful ministers, being all united in the same work as fellow laborers, and conspiring to the same design as fellow helpers to the grace of God, may be considered as one mystical person, that espouses the church as a young man espouses a virgin.[218]

---

216. Edwards, "117. To the Reverend John Erskine," *WJE* 16: 355.

217. Edwards, "117. To the Reverend John Erskine," *WJE* 16: 351.

218. Jonathan Edwards, "The Church's Marriage to Her Sons, and to Her God," in *Sermons and Discourses, 1743–1758*, The Works of Jonathan Edwards 25, ed. W. H. Kimnach (New Haven: Yale University Press, 2005), 173.

International Cooperation: Edwards's Grand Aspiration

The Puritan project in New England only gradually developed millennial thinking that was detached from primordial controls, for purity of polity was secured by a return rather than an advance.[219] The fixity of the pure model was to be found in retrieval; dynamic engagement with the world was synonymous with decline. Edwards, however, relativized the Congregational Way and revised his expectations of the life of the church by reflecting on its progress through human history in the course of his own ministry. Though increasingly enamored of the Presbyterian path, it too had its limits and was of secondary rank to the great evangelical doctrines of regeneration and salvation by grace and evangelistic fervor.[220] In his sermons on the parable of the net, for example, Edwards makes clear that church offices are only for this age,[221] also maintaining in commentary on the Psalter in the Blank Bible that the early ministries of deacons and priests are seen as meager compared with their "more glorious fulfillment in the future glorious times of the church."[222] Circumscribed are the orders of ministry but developing nonetheless. Reflection on the nature of ecclesiastical polity was gradually shaped by eschatological insights and motivations, though even a slow development was significant in the context of the New England project.

The revivals made an impact on polity in that they elevated the contribution of the laity (with some inevitable pushback from members of the clergy[223]) and accelerated the marginalization of local structures as the Spirit worked beyond them in ways surprising and yet often similar. They cultivated openness to international cooperative ventures that were less amenable to strict oversight and control. Indeed, though Edwards pursued a policy of purity to restrict communicant membership that provoked his dismissal, David Hall suggests that it was a local, lay, and regressive tribalism that galvanized the response to Edwards's sacramental views, which in sum were moving in the

---

219. Bozeman, *To Live Ancient Lives*, 221, 249.

220. McClymond and McDermott, *Theology of Jonathan Edwards*, 459. Edwards recognizes the limitations of any polity: "'Tis not all them that [p]rofess Christianity, 'tis not all . . . [t]hem [t]hat are Protestants . . . 'tis not all that are Presbyterians, 'tis not all that [c]ome to the sacrament that are [r]eally of the Church. . . . They are not all Israel." See Edwards, "358. Ephesians 5:25–27 (1735/1752)," *WJEO* 50: L. 2r.

221. Jonathan Edwards, *Fish Out of Their Element (On the Parable of the Net)*, Sermons by Jonathan Edwards on the Matthean Parables Volume III (Eugene: Cascade Books, 2012), 54.

222. Jonathan Edwards, "Ps. 132:15–16," in *The "Blank Bible,"* The Works of Jonathan Edwards 24, Part I, ed. S. J. Stein (New Haven: Yale University Press, 2006), 536.

223. Von Rohr, *Shaping of American Congregationalism*, 225–29.

direction of a conceptual unity significantly broader than the parish and its covenant and engendering progressive aspirations.[224] Edwards's own expansive vision of the work of redemption needs to be set alongside the painful local and neighborly conflicts that became the prime cause of discontent. Holifield makes this plain:

> Buildings constructed for rituals of harmony divided town after town into skirmishing factions.... The divisions during the great awakening were essentially over matters of ritual practice: who should preach, how sermons should be delivered, who should receive baptism, who should be admitted to the Lord's Supper, how much decorum should mark worship?[225]

Edwards is certainly concerned for the visible distinctiveness of the church, but with that is coupled an increasing desire for the church's progressive flexibility, dynamic advancement, and eschatological glory,[226] which if true of its heavenly condition, arguing from the greater to the lesser, is also true of the church on earth: "all the state of the church before, both in earth and in heaven, is a growing state."[227] It appears that for Edwards, the polity of the church should increasingly not just defend Gospel purity or experiential holiness, but also embody Gospel unity, or aspirational oneness. A greater concern for unity of believers was desired when revivals proved divisive, even though distinctions between types of membership put paid to a pure fellowship as an attainable ideal. It may be that conceptualities of contract would ultimately prove insufficient to capture the complexity and vision of any millennial ideal,[228] but in the meantime it provided a channel into, and a dam around, a more fluidly dangerous world.

These three thematic presentations of grounded ecclesiological practice in the ministry of Edwards serve not just for completion of the overview of

---

224. Hall, *Worlds of Wonder*, 155–56.

225. Holifield, "Peace, Conflict, and Ritual," 565, 568.

226. Janice Knight, *Orthodoxies in Massachusetts: Rereading American Puritanism* (Cambridge: Harvard University Press, 1994), 208–10.

227. Jonathan Edwards, "Misc." 371, in *The "Miscellanies" (Entry Nos. a–z, aa–zz, 1–500)*, Works of Jonathan Edwards 13, ed. T. A. Schafer (New Haven: Yale University Press, 1994), 442–43.

228. See Knight, *Orthodoxies in Massachusetts*, 2–4, where the language of contract is associated more closely with the Amesian school of Puritan ecclesiology, which privileges nationalism over internationalism.

Edwards's ecclesiology in this book, but function also as opportunities to test previous conclusions against these case studies. Edwards's espoused theology, avoiding both the Scylla of separatism and the Charybdis of formalism, finds its reflex here in an operational theology, which can be flexible and contextually aware, while nonetheless profoundly principled and theologically driven. His broader desire for dynamic order in the church is grounded in similar aspirations for worship and practical expressions of Christian obedience. His ecclesiology appears to cohere effectively within a larger embracing vision of reality shaped by the Gospel and the Kingdom.

6

Conclusion: Orderly But Not Ordinary

Edwards's Evangelical Ecclesiology

IN SURVEYING THE ministry of Edwards under the headings of order in his experience, world and practice, we have created a framework for understanding with new depth and freshness Edwards's ecclesiological commitments, as we will see below. These commitments are in evidence in our demonstration of the development within Jonathan Edwards's ecclesiological thought arising from the various potentially disordering situations in which he served. Furthermore, we have shown the constructive connection between his understanding of the church and other leading theological themes, which make of the church an essential entailment to Gospel preaching, rather than merely a pragmatic arrangement for passing needs.[1] For Edwards, the focus of fellowship amongst the regenerate is to be found in celebration of the Lord's Supper, which provides orderly nurture and visual confirmation of life in the Spirit. Edwards does not merely re-impose seventeenth century assumptions on congregational life in the eighteenth century, but importantly refashions ecclesiology in New England in his own day. His ecclesiology was generated by superimposing revivalist conditions and social aspirations onto Reformed convictions (sometimes with the revivalist strand eclipsing his patrimony), making it innovatively evangelical rather than generically Protestant.[2] It is not too much to say with Zakai that Edwards dedicated his life to "a defense of the Christian church."[3]

---

1. Vanhoozer would concur, making clear that "the church is 'analytic' in, an implication of, the gospel itself." See Kevin J. Vanhoozer, "Evangelicalism and the Church: The Company of the Gospel," in *The Futures of Evangelicalism: Issues and Prospects*, ed. C. Bartholomew, R. Parry and A. West (Grand Rapids: Kregel, 2003), 70.

2. Pauw suggests that Edwards departs occasionally from Calvin when he highlights revivalist eschatology. See Plantinga Pauw, "Practical Ecclesiology in John Calvin and Jonathan Edwards," in *John Calvin's American Legacy*, ed. Thomas J. Davis (Oxford: University Press, 2010), 106.

3. Zakai, *Jonathan Edwards's Philosophy of History*, 334.

Edwards's Comprehensive Ecclesiological Vision

Edwards understood the church within a grand divine scheme. In his earliest years he was concerned to review the place of his own experience of conversion within received accounts of preparation for salvation and faculty psychology, while during the period of the revivals from the mid-1730s until the early 1740s his center of attention is the church as the necessary framework for understanding and channeling spiritual ardor. The latter part of his ministry after the cooling of revivalist fervor finds his ecclesiological attention coalescing around international and eschatological visions. His apparent disappointment with the local congregation did not equate to a rejection of corporate Christian nurture in its entirety, but leads to its transposition into a new key. The value of conversion and experiential religion gave a new dynamic core to received ecclesiological norms, as the "affectional transposition of Christian doctrine" endemic to the eighteenth century found its toehold in Edwards's vision of the church.[4]

The overarching divine scheme showcases the church in systematic theological light as well. The extraordinary freedom of God in salvation is tempered by the expectation that the church will ordinarily help us to receive the experience of grace. The church is embedded within the order of creation, while at the same time it represents a down payment on the transformation of this world in the new creation. Edwards drew together divergent strands of Reformation thought to demonstrate the possibility of creating a purer fellowship for the regenerate, which is nevertheless nestled within a church whose social responsibility is wider than its membership. An ethical vision for human flourishing is tied into divine and dynamic trinitarian life within the church, and is not just based on an individual's rational autonomy. Union with God becomes not just a Reformed explanation of the beginnings of the Christian life (rather than its beatific end), but coheres with the very nature of church life as well, most evident in the solemnity of the Lord's Supper, which has at its heart communion with God. Revivalistic emphases, according to Edwards, must not necessarily undermine habituated ecclesiological forms, nor circumvent received theological norms. In short, Edwards confects a reconstitution of the life of the church with revivalistic emphases at its core.

Edwards's eschatological Gospel of the Kingdom had as its fruit not just regenerate lives but renewed social experience, penultimately in the church but ultimately for the world. He maintained that sponsoring the regeneration

---

4. Jaroslav Pelikan, *Christian Doctrine and Modern Culture (since 1700)*, The Christian Tradition: A History of the Development of Doctrine (Chicago: University of Chicago Press, 1989), 128.

of individuals would not necessarily lead to the fissiparous disordering of the community, as some feared, but the moral transformation of the community as it rediscovered its corporate moorings and thereby its social vision.[5] McLoughlin reminds us that "[r]evitalization of the individual led to efforts to revitalize society.... Religious revivalism, saving souls, is in this respect a political activity, a way of producing a reborn majority to remodel society according to God's will and with his help."[6] In New England, revival was intricately linked to the renewal of the covenant, for the "assumption on which the concept of a revival of religion rests is that God deals with entire communities as discrete moral entities."[7] Gerald McDermott is of the view that Edwards works to re-establish social cohesion through his ministry, even if his new conception of society is based not on traditional static hierarchy but on a dynamic and relational experiential order.[8] As Ward so succinctly suggests, any adjustment to the model of church as Edwards achieved would have significant repercussions, for "the New England parish was more than a device for paying a minister; it was a social ideal."[9] Even if the locus of religious authority was repositioned to occupy the seat of the human heart, it could still be possible to build a social vision around democratic religious expression, rather than clerical control.[10]

Edwards's Curtailed Ecclesiological Legacy

Edwards's ecclesiological vision was, however, rejected by the Northampton church. While local pastoral concerns may have colored his people's ability to reflect impartially on Edwards's teaching, the fact that they dismissed their minister, who saw himself as an objective representative of God's promises in that place, and thereby opted for a view of the Lord's Supper which did not assume the presence of the Lord in the Supper for the regenerate alone, substantially impacted Edwards's ecclesiological legacy, in Massachusetts and

---

5. Crawford, *Seasons of Grace*, 15, 124, 189.

6. William G. McLoughlin, *Revivals, Awakenings, and Reform: An Essay on Religion and Social Change in America, 1607–1977*, Chicago History of American Religion (Chicago: University of Chicago Press, 1978), 75.

7. Crawford, *Seasons of Grace*, 20. Crawford goes on to describe the ways in which New England differed from the Middle Colonies with its assumptions of "the outpouring of grace for the transformation of a community." Crawford, *Seasons of Grace*, 122–23, 247.

8. McDermott, *One Holy and Happy Society*, 137, 141.

9. Ward, *The Protestant Evangelical Awakening*, 277.

10. McDermott, *One Holy and Happy Society*, 153–54.

beyond.[11] It was Edwards's dynamic and contextually derived understanding of the place of the church within the historical purposes of God, which most resonated with his contemporaries, for in it their own adjustments to New World contingencies were most readily affirmed. Effectively, what his disputants did not do was reject the value of the church as an instrument of God's eschatological purposes, even if such a view, disconnected from Edwards's larger theological vision, had the potential to eviscerate its Gospel content and become unreconstructed activism.[12] His principled instrumentalism became in the hands of those less astute a pragmatic instantiation of the spiritual independence of the laity.

It is therefore often assumed that Edwards's Gospel was highly subjectivist, growing out of his commitment to religious affections, which were the location of true religion,[13] and that to preach the Gospel was merely to preach an individual experience of salvation from sin, or salvation from God's wrath as sin's consequence. William Abraham asserts with reference to Edwards that this "anthropocentric turn has been the undoing of modern evangelism,"[14] in which revivalist reductionism rules. Rather than the purveyor of a panoramic approach to world history, for which revivals were a dynamic motor, and the church a necessary carriage of divine encounter and nurture, Edwards is viewed as a fount of separatism, or the source of evangelicalism's antipathy towards ecclesiology. His own ecclesiological synthesis may not in the end have been sufficiently compelling in Northampton to compete with worldly blandishments, but he did nevertheless go a long way to create a vision for the church which was both theologically distinct and yet socially engaged: *distinctio sed separatio*. Edwards's own prophetic sensibility reinforced just such a vision.

Edwards's Gospel was not an attenuated theory of atonement, nor could it be summarized as the good news of an experience of rebirth. His Gospel was neither an idea without application, nor an experience without foundation. For Edwards, the assumptions of covenant life in New England, the millennial frame of his ministry, and his prophetic self-understanding position his preaching as more than an appeal to decision, but as a call to ecclesiological

---

11. It is of course true that Edwards's model of church exercised ecclesiological pre-eminence in New England until at least the Second Great Awakening through his New Divinity followers, even when the theological vision that generated this ecclesiology was somewhat attenuated.

12. Ian Stackhouse, "Revivalism, Faddism and the Gospel," in *On Revival: A Critical Examination*, eds. A. Walker and K. Aune (Carlisle: Paternoster Press, 2003), 244.

13. Edwards, *WJE* 2: 95.

14. William Abraham, *The Logic of Evangelism* (Grand Rapids: Eerdmans, 1989), 58.

renewal, eschatological expectation as well as spiritual revival. Here was simply no revivalist evangelicalism, but rather Edwards as the mouthpiece of a confessional evangelicalism with sweeping vision of the church, alongside passion and preaching and prayer for revivals in every land.

Edwards's Orderly but not Ordinary Ecclesiology

Edwards develops an approach to ecclesiology, which highlights the orderly processes but not the ordinary origins of the church's life. In a sense, then, his understanding of the church can be pictured as a company of the Gospel, which is a community embedded in the world though tracing its origins to disruptive divine life. The people of God are companions in fellowship with one another, especially evident when this takes place outside of the normal bounds of weekly meeting or is focused on an organization designed with particular evangelistic goals. Such a company has the dramatic responsibility of acting out before the eyes of the world the truth that it claims to embody, and the world that it proleptically represents, making its regenerate life as visible as possible. Edwards's company was also understood as a society that broke bread together, appealing to the literal etymology of the word to show how fellowship, visibility, and nurture might be expressed.[15] The Gospel as the animating center of the church, which births the need for a company at all, situates him in a Protestant tradition which continued to be reformed through the leverage of an unchanging Christological core. His own perceived role as a herald of the Gospel gave this company its marching orders and situated it temporally within a battle of cosmic proportions.

For Edwards, the order of the Word creates with the dynamism of the Spirit an elliptical account of the church's life, which makes it both orderly but not ordinary. The church is shaped by the Son and the Spirit, in as far as it can be described as the Body of Christ and the Temple of the Spirit simultaneously. Edwards's representation of the church is an exemplary model, not of traditional mechanistic ecclesiology, nor of revivalist and separatist ecclesiology, but of evangelical ecclesiology, which harnesses creative innovative missiological forms to received and systematically constructed Biblical truth. He holds together commitments to both light and truth, even where this threatens, in its own way, to sunder the stability of the church. His insights, scattered amongst his works, can be for us today a modest lamp for our path, even when we struggle to fulfill our own calling to be a city on a hill.

---

15. I acknowledge the source of this image in the writing of Vanhoozer, "Evangelicalism and the Church," 85–92. Debates in the ministry of Edwards around the breaking of the bread make this image particularly apt.

Bibliography

PRIMARY SOURCES

Ames, William. *The Marrow of Theology*. Translated by John E. Eusden. Grand Rapids: Baker, 1997.

Calvin, John. *Institutes of the Christian Religion*. Library of Christian Classics. Vols 21–22. Translated by F. L. Battles. Philadelphia: Westminster Press, 1960.

Edwards, Jonathan. "A Divine and Supernatural Light." Pages 405–26 in *Sermons and Discourses, 1730–1733*. The Works of Jonathan Edwards 17. Edited by Mark Valeri. New Haven: Yale University Press, 1999.

———. "A Faithful Narrative." Pages 97–211 in *The Great Awakening*. The Works of Jonathan Edwards 4. Edited by C. C. Goen. New Haven: Yale University Press, 1972.

———. "A Farewell Sermon Preached at the First Precinct in Northampton, after the People's Public Rejection of their Minister... on June 22, 1750." Pages 457–93 in *Sermons and Discourses, 1743–1758*. The Works of Jonathan Edwards 25. Edited by Wilson H. Kimnach. New Haven: Yale University Press, 2006.

———. *A History of the Work of Redemption*. The Works of Jonathan Edwards 9. New Haven: Yale University Press, 1989.

———. "A Letter to the Author of the Pamphlet Called an Answer to the Hampshire Narrative." Pages 91–163 in *Ecclesiastical Writings*. The Works of Jonathan Edwards 12. Edited by David D. Hall. New Haven: Yale University Press, 1994.

———. "A Sinner Is Not Justified in the Sight of God Except Through the Righteousness of Christ Obtained by Faith." Pages 60–66 in *Sermons and Discourses, 1723–1729*. The Works of Jonathan Edwards 14. Edited by Kenneth P. Minkema. New Haven: Yale University Press, 1997.

———. "An Appendix Containing Some Reflections and Observations on the Preceding Memoirs of Mr. Brainerd." Pages 500–41 in *The Life of David Brainerd*. The Works of Jonathan Edwards 7. Edited by Norman Pettit. New Haven: Yale University Press, 1985.

————. "An Humble Attempt to Promote Explicit Agreement and Visible Union of God's People in Extraordinary Prayer for the Revival of Religion and the Advancement of Christ's Kingdom on Earth, Pursuant to Scripture-Promises and Prophecies Concerning the Last Time." Pages 307–436 in *Apocalyptic Writings*. The Works of Jonathan Edwards 5. Edited by Stephen J. Stein. New Haven: Yale University Press, 1977.

————. *Apocalyptic Writings*. The Works of Jonathan Edwards 5. Edited by Stephen J. Stein. New Haven: Yale University Press, 1977.

————. "Charity and Its Fruits." Pages 123–397 in *Ethical Writings*. The Works of Jonathan Edwards 8. Edited by Paul Ramsay. New Haven: Yale University Press, 1989.

————. *Catalogues of Books*. The Works of Jonathan Edwards 26. Edited by Peter J. Thuesen. New Haven: Yale University Press, 2008.

————. "Christ, the Light of the World." Pages 533–46 in *Sermons and Discourses, 1720–1723*. The Works of Jonathan Edwards 10. Edited by Wilson H. Kimnach. New Haven: Yale University Press, 1992.

————. "Christians have Communion with Christ." Pages 134–50 in *Sermons on the Lord's Supper*. Edited by Don Kistler. Orlando: The Northampton Press, 2007.

————. "The Church's Marriage to Her Sons, and to Her God." Pages 164–96 in *Sermons and Discourses, 1743–1758*. The Works of Jonathan Edwards 25. Edited by Wilson H. Kimnach. New Haven: Yale University Press, 2005.

————. "Deacons to Care for the Body, Ministers for the Soul." Pages 93–109 in *The Salvation of Souls: Nine Previously Unpublished Sermons on the Call of the Ministry and the Gospel by Jonathan Edwards*. Edited by Richard A. Bailey and Gregory A. Wills. Wheaton, IL: Crossway Books, 2002.

————. "Diary." Pages 759–89 in *Letters and Personal Writings*. The Works of Jonathan Edwards 16. Edited by George S. Claghorn. New Haven: Yale University Press, 1998.

————. "Discourse on the Trinity." Pages 109–44 in *Writings on the Trinity, Grace and Faith*. The Works of Jonathan Edwards 21. Edited by Sang Hyun Lee. New Haven: Yale University Press, 2003.

————. "Dissertation I: Concerning the End for Which God Created the World." Pages 399–536 in *Ethical Writings*. The Works of Jonathan Edwards 8. Edited by John E. Smith. New Haven: Yale University Press, 1989.

————. "Dissertation II: The Nature of True Virtue." Pages 537–627 in *Ethical Writings*. The Works of Jonathan Edwards 8. Edited by John E. Smith. New Haven: Yale University Press, 1989.

————. "The Distinguishing Marks." Pages 213–88 in *The Great Awakening*. The Works of Jonathan Edwards 4. Edited by Clarence C. Goen. New Haven: Yale University Press, 1972.

————. *Ecclesiastical Writings*. The Works of Jonathan Edwards 12. Edited by David D. Hall. New Haven: Yale University Press, 1994.

————. *Fish Out of Their Element (On the Parable of the Net)*. Sermons by Jonathan Edwards on the Matthean Parables. Vol. 3. Eugene, OR: Cascade Books, 2012.

———. *Freedom of the Will*. The Works of Jonathan Edwards 1. Edited by Paul Ramsey. New Haven: Yale University Press, 1957.

———. "Glorious Grace." Pages 388–99 in *Sermons and Discourses, 1720–1723*. The Works of Jonathan Edwards 10. Edited by Wilson H. Kimnach. New Haven: Yale University Press, 1992.

———. "The Importance of a Future State." Pages 351–376 in *Sermons and Discourses, 1720-1723*. The Works of Jonathan Edwards 10. Edited by Wilson H. Kimnach. New Haven: Yale University Press, 1992.

———. "Jonathan Edwards's Singing Lecture Sermon." *Studies in Puritan American Spirituality* 8 (2004): 135–46.

———. "Lectures on the Qualifications for Full Communion in the Church of Christ." Pages 349–440 in *Sermons and Discourses, 1743–1758*. The Works of Jonathan Edwards 25. Edited by Wilson H. Kimnach. New Haven: Yale University Press, 2006.

———. "Letter to a Correspondent in Scotland, November 20, 1745." Pages 444–60 in *Apocalyptic Writings*. The Works of Jonathan Edwards 5. Edited by Stephen J. Stein. New Haven: Yale University Press, 1977.

———. "Letter to the Rev. Thomas Prince of Boston, December 12, 1743." Pages 544–57 in *The Great Awakening*. The Works of Jonathan Edwards 4. Edited by Clarence C. Goen. New Haven: Yale University Press, 1972.

———. *Letters and Personal Writings*. The Works of Jonathan Edwards 16. Edited by George S. Claghorn. New Haven: Yale University Press, 1998.

———. *The Life of Brainerd*. The Works of Jonathan Edwards 7. Edited by Norman Pettit. New Haven: Yale University Press, 1985.

———. "The Lord's Supper Ought to Be Kept Up and Attended in Remembrance of Christ." Pages 54–69 in *Sermons on the Lord's Supper*. Edited by Don Kistler. Orlando: The Northampton Press, 2007.

———. "The Means and Ends of Excommunication." Pages 64–79 in *Sermons and Discourses, 1739–1742*. The Works of Jonathan Edwards 22. Edited by Harry S. Stout, Nathan O. Hatch, and Kyle P. Farley. New Haven: Yale University Press, 2003.

———. "Mercy Not Sacrifice." Pages 111–35 in *Sermons and Discourses, 1739–1742*. The Works of Jonathan Edwards 22. Edited by Harry S. Stout, Nathan O. Hatch, and Kyle P. Farley. New Haven: Yale University Press, 2003.

———. "Misc." 2. Pages 197–99 in *The "Miscellanies" (Entry Nos. a–z, aa–zz, 1–500)*. The Works of Jonathan Edwards 13. Edited by Thomas A. Schafer. New Haven: Yale University Press, 1994.

———. "Misc." 26. Pages 212–13 in *The "Miscellanies" (Entry Nos. a–z, aa–zz, 1–500)*. The Works of Jonathan Edwards 13. Edited by Thomas A. Schafer. New Haven: Yale University Press, 1994.

———. "Misc." 86. Pages 250–51 in *The "Miscellanies" (Entry Nos. a–z, aa–zz, 1–500)*. The Works of Jonathan Edwards 13. Edited by Thomas A. Schafer. New Haven: Yale University Press, 1994.

————. "Misc." 189. Pages 331–32 in *The "Miscellanies" (Entry Nos. a–z, aa–zz, 1–500)*. The Works of Jonathan Edwards 13. Edited by Thomas A. Schafer. New Haven: Yale University Press, 1994.

————. "Misc. 207. Confirmation." Pages 341–42 in *The "Miscellanies" (Entry Nos. a–z. aa–zz, 1–500)*. The Works of Jonathan Edwards 13. Edited by Thomas A. Schafer. New Haven: Yale University Press, 1994.

————. "Misc." 262. Page 369 in *The "Miscellanies" (Entry Nos. a–z, aa–zz, 1–500)*. The Works of Jonathan Edwards 13. Edited by Thomas A. Schafer. New Haven: Yale University Press, 1994.

————. "Misc." 271. Page 374 in *The "Miscellanies" (Entry Nos. a–z, aa–zz, 1–500)*. The Works of Jonathan Edwards 13. Edited by Thomas A. Schafer. New Haven: Yale University Press, 1994.

————. "Misc." 317. Pages 397–400 in *The "Miscellanies" (Entry Nos. a–z, aa–zz, 1–500)*. The Works of Jonathan Edwards 13. Edited by Thomas A. Schafer. New Haven: Yale University Press, 1994.

————. "Misc." 325. Pages 404–05 in *The "Miscellanies" (Entry Nos. a–z, aa–zz, 1–500)*. The Works of Jonathan Edwards 13. Edited by Thomas A. Schafer. New Haven: Yale University Press, 1994.

————. "Misc." 338. Page 413 in *The "Miscellanies" (Entry Nos. a–z, aa–zz, 1–500)*. The Works of Jonathan Edwards 13. Edited by Thomas A. Schafer. New Haven: Yale University Press, 1994.

————. "Misc." 339. Page 414 in *The "Miscellanies," (Entry Nos. a–z. aa–zz, 1–500)*. The Works of Jonathan Edwards 13. Edited by Thomas A. Schafer. New Haven: Yale University Press, 1994.

————. "Misc." 356. Page 429 in *The "Miscellanies" (Entry Nos. a–z, aa–zz, 1–500)*. The Works of Jonathan Edwards 13. Edited by Thomas A. Schafer. New Haven: Yale University Press, 1994.

————. "Misc." 371. Pages 442–44 in *The "Miscellanies" (Entry Nos. a–z, aa–zz, 1–500)*. The *Works of Jonathan Edwards* 13. Edited by Thomas A. Schafer. New Haven: Yale University Press, 1994.

————. "Misc." 485. Page 527 in *The "Miscellanies" (Entry Nos. a–z, aa–zz, 1–500)*. The Works of Jonathan Edwards 13. Edited by Thomas A. Schafer. New Haven: Yale University Press, 1994.

————. "Misc." 689. Pages 251–52 in *The "Miscellanies" (Entry Nos. 501–832)*. The Works of Jonathan Edwards 18. Edited by A. Chamberlain. New Haven: Yale University Press, 2000.

————. "Misc." 948. Page 204 in *The "Miscellanies," (Entry Nos. 833–1152)*. The Works of Jonathan Edwards 20. Edited by Amy Plantinga Pauw. New Haven: Yale University Press, 2002.

————. "Misc." 1055. Page 394 in *The "Miscellanies," (Entry Nos. 833–1152)*. The Works of Jonathan Edwards 20. Edited by Amy Plantinga Pauw. New Haven: Yale University Press, 2002.

---------. "Misc." 1062. Pages 430–43 in *The "Miscellenanies" (Entry Nos. 833–1152)*. The Works of Jonathan Edwards 20. Edited by Amy P. Pauw. New Haven: Yale University Press, 2002.

---------. "Misc." 1263. Pages 201–12 in *The "Miscellanies" (Entry Nos. 1153–1360)*. The Works of Jonathan Edwards 23. Edited by Douglas A. Sweeney. New Haven: Yale University Press, 2004.

---------. "Misc." q. Pages 171–73 in *The "Miscellanies" (Entry Nos. a–z, aa–zz, 1–500)*. The Works of Jonathan Edwards 13. Edited by Thomas A. Schafer. New Haven: Yale University Press, 1994.

---------. "Misc." qq. Pages 188–89 in *The "Miscellanies" (Entry Nos. a–z, aa–zz, 1–500)*. The Works of Jonathan Edwards 13. Edited by Thomas A. Schafer. New Haven: Yale University Press, 1994.

---------. "Misc." rr. Page 189 in *The "Miscellanies," (Entry Nos. a–z, aa–zz, 1–500)*. The Works of Jonathan Edwards 13. Edited by Thomas A. Schafer. New Haven: Yale University Press, 1994.

---------. "Misc." ww. Pages 191–95 in *The "Miscellanies" (Entry Nos. a–z, aa–zz, 1–500)*. The Works of Jonathan Edwards 13. Edited by Thomas A. Schafer. New Haven: Yale University Press, 1994.

---------. "Misrepresentations Corrected, and Truth Vindicated." Pages 349–503 in *Ecclesiastical Writings*. The Works of Jonathan Edwards 12. Edited by David D. Hall. New Haven: Yale University Press, 1994.

---------. "Narrative of Communion Controversy." Pages 507–619 in *Ecclesiastical Writings*. The Works of Jonathan Edwards 12. Edited by David D. Hall. New Haven: Yale University Press, 1994.

---------. "None are Saved by Their Own Righteousness." Pages 329–56 in *Sermons and Discourses, 1723–1729*. The Works of Jonathan Edwards 14. Edited by Kenneth P. Minkema. New Haven: Yale University Press, 1997.

---------. *Original Sin*. The Works of Jonathan Edwards 3. Edited by John E. Smith. New Haven: Yale University Press, 1970.

---------. "The Perpetuity and Change of the Sabbath." Pages 217–50 in *Sermons and Discourses, 1730–1733*. The Works of Jonathan Edwards 17. Edited by Mark Valeri. New Haven: Yale University Press, 1999.

---------. "Personal Narrative." Pages 790–804 in *Letters and Personal Writings*. The Works of Jonathan Edwards 16. Edited by George S. Claghorn. New Haven: Yale University Press, 1998.

---------. "Praise One of the Chief Employments of Heaven." Pages 211–31 in *Altogether Lovely: Jonathan Edwards on the Glory and Excellency of Jesus Christ*. Edited by Don Kistler. Morgan: Soli Deo Gloria Publications, 1997.

---------. "Ps. 132:15–16." Pages 535–36 in *The "Blank Bible."* The Works of Jonathan Edwards 24, pt. 1. Edited by Stephen J. Stein. New Haven: Yale University Press, 2006.

---------. *Religious Affections*. The Works of Jonathan Edwards 2. Edited by John E Smith. New Haven: Yale University Press, 1969.

———. "Renewing Our Covenant with God." Pages 509–18 in *Sermons and Discourses, 1739–1742*. The Works of Jonathan Edwards 22. Edited by Harry S. Stout. New Haven: Yale University Press, 2003.

———. "Resolutions." Pages 753–59 in *Letters and Personal Writings*. The Works of Jonathan Edwards 16. Edited by George S. Claghorn. New Haven: Yale University Press, 1998.

———. "The Sacrament of the Lord Is the Communion of the Body and Blood of Christ." Pages 79–96 in *Sermons on the Lord's Supper*. Edited by Don Kistler. Orlando: The Northampton Press, 2007.

———. "The Sacrament of the Lord's Supper is a Very Sacred Ordinance." Pages 31–53 in *Sermons on the Lord's Supper*. Edited by Don Kistler. Orlando: The Northampton Press, 2007.

———. "Sacramental Union in Christ." Pages 582–89 in *Sermons and Discourses, 1743–1758*. The Works of Jonathan Edwards 25. Edited by Wilson H. Kimnach. New Haven: Yale University Press, 2006.

———. *Scientific and Philosophical Writings*. The Works of Jonathan Edwards 6. Edited by Wallace E. Anderson. New Haven: Yale University Press, 1980.

———. "Self-Examination and the Lord's Supper." Pages 264–72 in *Sermons and Discourses, 1730–1733*. The Works of Jonathan Edwards 17. Edited by Mark Valeri. New Haven: Yale University Press, 1999.

———. *Sermons and Discourses, 1720–1723*. The Works of Jonathan Edwards 10. Edited by Wilson H. Kimnach. New Haven: Yale University Press, 1992.

———. *Sermons by Jonathan Edwards on the Matthean Parables, vol. 1: True and False Christians (On the Parable of the Wise and Foolish Virgins)*. Eugene, OR: Cascade Books, 2012.

———. "Sin and Wickedness Bring Calamity and Misery on a People." Pages 484–505 in *Sermons and Discourses, 1723–1729*. The Works of Jonathan Edwards 14. Edited by Kenneth P. Minkema. New Haven: Yale University Press, 1997.

———. "Some Thoughts Concerning the Revival." Pages 289–530 in *The Great Awakening*. The Works of Jonathan Edwards 4. Edited by Clarence C. Goen. New Haven: Yale University Press, 1972.

———. "Sons of Oil, Heavenly Lights." Pages 257–74 in *Sermons and Discourses, 1743–1758*. The Works of Jonathan Edwards 25. Edited by Wilson H. Kimnach. New Haven: Yale University Press, 2005.

———. "The Spiritual Blessings of the Gospel Represented by a Feast." Pages 278–96 in *Sermons and Discourses, 1723–1729*. The Works of Jonathan Edwards 14. Edited by Kenneth P. Minkema. New Haven: Yale University Press, 1997.

———. "The Thing Designed in the Sacrament of the Lord's Supper is the Communion of Christians in the Body and Blood of Christ." Pages 1–30 in *Sermons on the Lord's Supper*. Edited by Don Kistler. Orlando: The Northampton Press, 2007.

———. "The Threefold Work of the Holy Spirit." Pages 371–436 in *Sermons and Discourses, 1723–1729*. The Works of Jonathan Edwards 14. Edited by Kenneth P. Minkema. New Haven: Yale University Press, 1997.

———. "They Sing a New Song." Pages 224–44 in *Sermons and Discourses, 1739–1742*. The Works of Jonathan Edwards 22. Edited by Harry S. Stout, Nathan O. Hatch, and Kyle P. Farley. New Haven: Yale University Press, 2003.

———. "To Col. John Pynchon, August 14, 1735." Pages 61–62 in *Letters and Personal Writings*. The Works of Jonathan Edwards 16. Edited by George S. Claghorn. New Haven: Yale University Press, 1998.

———. "To Deacon Lyman of Goshen, Connecticut (August 31, 1741)." Pages 533–34 in *The Great Awakening*. The Works of Jonathan Edwards 4. Edited by Clarence C. Goen. New Haven: Yale University Press, 1972.

———. "To Deacon Moses Lyman, May 10, 1742." Pages 101–03 in *Letters and Personal Writings*. The Works of Jonathan Edwards 16. Edited by George S. Claghorn. New Haven: Yale University Press, 1998.

———. "To Sir William Pepperrell, November 28, 1751." Pages 406–14 in *Letters and Personal Writings*. The Works of Jonathan Edwards 16. Edited by George S. Claghorn. New Haven: Yale University Press, 1998.

———. "To the Reverend Benjamin Colman." Pages 144–45 in *Letters and Personal Writings*. The Works of Jonathan Edwards 16. Edited by George S. Claghorn. New Haven: Yale University Press, 1998.

———. "To the Reverend John Erskine, July 5, 1750." Pages 347–56 in *Letters and Personal Writings*. The Works of Jonathan Edwards 16. Edited by George S. Claghorn. New Haven: Yale University Press, 1998.

———. "To the Reverend John Erskine, November 15, 1750." Pages 363–67 in *Letters and Personal Writings*. The Works of Jonathan Edwards 16. Edited by George S. Claghorn. New Haven: Yale University Press, 1998.

———. "To the Reverend John MacLaurin, May 12, 1746." Pages 203–07 in *Letters and Personal Writings*. The Works of Jonathan Edwards 16. Edited by George S. Claghorn. New Haven: Yale University Press, 1998.

———. "To the Reverend Robert Breck." Pages 221–22 in *Letters and Personal Writings*. The Works of Jonathan Edwards 16. Edited by George S. Claghorn. New Haven: Yale University Press, 1998.

———. "To the Reverend Thomas Foxcroft, May 24, 1749." Pages 282–86 in *Letters and Personal Writings*. The Works of Jonathan Edwards 16. Edited by George S. Claghorn. New Haven: Yale University Press, 1998.

———. "To the Trustees of the College of New Jersey, October 19, 1757." Pages 725–30 in *Letters and Personal Writings*. The Works of Jonathan Edwards 16. Edited by George S. Claghorn. New Haven: Yale University Press, 1998.

———. "True Nobleness of Mind." Pages 228–42 in *Sermons and Discourses, 1723–1729*. The Works of Jonathan Edwards 14. Edited by Kenneth P. Minkema. New Haven: Yale University Press, 1997.

————. "True Repentance Required." Pages 506-518 in *Sermons and Discourses, 1720-1723*. The Works of Jonathan Edwards 10. Edited by Wilson H. Kimnach. New Haven: Yale University Press, 1992.

————. *Typological Writings*. The Works of Jonathan Edwards 11. Edited by Wallace E. Anderson, Mason I. Lowance Jr., and David H. Watters. New Haven: Yale University Press, 1993.

————. "Unpublished Letter of May 30, 1735." Pages 99–110 in *The Great Awakening*. The Works of Jonathan Edwards 4. Edited by Clarence C. Goen. New Haven: Yale University Press, 1972.

————. "The Value of Salvation." Pages 308-336 in *Sermons and Discourses, 1720-1723*. The Works of Jonathan Edwards 10. Edited by Wilson H. Kimnach. New Haven: Yale University Press, 1992.

————. "151. Matthew 5:13 [Winter–Summer 1730]." L. 1r–16v in *Sermons, Series 2, 1729–1731*. The Works of Jonathan Edwards Online 45. Edited by The Jonathan Edwards Center at Yale. Accessed January 2013.

————. "182. Acts 8:22 [Fall 1730–Spring 1731]." Pages L. 1r–10r in *Sermons, Series 2, 1729–1731*. The Works of Jonathan Edwards Online 45. Edited by The Jonathan Edwards Center at Yale. Accessed January 2013.

————. "222. Ezekiel 23:37–39 [July–August 1731]." Pages L. 1r–16v in *Sermons, Series 2, 1731–1732*. The Works of Jonathan Edwards Online 46. Edited by The Jonathan Edwards Center at Yale. Accessed January 2013.

————. "287. Luke 22:30 (June 1733)." Pages L. 1r–9v in *Sermons, Series 2, 1733*. The Works of Jonathan Edwards Online 48. Edited by The Jonathan Edwards Center at Yale. Accessed January 2013.

————. "358. Ephesians 5:25–27 (1735/1752)." Pages L. 1r–35v in *Sermons, Series 2, 1735*. The Works of Jonathan Edwards Online 50. Edited by The Jonathan Edwards Center at Yale. Accessed January 2013.

————. "452. Unpublished Sermon on Haggai 2:7–9 (Dec. 1737)." L. 1r–25r. Accessed from the Jonathan Edwards Center at Yale, 2011.

————. "448. Matthew 25:1 (Nov. 1737)." Pages L. 1r–30v in *Sermons, Series 2, 1737*. The Works of Jonathan Edwards Online 52. Edited by The Jonathan Edwards Center at Yale. Accessed January 2013.

————. "482. Deuteronomy 29:18–21 (July 1738)." L. 1r–14v in *Sermons, Series 2, 1738, and Undated, 1734–1738*. The Works of Jonathan Edwards Online Volume 53. Edited by The Jonathan Edwards Center at Yale. Accessed January 2013.

————. "512. Acts 6:1–3 (June 1739)." L. 1r–16v in *Sermons, Series 2, 1739*. The Works of Jonathan Edwards Online 54. Edited by The Jonathan Edwards Center at Yale. Accessed January 2013.

————. "546. Hebrews 12:22–24(c) (April 1740)." Pages 1–22 in *Sermons, Series 2, January–June 1740*. The Works of Jonathan Edwards Online 55. Edited by The Jonathan Edwards Center at Yale. Accessed January 2013.

————. "591. Acts 14:23 (Jan. 1741)." L. 1r–14v in *Sermons, Series 2, January–June 1741*. The Works of Jonathan Edwards Online 57. Edited by The Jonathan Edwards Center at Yale. Accessed January 2013.

————. "613. Unpublished Sermon on Revelation 22:16–17 (May 1741)." L. 1r–18v. Accessed from the Jonathan Edwards Center at Yale, 2011.

————. "738. Unpublished Sermon on Colossians 1:24 (April 1744)." L. 1r–30v. Accessed from the Jonathan Edwards Center at Yale, 2011.

————. "812. Matthew 16:18 (March 1745/1746)." Pages L. 1r–20v in *Sermons, Series 2, 1746*. The Works of Jonathan Edwards Online 64. Edited by The Jonathan Edwards Center at Yale. Accessed January 2013.

————. "842. Unpublished Sermon on Ecclesiastes 5:1 (Oct. 1746)." L. 1r–18v. Accessed from the Jonathan Edwards Center at Yale, 2011.

————. "898. Deuteronomy 1:13–18 (June 1748)." L. 1r–19r in *Sermons, Series 2, 1748*. The Works of Jonathan Edwards Online 66. Edited by The Jonathan Edwards Center at Yale. Accessed January 2013.

————. "952. 1 Corinthians 10:17(a) (January 1749/1750)." L. 1r–12v in *Sermons, Series 2, 1750*. The Works of Jonathan Edwards Online 68. Edited by The Jonathan Edwards Center at Yale. Accessed January 2013.

Edwards, Jonathan, and Members of Ecclesiastical Council. "Advice to Mr. and Mrs. Kingsley, February 17, 1743." L. 1r–4v in *Church and Pastoral Documents*. The Works of Jonathan Edwards Online 39. Edited by The Jonathan Edwards Center at Yale. Accessed January 2013.

Hopkins, Samuel, ed. *The Life and Character of the Late Reverend Mr. Jonathan Edwards, President of the College at New-Jersey, Together With a Number of His Sermons*. 2nd ed. Glasgow: David Niven for James Duncan, 1785.

Norton, John. *The Orthodox Evangelist, or a Treatise Wherein Many Great Evangelical Truths (Not a Few Whereof Are Much Opposed and Eclipsed in This Perillous Hour of the Passion of the Gospel,) Are Briefly Discussed, Cleared, and Confirmed: As a Further Help, for the Begetting, and Establishing of the Faith Which Is in Jesus. As Also the State of the Blessed, Where; Of the Condition of Their Souls from the Instant of Their Dissolution: and of Their Persons after Their Resurrection*. London: John Macock, Henry Cripps, Lodowick Lloyd, 1654.

Spener, Philip Jacob. *Pia Desideria*. Seminar Editions. Translated by Theodore G. Tappert. Philadelphia: Fortress Press, 1964.

Winthrop, John. "A Modell of Christian Charity." Pages 138–46 in *The Puritan Tradition in America, 1620–1730*. Edited by Alden T. Vaughan. Hanover, NH: University Press of New England, 1972.

SECONDARY SOURCES

Abraham, William. *The Logic of Evangelism*. Grand Rapids: Eerdmans, 1989.

Adams, Doug. *Meeting House to Camp Meeting: Toward a History of American Free Church Worship from 1620 to 1835*. Saratoga: Modern Liturgy Resource Publications, 1981.

Avis, Paul D. L. *The Church in the Theology of the Reformers.* Atlanta: John Knox Press, 1981.

Bademan, R. Bryan. "The Edwards of History and the Edwards of Faith." *Reviews in American History* 34, no. 2 (2006): 131–49.

Bainton, Roland H. *Yale and the Ministry: A History of Education for the Christian Ministry at Yale from the Founding in 1701.* New York: Harper & Brothers, 1957.

Bebbington, David W. "Evangelical Christianity and the Enlightenment." Pages 66–78 in *The Gospel in the Modern World: A Tribute to John Stott.* Edited by Martyn Eden and David F. Wells. Leicester, UK: IVP, 1991.

———. *Evangelicalism in Modern Britain: A History from the 1730s to the 1980s.* London: Unwin Hyman, 1989.

Bogue, Carl W. "Jonathan Edwards on the Covenant of Grace." Pages 134–45 in *Soli Deo Gloria: Essays in Reformed Theology: Festschrift for John H. Gerstner.* Edited by R. C. Sproul. Nutley, NJ: Presbyterian and Reformed Publishing Company, 1976.

Bonomi, Patricia U. *Under the Cope of Heaven: Religion, Society, and Politics in Colonial America.* Updated ed. Oxford: Oxford University Press, 2003.

Bosch, David J. *Transforming Mission: Paradigm Shifts in Theology of Mission.* American Society of Missiology Series. Maryknoll, NY: Orbis Books, 2003.

Bozeman, Theodore Dwight. "Biblical Primitivism: An Approach to New England Puritanism." Pages 19–32 in *The American Quest for the Primitive Church.* Edited by Richard T. Hughes. Urbana and Chicago: University of Illinois Press, 1988.

———. *The Precisianist Strain: Disciplinary Religion and Antinomian Backlash in Puritanism to 1638.* Omohundro Institute of Early American History and Culture. Chapel Hill and London: University of North Carolina Press, 2004.

———. *To Live Ancient Lives: The Primitivist Dimension in Puritanism.* Chapel Hill: University of North Carolina Press, 1988.

Brand, Chad Owen, and R. Stanton Norman. "Introduction: Is Polity that Important?" Pages 1–23 in *Perspectives on Church Government: Five Views on Church Polity.* Edited by Chad Owen Brand and R. Stanton Norman. Nashville: Broadman & Holman, 2004.

Brand, David C. *Profile of the Last Puritan: Jonathan Edwards, Self-Love, and the Dawn of the Beatific.* American Academy of Religion Academy Series. Atlanta: Scholars Press, 1991.

Brauer, Jerald C. "Conversion: From Puritanism to Revivalism." *Journal of Religion* 58 no. 3 (1978): 227–43.

———. "The Nature of English Puritanism: Three Interpretations." *Church History* 23 no. 2 (1954): 99–108.

Breitenbach, William. "Piety *and* Moralism: Edwards and the New Divinity." Pages 177–204 in *Jonathan Edwards and the American Experience.* Edited by Nathan O. Hatch and Harry S. Stout. New York/Oxford: Oxford University Press, 1988.

Brekus, Catherine A. "Children of Wrath, Children of Grace: Jonathan Edwards and the Puritan Culture of Child Rearing." Pages 300–28 in *The Child in Christian Thought.* Edited by Marcia J. Bunge. Grand Rapids: Eerdmans, 2001.

Bremer, Francis J. *The Puritan Experiment: New England Society from Bradford to Edwards*. Rev. ed. Lebanon, NH: University Press of New England, 1995.

Brown, David C. "The Keys of the Kingdom: Excommunication in Colonial Massachusetts." *New England Quarterly* 67 no. 4 (1994): 531–66.

Brown, Robert E. *Jonathan Edwards and the Bible*. Bloomington: Indiana University Press, 2002.

Bushman, Richard L. *From Puritan to Yankee: Character and the Social Order in Connecticut, 1690–1765*. Cambridge: Harvard University Press, 1967.

Butler, Jon. "Enthusiasm Described and Decried: The Great Awakening as Interpretative Fiction." *Journal of American History* 69 no. 2 (1982): 305–25.

Byrd, James P. *Jonathan Edwards for Armchair Theologians*. Louisville: Westminster John Knox, 2008.

Caldwell, Patricia. *The Puritan Conversion Narrative: The Beginnings of American Expression*. Cambridge Studies in American Literature and Culture. Cambridge: Cambridge University Press, 1983.

Caldwell, Robert W. *Communion in the Spirit: The Holy Spirit as the Bond of Union in the Theology of Jonathan Edwards*. Studies in Evangelical History and Thought. Milton Keynes, UK: Paternoster Press, 2006.

Calvin, John. *Institutes of the Christian Religion*. The Library of Christian Classics. Translated by Ford Lewis Battles. Philadelphia: The Westminster Press, 1960.

"The Cambridge Platform." Pages 385–99 in *Creeds of the Churches: A Reader in Christian Doctrine from the Bible to the Present*. Edited by John H. Leith. Louisville: John Knox, 1982.

Carpenter, John B. "New England Puritans: The Grandparents of Modern Protestant Missions." *Missiology: An International Review* 30 no. 4 (2002): 519–32.

———. "Puritan Missions as Globalization." *Fides et Historia* 31 no. 2 (1999): 103–23.

Carr, Kevin C. "Jonathan Edwards and *A Divine and Supernatural Light*." *Puritan Reformed Journal* 2 no. 2 (2010): 187–209.

Carse, James. *Jonathan Edwards and the Visibility of God*. New York: Scribner's, 1967.

Chamberlain, Ava. "Bad Books and Bad Boys: The Transformation of Gender in Eighteenth-Century Northampton, Massachusetts." *New England Quarterly* 75 no. 2 (2002): 179–203.

———. "Brides of Christ and Signs of Grace: Edwards's Sermon Series on the Parable of the Wise and Foolish Virgins." Pages 3–18 in *Jonathan Edwards's Writings: Text, Context, Interpretation*. Edited by Stephen J. Stein. Bloomington and Indianapolis: Indiana University Press, 1996.

———. "Edwards and Social Issues." Pages 325–44 in *The Cambridge Companion to Jonathan Edwards*. Edited by Stephen J. Stein. Cambridge: Cambridge University Press, 2007.

———. "Self-Deception as a Theological Problem in Jonathan Edwards's 'Treatise Concerning Religious Affections.'" *Church History* 63 no. 4 (1994): 541–56.

———. "'We Have Procured One Rattlesnake': Jonathan Edwards and American Social History." Paper presented at the American Society of Church History Conference, Seattle, January 2005.

Cherry, Conrad. *The Theology of Jonathan Edwards: A Reappraisal.* Bloomington: Indiana University Press, 1990.

Claghorn, George S. "Introduction." Pages 741–52 in *Letters and Personal Writings.* The Works of Jonathan Edwards 16. Edited by George S. Claghorn. New Haven: Yale University Press, 1998.

Coffey, John, and Paul C. H. Lim. "Introduction." Pages 1–15 in *The Cambridge Companion to Puritanism.* Edited by John Coffey and Paul C. H. Lim. Cambridge: Cambridge University Press, 2008.

Coffey, John. "Puritanism, Evangelicalism and the Evangelical Protestant Tradition." Pages 252–77 in *The Emergence of Evangelicalism: Exploring Historical Continuities.* Edited by Michael A. G. Haykin and Kenneth J. Stewart. Nottingham, UK: Apollos, 2008.

Coffman, Ralph J. *Solomon Stoddard.* Boston: Twayne Publishers, 1978.

Cogley, Richard W. "John Eliot's Puritan Ministry." *Fides et Historia* 31 no. 1 (1999): 1–18.

Cohen, Charles L. *God's Caress: The Psychology of Puritan Religious Experience.* Oxford: Oxford University Press, 1986.

Conforti, Joseph A. "Jonathan Edwards's Most Popular Work: *The Life of David Brainerd* and Nineteenth-Century Evangelical Culture." *Church History* 54 no. 2 (1985): 188–201.

———. *Saints and Strangers: New England in British North America.* Regional Perspectives on Early America. Baltimore: The John Hopkins University Press, 2006.

Cooper, James F. *Tenacious of Their Liberties: The Congregationalists in Colonial Massachusetts.* Religion in America Series. Oxford: Oxford University Press, 1999.

Crawford, Michael. *Seasons of Grace: Colonial New England's Revival Tradition in Its British Context.* New York: Oxford University Press, 1991.

Crisp, Oliver D. "Jonathan Edwards and the Closing of the Table: Must the Eucharist be Open to All?" *Ecclesiology* 5 no. 1 (2009): 48–68.

———. *Jonathan Edwards and the Metaphysics of Sin.* Aldershot, UK: Ashgate, 2005.

Crocco, Stephen D. "Edwards's Intellectual Legacy." Pages 300–24 in *The Cambridge Companion to Jonathan Edwards.* Edited by Stephen J. Stein. Cambridge: Cambridge University Press, 2007.

Danaher, William J. "By Sensible Signs Represented: Jonathan Edwards' Sermons on the Lord's Supper." *Pro Ecclesia* 7 no. 3 (1998): 261–87.

———. *The Trinitarian Ethics of Jonathan Edwards.* Columbia Series in Reformed Theology. Louisville: Westminster John Knox, 2004.

Davidson, Edward H. *Jonathan Edwards: The Narrative of a Puritan Mind.* Cambridge: Harvard University Press, 1968.

Davidson, James West. *The Logic of Millennial Thought: Eighteenth-Century New England*. New Haven: Yale University Press, 1977.

De Jong, Peter Y. *The Covenant Idea in New England Theology: 1620–1847*. Grand Rapids: Eerdmans, 1945.

Delbanco, Andrew. *The Puritan Ordeal*. Cambridge: Harvard University Press, 1989.

DeProspo, R. C. "The 'New Simple Idea' of Edwards' Personal Narrative." *Early American Literature* 14 no. 2 (1979): 193–204.

Dillenberger, John. "The Ninety-Five Theses." Pages 489–500 in *Martin Luther: Selections from his Writings*. Edited by John Dillenberger. Garden City, NY: Anchor Books, 1961.

Doyle, Robert. "The Search for Theological Models: The Christian in His Society in the Sixteenth, Seventeenth and Nineteenth Centuries." Pages 27–72 in *Christians in Society*. Explorations 3. Edited by Barry G. Webb. Homebush West, NSW: Lancer, 1988.

Erikson, Kai T. *Wayward Puritans: A Study in the Sociology of Deviance*. Needham Heights, MA: Macmillan, 1966.

Eskew, Harry, and Hugh T. McElrath. *Sing with Understanding: An Introduction to Christian Hymnology*. 2nd, rev., and expanded ed. Nashville: Church Street Press, 1995.

Fiering, Norman S. *Jonathan Edwards's Moral Thought in Its British Context*. Chapel Hill: University of North Carolina Press, 1981.

———. "Will and Intellect in the New England Mind." *William and Mary Quarterly* 29 no. 4 (1972): 515–58.

Fitzgerald, Monica, D. "Drunkards, Fornicators, and a Great Hen Squabble: Censure Practices and the Gendering of Puritanism." *Church History* 80 no. 1 (2011): 40–75.

Foster, Stephen. *The Long Argument: English Puritanism and the Shaping of New England Culture, 1570–1700*. Chapel Hill: University of North Carolina Press, 1991.

Francis, Richard. *Judge Sewall's Apology: The Salem Witch Trials and the Forming of an American Conscience*. New York: Harper Perennial, 2005.

Gilpin, W. Clark. "'Inward, Sweet Delight in God': Solitude in the Career of Jonathan Edwards." *Journal of Religion* 82 no. 4 (2002): 523–38.

Goen, Clarence C. "Editor's Introduction." Pages 1–95 in *The Great Awakening*. The Works of Jonathan Edwards 4. Edited by Clarence C. Goen. New Haven: Yale University Press, 1972.

———. "Jonathan Edwards: A New Departure in Eschatology." *Church History* 28 no. 1 (1959): 25–40.

———. *Revivalism and Separatism in New England, 1740–1800: Strict Congregationalists and Separate Baptists in the Great Awakening*. Middletown, CT: Wesleyan University Press, 1987.

Goodwin, Gerald J. "The Myth of 'Arminian-Calvinism' in Eighteenth-Century New England." *New England Quarterly* 41 no. 2 (1968): 213–37.

Grabo, Norman S. "Jonathan Edwards' *Personal Narrative*: Dynamic Stasis." *Literatur in Wissenschaft und Unterricht* 2 no. 3 (1969): 141–48.

Grasso, Christopher. "Misrepresentations Corrected: Jonathan Edwards and the Regulation of Religious Discourse." Pages 19–39 in *Jonathan Edwards's Writings: Text*, Context, Interpretation. Edited by Stephen J. Stein. Bloomington/Indianapolis: Indiana University Press, 1996.

Guelzo, Allen C. "The Return of the Will: Jonathan Edwards and the Possibilities of Free Will." Pages 87–110 in *Edwards in Our Time: Jonathan Edwards and the Shaping of American Religion*. Edited by Sang Hyun Lee and Allen C. Guelzo. Grand Rapids: Eerdmans, 1999.

Gura, Philip F. "Edwards and American Literature." Pages 262–79 in *The Cambridge Companion to Jonathan Edwards*. Edited by Stephen J. Stein. Cambridge: Cambridge University Press, 2007.

———. *Jonathan Edwards: America's Evangelical*. New York: Hill & Wang, 2005.

Haight, Roger. *Christian Community in History: Comparative Ecclesiology*. New York: Continuum, 2005.

Hall, David D., ed. *The Antinomian Controversy, 1636–1638: A Documentary History*. 2nd ed. Durham: Duke University Press, 1990.

———. "Editor's Introduction." Pages 1–90 in *Ecclesiastical Writings*. The Works of Jonathan Edwards 12. Edited by David D. Hall. New Haven: Yale University Press, 1994.

———. *The Faithful Shepherd: A History of New England Ministry in the Seventeenth Century*. Chapel Hill: University of North Carolina Press, 1972.

———. "The New England Background." Pages 61–79 in *The Cambridge Companion to Jonathan Edwards*. Edited by Stephen J. Stein. Cambridge: Cambridge University Press, 2007.

———. *Worlds of Wonder, Days of Judgment: Popular Religious Belief in Early New England*. Cambridge: Harvard University Press, 1989.

Hall, Timothy D. *Contested Boundaries: Itinerancy and the Reshaping of the Colonial American Religious World*. Durham: Duke University Press, 1994.

Hambrick-Stowe, Charles E. *The Practice of Piety: Puritan Devotional Disciplines in Seventeenth-Century New England*. Chapel Hill: University of North Carolina Press, 1982.

Hall, Richard A. S. *The Neglected Northampton Texts of Jonathan Edwards: Edwards on Society and Politics*. Studies in American Religion 52. Lewiston, NY: Edwin Mellen Press, 1990.

Haroutunian, Joseph. *Piety Versus Moralism: The Passing of New England Theology from Edwards to Taylor*. Eugene, OR: Wipf and Stock, 1932.

Hart, Darryl G. "The Church in Evangelical Theologies, Past and Future." Pages 23–40 in *The Community of the Word: Toward an Evangelical Ecclesiology*. Edited by M. Husbands and D. J. Treier. Downers Grove, IL: IVP, 2005.

Hart, D. G., and John R. Muether. *Seeking a Better Country: 300 Years of American Presbyterianism*. Phillipsburg, NJ: Presbyterian & Reformed Publishing, 2007.

Hastings, W. Ross. "Discerning the Spirit: Ambivalent Assurance in the Soteriology of Jonathan Edwards and Barthian Correctives." *Scottish Journal of Theology* 63 no. 4 (2010): 437–55.

Haykin, Michael A. G. "Evangelicalism and the Enlightenment: A Reassessment." Pages 37–60 in *The Emergence of Evangelicalism: Exploring Historical Continuities*. Edited by Michael A. G. Haykin and Kenneth J. Stewart. Nottingham, UK: Apollos, 2008.

———. *Jonathan Edwards: The Holy Spirit in Revival: The Lasting Influence of the Holy Spirit in the Heart of Man*. Emmaus Series. Darlington: Evangelical Press, 2005.

Haykin, Michael A. G., and Kenneth J. Stewart, eds. *The Emergence of Evangelicalism: Exploring Historical Continuities*. Nottingham, UK: Apollos, 2008.

Heimert, Alan. *Religion and the American Mind: From the Great Awakening to the Revolution*. The Jonathan Edwards Classic Studies Series. Eugene, OR: Wipf and Stock, 2006.

Hindmarsh, Bruce. "The Great Awakening Revisited." *Evangelical Studies Bulletin* 68 (2008): 1–5.

———. "Is Evangelical Ecclesiology an Oxymoron? A Historical Perspective." Pages 15–37 in *Evangelical Ecclesiology: Reality or Illusion?* Edited by John G. Stackhouse Jr. Grand Rapids: Baker Academic, 2003.

———. *John Newton and the English Evangelical Tradition: Between the Conversions of Wesley and Wilberforce*. Grand Rapids: Eerdmans, 1996.

Holifield, E. Brooks. *The Covenant Sealed: The Development of Puritan Sacramental Theology in Old and New England, 1570–1720*. Eugene, OR: Wipf and Stock, 1974.

———. *God's Ambassadors: A History of the Christian Clergy in America*. Pulpit & Pew. Grand Rapids: Eerdmans, 2007.

———. "Peace, Conflict, and Ritual in Puritan Congregations." *Journal of Interdisciplinary History* 23 no. 3 (1993): 551–70.

———. *Theology in America: Christian Thought from the Age of the Puritans to the Civil War*. New Haven: Yale University Press, 2003.

Holmes, Stephen R. *God of Grace and God of Glory: An Account of the Theology of Jonathan Edwards*. Edinburgh: T&T Clark, 2000.

Hoopes, James. "Jonathan Edwards's Religious Psychology." *Journal of American History* 69 no. 4 (1983): 849–65.

Hughes, Richard T., and C. Leonard Allen. *Illusions of Innocence: Protestant Primitivism in America, 1630–1875*. Chicago and London: University of Chicago Press, 1988.

Jamieson, John F. "Jonathan Edwards's Change of Position on Stoddardeanism." *Harvard Theological Review* 74 no. 1 (1981): 79–99.

Jenson, Robert W. *America's Theologian: A Recommendation of Jonathan Edwards*. New York/Oxford: Oxford University Press, 1988.

Johnson, John E. "The Prophetic Office as Paradigm for Pastoral Ministry." *Trinity Journal* 21 no. 1 (2000): 61–81.

Jones, James W. *The Shattered Synthesis: New England Puritanism before the Great Awakening.* New Haven: Yale University Press, 1973.

Jue, Jeffrey K. "Puritan Millenarianism in Old and New England." Pages 259–76 in *The Cambridge Companion to Puritanism.* Edited by John Coffey and Paul C. H. Lim. Cambridge: Cambridge University Press, 2008.

Kärkkäinen, Veli-Matti. *An Introduction to Ecclesiology: Ecumenical, Historical and Global Perspectives.* Downers Grove, IL: IVP, 2002.

Kamensky, Jane. *Governing the Tongue: The Politics of Speech in Early New England.* New York/Oxford: Oxford University Press, 1997.

Kidd, Thomas S. *The Great Awakening: The Roots of Evangelical Christianity in Colonial America.* New Haven: Yale University Press, 2007.

———. *The Protestant Interest: New England after Puritanism.* New Haven: Yale University Press, 2004.

———. "'The Very Vital Breath of Christianity': Prayer and Revival in Provincial New England." *Fides et Historia* 36 no. 2 (2004): 19–33.

Kimnach, Wilson H., Caleb J. D. Maskell, and Kenneth P. Minkema. *Jonathan Edwards's Sinners in the Hands of an Angry God: A Casebook.* New Haven: Yale University Press, 2010.

———. "Preface to the New York Period." Pages 259–93 in *Sermons and Discourses, 1720–1723.* The Works of Jonathan Edwards 10. Edited by Wilson H. Kimnach. New Haven: Yale University Press, 1992.

———. "Preface to the Period." Pages 3–46 in *Sermons and Discourses, 1743–1758.* The Works of Jonathan Edwards 25. Edited by Wilson H. Kimnach. New Haven: Yale University Press, 2006.

Kish Sklar, Kathryn. "Culture Versus Economics: A Case of Fornication in Northampton in the 1740s." *University of Michigan Papers in Women's Studies* 3 no. 1 (1978): 35–56.

Knight, Janice. *Orthodoxies in Massachusetts: Rereading American Puritanism.* Cambridge: Harvard University Press, 1994.

Kobrin, David. "The Expansion of the Visible Church in New England: 1629–1650." *Church History* 36 no. 2 (1967): 189–209.

Lambert, Frank. *Inventing the "Great Awakening."* Princeton: Princeton University Press, 1999.

Landsman, Ned C. *From Colonials to Provincials: American Thought and Culture, 1680–1760.* Ithaca: Cornell University Press, 1997.

Latourette, Kenneth Scott. *A History of Christianity.* London: Eyre & Spottiswoode, 1954.

Laurence, David. "Jonathan Edwards, Solomon Stoddard, and the Preparationist Model of Conversion." *Harvard Theological Review* 72 nos. 3–4 (1979): 267–83.

Lee, Sang Hyun. "Editor's Introduction." Pages 1–106 in *Writings on the Trinity, Grace, and Faith.* The Works of Jonathan Edwards 21. Edited by Sang Hyun Lee. New Haven: Yale University Press, 2003.

————. "Grace and Justification by Faith Alone." Pages 130–46 in *The Princeton Companion to Jonathan Edwards*. Edited by Sang Hyun Lee. Princeton and Oxford: Princeton University Press, 2005.

Lee, Sang Hyun, ed. *The Princeton Companion to Jonathan Edwards*. Princeton: Princeton University Press, 2005.

Lesser, Max X. *Reading Jonathan Edwards: An Annotated Bibliography in Three Parts, 1729–2005*. Grand Rapids: Eerdmans, 2008.

Levesque, George G. "Quaestio: Peccator non Iustificatur Coram Deo Nisi per Iustitiam Christi Fide Apprehensam." Pages 47–66 in *Sermons and Discourses, 1723–1729*. The Works of Jonathan Edwards 14. Edited by Kenneth P. Minkema. New Haven: Yale University Press, 1997.

Littell, F. H. *The Origins of Sectarian Protestantism: A Study of the Anabaptist View of the Church*. New York: Macmillan, 1964.

Locke, John. *An Essay Concerning Human Understanding*. The Clarendon Edition of the Works of John Locke. Oxford: Clarendon Press, 1975.

Lovejoy, David S. *Religious Enthusiasm in the New World: Heresy to Revolution*. Cambridge: Harvard University Press, 1985.

Lowance, Mason I. Jr. *The Language of Canaan: Metaphor and Symbol in New England from the Puritans to the Transcendentalists*. Cambridge: Harvard University Press, 1980.

Lowell, Robert. "Jonathan Edwards in Western Massachusetts." Pages 40–43 in *Life Studies and For the Union Dead*. New York: Farrar, Straus and Giroux, 2007.

Lucas, Sean M. *God's Grand Design: The Theological Vision of Jonathan Edwards*. Wheaton, IL: Crossway, 2011.

MacGregor, Geddes. *Corpus Christi: The Nature of the Church According to the Reformed Tradition*. London: Macmillan, 1959.

Marini, Stephen. "Hymnody as History: Early Evangelical Hymns and the Recovery of American Popular Religion." *Church History* 71 no. 2 (2002): 273–306.

Marini, Stephen A. "Rehearsal for Revival: Sacred Singing and the Great Awakening in America." Pages 71–91 in *Sacred Sound: Music in Religious Thought and Practice*. Edited by Joyce Irwin. Chico, CA: Scholars Press, 1983.

Marsden, George M. "Challenging the Presumptions of the Age: The Two Dissertations." Pages 99–113 in *The Legacy of Jonathan Edwards: American Religion and the Evangelical Tradition*. Edited by Darryl G. Hart, Sean Michael Lucas, and Stephen J. Nichols. Grand Rapids: Baker Academic, 2003.

————. *Jonathan Edwards: A Life*. New Haven: Yale University Press, 2003.

————. *A Short Life of Jonathan Edwards*. Library of Religious Biography. Grand Rapids: Eerdmans, 2008.

Marshall, Madeleine Forell, and Janet Todd. *English Congregational Hymns in the Eighteenth Century*. Lexington: University of Kentucky Press, 1982.

Marty, Martin E. "Two Kinds of Two Kinds of Civil Religion." Pages 139–57 in *American Civil Religion*. Edited by Donald G. Jones and Russell E. Richey. San Francisco: Mellen Research University Press, 1990.

May, Henry F. *The Enlightenment in America.* New York: Oxford University Press, 1976.

McClymond, Michael J. *Encounters with God: An Approach to the Theology of Jonathan Edwards.* New York: Oxford University Press, 1998.

————. "Spiritual Perception in Jonathan Edwards." *Journal of Religion* 77 no. 2 (1997): 195–216.

McClymond, Michael J., and Gerald R. McDermott. *The Theology of Jonathan Edwards.* New York: Oxford University Press, 2011.

McConnell, Walter. "Facing New Paradigms in Worship: Learning New Lessons from Old Masters." *Evangelical Review of Theology* 29 no. 4 (2005): 331–46.

McDermott, Gerald R. *Jonathan Edwards Confronts the Gods: Christian Theology, Enlightenment Religion, and Non-Christian Faiths.* Oxford: Oxford University Press, 2000.

————. "Jonathan Edwards and the National Covenant: Was He Right?" Pages 147–57 in *The Legacy of Jonathan Edwards: American Religion and the Evangelical Tradition.* Edited by D. G. Hart, S. M. Lucas, and S. J. Nichols. Grand Rapids: Baker, 2003.

————. "Missions and Native Americans." Pages 258–73 in *The Princeton Companion to Jonathan Edwards.* Edited by Sang Hyun Lee. Princeton: Princeton University Press, 2005.

————. *One Holy and Happy Society: The Public Theology of Jonathan Edwards.* University Park: Pennsylvania State University Press, 1992.

McKee, Elsie Anne. "The Offices of Elders and Deacons in the Classical Reformed Tradition." Pages 344–53 in *Major Themes in the Reformed Tradition.* Edited by Donald K. McKim. Grand Rapids: Eerdmans, 1992.

McLoughlin, William G. *Revivals, Awakenings, and Reform: An Essay on Religion and Social Change in America, 1607–1977.* Chicago History of American Religion. Chicago: University of Chicago Press, 1978.

McNeill, John T. "The Church in Post-Reformation Reformed Theology." *Journal of Religion* 24 no. 2 (1944): 96–107.

Meigs, James T. "The Half-Way Covenant: A Study in Religious Transition." *Foundations* 13 no. 2 (1970): 142–58.

Miller, Perry. *Errand into the Wilderness.* Cambridge: Harvard University Press, 1956.

————. *Jonathan Edwards.* Lincoln: University of Nebraska Press, 2005.

————. *The New England Mind: From Colony to Province.* Cambridge: The Belknap Press of Harvard University Press, 1953.

————. *Orthodoxy in Massachusetts 1630–1650.* Boston: Beacon Press, 1959.

————. "Solomon Stoddard, 1643–1729." *Harvard Theological Review* 34 no. 4 (1941): 277–320.

Minkema, Kenneth P. "Jonathan Edwards: A Theological Life." Pages 1–15 in *The Princeton Companion to Jonathan Edwards.* Edited by Sang H. Lee. Princeton: Princeton University Press, 2005.

————. "Old Age and Religion in the Writings and Life of Jonathan Edwards." *Church History* 70 no. 4 (2001): 674–704.

————. "Personal Writings." Pages 39–60 in *The Cambridge Companion to Jonathan Edwards*. Edited by Stephen J. Stein. Cambridge: Cambridge University Press, 2007.

————. "Preface to the Period." Pages 3–46 in *Sermons and Discourses, 1723–1729*. The Works of Jonathan Edwards 14. Edited by Kenneth P. Minkema. New Haven: Yale University Press, 1997.

Moody, Josh. *Jonathan Edwards and the Enlightenment: Knowing the Presence of God*. Lanham, MD: University Press of America, 2005.

Moore, Susan Hardman. *Pilgrims: New World Settlers and the Call of Home*. New Haven: Yale University Press, 2007.

Morgan, Edmund S. *The Puritan Family: Religion and Domestic Relations in Seventeenth-Century New England*. New, revised, and enlarged ed. New York: Harper & Row, 1966.

————. *Visible Saints: The History of a Puritan Ideal*. Ithaca: Cornell University Press, 1963.

Morris, William Sparkes. *The Young Jonathan Edwards: A Reconstruction*. The Jonathan Edwards Classic Studies Series. Eugene, OR: Wipf and Stock, 2005.

Murray, Iain H. *Jonathan Edwards: A New Biography*. Edinburgh: The Banner of Truth Trust, 1987.

Music, David W. "Jonathan Edwards and the Theology and Practice of Congregational Song in Puritan New England." *Studies in Puritan American Spirituality* 8 (2004): 103–33.

Neele, Adriaan C. *The Art of Living to God: A Study of Method and Piety in the Theoretico-Practica Theologia of Petrus van Mastricht (1630–1706)*. Perspectives on Christianity 8:1. Pretoria: Department of Church History, University of Pretoria, 2005.

Nichols, Stephen J. "Last of the Mohican Missionaries: Jonathan Edwards at Stockbridge." Pages 47–36 in *The Legacy of Jonathan Edwards: American Religion and the Evangelical Tradition*. Edited by D. G. Hart, Sean Michael Lucas, and Stephen J. Nichols. Grand Rapids: Baker, 2003.

Niebuhr, H. Richard. *The Kingdom of God in America*. First Wesleyan ed. Middletown, CT: Wesleyan University Press, 1988.

Noll, Mark A. *America's God: From Jonathan Edwards to Abraham Lincoln*. Oxford: Oxford University Press, 2002.

Nuttall, Geoffrey F. *The Holy Spirit in Puritan Faith and Experience*. Oxford: Basil Blackwell, 1947.

O'Brien, Susan. "A Transatlantic Community of Saints: The Great Awakening and the First Evangelical Network, 1735–1755." *American Historical Review* 91 no. 4 (1986): 811–32.

O'Donovan, Oliver. *Resurrection and Moral Order: An Outline for Evangelical Ethics*. Leicester, UK: Apollos, 1994.

Oberholzer, Emil Jr. *Delinquent Saints: Disciplinary Action in the Early Congregational Churches of Massachusetts*. Columbia University Studies in the Social Sciences. New York: AMS Press, 1968.

Okholm, Dennis L. "The Fundamental Dispensation of Evangelical Ecclesiology." Pages 41–62 in *The Community of the Word: Toward an Evangelical Ecclesiology*. Edited by Mark Husbands and Daniel J. Treier. Downers Grove, IL: IVP, 2005.

Oliphint, K. Scott. "Jonathan Edwards on Apologetics: Reason and the Noetic Effects of Sin." Pages 131–46 in *The Legacy of Jonathan Edwards and the Evangelical Tradition*. Edited by D. G. Hart, Sean Michael Lucas, and Stephen J. Nichols. Grand Rapids: Baker Academic, 2003.

Packer, James I. "A Puritan Perspective: Trinitarian Godliness according to John Owen." Pages 91–108 in *God the Holy Trinity: Reflections on Christian Faith and Practice*. Edited by Timothy George. Grand Rapids: Baker, 2006.

———. "The Puritan View of Preaching the Gospel." Pages 11–21 in *How Shall They Hear? A Symposium of Papers Read at the Puritan and Reformed Studies Conference, December 1959*. London: Evangelical Magazine, 1960.

Pauw, Amy Plantinga. "Editor's Introduction." Pages 1–39 in *The "Miscellanies," (Entry Nos. 833–1152)*. The Works of Jonathan Edwards 20. Edited by Amy Plantinga Pauw. New Haven: Yale University Press, 2002.

———. "Edwards as American Theologian: Grand Narratives and Personal Narratives." Pages 14–24 in *Jonathan Edwards at 300: Essays on the Tercentenary of his Birth*. Edited by Harry S. Stout, Kenneth P. Minkema, and Caleb J. D. Maskell. Lanham, MD: University Press of America, 2005.

———. "Jonathan Edwards' Ecclesiology." Pages 175–86 in *Jonathan Edwards as Contemporary: Essays in Honor of Sang Hyun Lee*. Edited by Don Schweitzer. New York: Peter Lang, 2010.

———. "Practical Ecclesiology in John Calvin and Jonathan Edwards." Pages 91–110 in *John Calvin's American Legacy*. Edited by Thomas J. Davis. Oxford: Oxford University Press, 2010.

———. *"The Supreme Harmony of All": The Trinitarian Theology of Jonathan Edwards*. Grand Rapids: Eerdmans, 2002.

Pelikan, Jaroslav. *Christian Doctrine and Modern Culture (Since 1700)*. The Christian Tradition: A History of the Development of Doctrine. Chicago and London: University of Chicago Press, 1989.

———. *Reformation of Church and Dogma (1300–1700)*. The Christian Tradition: A History of the Development of Doctrine. Chicago and London: University of Chicago Press, 1984.

Persons, Stow. "The Cyclical Theory of History in Eighteenth Century America." *American Quarterly* 6 no. 2 (1954): 147–63.

Pettit, Norman. "Editor's Introduction." Pages 1–85 in *The Life of Brainerd*. The Works of Jonathan Edwards 7. Edited by Norman Pettit. New Haven: Yale University Press, 1985.

———. *The Heart Prepared: Grace and Conversion in Puritan Spiritual Life*. 2nd ed. Middletown, CT: Wesleyan University Press, 1989.

Porter, Roy. *Enlightenment: Britain and the Creation of the Modern World*. London: Penguin, 2000.

Post, Stephen. "Disinterested Benevolence: An American Debate over the Nature of Christian Love." *Journal of Religious Ethics* 14 (1986): 356–68.

Proudfoot, Wayne. "Perception and Love in Religious Affections." Pages 122–36 in *Jonathan Edwards's Writings: Text, Context, Interpretation*. Edited by Stephen J. Stein. Bloomington and Indianapolis: Indiana University Press, 1996.

Ramsay, Paul. "Editor's Introduction." Pages 1–121 in *Ethical Writings*. The Works of Jonathan Edwards 8. Edited by Paul Ramsay. New Haven: Yale University Press, 1989.

———. "Editor's Introduction." Pages 1–128 in *Freedom of the Will*. The Works of Jonathan Edwards 1. Edited by Paul Ramsay. New Haven: Yale University Press, 1957.

Rightmire, R. David. "The Sacramental Theology of Jonathan Edwards in the Context of Controversy." *Fides et Historia* 21 no. 1 (1989): 50–60.

Rivera, Ted. *Jonathan Edwards on Worship: Public and Private Devotion to God*. Eugene, OR: Pickwick, 2010.

Sairsingh, Krister. "Jonathan Edwards and the Idea of Divine Glory: His Foundational Trinitarianism and Its Ecclesial Import." Unpublished doctoral diss., Harvard University, 1986.

Schafer, Thomas A. "Jonathan Edwards' Conception of the Church." *Church History* 24 no. 1 (1955): 51–66.

———. "Solomon Stoddard and the Theology of the Revival." Pages 328–61 in *A Miscellany of American Christianity: Essays in Honor of H. Shelton Smith*. Edited by Stuart C. Henry. Durham: Duke University Press, 1963.

Scheick, William J. "Family, Conversion, and the Self in Jonathan Edwards' *A Faithful Narrative of the Surprising Work of God*." *Tennessee Studies in Literature* 18 (1973): 79–89.

———. "The Grand Design: Jonathan Edwards' History of the Work of Redemption." Pages 177–88 in *Critical Essays on Jonathan Edwards*. Edited by William J. Scheick. Boston: G. K. Hall & Co., 1980.

———. *The Writings of Jonathan Edwards: Theme, Motif and Style*. College Station: Texas A & M University Press, 1975.

Schmidt, Leigh E. *Holy Fairs: Scotland and the Making of American Revivalism*. 2nd ed. Grand Rapids: Eerdmans, 1989.

Schmotter, James W. "The Irony of Clerical Professionalism: New England's Congregational Ministers and the Great Awakening." *American Quarterly* 31 no. 2 (1979): 148–68.

———. "Ministerial Careers in Eighteenth-Century New England: The Social Context, 1700–1760." *Journal of Social History* 9 no. 2 (1975): 249–67.

Seeman, Erik R. *Pious Persuasions: Laity and Clergy in Eighteenth-Century New England. Early America: History, Context, Culture*. Baltimore and London: Johns Hopkins University Press, 1999.

Smith, John E. "Editor's Introduction." Pages 1–83 in *Religious Affections*. The Works of Jonathan Edwards 2. Edited by John E. Smith. New Haven: Yale University Press, 1959.

———. "Jonathan Edwards: Piety and Practice in the American Character." *Journal of Religion* 54 no. 2 (1974): 166–80.

———. "Religious Affections and the 'Sense of the Heart'." Pages 103–14 in *The Princeton Companion to Jonathan Edwards*. Edited by Sang Hyun Lee. Princeton and Oxford: Princeton University Press, 2005.

Smolinski, Reiner. "Apocalypticism in Colonial North America." Pages 36–71 in *The Encyclopedia of Apocalypticism. Apocalypticism in the Modern Period and the Contemporary Age*. Edited by Stephen J. Stein. Vol. 3. New York: Continuum, 2003.

Spohn, William C. "Spirituality and Its Discontents: Practices in Jonathan Edwards's *Charity and Its Fruits*." *Journal of Religious Ethics* 31 no. 2 (2003): 253–76.

Stackhouse, Ian. "Revivalism, Faddism and the Gospel." Pages 239–51 in *On Revival: A Critical Examination*. Edited by Andrew Walker and Kristin Aune. Carlisle, UK: Paternoster Press, 2003.

Stein, Stephen J., ed. *The Cambridge Companion to Jonathan Edwards*. Cambridge: Cambridge University Press, 2007.

———. "Editor's Introduction." Pages 1–93 in *Apocalyptic Writings*. The Works of Jonathan Edwards 5. Edited by Stephen J. Stein. New Haven: Yale University Press, 1977.

———. "Providence and the Apocalypse in the Early Writings of Jonathan Edwards." *Early American Literature* 13 no. 3 (1978): 250–67.

Stoever, William K. B. "The Godly Will's Discerning: Shepard, Edwards, and the Identification of True Godliness." Pages 85–99 in *Jonathan Edwards's Writings: Text*, Context, Interpretation. Edited by Stephen J. Stein. Bloomington and Indianapolis: Indiana University Press, 1996.

Stout, Harry S. "Liturgy, Literacy, and Worship in Puritan Anglo-America, 1560–1679." Pages 11–35 in *By the Vision of Another World: Worship in American History*. Edited by James D. Bratt. Grand Rapids: Eerdmans, 2012.

———. *The New England Soul: Preaching and Religious Culture in Colonial New England*. New York: Oxford University Press, 1986.

———. "The Puritans and Edwards." Pages 274–91 in *The Princeton Companion to Jonathan Edwards*. Edited by Sang Hyun Lee. Princeton: Princeton University Press, 2005.

———. "Word and Order in Colonial New England." Pages 19–38 in *The Bible in America: Essays in Cultural History*. Edited by Nathan O. Hatch and Mark A. Noll. New York/Oxford: Oxford University Press, 1982.

Strange, Alan D. "Jonathan Edwards on Visible Sainthood: The Communion Controversy in Northampton." *Mid-America Journal of Theology* 14 (2003): 97–138.

Strobel, Kyle. "Jonathan Edwards and the Polemics of *Theosis*." *Harvard Theological Review* 105 no. 3 (2012): 259–79.

Studebaker, Steve. "Jonathan Edwards's Social *Augustinian* Trinitarianism: An Alternative to a Recent Trend." *Scottish Journal of Theology* 56 no. 3 (2003): 268–85.

Sweeney, Douglas A. "The Church." Pages 167–89 in *The Princeton Companion to Jonathan Edwards*. Edited by Sang Hyun Lee. Princeton/Oxford: Princeton University Press, 2005.

———. "Evangelical Tradition in America." Pages 217–38 in *The Cambridge Companion to Jonathan Edwards*. Edited by Stephen J. Stein. Cambridge: Cambridge University Press, 2007.

———. *Jonathan Edwards and the Ministry of the Word: A Model of Faith and Thought*. Downers Grove, IL: IVP Academic, 2009.

Thuesen, Peter J. "Edwards' Intellectual Background." Pages 16–33 in *The Princeton Companion to Jonathan Edwards*. Edited by Sang Hyun Lee. Princeton: Princeton University Press, 2005.

Tipson, Baird. "Invisible Saints: The 'Judgment of Charity' in the Early New England Churches." *Church History* 44 no. 4 (1975): 460–71.

Torrance, James B. "Covenant or Contract? A Study of the Theological Background of Worship in Seventeenth-Century Scotland." *Scottish Journal of Theology* 23 no. 1 (1970): 51–76.

Torrance, Thomas F. "Eldership in the Reformed Church." Pages 182–200 in *Gospel, Church, and Ministry: Thomas F. Torrance Collected Studies I*. Edited by Jock Stein. Eugene, OR: Pickwick Publications, 2012.

Tracy, Patricia J. *Jonathan Edwards, Pastor: Religion and Society in Eighteenth-Century Northampton*. The Jonathan Edwards Classic Studies Series. Eugene, OR: Wipf and Stock, 2006.

Vanhoozer, Kevin J. "Evangelicalism and the Church: The Company of the Gospel." Pages 40–99 in *The Futures of Evangelicalism: Issues and Prospects*. Edited by Craig Bartholomew, Robin Parry, and Andrew West. Grand Rapids: Kregel, 2003.

Vaughan, Alden T., ed. *The Puritan Tradition in America, 1620–1730*. Rev. ed. Hanover, NH: University Press of New England, 1972.

Vetö, Miklos. "Spiritual Knowledge According to Jonathan Edwards." Translated by Michael J. McClymond. *Calvin Theological Journal* 31 no. 1 (1996): 161–81.

von Rohr, John. "Extra Ecclesiam Nulla Salus: An Early Congregational Version." *Church History* 36 no. 2 (1967): 107–21.

———. *The Shaping of American Congregationalism, 1620–1957*. Cleveland: Pilgrim Press, 1992.

Vodola, Elisabeth. *Excommunication in the Middle Ages*. Berkeley: University of California Press, 1986.

Walker, G. S. M. "Calvin and the Church." *Scottish Journal of Theology* 16 no. 4 (1963): 371–89.

Walls, Andrew F. "The Eighteenth-Century Protestant Missionary Awakening in Its European Context." Pages 22–44 in *Christian Missions and the Enlightenment*. Edited by Brian Stanley. Grand Rapids: Eerdmans, 2001.

———. "Missions and Historical Memory: Jonathan Edwards and David Brainerd." Pages 248–65 in *Jonathan Edwards at Home and Abroad: Historical Memories, Cultural Movements, Global Horizons*. Edited by David W. Kling and Douglas A. Sweeney. Columbia: University of South Carolina Press, 2003.

Ward, Roger. "The Philosophical Structure of Jonathan Edwards's Religious Affections." *Christian Scholar's Review* 29 no. 4 (2000): 745–68.

Ward, W. Reginald. *Early Evangelicalism: A Global Intellectual History, 1670–1789*. Cambridge: Cambridge University Press, 2006.

———. *The Protestant Evangelical Awakening*. Cambridge: Cambridge University Press, 1992.

Westerkamp, Marilyn J. *Women and Religion in Early America, 1600–1850: The Puritan and Evangelical Traditions*. Christianity and Society in the Modern World. London and New York: Routledge, 1999.

Westermeyer, Paul. *Te Deum: The Church and Music: A Textbook, a Reference, a History, an Essay*. Minneapolis: Fortress, 1998.

Westra, Helen P. "Divinity's Design: Edwards and the History of the Work of Revival." Pages 131–57 in *Edwards in our Time: Jonathan Edwards and the Shaping of American Religion*. Edited by Sang Hyun Lee and Allen C. Guelzo. Grand Rapids: Eerdmans, 1999.

———. "Jonathan Edwards and 'What Reason Teaches.'" *Journal of the Evangelical Theological Society* 34 no. 4 (1991): 495–503.

Wheeler, Rachel. "Edwards as Missionary." In *The Cambridge Companion to Jonathan Edwards*. Edited by S. J. Stein. Cambridge: Cambridge University Press, 2007.

———. "'Friends to Your Souls': Jonathan Edwards' Indian Pastorate and the Doctrine of Original Sin." *Church History* 72 no. 4 (2003): 736–65.

———. "Lessons from Stockbridge: Jonathan Edwards and the Stockbridge Indians." In *Jonathan Edwards at 300: Essays on the Tercentenary of His Birth*. Edited by H. S. Stout, K. P. Minkema, and C. J. D. Maskell. Lanham, MD: University Press of America, 2005.

Williams, David R. "Horses, Pigeons, and the Therapy of Conversion: A Psychological Reading of Jonathan Edwards's Theology." *Harvard Theological Review* 74 no. 4 (1981): 337–52.

Williams, Garry J. "Enlightenment Epistemology and Eighteenth-Century Evangelical Doctrines of Assurance." Pages 361–63 in *The Emergence of Evangelicalism: Exploring Historical Continuities*. Edited by M. A. G. Haykin and K. J. Stewart. Nottingham, UK: Apollos, 2008.

Wilson, John F. "Editor's Introduction." Pages 1–109 in *A History of the Work of Redemption*. The Works of Jonathan Edwards 9. Edited by John F. Wilson. New Haven: Yale University Press, 1989.

————. "History." Pages 210–25 in *The Princeton Companion to Jonathan Edwards*. Edited by Sang Hyun Lee. Princeton: Princeton University Press, 2005.

————. "History, Redemption, and the Millennium." Pages 131–41 in *Jonathan Edwards and the American Experience*. Edited by Nathan O. Hatch and Harry S. Stout. New York: Oxford University Press, 1988.

————. "Jonathan Edwards as Historian." *Church History* 46 no. 1 (1977): 5–18.

Winiarski, Douglas L. "Jonathan Edwards, Enthusiast? Radical Revivalism and the Great Awakening in the Connecticut Valley." *Church History* 74 no. 4 (2005): 683–739.

————. "The Newbury Prayer Bill Hoax: Devotion and Deception in New England's Era of Great Awakenings." *The Massachusetts Historical Review* 14 (2012): 53–86.

Winship, Michael P. "Behold the Bridegroom Cometh! Marital Imagery in Massachusetts Preaching, 1630–1730." *Early American Literature* 27 no. 3 (1992): 170–84.

Winslow, Ola Elizabeth. *Jonathan Edwards 1703–1758: A Biography*. New York: Macmillan, 1941.

Withrow, Brandon G. "A Future of Hope: Jonathan Edwards and Millennial Expectations." *Trinity Journal* 22 no. 1 (2001): 75–98.

Wren, Brian. *Praying Twice: The Music and Words of Congregational Song*. Louisville: Westminster John Knox, 2000.

Youngs, J. William T. *God's Messengers: Religious Leadership in Colonial New England, 1700–1750*. Baltimore: The Johns Hopkins University Press, 1976.

Zakai, Avihu. "The Conversion of Jonathan Edwards." *Journal of Presbyterian History* 76 no. 2 (1998): 127–38.

————. *Exile and Kingdom: History and Apocalypse in the Puritan Migration to America*. Cambridge Studies in Early Modern British History. Cambridge: Cambridge University Press, 1992.

————. "The Gospel of Reformation: The Origins of the Great Puritan Migration." *Journal of Ecclesiastical History* 37 no. 4 (1986): 584–602.

————. "Jonathan Edwards, the Enlightenment, and the Formation of Protestant Tradition in America." Pages 182–208 in *The Creation of the British Atlantic World*. Edited by Elizabeth Mancke and Carole Shammas. Baltimore and London: The Johns Hopkins University Press, 2005.

————. *Jonathan Edwards's Philosophy of History: The Reenchantment of the World in the Age of Enlightenment*. Princeton: Princeton University Press, 2003.

Zimmerman, Philip D. "The Lord's Supper in Early New England: The Setting and the Service." Pages 124–34 in *New England Meeting House and Church: 1630–1850*. Edited by Peter Benes and Jane M. Benes. The Dublin Seminar for New England Folklife: Annual Proceedings 1979. Boston: Boston University, 1980.

Zylla, Phil C. *Virtue as Consent to Being: A Pastoral-Theological Perspective on Jonathan Edwards's Construct of Virtue*. McMaster Ministry Studies Series. Eugene, OR: Pickwick, 2011.

Index

Hume, David, 205n282
Humility, virtue of, Edwards on, 85–86
Hutchinson, Abigail, 75, 135
   conversion of, 73–74
Hutchinson, Anne (1591–1643), 15, 18, 115
Hutchinson, William (1586–1641), 15
Hymnody, 217–218
   evangelical, 219n29
Hymns
   advantage of, 220n40
   in contexts other than Sunday
      worship, 224
   Edwards's views on, 222–224
   introduction into Northampton
      church, 221, 223–225
   power to displace psalmody, 221
   Watts's, 221–224, 222n51–222n52
   Wesley's, 222–223
Hymn-singing
   congregation's, 220n38
   in revivals, 220n39, 222
Hypocrites, legal vs evangelical,
   Edwards on, 136

Images of Divine Things (Edwards), 101
Immediacy, Edwards's language of,
   130–131, 131n305, 134
Inclinations, 129–130. *See also*
   Affections
Independence of mind, Edwards's,
   28, 33
Indians
   Brainerd's missionary work among,
      149, 160–162, 165. *See also The
      Life of Brainerd* (Edwards)
   colonial pressures and, 160–161
   contacts with Europeans, 160–161,
      160n83
   dignity and equality of, Puritan
      assumptions about, 161
   early missions among, 163–164
   education of, music in, 219n31

European diseases and, 24
French incursions into New England
   and, 152
ministry to, 159–160
Puritans and, 24
as refugees in Massachusetts, 152
rights of, Edwards's defense of, 200
in Stockbridge, Edwards's work
   among, 199–201
taught English, 201, 201n254
Indigenous North Americans. *See*
   Indians
Individualism, preparationist, 78
Inner testimony, Edwards's appeal to,
   133, 133n318
Instruments, 206n285
"Intellectual Fathers," 16, 54
Internationalism, 16, 79, 116, 253–255,
   254n228
   church and, 44
Isaiah
   11:9, Edwards's preaching from,
      147n12
   51:8, Edwards's sermon series on, 91,
      96. *See also A History of the Work
      of Redemption* (Edwards)
   60:2–4, Edwards's preaching from, 147
Israel, 91, 100, 106
   covenants with, 13
   elders of, elders of church likened
      to, 246
   social structure of, as model, 243
   in wilderness, model of, 23–24
Itinerancy, 114–117, 135n325
   Edwards's attitude toward, 2, 116–117

James 2:19, 130
James I (1603–1625), 7
James II (1685–1688), 25–26
Jamieson, John F., 175n137
Jefferson, Thomas (1743–1826), 205n282
Jenson, Robert W., 65, 65n188

Satan, 107
  and Christ, suprahistorical battle
    between, 152
Saybrook Platform (1708), 9, 30, 117,
    174, 247
Schafer, Thomas A., x, 2n8, 14n55,
    30n12, 31n15, 32n27, 32n30,
    209n300, 210n301–n306,
    211n307, 211n309
  on Edwards's ecclesiology, 209–211
Scheick, William J., 69n7, 71n17,
    72n19, 94n131, 105n180,
    106n185, 171n125, 196n233
Schmidt, Leigh E., 75n40, 106n186,
    189n200
Schmotter, James W., 171n124,
    192n210, 192n213
Science
  Edwards's writings on, 32n29
  in Watts's hymnody, 222n52
Scotland
  Edwards's correspondent in. *See*
    MacLaurin, John
  Edwards's ministerial opportunities
    in, 200
  revivals in, 189n200
Scripture, translation into Algonquin,
    24
"Seasons of awakening," Edwards's,
    33, 35
Second Great Awakening, 259n11
Seeman, Erik R., 113n219, 117,
    117n241, 118n243–n244, 123,
    123n270, 124n276
Self-deception, 137–138
Self-love, Edwards on, 82–83, 141
Self-seeking, vs disinterested action, 141
Sense perception. *See also* "New sense"
  Edwards on, 155
Separatism, xi, 13, 24, 173–176,
    175n139, 259
  Edwards and, 210–211

  ideological support for, 173
  rejection of national covenant,
    implications of, 176
Sermon(s)
  on Acts 8:22 (Edwards), 230, 230n101
  "A Modell of Christian Charity"
    (Winthrop), 23, 23n97–23n98
  "Charity contrary to a selfish spirit"
    (Edwards), 82
  on 1 Corinthians (Edwards), 83–85,
    87, 89, 91
  on 2 Corinthians (Edwards), 190–198
  "Deacons to Care for the Body,
    Ministers for the Soul"
    (Edwards), 243–244
  and declension of colonies, 9n38
  on Deuteronomy 1:13–18 (Edwards),
    248–250
  on Deuteronomy 29 (Edwards),
    84n79, 231
  "A Divine and Supernatural Light"
    (Edwards), 127n287
  Edwards's, 40, 190. *See also Charity
    and Its Fruits* (Edwards); "A
    Farewell Sermon" (Edwards); *A
    History of the Work of Redemption*
    (Edwards); *specific sermon*
  on Ephesians 5 (Edwards), 81
  on excommunication (Edwards),
    231–232
  on Hebrews 12:22–24 (Edwards), 79
  on Isaiah 51:8 (Edwards), 91, 96.
    *See also A History of the Work of
    Redemption* (Edwards)
  "Love is more excellent than
    extraordinary gifts of the Spirit"
    (Edwards), 84–85
  "The Means and Ends of
    Excommunication" (Edwards),
    84n79, 231–232
  on parable of net (Edwards), 253
  on practice of love (Edwards), 81